WITHDRAWN

"HAUGHTY CONQUERORS"

"HAUGHTY CONQUERORS"

Amherst and the Great Indian Uprising of 1763

William R. Nester

Westport, Connecticut
London

Library of Congress Cataloging-in-Publication Data

Nester, William R., 1956–
   "Haughty conquerors" : Amherst and the great Indian uprising of 1763 / William R.
Nester.
     p. cm.
   Includes bibliographical references and index.
   ISBN 0–275–96770–0 (alk. paper)
   1. Pontiac's Conspiracy, 1763–1765. 2. Pontiac, Ottawa Chief, d. 1769. 3. Amherst,
Jeffrey Amherst, Baron, 1717–1797. 4. Great Britain—Colonies—America. I. Title.
E83.76.N47 2000
973.2'7—dc21   99–055020

British Library Cataloguing in Publication Data is available.

Library of Congress Catalog Card Number: 99–055020
ISBN: 0–275–96770–0

First published in 2000

Praeger Publishers, 88 Post Road West, Westport, CT 06881
An imprint of Greenwood Publishing Group, Inc.
www.praeger.com

Printed in the United States of America

The paper used in this book complies with the
Permanent Paper Standard issued by the National
Information Standards Organization (Z39.48–1984).

10 9 8 7 6 5 4 3 2 1

Contents

Introduction

Do not be angry father, you are going to the other side of the great lake. We shall get rid of the English.
—Indian reply to Captain Pierre Pouchot when he criticized them for abandoning the French, 1760[1]

Although that anonymous Indian's role in the uprising from 1763 to 1764 known as Pontiac's War can never be known, his words were prescient. During that time a loose coalition of tribes from the Appalachian Mountains to the Mississippi River and from the Ohio valley to the Great Lakes did briefly manage to "rid" themselves of nearly all the British in their midst. Indeed, that effort ranks with the 1680 Pueblo revolt as the most successful Indian war in Native American history. Not only did they assault and capture nine frontier forts, kill as many as 2,500 whites, and besiege Forts Detroit and Pitt for months, but, most importantly, they negotiated a peace with the British that realized most of their demands. Nonetheless, those Indians would only briefly savor their victory.

What sparked that uprising against British rule imposed only three years earlier? Britain's conquest of New France in 1760, codified by the 1763 Treaty of Paris, terrified virtually all Indians east of the Mississippi River. In the previous century and a half of expanding French and British settlement in North America, most of the tribes that had survived the epidemics and wars brought by the Europeans had actually prospered. By playing off those imperial powers against each other, they extracted the best trade and alliance terms from both. Indian living standards had risen with the meshing of muskets, iron traps and pots, wool blankets and clothing, and a host of other manufactured goods into their cultures.

Although France officially owned all lands between the Appalachians and the Mississippi until 1763, its imperial presence was light—only a score of trading posts and missions were scattered across that vast realm. French imperialism was actually a misnommer. The French never truly conquered most tribes living in their "empire"—they simply paid access fees to trade and proselytize in the region. But that alone was not enough to survive, let alone prosper. By necessity, the French learned Indian languages and customs, intermarried, and strove to flatter the prevailing sentiments.

Even then sensitivity was not enough. France's hold over that land would be challenged. Starting in the 1720s, an increasing number of intrepid British traders ventured into the region with goods that were less expensive and of better quality than those supplied by the French, and Indians could go to the British via Fort Oswego on Lake Ontario or down the Lake Champlain route to Albany itself.

Yet, despite the increasingly stiff competition, the French continued to dominate the trade, and during their wars with Britain rallied most warriors to their side. Although their goods may have been shoddy and overpriced, the French economic presence remained overwhelming. Not only did it not pay to bite the hand that best fed it, but the tribes grudgingly accepted France's dominant military power, mostly based on its ability to manipulate tribal animosities. Earlier in that century the French and their allies had nearly exterminated the Fox and Natchez when those tribes challenged their rule. And most importantly, the French contained the more ominous British Empire east of the Appalachian Mountains. As long as only French and British traders circulated west of that mountain wall, the tribes were content. In all, although British goods may have been superior, the Indians preferred the French as their formal "Great Father."

British imperialism contrasted severely with the French version. The Indians were well aware of the fate of most tribes east of the Appalachians. With their superior numbers the British had eventually crushed any native resistance there. Rather than salt the earth of the vanquished, the British seeded it with ever growing settlements. Those western Indians feared that they would suffer that same fate if the British took their land.

Indeed, that is what happened. Immediately after New France's surrender in September 1760, the British rapidly dispatched troops to occupy the French posts throughout the Great Lakes. The British came as "Haughty Conquerors," an arrogance mingled with the belief that they had liberated the natives from France's shoddy goods and "Popism" while seizing territory that was rightfully theirs.[2] Gone was the French sensitivity to Indian customs and needs; the British overlords imposed on their new subjects increasingly onerous demands and regulations. The haughtiness of the conquerors was insulting enough. But the Indians feared that settlers would soon follow in the wake of the soldiers and traders.

The war which followed was not inevitable. Different, wiser policies could have avoided it. What is popularly known as "Pontiac's War" could better be called "Amherst's." Those British officials assigned to the region were simply following the lead of the commander of His Majesty's Forces in North America since 1759, Sir Jeffrey Amherst. Against the protests of Indian Superintendent Sir William Johnson and other agents, along with the Indians themselves, Amherst pursued a "penny wise, pound foolish" policy whereby he cut back gifts and munitions to the Indians in order at once to pare administrative costs, weaken native military abilities, and strengthen Indian self-sufficiency by forcing them to relearn the art of hunting with bows and arrows. What Amherst viewed as unnecessary "presents" the tribes asserted were "payments" for access to their lands. Meanwhile, traders and land company agents swarmed over the region, cheating the Indians of their furs and homes.

Amherst got plenty of warnings about what would happen if he pursued his policies. At various councils the chiefs would either subtly or bluntly echo Delaware Chief Kittiuskund's warning that "all the nations had jointly agreed to defend their hunting place at Alleghenny, and suffer nobody to settle there. . . . And if the English would draw back over the mountains, they would get all the other nations into their interest; but if they stayed and settled there, all the nations would be against them; and he was afraid it would be a great war, and never come to a peace again."[3]

Thus did a smoldering resentment of British arrogance and conquest finally explode into an all-out war. Although it has been popularly called "Pontiac's War," the Seneca were most active in nurturing resentments and encouraging a concerted rebellion against the British. As early as December 1760 the Seneca circulated warbelts and envoys among the Ohio valley and Great Lakes tribes to unite them in war against the British. But that effort fizzled. After seven years of war most Indians were eager for peace; they adopted a wait-and-see attitude toward their new overlords. Shortly thereafter the Delaware prophet Neolin began preaching a vision of all Indians uniting to purify themselves and drive the whites from North America. Inspired by his words, the Seneca again circulated warbelts in early 1763. This time the coalition not only jelled, but the subsequent attacks were stunningly successful. Nearly all the war chiefs brilliantly planned and led surprise attacks on most frontier forts and relief expeditions.

How important was Ottawa Chief Pontiac to the Indian war of liberation?[4] Although Pontiac was a major leader during the war, he by no means organized or led the uprising. He was but one of many chiefs who took up the Seneca war cry and inspired the local tribes to revolt against the British among them. Yet his role at Detroit was decisive. In 1762, the Detroit area tribes once again coolly received the Seneca envoys; though angered by

British insults, most hesitated to revolt. It was Pontiac who fanned those embers of resentment into the bonfire of war, first among the Detroit tribes and then those in the surrounding region. When the revolt sputtered out, he sent out dozens of runners to different tribes and himself traveled among the villages, from 1764 through 1766, to revive resistance. Ironically, given the prominence in the war which historians have attributed to him, Pontiac's alliance among local tribes, the siege of Fort Detroit, and even leadership of his village eventually collapsed.

Did a "conspiracy" precede the uprising? Historians have debated whether that is a valid label. The controversy began when Francis Parkman titled his book *The Conspiracy of Pontiac*. Wilbur Jacobs, among others, argues that "war of liberation" rather than "conspiracy" is more appropriate, since the latter implies that what the Indians did was somehow wrong. Jacobs rightfully criticizes "Parkman and other writers" who "failed to do justice to American Indian aspirations for self-determination."[5]

That is unquestionable. Nonetheless, the sentiments of those who have joined the "conspiracy controversy" are well-intentioned but misplaced. Of course, what the Indians did between 1761 and 1763 was to engage in several conspiracies (defined as clandestine plots to commit an illegal act). Following Canada's conquest the British Empire and its laws theoretically ruled all Indians from the Atlantic Ocean through the Great Lakes and Ohio valley. The 1763 Treaty of Paris extended the British Empire to all lands between the Atlantic Ocean and the Mississippi River. Rebellion was illegal according to British law. But the Indians were thoroughly within their rights, as Americans understand them, to rebel against unjust, exploitive rule. For their war of liberation to succeed, they did indeed have to conspire. That was their natural right as conquered, dispossessed peoples. The Indian rebellion can best be understood as a war of independence, preceded by a conspiracy. Thus Chapter 2 of this book is unashamedly titled "Conspiracies."

Those dazzling Indian victories of late spring 1763 proved to be fleeting by late summer. The enthusiasm for the war steadily dwindled. Indian warfare traditionally involved raids which garnered scalps, prisoners, and loot with few or no losses. The prolonged sieges ran counter to Indian notions of how war should be conducted. Even more discouraging was the ability of the relief expeditions led by Colonel Henry Bouquet and Captain James Dalyell to break through to Forts Pitt and Detroit, respectively. Perhaps most importantly, once the flush of victory had faded, the Indians faced sober dread about the future. Those supplies captured with the forts would last only so long. The war had diverted most Indians from the hunt. The cutoff of powder, shot, and other provisions was starting to pinch. Having become dependent on the white man's technology and trade, how could the Indians survive that winter without starvation, let alone thereafter?

The British, meanwhile, stewed in their own troubles. The eruption of the Indian rebellion and capture of those nine forts were severe blows to Britain's empire and pride. The attacks had occurred when most regular troops in North America remained in the Caribbean following the conquest of Cuba and other enemy islands. There was no possibility of mounting a major counterattack that year. Finally, having been most responsible for sparking the war, Amherst turned his back on it. In November he sailed for England, leaving the war in the hands of his second in command, Major General Thomas Gage.

Although the British managed to quell the uprising in 1764, they did so largely by diplomacy rather than the indecisive wilderness campaigns led by Colonels Henry Bouquet and John Bradstreet. And they paid a high political price for peace. Treaties were negotiated which conceded nearly every Indian demand.

Ironically, just as the war erupted the British government was debating a measure that would become known as the Proclamation of 1763. The law forbade American settlements in Indian lands west of the Appalachian Mountains or any exclusive trade between one colony and any tribes. Thus could the Indians avoid the creeping imperialism of settlements while playing off the traders against one another. That policy was codified in treaties with various tribes in 1764.

But the policy was no sooner enacted than colonial pressures began to erode it. Treaties in 1765, 1766, and 1768 tore loose the first chunks of Indian lands west of the Appalachians. Even those concessions were not enough for the land companies which demanded ever more vast regions for themselves. The continuing restrictions on most land acquisitions were one of the more rankling grievances that would inspire the American War of Independence.

The war brought out the very worst in those who fought it. The Indians committed their usual array of fiendish tortures on many of those they captured; cannibalism of the victim often followed. The British were no less cruel. Sir Jeffrey Amherst called for exterminating the Indians with fire, sword, musket, and even smallpox, to be spread among them by giving them infected blankets. Pennsylvanian militia murdered a score of peaceful Indians at Conestoga and Lancaster. It was during Amherst's War that the expression "The only good Indian is a dead Indian" first appeared. It would be passionately echoed for another 125 years of frontier warfare.

Throughout America's frontier history those empowered with Indian policy would continually relearn and promptly forget the same blood-soaked lesson—it cost far less in money and lives to feed than fight the Indians. Generous fulfillment of Indian demands and needs kept the peace and allowed merchants, settlers, and other entrepreneurs to reap profit from native lands and hands. In contrast, harsh, repressive, and rapacious policies tended to provoke uprisings which were exorbitantly expensive to crush. In short, appeasement helped and punishment hurt imperial interests.

Most of the officers and Indian agents charged with implementing government policies understood that truism. But policy was made far from the frontier in confortable East Coast cities by officials beset by various constraints. Those could include the officials' own prejudices, ignorances, and greed, their superiors' demands to pare costs, and groups demanding ever more access to native lands and willing to bribe for the privilege. Almost invariably, short-term, special interests tended to outweigh long-term national interests. The Great Uprising was the first of several score frontier wars which repeated that tragic pattern.[6]

Despite the war's severity, complexity, and importance, only three authors have explored it with books. Francis Parkman's *The Conspiracy of Pontiac* is a classic in style, scholarship, and attitude dating from the late 19th century. Howard Peckham's *Pontiac and the Indian Uprising* introduces some new material in a short book written in 1947. Allan Eckert's *The Conquerors* is much longer and wide-ranging. While all three books are informative, they are limited to varying degrees by the emphasis they put on Pontiac and the fleeting attention they pay to other prominent personalities and larger political, economic, and cultural forces.[7]

By making Pontiac the center of their narratives, Parkman and Peckham inflate his influence and overshadow other important leaders at Detroit and elsewhere. The titles explain their bias. It was Pontiac's conspiracy for Parkman and Pontiac's uprising for Peckham. Parkman believed that Pontiac planned and directed the entire war.[8] A century later, Peckham asks, in his book's foreword, how Pontiac "could lead four tribes to war and inspire the revolt of twice that number? Why was he able to capture nine British forts, force the abandonment of a tenth, and besiege two more?"[9] Actually, Pontiac and his followers could not even capture the fort in their midst, Detroit, and had little or no role in destroying those other forts. Curiously, after pursuing this argument throughout his book, Peckham then turns it on its head in a long footnote where he criticizes Parkman and backs off his own earlier claim that Pontiac was the uprising's mastermind.[10] There is also the problem of attitude. Parkman, writing in the mid-19th century, and Peckham a century later reflect the racism of their times by lauding the British and denigrating the Indians and Canadians as "savages" and "rascals." Peckham dismisses the Delaware prophet Neolin as "psychopathic."[11]

In contrast, Eckert places Pontiac in perspective by giving a balanced view of all the major characters. Yet while he provides vivid, well-researched narratives, his interpretation often blends fact and fiction. His books are wonderful to read but unfortunately must be considered outstanding historical novels rather than histories. Not only are the dialogues made up but even the documents "quoted" are often gross distortions and sometimes outright fabrications of the originals. Thus, all his quotations are suspect. Sometimes, perhaps from a desire for dramatic effect, he gets his facts wrong or does not give the full picture.

It is fashionable for academics to skewer the works of Allan Eckert. Despite what I have written above, most criticisms of him are overblown. What explains the animosity? Jealousy may play a role. Eckert is a popular writer with hundreds of thousands of his books sold over the decades. Academics should see Allan Eckert as a valuable ally rather than an enemy. Eckert taps into and expands a mass interest in frontier history. His critics should be grateful to him for providing a large, informed audience, provocative interpretations to ponder, and fodder for critical reviews.

"Haughty Conquerors" will systematically analyze the war's underlying causes, the course and nature of the fighting, the leaders who shaped the struggle, and the far-reaching consequences. To do so it will explore the rich range of primary sources on the subject, something previous books tapped but sparingly and unevenly, along with the profusion of secondary studies. It is time for a fresh look at a familiar tale.

The titles of the book and chapters come from lines spoken by the Ottawa Indian Chief Pontiac in the stunning play *Ponteach*, written in 1766 and attributed to the intrepid ranger leader Robert Rogers. In this speech, Pontiac rues the French defeat, the British conquest, and the destruction of his people's way of life:

> Where are we now? The French are all subdued,
> But who are in their stead to become our Lords? . . .
> Whom see we now, their haughty conquerors . . .
> Big with their Victories so often gained;
> On us they Look with deep Contempt and Scorn . . .
> Nay think us conquered, and our Country theirs,
> Without a Purchase, or ev'n asking for it . . .
> I'd be content, would he keep his own Sea,
> And leave these distant Lakes and Streams to us . . .
> To be a Vassal to his low Commanders,
> Treated with Disrespect and public Scorn
> By Knaves, by Miscreants, Creatures of his Power . . .
> No, I'll assert my Right, the Hatchet raised,
> And drive these Britons hence like frightened Deer.
> Destroy their Forts, and make them rue the Day
> That to our fertile Land they fought the Way.[12]

NOTES

1. Brian Leigh Dunnigan, ed., *Memoirs on the Late War in North America Between France and England, by Pierre Pouchot* (Youngstown, N.Y.: Old Fort Niagara Association, 1994), 316.

2. That appropriate sobriquet was put in Pontiac's mouth in a play attributed to the brilliant American ranger leader Robert Rogers. Robert Rogers, *Ponteach or the*

Savages of America: A Tragedy (London: J. Millan, 1766), edited by Allan Nevins (1914) (New York: Lenox Hill, 1971), 201.

3. Post's "second journal," entries of November 28 and 29, 1758, in Proud, *History of Pennsylvania*, 2:app., 121, 124, quoted in Francis Jennings, *Empire of Fortune: Crowns, Colonies, & Tribes in the Seven Years War in North America* (New York: W. W. Norton & Company, 1988), 430.

4. For an especially revealing account of just which tribes and leaders were most responsible for the revolt, see Aaron the Mohawk to William Johnson, December 1, 1763, in James Sullivan and A. C. Flick, eds., *The Papers of William Johnson*, 14 vols. (Albany: State University of New York, 1921–1965), 10:939.

5. Wilbur R. Jacobs, *Dispossessing the American Indian: Indians and Whites on the Colonial Frontier* (New York: Charles Scribner's Sons, 1972), 90, 13.

6. For the most comprehensive study of this pattern see Paul Prucha, *The Great Father: The United States Government and the American Indians* (Lincoln: University of Nebraska Press, 1984).

7. Francis Parkman, *The Conspiracy of Pontiac and the Indian War after the Conquest of Canada* (1969) (reprint, Lincoln: University of Nebraska Press, 1994); Howard H. Peckham, *Pontiac and the Indian Uprising* (1947) (reprint, Chicago: University of Chicago Press, 1961); Allan Eckert, *The Conquerors: A Narrative* (1970) (reprint, New York: Bantam, 1981).

8. As the title of his book *The Conspiracy of Pontiac* reveals, Parkman believed Pontiac was the rebellion's mastermind. Francis Parkman, *Pontiac's War* (1886) (reprint, New York: Da Capo Press, 1991); but Parkman apparently based his argument on one letter written by Louisiana Governor d'Abbadie in 1764 which no longer exists, a rather flimsy foundation for such a powerful assertion. See Jacobs, *Dispossessing the American Indian*, 90. Howard Peckham saw no "grand conspiracy or preconcerted plan on [Pantiac's] part embracing all the western tribes." Peckham, *Pontiac and the Indian Uprising*, 11.

9. Peckham, *Pontiac and the Indian Uprising*, viii.

10. Ibid., nn. 108–11.

11. Ibid., 98.

12. Nevins, *Ponteach, or the Savages of America*.

1

Conquest

"Where Are We Now? The French Are All Subdued"

I was come to take Canada and I did not intend to take anything less.
—Sir Jeffrey Amherst

I have served over 22 years but I have never seen such . . . rebels, bandits, and hamstringers, especially the grenadiers.
—Captain Simeon Ecuyer

Drive off your land those dogs clothed in red who will do you nothing but harm.
—The Master of Life to Neolin

In early September 1760, three British armies converged on Montreal. General William Haviland's 3,400 troops approached from Albany, General James Murray's 2,500 troops from Quebec, and General Jeffrey Amherst's 10,350 troops from Lake Ontario. Amherst, His Majesty's commander in chief for North America, had engineered that rendezvous. He boasted that never before did "three Armys, setting out from different & very distant Parts from each other joyned in the Center, as was intended, better than we did."[1]

For Montreal's defenders, the odds of fending off that huge army were bleak. The 2,200 French troops, stretched thin along the parapets, stared out at the camps of 16,250 British troops.[2] Ammunition and food were nearly exhausted. British artillery would soon blast Montreal's high thin walls to rubble. Thousands of redcoats would then pour through the breaches to sack the city and slaughter its defenders and civilians alike. With a British fleet plugging the St. Lawrence, the French could expect no more reinforcements or supplies, let alone a last minute rescue by a fresh army. British entrenchments straddled all escape routes. The French were completely cut off. Facing such odds, the only sensible choice was surrender.

New France's governor, Pierre de Marquis de Rigaud de Vaudreuil de Cavagnial, proposed just that at a September 6 council of war. He then submitted to General Francois-Gaston de Duc de Levis and his staff a 55-clause surrender document that he had penned, which would guarantee Canadian religious and property rights under the new regime. Levis and most other officers protested that Canada could not be surrendered that easily. Their honor as French aristocrats was at stake. Honor demanded resistance at least until the wall was breached. Vaudreuil countered that after six years of fighting, those officers had amply secured their honor in Canada's defense. The officers muttered protests but went along. The war had exhausted them as much as everyone else.

The following day, Vaudreuil sent Colonel Louis Antoine de Bougainville to the British lines to negotiate his document with Amherst. The British general accepted all terms except one—French troops would not be granted honors of war, which allowed them to march out with flags flying, drums beating, and muskets shouldered. French atrocities during the war, Amherst insisted, mocked any notion of honor. Bougainville hurried back to Montreal with the demand. Vaudreuil was dismayed, Levis incensed. The French would fight on until honor was accepted. Bougainville carried that message back to Amherst's headquarters. The general was unyielding. A third attempt to sway him, this time by another French officer, met the same irritated rejection. During the heated negotiations, when Amherst was asked just what he wanted, he replied, "I was come to take Canada and I did not intend to take anything less."[3]

He got it. On September 8, 1763, Governor Vaudreuil signed a document which surrendered all of Canada. The French troops burned their colors rather than see them in British hands. They were soon packed on transports and sailed back to France.

Surrender was not enough. Occupation would follow. That essential task was easier than had been expected. The 62,000 Canadians did not quite view the British as liberators. But they were so relieved that the harsh years of malnutrition, poverty, and death had finally ended that no one resisted. Shortly after the surrender Amherst assigned Brigadier Generals James Murray and Thomas Gage, and Colonel Burton to serve as the respective governors general of Montreal, Quebec, and Trois-Rivieres. Regiments were quartered on those populations and in the forts.

The British army would govern Canada from September 8, 1760 until August 10, 1764, when a civilian government was imposed.[4] It was a benevolent and properous occupation for the Canadians. The economy was soon booming. British merchant ships disgorged inexpensive goods onto the docks. Tens of thousands of furs which had accumulated in warehouses during the war were loaded onto those same ships. The influx of coin spent by thousands of soldiers further invigorated Canada's economy. With the new prosperity those Canadians living in the St. Lawrence valley could muster no passion to revolt against their new masters, even if they had enjoyed the means of doing so. That sentiment would not be shared by those peoples living across the Great Lakes of "upper" Canada.

That vast region's occupation was soon under way. Four days after the surrender, on September 12, 1760, Amherst assigned Major Robert Rogers the duty of receiving the surrender of French forces in the Great Lakes.[5] Rogers was an excellent choice to lead that mission. No man on either side during the war had acquired a more brilliant record. Rogers had grown up on the New Hampshire frontier and was a seasoned woodsman when at age 24, in 1755, he recruited a company for his province's regiment. As captain, he led his company on repeated patrols against marauding French and Indian war parties when other British regular and provincial officers sheltered in their camps. In March 1756, William Shirley, then the British commander in chief for North America, was so impressed that he asked Rogers to recruit and lead an independent ranger company. Over the next four years, Rogers led first one and eventually a half dozen companies on more than a score of raids against the enemy, even in the depths of winter and through blinding snowstorms.

Yet, despite being a genuine hero, Rogers had a dark side. He had a well-deserved reputation for gambling, boozing, and wenching to excess. Even worse were accusations that Rogers at times lied, cheated, and stole. Before the war he was arrested, though not sentenced, for counterfeiting. Whatever temptations he would encounter in late 1763, Rogers would suppress them and admirably accomplish his mission. But the temptations would later overwhelm him when he received command of Fort Michilimackinac.

The next day Rogers packed 200 rangers in fifteen whaleboats and set off up the St. Lawrence River. They halted at Presque Isle where the troops awaited supplies while Rogers journied with orders for Colonel Robert Monckton at Fort Pitt. He arrived there on October 16.[6]

Among Monckton's orders from Amherst was to select a competent officer to command Detroit, the most important fort of the Great Lakes. Monckton chose Captain Donald Campbell of the 60th Royal Americans. Bright, energetic, and courageous, Campbell was a first-rate officer. Alas, nearsightedness and girth restricted his movements on the battlefield. Instead he excelled at administrative work. He had received a lieutenant's commission in March 1756 and was appointed quartermaster the following month. The vigor, skill, and cheer with which he fulfilled his assignments got him promoted to captain lieutenant on April 17, 1758 and captain on August 29, 1759.

Campbell's orders were to assist Rogers in disarming the French troops and sending them to Quebec where they would be shipped to Britain, securing loyalty oaths from the Canadians, freeing as many prisoners from the Indians as possible, and dispatching troops to occupy the forts throughout the upper Great Lakes. Once that was accomplished, Rogers would return. Campbell would stay on as Detroit's commander, and send back detailed intelligence reports on the region's Indians, Canadians, and potential wealth.[7]

Deputy Indian Superintendent George Croghan would accompany Campbell. As a master of wilderness survival, trading, and Indian ways, Croghan was a frontier legend. He probably reached America from Ireland in 1741 when he immediately plunged into the Indian trade throughout the Ohio valley and south shores of Lake Erie. Although he worked deep in enemy territory with a price on his head, he prospered because he offered the Indians goods that were less expensive, better made, and more abundant than French goods, backed by his daring and diplomatic skills. By the 1750s he employed a score of traders throughout that region. Croghan's Indian expertise prompted the Pennsylvania and Virginia colonies to hire him to help negotiate treaties and deliver gifts. After the war broke out he continued to serve the colonies and joined Colonel George Washington's 1754 Fort Necessity campaign and General Edward Braddock's 1755 campaign. At their first meeting, Indian Superintendent William Johnson tapped Croghan to be his deputy at a salary of 200 pounds a year. Croghan would serve in that indispensable role for fifteen years, during which he attended scores of councils and negotiated dozens of agreements. He was renowned not just for his bravery and diplomatic skills but also for his charm, wit, and generosity to friendly Indians and impoverished settlers alike. Less laudably, he also had a well-deserved reputation as a land speculator, gaudy dresser, profligate spender, heavy drinker, snuff snorter, double dealer, and extravagant liar. Like nearly all humans, "self-interest was the sole guide of his life."[8]

Whether two such frontier heroes and ample egos like Rogers and Croghan got along is unknown. But their skills would prove perfectly complementary. At Fort Presque Isle, reinforcements swelled the expedition to about 275 men of whom roughly 200 were Queen's Rangers and 75 were 60th Royal Americans. The expedition disembarked before Fort Pontchartrain at Detroit on November 29, 1760.

Captain François-Marie Picote de Belestre commanded Fort Pontchartrain with its 37 regulars and 800 militia. He was not surprised when the British troops appeared at his fort's gate. Having received word that Vaudreuil had surrendered Canada, he knew it was only a matter of time before he would have to haul down his colors. Still, the experience was a humilating shock. The only choice left to him was to conduct the transfer of power with all the dignity he could muster. According to Campbell, Belestre "did everything with good grace."[9]

Rogers swiftly took command. He dispatched Belestre and his troops east with a 32-man escort along with seventeen former British captives, a Dutch boy, and two blacks. Fort Pontchartrain was renamed Fort Detroit. Lieutenant John Butler and troops embarked in bateaux to occupy Forts Miami and Ouiatenon. The most important measures for securing British rule depended on inducing the loyalty and dependence of the Canadians and Indians.[10]

The Canadians were given a choice: either swear an oath of allegiance to the British Crown or leave Canada. Nearly all chose to stay in their homes in return for promising their loyalty to George II: "I will defend him and his in this country with all my power against his or their enemies; and further I swear to make Known and revail to His Majesty, His General, or their assistants in place present, as much as depends of me all Traitors, or all conspirations that could be formed against his Sacred person, his Country, or his Government."[11] Those 500 Canadian men who mumbled the oath also surrendered 400 muskets.[12]

Ironically, the Canadians had sworn allegiance to a dead king. George II passed away on October 25, 1760. His grandson, who took the throne, would be known to history as George III, whose subordinates would provoke uprisings in Canada and later America. Ironically, most Canadians would adhere to their oaths despite the temptations posed by the Indian uprising three years later and American Revolution fifteen years after that.

Indeed, the Canadians appeared to greet the British as liberators rather than conquerors. Relief that the war with its death, shortages, and isolation appears to have overwhelmed any patriotism the Canadians may still have felt at the conquest. Campbell reported that the "inhabitants seem very happy at the change of government, but they are in want of everything. It has been a very flourishing place before the war, plenty of everything."[13]

The imposition of British rule was greatly eased by Campbell's sincerity and geniality. Nearly everyone—his troops, the Canadians, and Indians— adored him: "he is the pride and joy of Detroit and I can say that he is loved and respected by all those living in this country. It is the same with the officers of his corps."[14] Campbell's humanitarianism would ultimately lead to his destruction.

How did the Indians feel about the new regime? After all, it was their land which the Canadians had surrendered. Croghan employed every diplomatic means possible to secure their loyalty to the British during a council he convened with the three local tribes, the Huron, Ottawa, and Potawatomi, from December 3 to 5, 1760. First he promised the chiefs that they would enjoy "a free open trade" as long as they remained loyal to Britain and returned all of their prisoners. Recognizing the warriors' "martial spirit" that "must be employed at war," he pointed them southeast against the Cherokee, whom the British were then fighting: "There your warriors will find diversion & there they may go; they have no other place to go as all nations [have] become the subjects of Great Britain." He also warned the chiefs to protect any Canadian settlers or British traders in their midst "as I shall look on any insult . . . as if done to me as they are under my protection." With this short speech Croghan enlisted the tribes as Britain's economic and military allies, to be rewarded with free trade that would meet all their needs.[15]

The chiefs then rose and spoke, each promising to fulfill Croghan's demands. They equivocated only over the whites living among them, many of whom were no longer prisoners but tribal and family members: "You shall have them as soon as possible tho we do not choose to force them that have a mind to live among us." They did hand over 42 prisoners eager for release and promised that peace between them would last for "as long as the sun and moon give light."[16] Croghan left for Fort Pitt on December 11.

Only one more mission remained unfilled—Fort Michilimackinac's possession. Rogers tried to reach that distant post before the waters iced over. He set off with 35 rangers, Indian Captain Andrew Montour, a half dozen Indians, and some Canadians on December 8. In all his endeavors Rogers had always plowed ahead despite the risks. But he could not control nature. The temperatures plummeted. The ice forming on the lake threatened their frail canoes with destruction. On December 16, Rogers reluctantly gave the order to head back. They reached Fort Detroit's safety three days and 95 miles later. The occupation of the upper Great Lakes forts would have to await spring and another commander. On December 23, Rogers embarked with an escort for Fort Pitt. It would not be Rogers' last time at Detroit.[17]

Campbell had reason to feel satisfied as he and his men settled in for a long, harsh winter. The Canadians and Indians appeared to have accepted the transfer of power with grace, enthusiasm, and hope. Sunday night parties at his headquarters among his officers and 20 or so of the local elite alleviated the winter gloom. The shortage of provisions and ammunition was annoying rather than critical. At worst the troops might have to tighten their belts until supply convoys arrived with the spring melt.

Taking Detroit, of course, was only the first essential step in seizing control of the region. As for the rest of upper Canada, detachments had already secured Forts Miami and Ouiatenon. During the spring of 1761, the British would resume their efforts to assert control over the rest of their newly won empire. Troops would occupy the upper Great Lakes posts the next summer.

Power rather than sentiment explains the swift acquiescence of Canadians and Indians to British rule. Those former French subjects had little choice as to whom they promised their loyalty. The British had thoroughly beaten the French on the battlefield and accepted Canada's surrender. It was quite likely that they would soon capture Louisiana as well. Those conquests would most likely be enshrined in treaty at the diplomatic table. If so the loyalty oaths might become permanent. If not, then nothing was lost. The Canadians and Indians would be French again when the fleur de lis again flew over the region. Regardless, all the Canadians had done was mouth consent to words they did not understand.

But behind the compliance were muted rumbles of discontent which would steadily worsen. At Detroit and elsewhere throughout the region the biggest problem was want of provisions. The Canadians had suffered a poor harvest and had a meager surplus to sell to the British. Ammunition was scarce, something the Indians especially lamented. The British had little to spare. Only weeks after the council Campbell reported that all the Indians complained that they lacked powder and ball for hunting and several distant tribes arrived at Detroit "absolutely starving."[18] Those shortages and complaints would worsen. Annoyance would boil into rage and eventually into violence.

That violence might have been prevented. From late 1760 until spring 1763 ever more frontier officers and Indian agents warned Amherst of the worsening danger. But the general, his head swollen with victories and prejudices, dismissed all their entreaties. Amherst had fulfilled his vow to take Canada. Alas, he failed to understand how to keep it. Three years after he won that empire, he nearly lost it, or at least its western reaches. Thousands of British subjects would die, suffer captivity, and see their homes and livelihoods destroyed. It was Amherst's policies of suppressing the Indians that sparked that wilderness conflagration. Why did he lead the empire down that path to destruction?

Jeffrey Amherst would be 46 years old when the uprising erupted in 1763. He had spent most of his life in uniform.[19] As a young officer, his administrative skills and loyalty brought him to the attention of ranking generals whose staff he joined. From that relative safety he witnessed the battles of Dettingen in 1743, Fontenoy in 1745, Lauffeldt in 1747, and Hastenbeck in 1757. In 1756 he received his first independent command as colonel of the 15th regiment. Impressed by Amherst's experiences, William Pitt, the government's leader, appointed him to lead the Louisbourg campaign in 1758. Amherst's army did take Louisbourg that year, and then marched or rowed on to occupy Fort Carillon in 1759, and Fort Levis and Montreal in 1760.

Amherst presided over rather than led those campaigns that eventually crushed the French Empire. The grand strategy was that of William Pitt. The tactics were those proposed by subordinates. Nonetheless, no army commanded by Amherst ever lost a battle.

A grateful Whitehall heaped honors upon him. On September 30, 1758, he was named colonel of the 60th regiment, a sinecure that accompanied serving as commander in chief along with Virginia's governorship which paid 1,500 pounds, though he never sat at Williamsburg. On January 19, 1761, he would be promoted to lieutenant general and in March made a Knight of Bath. Astonishingly, even after the uprising and his recall to England, he would receive higher honors.

All that lay in the future. Immediately following Canada's surrender, he briefly visited Quebec, then hurried back to Fort George, the star-shaped stone fortress on Manhattan's southern tip that was his New York headquarters. For the next three years he cocooned himself there, directing affairs by exchanging letters with his field commanders. The realm he commanded was vast. Once the Treaty of Paris was signed in February 1763, it expanded to cover half a continent, all of North America south of Hudson Bay and east of the Mississippi River except New Orleans, as well as the Bahamas and Bermuda.

What manner of man was Amherst? At best he was a plodding mediocrity, a characteristic which was painfully obvious even to him. He was a petty bureaucrat rather than an administrator, obsessed with obeying rules and cutting costs rather than alleviating problems. In all, he would have made a much better accountant than general.

Many astute observers feared Amherst was just not terribly bright. Horace Walpole believed that the general was at least smart enough to know he was not very smart: "Whether being conscious of his own defects, and of being incompetent to converse with men whom he knew enlightened, he seemed determined to bury his deficiency in obstinate silence; or else his pride and vanity, of which he had a tolerable share, made him disdain to communicate his paucity of ideas."[20]

Unfortunately, he compensated for that inadequacy by insisting that his word was law. If he lacked the flair or skills of other generals, he could at least command obedience which often meant dismissing advice when it conflicted with his own conceits or ignorances. His pigheaded refusal to listen to expert views on vital issues certainly revealed him to be both emotionally and intellectually stunted. That was especially true when it came to Indians, a people whom he utterly loathed but unfortunately did not fear. In his years in America he had never witnessed an Indian battle. He assumed Indians were effective merely at robbing and murdering isolated settlers or captive soldiers. That would be a fatal mistake.

Aside from the Louisbourg campaign, Amherst's only serious fighting in North America occurred at Fort Levis in August 1760, where Captain Pierre Pouchot put up a spirited defense for several days before finally giving up. It was at Fort Levis perhaps more than anywhere else that Amherst served in America that his image of Indians as cowardly loafers jelled. When Fort Levis was surrendered on August 25, 1760, he prevented the Indians from charging into the fort to loot it and massacre the garrison. Denied those fruits of victory, over 500 Indians, whom Indian Superintendent William Johnson had spent months and a considerable sum wooing, angrily packed up and disappeared into the forest. Neither they nor Amherst would bury the rage provoked by that incident.

Amherst did reward the 182 Indians who stayed with him by having as many silver medals struck and given to each "to wear as a proof as His

Majesty's satisfaction of their zeal & bravery, that they may be distinquished by this token whenever they shall come to any of the forts or posts, from those unworthy Indians who so shamefully abandoned the army after it left Oswego, & the General expects that when any of the Indians wearing these medals come to any of the forts or posts, they be freely admitted and kindly received; & the commanding officers are desired to shew them all marks of favour in their power."[21]

Had Amherst been as generous to all Indians the uprising of 1763 would never have erupted. Instead, his policy was anchored in the belief that idle hands breed mischief. In the general's mind the French had spoiled the Indians, who expected the British to be just as indulgent. This Amherst vehemently rejected. He called for giving the Indians only "a little clothing, some arms & ammunition to hunt with . . . but . . . when the intended trade is once established, they will be able to supply themselves with these from the traders for their furs. I do not see why the Crown should be put to that expense. I am not for giving them any provisions; when they find they can get it on asking . . . they will grow remiss in hunting, which should industriously be avoided; for so long as their minds are intent on business they will not have leisure to hatch mischief." He rejected the notion of "purchasing the good behavior either of Indians, or any others. . . . When men of that race so ever behave ill, they must be punished but not bribed."[22]

This policy, he believed, killed two birds with one stone. First of all, the weaker the Crown kept the tribes the less likely they were to revolt. To supply them with ammunition would simply encourage aggression. Indians forced to hunt for their livelihood could not easily take the warpath. That policy of denial also alleviated Britain's national debt which had soared through nine years of world war. The general was simply following Pitt's orders to pare expenses.

What seemed logical to Amherst was disastrous to those who understood Indians. The general completely misunderstood the nature of Indian diplomacy. No Indian treaty was definitive. Once forged, a convenant chain of friendship had to be continually polished and repolished. Major agreements had to be reinforced with endless minor reagreements and their accompanying councils, speeches, ceremonies, banquets, and gifts. Diplomacy included the essential painstaking process of satisfying the ambitions, vanities, and pride of each tribe's many chiefs.

Indian councils followed a very strict protocol. They opened with condolences for those who had recently died and the symbolic covering with gifts of their graves. The leader or group who called a council was the first to speak. Wisely, the Indians only allowed a response to a speaker to occur the following day, hopefully after passions had cooled and the matter had been thoroughly discussed by all. Each speaker presented a belt or string of wampum with each significant point, depending on its gravity. Indians would shout their approval with each belt presented. The greater the number of nations represented at a council, the more time it took for interpretations and responses. When a council ended, its proceedings were recorded in wampum belts.

Gift-giving was essential to Indian morality, as well as diplomacy. The Indians viewed the goods given at council not as gifts but as payment for the right to inhabit but not own land exchanged by treaty, or simply as an ethic that those with more wealth naturally give to those with less. The French understood this. Missionaries and captains were constantly handing out clothing, blankets, muskets, munitions, and dozens of lesser goods. The Indians reciprocated. A guest was to be fed, lodged, and even satisfied carnally if need be.

Those moral values were beyond Amherst's comprehension. What Amherst dismissed as presents the Indians considered rent for access to their territory. If Amherst cut off the rent the British were expected to pay, the Indians would naturally try to evict them. Not only that, but a war had just ended in which hundreds of Indians had died on the battlefield or from disease. The survivors of those killed by enemies must be either avenged or compensated. With the conquest of New France and overwhelming British power, the Indians could not realistically hope to avenge their dead by killing more of their enemies. The rage and sorrow of the vanquished could only be assuaged by the generosity of the new "Great Father." Thus the British could not enjoy peace until they conformed to the Indian etiquette of "covering the dead" with gifts. Experts on Indians understood this; Amherst and most other British officers did not.

No one realized this more clearly than the Indian Superintendent for the northern district, Sir William Johnson, the Cassandra of Amherst's War. With exquisite politeness, he repeatedly warned Amherst that his policy of cutting off gifts and munitions to the Indians could lead to disaster. A chain of friendship must be continuously polished with gifts; otherwise it will rust away. Indians give loyalty and measure friendship in proportion to the generosity of the strong for the weak partner. The Indians interpreted Amherst's cutbacks, especially of ammunition, not simply as a profoundly unfriendly act, but as a deliberate British plot to destroy them as a people.

Johnson gently suggested that "a little generosity & moderation will tend more to the good of His Majesty's Indian interest than the reverse, which would raise their jealousy much more than it is now." To that end he advocated a strict "law passed for keeping traders within due bounds." That law would fix prices, require all traders to apply for licenses and post bonds before they set foot on Indian land, and empower fort commanders to regulate trade with and dispense gifts to the Indians. But most importantly, the Indians must receive gunpowder, for "they must suffer greatly if they can't have some from you—refusing them now will increase their jealousy and make them all very uneasy I am certain, this Sir, I think my duty to make known to you."[23]

Privately, Johnson worried that "the General is too indifferent about & severe to all Indians, which I greatly dread, will prove of very bad consequence to His Majesty's Indian interest now so well established, as well as his subjects living" on the frontier.[24] Amherst "is not at all a friend of Indians which I am afraid will have bad consequences."[25]

Amherst just as often rejected warnings from Johnson and others. His penny-wise and pound-foolish policies would spark the most wide-ranging and bloody Indian war in American history.

Yet there was an authority higher than either Amherst or Johnson. Ultimately, of course, those men were mere servants of the Crown. The king's official residence was St. James Palace. His government was located in Whitehall Palace. Two institutions within that government were chiefly responsible for proposing and implementing policies toward North America, the Southern Department and the Board of Trade. The Board of Trade included a president and four other members. That body compiled information and developed proposals for better managing the colonies. A secretary of state headed the half dozen staff members of the Southern Department which was responsible not just for North America but southern Europe and the Mediterranean as well.

Those two institutions would submit proposals to the Cabinet which would debate and decide them. Decisions would then be approved by King George III, who mostly rubberstamped them. If a policy needed a law to be effective, the Cabinet then drew up one and submitted it to Parliament where enough votes could usually be bribed or convinced for its passage. Whitehall then sent the edict or law to the appropriate institution for implementation, the commander in chief, Indian Superintendents, or colonial governors.

Contrary to popular belief, Whitehall sympathized with the Indians and condemned efforts by colonial governments and speculators to steal their land. More than the desire to avoid Indian wars lay behind those sentiments. British officials genuinely believed that the Indians had a right to their land and that only the Crown should be able to buy it from them. Whitehall was determined to "prevent the many evils and great discouragement to cultivation which arose from persons obtaining extravagent grants of land . . . by fraudulent conveyances & other indirect practices."[26]

But those sentiments and even laws and edicts which reflected them weakened after they had crossed the Atlantic. The duties for conducting diplomacy, trade, and war with the Indians overlapped among the commander in chief, Indian Superintendents, and colonial governors. With the Proclamation of October 7, 1763, there would be seventeen separate colonial governments in North America—Nova Scotia, Canada, New Hampshire, Massachusetts, Connecticut, Rhode Island, New York, New Jersey, Pennsylvania, Delaware, Maryland, Virginia, North Carolina, South Carolina, Georgia, East Florida, and West Florida.

Those colonial governments were simliar. The king appointed the governor, who was advised by a council of leading colonists. A popularly elected assembly voted on the colony's laws and approved the council members. Voter and office eligibility laws varied in each colony but were generally confined to white men of property. The governor could veto assemby laws. The assembly could vote down the governor's initiatives.

Bitter conflicts almost invariably arose between the governor and powerful factions in the assembly, especially regarding the interrelated issues of war, taxes, and Indians. Governors were trapped between conflicting imperial and assembly demands. During wars, Whitehall sought to maximize, while the assemblies sought to minimize the amount of taxes and troops raised by that colony. As for troops, the colonial assemblies were in a strong bargaining position. Whitehall needed all the provincial soldiers and other support it could get. For most colonies the battlefields were far away. Even colonies whose frontiers were ravaged by raids usually had some regular army protection. To sweeten its demands for provincial troops, Whitehall would promise to split the costs. Parliament would pay for their equipment and transportation while the colony would take care of their pay. Taxes were even more contentious. Whitehall and Parliament could try to impose taxes. But the colonists could refuse to pay while protesting "no taxation without representation"; no colonial representatives sat in Parliament. Every colony had an "Indian problem" and wilderness frontier except Rhode Island. Land speculators and traders exerted pressure on assemblymen to pass laws and policies that promoted their interests, even when they conflicted with imperial laws and policies.

Traditionally, the colonial governors had conducted all Indian diplomacy. They were responsible for negotiating treaties with the Indians that took their land, bought peace, and ended wars. But as the colonies expanded, their interests and land claims increasingly overlapped and conflicted. The Indians played off the colonies and the French against each other to get better deals. Diplomacy grew more expensive with the competition. Ever more colonial leaders demanded a higher authority appointed by the Crown who could assume diplomatic costs and adjudicate differences among the colonies and with the Indians.

The Board of Trade did not act on the pressure until 1721, when it proposed creating a governor general who would serve as supreme military commander and Indian diplomat. But Whitehall was cool to the idea and nothing came of it. The idea for establishing an Indian Superintendent emerged at the 1754 Albany Congress where various schemes of colonial union were debated. While Whitehall rejected the Union plan adopted at Albany, it did agree to create the office of Indian Superintendent and named William Johnson to head it. On April 14, 1755, General Edward Braddock handed William Johnson his commission as Indian Superintendent. In a February 17, 1756 order, Whitehall split the Indian superintendency between a northern department under Johnson and a southern department under Edmund Atkin, with the dividing line at the border between Maryland and Pennsylvania and along the Ohio River.

Although automous, the Indian Superintendent was subordinate to North America's commander in chief. Money for personnel and gifts came from the military budget. This gave the commander potential veto power over Indian policies. Sir Jeffrey Amherst wielded that power to dictate policy. In contrast, his successor, General Thomas Gage, deferred to the superintendents' judgments. Indian policy was thus a tug of war into which the superintendents were dragged by the general when Amherst ruled. Under Gage, Indian policy was a dance in which the superintendents led.

Nonetheless, all along the superintendents considered themselves primarily responsible to Whitehall rather than the commander in chief. They corresponded with both the general at his New York City headquarters and ministers in London, primarily the Board of Trade and Secretary for the Southern Department, with their overlapping duties for the North America colonies. From 1755 until 1763, that relationship was informal. On August 5, 1763, Whitehall officially subordinated the superintendents to the Board of Trade. But it was not until 1768 that Whitehall estabished a ministry of colonial affairs and a separate budget for the superintendents, although it remained drawn from the commander in chief's coffer. The colonial secretary still sat with the Board of Trade.

The work of the superintendent and his agents was never done. They constantly reknit unraveling relations. It was endless, tedious, frustrating work, especially for someone as conscientious as Johnson: "I have inexpressible trouble, every room & corner in my house constantly full of Indians, each individual of whom has a thousand things to say & ask and any person who choses to gain their affections or obtain an ascendancy over them must be the greatest slave living & listen to them all at any hour."[27]

While the superintendent's duties were great, his powers were limited. Amherst sharply cut back the most important power they could wield, the generous bestowing of gifts upon cooperative Indians. Nor could the superintendent credibly threaten military reprisal against miscreants. The dozen forts scattered across the Indian lands posed no military threat to the local tribes. Those tiny garrisons were mere symbols of British power. Exacerbating traditional jealousies among the tribes might briefly offer the British respite from their collective demands. But that strategy was ultimately self-defeating. It could not long conceal the reality that Indian grievances with the British far exceeded those among themselves. Any threat to withhold vital munitions and other supplies would only escalate the plunge into war.

In all, superintendents presided over their regions. Real power was splintered among them, the commander in chief, the provincial governors and assemblies, and companies with business interests and land claims in Indian territory. Thus was a superintendent's prudent diplomacy continually frustrated by an inability to prevent other colonial powers from asserting their interests against the Indians.

So just how could a superintendent keep the tribes passive and cooperative? Like a good father, he mediated conflicts among the tribes and between them and whites. Shorn of the ability to threaten military or economic reprisal or deliver generous gifts, success depended on his power to persuade those involved in a conflict to find a mutually satisfactory resolution. The greater the superintendent's reputation for fairness, the more likely those involved would listen and follow his advice. In this sense the superintendent was the chief of chiefs, whose authority rested on his ability to exude wisdom, justice, and dignity.

Two men had successively presided over the southern district. In 1756, Edmund Atkin seemed to Whitehall the best man for the job. He was first named to South Carolina's council in 1738 and served there until 1750 when he moved to England for six years. Having traded with the Indians for well over two decades, he had gained a deep and sympathetic knowledge of them. In London he wrote two influential tracts on Indian policy, the "Historical Account of the Choctaw Indians . . ." (1753) and the *Edmund Atkin Report* of 1755. It was then that an impressed Whitehall appointed him superintendent for the southern district.

It was not until October 1756 that Atkin returned to South Carolina where he would serve until his death in 1761. His tenure was controversial. Many denounced him as pompous, lethargic, and inefficient. He failed to prevent the Cherokee uprising of 1758 which was not crushed until 1761. His most noted if fleeting successes were convincing the Cherokee and Catawba to war against the French and their allied Indians in 1758 and 1759. The resulting raids were mere pinpricks and most of the southern Indians who joined General John Forbes' campaign against Fort Pitt in 1758 soon deserted. More durable were his efforts at setting up and maintaining the office which was eventually taken over by a far more capable superintendent.[28]

The office was vacant for nearly a year until Whitehall tapped John Stuart to serve as southern Indian Superintendent in 1762. Stuart would be a much better superintendent. He was energetic, diplomatic with Indians and whites alike, and far-sighted in his policies. Stuart and Johnson worked closely to coordinate their diplomacy. They agreed on the broad outlines of British policy, though at times they differed over details.

Stuart had his hands full. Warriors in the southern district numbered perhaps 12,000 by mid-century.[29] Two tribes posed the greatest threat to the southern colonies. The Cherokee had perhaps 2,750 warriors in four clusters in the western Carolinas, northern Georgia, and eastern Tennessee. The Upper and Lower Creek or Muskogee numbered 2,665 warriors in western Georgia and eastern Alabama. With 5,000 warriors the Choctaw were the largest southern tribe but posed little immediate threat to the colonies from their villages in southern Mississippi. Even more distant were the Chickasaw with 480 warriors in northern Mississippi and western Tennessee. All of those tribes, to varying degrees, were potential enemies to British rule.

In contrast, two small tribes in the western Carolinas, the Catawba with 320 warriors and Tuscarora with about 100, were firm British allies by necessity. Their villages were only a few days' march from the settlements. British power could either shelter or crush them. Those tribes served as a buffer between the colonists and war parties of Cherokee or any northern tribes striding down the warrior path along the Appalachian Mountain spine.

Scattered among those larger tribes were smaller ones like the Alabama on the river named for them, the Yamassee and Seminole of northern Florida, the Nottoway and Spanoney of southern Virginia and upper North Carolina, the Southern Shawnee who lived among the Upper Creek, and a cluster of Tunica, Biloxi, Houma, Atakapa, Quapaw, Opelosa, Bayagoula, and Pascagoula among the Choctaw in western Mississippi. Those tribes simply tried to survive without being trampled or devoured by their more powerful neighbors. Handfuls of their warriors may have occasionally slipped away on raids, but the village elders insisted on peace. A tribe's population was roughly five times its number of warriors. Thus, as many as 55,000 Indians were scattered in villages across the southeast.

Until 1763, the dynamics of a classic balance of power governed relations among the southern tribes and the British, French, and Spanish. Interests rather than sentiments shaped relations. Each colonial power or tribe conducted diplomacy, trade, and war to advance its respective interests. Alliances shifted with threats. An enemy one day could be an ally the next. The enemy of one's enemy was often one's friend.

Still, some animosities persisted. The French just could not nail down enduring frienships with the Choctaw or Chickasaw, nor could the British with the Creek or Cherokee. Those tribes naturally leaned toward the imperial power which was less immediately threatening. Indian council fires denied to one side were often but not always opened to the other.

What role did Spain play in the region? Spain was an imperial has-been in southeastern North America. Its colonies there were financial black holes. Throughout the 1750s and 1760s, the Spanish simply clung to the shelter of St. Augustine, Pensacola, and a few other tiny settlements.

The southern superintendent's counterpart was Louisiana's governor at New Orleans. The French governor remained diplomatically active among the tribes even after the British began occupying the region east of the Mississippi River in 1763. Officially, Governor Jean-Jacques Blaise d'Abbadie and his successor Charles-Philippe Aubry cooperated with the British after the Paris Treaty was signed on February 10, 1763. But they played a double game when British backs were turned. The livelihoods of hundreds of traders and prominent New Orleans merchants depended on keeping those southern tribes loyal to French interests. Just how far the French went toward maintaining their economic and diplomatic ties was and remains controversial. Did Governor d'Abbadie encourage the Tunica and other small tribes to attack a British expedition rowing laboriously up the Mississippi River in 1764? British officials certainly leveled that accusation. Governor d'Abbadie vociferously denied the charge.

When the Indian uprising erupted across the northern frontier in May 1763, it was greatly feared that the southern tribes would join with the rebels to forge one grand alliance dedicated to throwing the British back across the Appalachians, or to the tidewater. Tensions seemed just as hot with the southern as the northern tribes. The Cherokee had warred against the southern colonies from 1758 to 1761; an unstable truce had ended the fighting but animosities lingered. As in the north, traders swarmed over the region to ply the Indians with drink and cheat them of their furs. Squatters stole Indian lands and then demanded protection from their colonial government. Southern Indian Superintendent John Stuart was instrumental in keeping those tribes off the warpath.

Skilled as Stuart was, neither he nor anyone else in North America was as experienced in Indian diplomacy as Sir William Johnson.[30] Johnson had first arrived in America in 1738 from Ireland, his boyhood home. His uncle, Peter Warren, had sent for him to manage his vast lands in the lower Mohawk valley. Johnson proved worthy of the task, skillfully promoting peace and prosperity among the melange of Irish, Dutch, German, and English families, and the neighoring Mohawk and other tribes. He steadily amassed a fortune as a merchant, fur trader, and land speculator, but in harmony with rather than at the expense of the Indians. The Mohawk so esteemed Johnson for his fairness, sympathy, and generosity that they adopted him as the sachem Warraghiyagey or "The Man Who Undertakes Great Things." As a sachem he was entitled to sit in the Iroquois council at Onondaga. He would receive similar honors from a grateful and impressed New York government which named Johnson justice of the peace in 1745, militia colonel and Indian agent in 1746, and council member in 1751.

Johnson's Iroquois ties and diplomatic skills paid off for Britain during King George's War from 1745 to 1748. He not only managed to keep most Iroquois neutral but rallied many warriors against the French. In 1747 he led a war party to Lake George, though they never encountered the enemy. During the French and Indian War, General Edward Braddock named him Indian Superintendent and commander of the British expedition against the French on Lake Champlain on April 14, 1755. Under his command, a provincial army defeated a French and Indian attack on his Lake George camp on September 7, 1755. During the battle a musket ball tore into his thigh and would remain painfully lodged there for the remainder of his life. He received his command to return to his home, Johnson Hall, and concentrate on Indian diplomacy and serve as militia colonel. Learning of his victory, a grateful Whitehall bestowed upon him the title of baronet. He would henceforth be Sir William Johnson. During 1758 he led nearly 400 Indians on General James Abercromby's disastrous assault on Fort Carillon. At the siege of Fort Niagara in 1759, he took command of British forces when General John Prideaux was killed. He presided over the British defeat of a French relief force and Fort Niagara's surrender. In 1760, he rallied over 500 Indians for Amherst's campaign. He fumed as Amherst alienated most of them. But he was present at Montreal's surrender in September 1760.

With Canada conquered, the northern superintendent was eager to retire. In October 1760, he asked Amherst to consider "that having now discharged my duty during the war to the utmost of my ability, I should be glad to be freed from the discharge of an office so fatigueing in which I have greatly impaired my constitution & negected my concerns . . . which I would willingly apply the remainder of my life to retrieve."[31]

Permission was denied. The French may have surrendered Canada but the war dragged on. Rule had to be imposed on dozens of new tribes, most of which had fought against Britain during the war. Hundreds of those Indians had returned to their villages with British scalps, prisoners, and plunder, and still burned with animosity and distrust. The northern superintendent was essential to forging chains of friendship with those tribes and liberating their captives. Johnson reluctantly agreed to stay on.

Few men equaled and none surpassed Johnson in fulfilling the role of public servant. Yet he privately admitted that he was "not naturally fond of making any parade of my endeavors to serve my country. It is not easy to conceive my trouble & fatigue & neglect of domestic concerns . . . [I] have nothing more at heart than to make my labours of still more benefit to the public."[32] Yet, he knew his limits. When his name was proposed for New York governor in 1761, Johnson politely dismissed the nomination, claiming that he was "sensible of my inability for the execution of so important a trust."[33] Being an Indian Superintendent was an exhausting, Sisyphean task. Unlike so many others, Johnson did not reap private gain from public office, and he deplored those who did. He sacrificed enormous wealth and leisure during his decades of service. Writing in 1768, he revealed that his "income has never been half what it was before my appointment, & my acting in a regular military capacity brought me a considerable additional charge foreign to my civil commission . . . I have been a loser by the service, whilst I have totally neglected the many fair opportunitys which my situation & interest afforded me."[34]

Johnson was a highly intelligent and self-educated man who revelled in stimulating discussion. But try as he might it was difficult to establish a salon at Johnson Hall at the edge of the wilderness. A friend expressed his wish "to spend a week or two with you & assist you in fixing up some little philosophical aparatus that might amuse you in your hours of leisure & retirement."[35] That never came to pass.

Johnson, of course, could not conduct Indian diplomacy alone. He depended on a score of deputies, agents, interpreters, and others. Typical were his personnel expenses from August 1, 1762 to March 24, 1763 which included salaries of 823 pounds for nine employees, 39 pounds to rent a storehouse at Schenectady, and 1,346 pounds for himself.[36] All of his men were vital. Only one, however, was irreplaceable.

George Croghan was William Johnson's right-hand man. They first met at an Indian council at Fort Johnson, the Indian Superintendent's home in June 1756. The two men quickly hit it off. With a common age and Anglican Irish heritage they had immigrated to America as young men and had risen as successful traders, Indian experts, and womanizers. Croghan was not, however, an adopted member of any tribe as was Johnson among the Iroquois. Nor had he ever represented their interests as Johnson did before the French and Indian War broke out. Yet, after Johnson, probably no British subject had more experience with Indians.

The northern superintendency was responsible for fewer Indians but more tribes and a much more complex distribution of power than the southern district.[37] By the most accurate head count, at least 11,980 warriors in Canada, New York, the Ohio valley, and Great Lakes may have been available to war against the British. Most of them would join the 1763 uprising.

No tribe was more influential than the Iroquois, although its power had peaked a century earlier during the "Beaver Wars" of the 17th century when war parties ranged as far as the Mississippi River in an attempt to conquer all those tribes and win the fur trade for themselves. Those wars eventually exhausted all the tribes including the Iroquois. The age of Iroquois imperialism sputtered out by the early 18th century. Nonetheless, the Iroquois insisted that they remained the suzerain overlords of that region, and most tribes at least nominally went along with that notion. The messages of Iroquois envoys were greeted with respect if not automatic compliance.

The six bands of the Iroquois "longhouse" lived in village clusters across New York with the Mohawk, now reduced to 160 warriors, guarding the eastern door on the middle Mohawk valley, the Oneida with 250 warriors just upstream, the Onondaga with 150 warriors tending the council fire in the center; then the 200 Cayuga and 140 Tuscarora warriors, and finally the Seneca, 1,050 strong anchoring the western door in the Genesee valley. Colonies of Iroquois had settled elsewhere including 80 Oswegatchie warriors on the St. Lawrence River, and several hundred Mingo, mostly former Seneca, scattered in the upper Ohio River valley. Those tribes remained loosely allied with the Six Nations.

The mission Indians in lower Canada were called the Seven Nations. There were 300 Caughnawaga warriors at Sault St. Louis near Montreal, 150 Cansadaga, Arundac, and Algonkin at Lac de Deux Montagnes near the Ottawa River mouth, 100 Abenakin at the St. Francis mission, 40 Skaghquanoghrono at Trois-Rivieres, and 40 Huron at La Lorette near Quebec.

Those tribes had supplied a stream of war parties against the British. During Amherst's War they would remain British allies.

After the Seneca the Shawnee fielded the most warriors, 800 in villages along the upper Ohio, Muskingum, and Scioto River valleys. With 600 warriors the Delaware also were numerous although scattered in villages in the upper Susquehanna and Muskingum River valleys. With several hundred Mingo scattered among them, the Shawnee and Delaware listened carefully to decisions of the Six Nations council. When that council split, as it did during the 1763 uprising, the Shawnee and Delaware joined the faction that best reflected their own interests. Mingled with the Delaware in the upper Susquehanna River were 200 related Nanticoke, Conoy, Tutecoe, and Sapony.

At one time the Algonquian-speaking Ottawa, Chippewa, and Potawatomi were one tribe which splintered but remained associated as "the three fires." When the uprising broke out the Potawatomi and Ottawa still referred to the Chippewa as their "Elder Brothers." Those tribes were scattered across the Michigan penninsula and the shores of upper Lakes Huron and Michigan, and eastern Superior. Three tribes straddled Detroit, the Huron with 250 warriors, the Potawatomi with 150, and the Ottawa with 300, along with 320 Mississauga Chippewa not far away. Ever more Chippewa would join the Ottawa village near Detroit in the months leading up to the war's outbreak and thereafter. Near Fort St. Joseph there were 150 Ottawa and 200 Potawatomi. At Michilimackinac there were 250 Ottawa and 400 Chippewa.

Elsewhere in the upper Great Lakes there were about 200 Wyandot Huron warriors at Sandusky on Lake Erie, 110 Menominee, 110 Folsavoin, 360 Puan or Winnebago, 300 Sauk, and 320 Fox near Fort La Baye at Green Bay on Lake Michigan, 230 Miami or Twightwee near Fort Miami, and 180 Kickapoo, 90 Mascouten, 100 Piankeshaw, and 200 Wawiaghtono near Fort Ouiatenon. The Illinois tribe along the Illinois River had about 500 warriors among the Peoria, Kaskaskia, Cahokia, and other bands.

British actions following the conquest provoked anger in each of those villages. Johnson and his men did what they could to prevent that anger from exploding into violence. But powerful forces beyond their control would overwhelm their efforts.

After Canada's surrender ambitious traders raced to be first to the villages in the Ohio valley and Great Lakes. Johnson feared that Indian resentment would rise as unscrupulous traders cheated them. He ordered his deputy and agents to enforce fixed prices, required licenses, forbade the sale of alcohol, and imposed other regulations. Those who traded without a license or violated the rules faced the confiscation of their goods if caught. George Croghan admonished his own traders "to dispose of your goods at prices agreed on and be careful to cultivate a good understanding with the Indians at the different nations by doing them strict justice in the course of your trade with them."[38] Hardnosed realism rather than sentiment justified such policies. Exploitation of the Indians prompted hatreds to swell to the exploding point which in turn jeopardized not just profits but the newly won empire itself.

Nonetheless, traders protested the rules. The war had disrupted supplies to the Indians. The pent-up demand for goods was enormous. The traders could reap vast profits if they were allowed to charge whatever the market would bear. The trouble was that such potential "killer" profits might become literally true.[39] The more honest merchants objected that their compliance with the regulations lost them profits to unscrupulous rivals. Nearly all traders charged George Croghan with conflict of interests with his simultaneous activities as a deputy to the Indian Superintendent and trader. Fort Pitt merchant John Langdale blistered Croghan as "the most implacable enemy to the province."[40] Honest traders apparently were few. At Detroit Captain Campbell reported that the Indians "complain of our prices and that we do not take all their peltries from them. They all go to Niagara where there is no control on selling rum . . . and neglect to purchase ammunition for their subsistence, and then become a burden on the officer who commands here."[41]

No trade good was more common than rum. Indians at once despised and demanded alcohol. They deplored its pernicious effects but many were addicted to its abuse. Addicts impoverished themselves and their families by trading away a winter's worth of skins for a few cupfuls. Drunkards committed vicious murders and mayhem.

Rum had been a vital product for those British traders who had sneaked into French territory to wring profits from the Indians before the war. To avoid rum's debilitating effects the French government had tried to ban its sale by Canadians to the Indians. Now that the British were trying to manage their own empire rather than destroy that of the French, Amherst accepted Johnson's plea that rum be banned. But bans must be enforced. British fort commanders and Indian agents did so sparingly.

Poaching was another source of Indian rage. Like rum it was forbidden to hunt on Indian lands. But hundreds of long hunters did so anyway. Colonel Henry Bouquet was determined to stamp it out. To Fort Cumberland's commander, Major James Livingstone, he angrily complained that "notwithstanding my orders against hunting a number of white men have been out the whole season and destroyed a great quantity of game. As that infamous practice will occasion some disturbance I recommend to you to endeavour to seize some of those villains that a satisfactory example may be made of them."[42] But like rum smugglers, few poachers were caught.

Then there were those who stole the land from beneath the Indians whose ancestors had lived there for generations. In western Virginia, Pennsylvania, and New York, squatters swarmed into one valley after another and defied anyone, red or white, to expel them. In February 1762, Colonel Bouquet wrote Virginia governor Francis Fauquier that "for two years past these lands have been overrun by a number of vagabonds who under pretence of hunting were making settlements in several parts of them which the Indians made grievous & repeated complaints as being contrary to the treaty made with them at Easton."[43] Once again, squatting may have been illegal but the law was unenforceable.

Not one but two land disputes between the British and Indians bedeviled relations in New York. The Kayaderosseras patent was fradulently taken from the Mohawk in 1708 and was interpreted by the investors to include a vast wedge of 700,000 acres between the Hudson and Mohawk Rivers. New York Lieutenant Governor Cadwallader Colden bluntly told William Johnson that "it will be impossible for you to please both the Indians and the Pattentees of the great tracts. I believe not one of the great tracts were fairly purchased."[44] That dispute would rage for years before it was finally settled.

Johnson's power was embarrassingly limited in his own backyard. For decades he had been an Iroquois sachem and had carved out a huge fief of land straddling the Mohawk valley. But his neighbor, Ury Klock, persistently antagonized the Iroquois by trying to steal their land and debauch their people with rum. In January 1761, Klock took title to 800 acres of land north where Canada Creek flows into the Mohawk River. He obtained it with his usual tactics. After plying several prominent Mohawks with rum he got them to sign the deed. Upon hearing of the trick, the Mohawks counciled and condemned Klock and those he had corrupted. They protested to Indian Superintendent Johnson. He assured the Mohawks that "Klock's villainous proceeding will not be allowed."[45] He appealed to New York's governor and council to bring Klock to justice.

But the government's hands were tied and they could do nothing. Klock's swindle was nothing new. For years he had nibbled away at Mohawk lands by taking advantage of Indian weaknesses for drink and gifts. In doing so he theoretically violated vague laws forbidding such deceits. But the law meant little on the frontier and Klock's lawyers were adept at confounding any attempt to enforce it.

Johnson was motivated by more than his dedication to his Mohawk brothers and justice in bringing Klock to bay. While he was a conscientious, tireless, and just advocate for reconciling British and Indian interests, at times his own interests intruded. Throughout his decades of public service, he gained a land empire of baronial proportions. His wealth depended on his tenants' rent. The more land he could amass and the more people he could settle, the richer he became. In 1760, the Iroquois gave him a huge tract of 66,000 acres north of the Mohawk River in gratitude for his decades of faithful advocacy. Johnson then gave them 1,200 pieces of eight to seal the "grant." So far, so good. But there was a catch. That land included some claimed by Klock. And both men had violated laws which forbade anyone but the Crown from buying land from Indians. Legal tangles, bureaucratic inertia, and political squabbles would block any resolution of that conflict for another seven years.[46]

Elsewhere disputes arose even over lands which the Indians had seemingly ceded by treaty. For Indians habitation and ownership differed. Circumstances might cause different peoples to occupy the same patch of land at different times. But no humans owned that land. Only the Master of Life who created the world could possibly hold title. Those who inhabited land acquired duties toward it. They could transfer their right to live on some land to others but that did not imply or confer ownership. Indians retained the right to cross and even hunt the lands they "sold" to the whites.

Land disputes did not just entangle the British and Indians. Within colonies different land companies battled over titles or with the government over swaths of territory. Nearly all the colonies asserted conflicting land claims. New York, Massachusetts, and New Hampshire overlapped between the Hudson and Connecticut Rivers. Connecticut settlers squatted in the upper Susquehanna valley of Pennsylvania. Provincial governments justified their claims by citing ancient royal charters and treaties with Indians. At times those involved submitted their dispute to Whitehall to decided. But the royal ministers were notoriously slow and indecisive both because they lacked an understanding of the issues' complexities and feared alienating important constituents.[47]

The most notorious land dispute between colonies arose in the Wyoming valley of the upper Susquehanna River. Connecticut's Susquehanna Company claimed that land based on the 1662 Connecticut Charter, which asserted a "sea to sea" territory and a fraudulent deal struck with some minor and drunken Iroquois chiefs at the 1754 Albany Congress. In 1761, the Susquehanna Company built a road through the sparsely populated territory between the upper Delaware and Susquehanna Rivers to reach Wyoming and began clearing land there. The local tribes, their Iroquois overlords, and Pennsylvania's government protested but could not deter the Susquehanna Company's claim and settlers.[48]

Enforcement of laws against unfair trade, poaching, and squatting was difficult if not impossible in a vast wilderness broken by a dozen far-flung forts. The French had founded the post system to promote and regulate trade, rally the Indians in wars against the British, and troll for Christian converts. The British inherited the system and felt compelled to retain it. But it was expensive to maintain and the British lacked the French ability to understand and thus ingratiate themselves with the Indians. Each frontier fort commander was responsible for enforcing trade regulations. That worked or failed depending on the skills and determination of the commander.

But Amherst's policy of denial hamstrung even the most conscientious post commanders. At Detroit Captain Campbell wearily reported that "the Indians expect presents from us. I have done everything in my power to keep them in temper. I have been obliged to give them provisions and small presents (tho without orders). I hope the generals will approve of it as the necessity of the service requires it . . . depriving them of all assistance might have been attended with fatal consequences."[49]

Those problems and the Indian rage they provoked would worsen as British officials, officers, and Indian agents proved incapable of resolving them. Amherst was unfazed by the ever more dire reports of Indian unrest and the rising possibility of rebellion. He believed that the British army would deter any uprising even when the hodgepodge of regulations and councils failed. That hope would be severely misplaced.

The British army in North America was unprepared to fight a wilderness war.[50] What was surprising to many was that any army at all remained there. In 1763, William Pitt made a crucial decision—the army would stay in North America. More than a little irony accompanied that decision. In its previous wars with the French in North America, Whitehall sent over few if any troops and quickly withdrew them once the guns fell silent. But now that the French Empire was conquered, Pitt decided to maintain regiments there. Some troops, of course, were needed to man posts across Canada and the wilderness empire. Most, however, were stationed in American cities and towns.

Aside from the questionable distribution of troops, there was a problem with the type of regiments left in America. While regular regiments would have been appropriate for Canadian cities, if occupying the newly conquered lands were the priority, then Whitehall logically would have deployed there the best units for the task, the ranger companies and 80th Light Infantry. Instead the ranger units were disbanded shortly after Canada was surrendered and the 80th was scheduled to be dissolved in 1763.

Did that policy reflect a Whitehall fear of rebellion as much from Americans as Canadians? If so, the Crown unwittingly launched the very policy that would eventually provoke the American Revolution. Maintaining a half dozen regiments in America was very expensive. Whitehall thought it only fair that the Americans pay a share of their own defense. Most Americans would see the issue quite differently—the troops and taxes were deliberate Whitehall means of repressing them.[51]

Nonetheless, the number of regiments and troops stationed in North America plummeted from 1760 to 1763. At the conquest there were 32 regiments with 30,000 troops in North America.[52] Shortly thereafter Whitehall ordered Amherst to cut the four battalions of the 60th Royal Americans to 700 enlisted men, 20 drummers, and 60 noncommissioned each. Troops would be reassigned among the companies to give each a roughly equal number.[53] Then, in 1761 and 1762, North America was stripped of troops, supplies, and ships for various campaigns in the Caribbean and later the occupation of the Floridas. In May 1762, Amherst sent Lord Rollo with 2,000 troops to occupy Dominica. On November 19, 1761 General Robert

Monckton sailed with an eleven-battalion and 173-ship expedition from New York toward Martinique, which was reached on January 7, 1762. That army, reinforced and commanded by George Keppel, the Earl of Albemarle, sailed on to besiege Havana in the summer of 1762. In September 1762, Amherst sent his younger brother, Lieutenant Colonel William Amherst, to lead an expedition to retake Newfoundland, which the French had captured. Most of the regiments in those distant campaigns were occupying those conquered lands when the 1763 uprising exploded.

Once the Treaty of Paris was signed on February 10, 1763, maintaining a large army in North America naturally seemed wasteful to Whitehall. On May 18, 1763, Amherst received orders to disband the 60th Royal Americans' 3rd and 4th battalions and reduce its 1st and 2nd battalions to 500 troops in nine 55-man companies in each battalion. The 42nd Highlanders would also be reduced to one grenadier, one light, and seven line companies of roughly 55 men each. The 80th Light Infantry regiment would be completely disbanded and its troops dispersed among other regiments.[54]

The British army in North America was stretched thin when the uprising exploded in 1763. There were about 8,000 troops overall, of which 3,650 were in Canada, 1,700 in Nova Scotia, Cape Breton, and Newfoundland, 1,250 on the New York frontier, 400 in western Pennsylvania, 350 in the upper Great Lakes posts, 450 in South Carolina and Georgia, and several hundred in New York City.[55]

Numbers and deployment were not the only weaknesses. The regiment was the British army's core. The Crown appointed a regiment's colonel. Most were given to experienced, skilled officers; some were sinecures. But the colonel was the regiment's "proprietor" who was responsible for nurturing it. Nearly all British regiments held only one battalion. With four battalions the 60th Royal Americans was a unique exception. The number of companies in each battalion also varied, with eight, nine, ten, or twelve the most common. Of those companies, one was composed of grenadiers and the other of light infantry.

In North America, the company rather than the regiment was the most important unit. Regiments were broken up and their companies sent to distant posts. Companies rarely joined to train to march and fight as a battalion. There were also some New York and South Carolina Independent Companies raised to garrison distant posts. Invalids composed the bulk of those units. Those scattered posts were as much a liability as an asset. They were expensive to maintain and easy to take by surprise. They did not deter Indian aggression, they provoked it.

Regiments were chronically understrength, especially on campaign when death, disease, and desertion drained away men. It was estimated that a regiment had to recruit 1.5 percent of its strength a month during peace and 2.1 percent during war.[56] Regiments were responsible for filling their own ranks. Recruitment was perenial but was especially prevalent during the winter months after the harvest was done and idle hands restless. A recruiting party usually included a subaltern, a sergeant, and a drummer boy. They employed fair means and foul to snare a recruit. Appeals to patriotism or adventure in crowded taverns or market squares gained only so many volunteers. Enlistment bounties enticed others, especially when the "King's shilling" was found at the bottom of a drained mug of rum. But most of those who signed up were riff-raff and misfits of all sorts. Vagrants, debtors, and hardened criminals could escape prison or the hangman's noose by promising to serve the king. In a pinch, regiments ordered to embark for distant campaigns could draft men from those which remained at home.

As if the thin red line were not thin enough, desertion further depleted the ranks. Those able to slip away from camp could usually find refuge in American towns and farms. While ever more Americans despised the army, they sympathized with the plight of common soldiers. Many a British officer echoed General Thomas Gage's complaint that "the Mutiny Act does not extend to America. . . . Soldiers are seduced from the King's service, deserters are protected and secreted, arms, cloaths, &c purchased. Quarters and carriages refused, without incurring any penalty. Officers have been persecuted and fined for seizing deserters, seduced from their regiments, and indented as private servants; sent to jail for being in the quarters which had been allotted for them, and prosecuted for getting carriges on their march."[57]

Desertion was not the only problem plaguing the army. Drunkenness, theft, insubordination, and other crimes teetered regiments at the brink of anarchy. Fort Bedford's commander, Lieutenant Lewis Ourry, admitted "that the men of this garrison are lost to all discipline and continually guilty of drunkeness and theft, they have burnt great part of the rails of the enclosure, and the poles that make the floors of the stores over their barracks; the meat and the liquor have lately been broke open and robbed, as also some houses in the town."[58] Officers were often helpless to prevent or punish such serious infractions.

Just as many troops ignored the strict regulations that supposedly governed their lives, they got little out of training. The 1756 Regulations streamlined platoon exercises to 24 motions from the bewildering 63 motions of the 1728 Regulations. Each motion was accompanied by a drumbeat. When marching on parade or in battle the British army goose-stepped stiff-legged at 120 steps a minute. Fife and drum music provided rhythm for the march.

In battle, the grenadier company was split between two platoons which sandwiched the battalion's line, while the light infantry was detached as skirmishers on the battalion's front or flanks. Troops fired by platoons, starting with the platoon on the left flank and rippling across the line to the right. After one rank had fired, the next took their place. Ideally, the first platoon had reloaded by the time the last had fired so that there was a continuous rolling succession of volleys. During the late 1750s, ever more battalions adopted a more complicated version of this known as "alternate fire," which involved every third platoon firing at once. But the initial training in these elaborate exercises was rudimentary and rarely practiced thereafter, once a regiment was on the march or at a post.

The troops were no more adept with their firearms than they were their maneuvers. They were armed with the .75 caliber Land Pattern Musket, affectionately known as the "Brown Bess." The production of muskets had been standardized ever since the 1715 ordnance system was inaugurated. Mass quantities of parts were ordered from different sources and then assembled at the Tower of London and Dublin arsenals. The Brown Bess was a rugged, well-made musket. Gunpowder was also carefully manufactured by standards developed at the Royal Laboratory at Woolwich. During the 1730s, powder was developed that could be used both for priming the pan and seating the ball; until that time a finer priming powder was used which complicated loading. The ball and exact measures of the powder were rolled in a paper cartridge with each end twisted. Cartridges were kept in a wooden block with eighteen holes drilled and encased in waterproof black leather. The rate and ease of loading and firing were further improved in the 1750s when battalions began to replace wooden with steel ramrods. Troops were also issued bayonets and hangers or light swords.

Unfortunately, several factors prevented the soldiers from becoming good shots. Although each battalion was annually issued 45,000 charges, or 60 to 120 shots per soldier, the troops were not issued enough lead to allow them to practice. All they could do was burn powder or "squibs" in simulated firings. Muskets had only front sights which, when used, caused soldiers to fire high. Finally, soldiers were taught to point rather than aim their muskets toward the enemy before pulling the trigger.

Discipline and training was poor because many officers simply were not fit for command. Roughly two-thirds of the officer commissions from the rank of lieutenant colonel to ensign in the British army were purchased and the rest earned by promotion. Royal Warrants of 1720 and 1722 fixed prices for each officer rank. The Crown fixed the number of officers in each regiment and approved all commissions. Vacancies occurred through retirement, transfers, or death. That set off a chain reaction. One could not go up without selling down. The office could be sold only to someone from the rank just below. Buyers got the rank but not the seniority. They entered that rank as junior officers and advanced as their seniors moved elsewhere. The regiment's proprietary colonel recommended one of the applicants for each vacancy to the Crown, who usually approved it. Death, however, opened a vacancy that the king could fill at his whim. Usually, a man with merit was vaulted into that position.

The nobility accounted for about one-quarter of the officers and one-half of the colonels and generals. Untitled merchants or landed gentry accounted for nearly half of officers. Foreigners composed another quarter of the corps. A handful of officers originated as privates. Outstanding bravery and leadership could pull them upward as noncommissioned officers and even higher.

Officers learned their trade from experience and study. Veteran officers passed on their skills to new arrivals. That knowledge was supplemented by a half dozen books on military science which were considered essential reading, including Humphrey Bland's *Treatise on Military Discipline* (1727), Richard Kane's *Campaigns* (1745), Turpin de Crisse's *Art of War* (1754), Thomas More Molyneaux's *Conjunct Expeditions* (1759), Campbell Dalrymple's *Military Essay* (1761), and Maurice de Saxe's *Reveries, or Memories upon the Art of War* (1757). These books covered every conceivable aspect of military life from barracks to battles.

But feeding their troops rather than fighting the enemy preoccupied every officer. That problem was especially acute in North America. Supplying the distant forts was an unrelenting challenge. A rutted wagon road ran the 308 miles from Philadelphia to Fort Pitt. Even during peacetime it was tough enough scraping up enough wagons and draft animals to keep Fort Pitt and the forts en route provisioned; during war it took months to gather what was needed to sustain a campaign along that axis with Indian war parties haunting the surrounding forests. A similar problem afflicted the 210 miles of water roads from Albany to Oswego on Lake Ontario. During the summer the watershed waters where the Mohawk River and French Creek nearly touched each other dried to trickles. Supplies had to be hauled by wagon for ever longer stretches of road linking the navigable points of those two water courses. Winter severed the Great Lakes forts from the east for four or five miserable months. Boating supplies to the forts was a long, tedious and sometimes dangerous undertaking even after the lake ice had melted. The slow breakup of the ice each spring was a momentous event for the stranded garrisons. Fort Presque Isle's commander, Ensign John Christie, reported that "the lake began to open about the 20th of March but perceived mountains of ice for ten days after."[59]

Supplies, of course, had to be procured before they could be sent. It cost 200,000 pounds sterling to feed the 15 battalions in North America for a year, and another 200,000 to pay for transporting them and their supplies and maintaining their forts. The ordnance bill was another 45,000 pounds.[60]

Like most armies throughout history, Britain's suffered from rapacious, corrupt, inefficient contractors. Each regiment had in London a civilian agent who purchased equipment, lobbied Whitehall, managed finances, and drew funds for the troops' pay from the paymaster general. The agent forwarded all equipment and pay to the regiment's quartermaster in America. Agents placed their orders with private contractors who received their commissions by submitting the lowest bid to Whitehall. The commissary general for North America, Robert Leake during this time, was responsible for negotiating and implementing contracts with the contractors. In England those who received contracts were usually wealthy, powerful members of

Parliament or their financial backers. Agents in the colonies enjoyed a similar happy marriage of economic and political power. All that sounds clear-cut enough. But for British quartermasters implementing contracts was an endless nightmare of missed deadlines, shoddy goods, and padded bills.

Since 1760 the British treasury had relied on the London firm of George and James Colebrook, Arnold Nesbit, and Moses Franks to supply the army in North America. That firm's agents in America were William Plumsted and David Franks of Philadelphia. Bidding reopened when that contract expired on November 5, 1763. It took another five months before Whitehall could find a new supplier. On April 13, 1764, the partners Sir Samuel Fludyer and John Drummond won the contract by promising to deliver the goods considerably cheaper than the original firm. Robert Callender was the North American agent for the new firm. These turnovers delayed shipments and raised costs.

These interrelated problems of ill-trained troops and officers, poor morale and discipline, thinning ranks, and inadequate supply were debilitating enough. Even worse, the army had only gradually and partially adapted to North American warfare since the French and Indian War broke out in 1754. The lessons, especially General Edward Braddock's debacle at the Monongahela in 1755, had been harsh and inadequately learned.

The most important innovation was the creation of independent ranger companies and light infantry companies in each battalion. Hardened frontiersmen filled ranger companies. Each battalion's best marksmen and most agile runners were organized into the light infantry company. An entire regiment, the 80th, was composed of light infantrymen. Yet these units remained the neglected stepchildren of the British army.

Tactics remained rooted in European-style battles in open fields rather than North American forests. To his credit, General Jeffrey Amherst did adopt a more practical two- rather than three-line formation, probably in 1759. The enemy's ability to outflank the British was thus rendered more difficult with redcoat ranks extended by a third. With the front and rear ranks taking turns firing and loading, the enemy was still blasted with a nearly continuous storm of lead. Unfortunately, the two-rank formation was ineffective against Indians in a wilderness battle.[61]

Amherst and most officers spurned the advice of wilderness warfare experts. Two books were actually written on North American warfare by participants. Unfortunately, both books by Robert Rogers, *The Journals of Robert Rogers: Containing an Account of the several Excusions . . . upon the Continent of North America* (1765) and William Smith, *An Historical Account of the Expedition Against the Ohio Indians* (1766) did not appear until just after Amherst's War. Of course, it is unlikely that Amherst and other like-minded officers would have read those books had they been published earlier. Snobbery explains the attitude. It was inconceivable that such unconventional units, especially provincial rangers, were better suited than regular line regiments to North American warfare.

The army was just as straitjacketed by strategy. It was excruciatingly difficult for regular troops to reach let alone take distant villages by surprise. Woodland tribes settled in clusters of villages to till their crops. They remained in their homes for years and often decades until the soil was exhausted or war forced them elsewhere. Trails linked each village in the cluster and the clusters with one another and with the distant white settlements upon which they depended for trade goods. The white traders knew where the villages were and how to get there. This appeared to make the villages vulnerable to attack.

An enemy attack, however, especially if it was a British or French expedition, rarely caught a village by surprise. Travelers along those well-traveled trails usually brought word of a white expedition even as it mustered troops and supplies at some frontier fort. The inhabitants of a targeted village usually had ample time to gather their belongings and flee. Once the expedition arrived in the deserted village it could do nothing more than burn the dwellings and crops. Yet if the expedition destroyed the crops of enough villages the tribe faced a winter of starvation. Their fate then depended on the generosity of allied tribes.

The greatest Indian weakness was their dependence on muskets, powder, and shot, none of which they could manufacture themselves. That dependence was not grave as long as the French and British Empires vied with one another for Indian furs and alliances. By playing those enemies off against one another, most tribes enjoyed a relatively steady supply. That changed once the British conquered France's North American empire and merged it with its own. The tribes now faced a monopoly with an iron grip over nearly all prices and supplies, although a trickle of French munitions from New Orleans reached the tribes.

Given all the limitations on British military power, it was easier and cheaper to feed than fight the Indians. As long as the British honored their agreements, the Indians reciprocated. Few white men understood Indian faults and virtues as well as George Croghan. While he admitted that "Indians are of a fickle, uncertain temper," he noted it "remarkable that altho they are thus capricious, yet to their honor . . . it was never known they ever attempted to dissolve a contract, justly and plainly made with them."[62] William Johnson observed that same reality. In peacetime Indians held "theft in contempt; so that they are rarely guilty of it though tempted by articles of much value."[63] Ironically, that could not be said for the British, despite their legalistic culture that exalted written contracts.

But one challenge to Indian diplomacy was knowing with whom to strike an agreement. Like any community, each village was often a boiling caldron of conflicting personalities, clans, and interests. All the white conquerors had trouble understanding a society where authority was so decentralized and ambivalent. To alleviate that problem, the Indian agents would appoint a "medal chief" upon whom was vested power and responsibility for relations between Indians and whites. But even then a chief reigned rather than ruled. The chief's task was to forge a consensus among different factions. A village was often split between war and peace factions. Successful British diplomacy depended on knowing who was in which faction. Generous gifts to members of the faction most opposed to British interests could tip the political balance.

Thus was diplomacy geared to village chiefs rather than tribes, which refer mostly to linguistic and cultural rather than political groupings. A tribal band with a chief might be limited to one village or embrace several. The bands of a tribe were not so much allied as agreed not to war against one another. For some tribes caught on the frontier between the British and French Empires, their nonaggression pacts could break down during war as competing agents arrived at their councils with gifts and promises. During the 1763 uprising, the Six Nations Iroquois split between the Seneca, who warred against the British and the other five, who first stayed neutral and then allied with the British.

In 1760, Britain may have conquered Canada but the global war was far from won. The war would drag on for another three years that drained the belligerents of blood and treasury. Fighting with France raged elsewhere in Europe, the Caribbean, India, and on the high seas. Indeed, the war would widen before it ended; Spain allied with France in August 1761.

Louisiana, which stretched up the Mississippi River and to the southern Appalachian Mountains, remained a French stronghold and the back door to the Great Lakes and Ohio valley. On the upper Mississippi River, Fort de Chartres supplied local tribes and was only a two weeks' hard walk to Detroit. The just subjected tribes of the region clug to hope that a French army was coming to their rescue. Along the British frontier rumors of French agents, warbelts, and secret councils proliferated.

The French in Louisiana were certainly within their rights to press war against the British. They had not signed loyalty oaths and their country was still at war with Britain. They lacked not the justification but the means of waging war. At best Captain Villiers, Fort de Chartres' commander, could distribute some of his meager supplies and circulate warbelts among the tribes. Aware that the Canadians had signed loyalty oaths whose violation might result in their execution for treason, the French were circumspect in encouraging them to join any Indian rebellions.

Yet in the occupied territory, however much the war had exhausted them and despite the loyalty oaths the British forced them to swear, most Canadian men were still armed and potentially dangerous. France's Indian allies were unbeaten and unbound to any sovereign but their own fierce independence, no matter what platitudes they might utter at councils to their new "Great Father" across the sea. Most of those Indians mourned Canada's surrender and despised and feared the conquerors; their hearts burned with deepening rage. British arrogance combined with the shortage and high prices of goods was shoving those tribes to the breaking point.

Indian Superintendent William Johnson and other Indian agents understood this; Commander in Chief Jeffery Amherst did not. Amherst ruled over the empire with the advice and diplomacy of the two next most powerful men in the American colonies, the northern and southern Indian superintendents. The tragedy was that he rejected their advice. To Croghan, Johnson wrote that it is "clear that too much economy ought not to be thought of as yet with the Indians, if we expect to keep them in temper & maintain our posts—but it is not in my power to convince the General thereof."[64]

NOTES

1. Clarence J. Webster, ed., *The Journal of Jeffrey Amherst, Recording the Military Career of General Amherst in America from 1758 to 1763* (hereafter cited as *Amherst Journal*) (Chicago: Ryerson Press, 1931), 247.

2. Lawrence Henry Gipson, *The British Empire before the American Revolution*, 15 vols. (New York: 1936–1970), vol. 7, *The Great War for Empire: The Victorious Years, 1758–1760* (New York: Alfred A. Gipson, 1949), 448–49, 457.

3. Webster, *Amherst Journal*, 246.

4. For a good overview of scholarly perspectives on the English occupation and Canadian response, see Cameron Nish, ed., *The French Canadians, 1759–1766: Conquered? Half-Conquered? Liberated?* (Montreal: Copp Clark Publishing Company, 1966).

5. John R. Cuneo, *Robert Rogers of the Rangers* (Ticonderoga, N.Y.: Fort Ticonderoga Museum, 1988).

6. Jeffrey Amherst to Robert Rogers, September 12, 1760, in Sylvester K. Stevens, Donald H. Kent, Autumn L. Leonard, Louis M. Waddell, and John Totteham, eds., *The Papers of Henry Bouquet* (hereafter cited as *Bouquet Papers*), 6 vols. (Harrisburg: Pennsylvania Historical and Museum Commission, 1972–1994), 5:33–35. For Rogers's own sometimes varying and contradictory accounts of his mission, see V. H. Paltsits, ed., "Journal of Robert Rogers," *Bulletin of the New York Public Library* (New York: New York Public Library, April 1933); Robert Rogers, *A Concise Account of North America* (London, 1765).

7. Robert Monckton to Donald Campbell, October 19, 1760, *Bouquet Papers*; Robert Monckton to Robert Rogers, October 19, 1760, ibid., 5:78–81.

8. Nicolas B. Wainwright, *George Croghan: Wilderness Diplomat* (Chapel Hill: University of North Carolina Press, 1959), 4.

9. Donald Campbell to Henry Bouquet, December 2, 1760, *Bouquet Papers*, 5:141–43; Robert Rogers to Henry Bouquet, December 1, 1760, ibid., 5:138.

10. Return of Detroit Prisoners, December 26, 1760, *Bouquet Papers*, 5:210; Henry Bouquet to Robert Monckton, December 25, 1760, ibid., 5:204–5.

11. Oath of Allegiance, October 19, 1760, *Bouquet Papers*, 5:80.

12. Jeffrey Amherst to William Johnson, February 1, 1761, in James Sullivan and

A. C. Flick, eds., *The Papers of William Johnson* (hereafter cited as *Johnson Papers*), 14 vols. (Albany: State University of New York, 1921–1965), 4:315–18.

13. Donald Campell to Henry Bouquet, December 2, 1760, *Bouquet Papers*, 5: 142.

14. Eustache Gamelin to Henry Bouquet, December 23, 1760, *Bouquet Papers*, 5:198. See also James MacDonald to Henry Bouquet, March 10, 1761, ibid., 5:342.

15. Proceedings of Indian Conference, December 3–5, 1760, *Johnson Papers*, 10: 198–207.

16. Indian Conference at Detroit, December 3, 1760, *Bouquet Papers*, 5:151.

17. George Croghan to William Johnson, January 13, 1761, *Johnson Papers*, 4: 301–4; Jeffrey Amherst to William Johnson, February 1, 1761, ibid., 4:315–18.

18. Donald Campbell to Henry Bouquet, December 23, 1760, *Bouquet Papers*, 5:196; Donald Campbell to Henry Bouquet, December 11, 1760, March 10, 1761, ibid., 5:170–72, 340–41; Henry Bouquet to Robert Monckton, March 20, April 22, 1761, ibid., 5:352–56, 435–39.

19. J. C. Long, *Lord Jeffrey Amherst: A Soldier of the King* (New York: Macmillan, 1933).

20. Horace Walpole, *Memoirs of George II*, John Brooke, ed. (New Haven, Conn.: Yale University Press, 1985), 3:283–87.

21. Amherst's General Orders, April 19, 1761, *Bouquet Papers*, 5:455–56.

22. Jeffrey Amherst to William Johnson, February 22, 1761, *Johnson Papers*, 4: 345, 343–47.

23. William Johnson to Jeffrey Amherst, March 21, 1761, *Johnson Papers*, 10:244, 243–27. See also William Johnson to Jeffrey Amherst, June 21, 1761, ibid., 10:291–92; William Johnson to Jeffrey Amherst, January 21, 1763, ibid., 10:611–13.

24. William Johnson to Daniel Claus, May 1, 1761, *Johnson Papers*, 10:262.

25. William Johnson to Daniel Claus, *Johnson Papers*, 4:354, 352–56.

26. Lords of Trade to William Pitt, February 21, 1760, in E. B. O'Callaghan and Berthold Fernow, eds., *Documents Relative to the Colonial History of the State of New York* (hereafter cited as NYCD), 15 vols. (Albany, N.Y.: Weed, Parsons, and Co., 1856–1887), 7:429, 428–29.

27. William Johnson to Thomas Gage, March 16, 1764, *Johnson Papers*, 4:370, 367–72.

28. Wilbur R. Jacobs, ed., *The Appalachian Indian Frontier: The Edmond Atkin Report and Plan of 1755* (Lincoln: University of Nebraska Bison Book, 1967), xv–xxxvi.

29. Stuart's List of Indians in Southern District, 1764, Gage collection, William L. Clements Library, Ann Arbor, Mich. (hereafter cited as CL). See also Louis De Vorsey, *The Indian Boundary in the Southern Colonies, 1763–1775* (Chapel Hill: University of North Carolina Press, 1961), 7–27; John Richard Alden, *John Stuart and the Southern Colonial Frontier: A Study of Indian Relations, War, Trade, and Land Problems in the Southern Wilderness, 1754–1775* (1944) (reprint, New York: Gordian Press, 1966), 7.

30. For two good accounts of his life, see James Thomas Flexner, *Mohawk Baronet: A Biography of Sir William Johnson* (Syracuse, N.Y.: Syracuse University Press, 1959); Milton W. Hamilton, *Sir William Johnson: Colonial American, 1715–1763* (Port Washington, N.Y.: Kennikat Press, 1976).

31. William Johnson to Jeffrey Amherst, October 24, 1760, *Johnson Papers*, 4: 269–75.

32. William Johnson to William Smith, January 30, 1766, *Johnson Papers*, 5:24.

33. William Johnson to Thomas Pownall, January 28, 1761, *Johnson Papers*, 4: 314–15.

34. William Johnson to Thomas Penn, February 5, 1768, *Johnson Papers*, 6:94.

35. Thomas Barton to William Johnson, October 31, 1766, *Johnson Papers*, 5: 402.

36. Memorandum of Officers' Pay, March 24, 1763, *Johnson Papers*, 10:637.

37. Enumeration of Indians within Northern Department, November 18, 1763, NYCD 7:582–84; List of Indian Nations by Thomas Hutchins, George Croghan to Jeffrey Amherst, October 5, 1762, *Johnson Papers*, 10:544–46; Memorandum on Six Nations and Other Confederacies, *Johnson Papers*, 4:240–45; List of Fighting Men, Dr. Franklin, 1762, Shelburne collection, CL, 48:31.

38. George Croghan to William Trent and Alexander Lowry, February 5, 1761, *Bouquet Papers*, 5:282; Croghan Indian Trade Prices at Detroit, February 5, 1761, ibid., 5:283.

39. Fort Pitt Traders to Henry Bouquet, February 27, 1761, *Bouquet Papers*, 5: 315.

40. John Langdale to Henry Bouquet, March 5, 1761 (two letters), *Bouquet Papers*, 5:330, 328–31, 332–33.

41. Donald Campbell to Henry Bouquet, May 21, 1761, *Bouquet Papers*, 5:491–92.

42. Henry Bouquet to James Livingstone, February 6, 1762, *Bouquet Papers*, 6: 43.

43. Henry Bouquet to Francis Fauquier, February 8, 1762, *Bouquet Papers*, 6:44, 44–45.

44. Cadwallader Colden to William Johnson, June 13, 1765, *Johnson Papers*, 1: 788, 786–89; William Johnson to Thomas Gage, May 4, 1765, ibid., 11:711–14; Committee of Kayaderosseras Proprietors, July 22, 1765, ibid., 11:864–66; John Tabor Kempe to William Johnson, August 12, September 7, 23, 1765, ibid., 11: 886–89, 923–27, 948–51.

45. William Johnson to Alexander Colden, January 28, 1761, *Johnson Papers*, 4: 313, 311–14; Alexander Colden to William Johnson, January 18, 1761, ibid., 4: 306–8; Cadwallader Colden to William Johnson, February 20, 1761, ibid., 4:338–41; Journal of Indian Affairs, March 4, 1761, ibid., 10:227–29.

46. Goldsbrow Banyar to William Johnson, February 2, 1761, *Johnson Papers*, 4: 319–21; William Johnson to Goldsbrow Banyar, February 10, 1761, ibid., 4:326–29.

47. For example, see Cadwallader Colden to Lords of Trade, February 28, 1761, March 1, 1762, NYCD 7:455–58, 490–94.

48. James Hamilton to William Johnson, February 10, 1761, *Johnson Papers*, 10: 210–13; Richard Peters to William Johnson, February 12, 1761, ibid., 10:213–16; William Johnson to James Hamilton, March 4, 1761, ibid., 10:230–31; Richard Peters to William Johnson, May 18, 1761, ibid., 10:266–68; William Johnson to Richard Peters, March 4, 1764, ibid., 10:231–32.

49. Donald Campbell to Henry Bouquet, June 1, 1761, *Bouquet Papers*, 5:517.

50. John Shy, *Toward Lexington: The Role of the British Army in the Coming of the American Revolution* (Princeton, N.J.: Princeton University Press, 1965); J. A Houlding, *Fit for Service: The Training of the British Army, 1715–1795* (Oxford: Clarendon Press, 1981).

51. Bernard Knollenberg, *Origin of the American Revolution, 1759–1766* (New York: 1969); Shy, *Toward Lexington*, 45–83.

52. Shy, *Toward Lexington*, 35.

53. Jeffrey Amherst to Henry Bouquet, March 20, 1761, *Bouquet Papers*, 5:357–59; Henry Bouquet to Jeffrey Amherst, April 21, 1761, ibid., 5:432–33; Lewis Ourry to Henry Bouquet, March 22, 1761, ibid., 5:363–65; Charles Heathcott to Henry Bouquet, April 1, 1761, ibid., 5:383–84.

54. Ellis Orders to Reduce Army, May 18, 1763, *Bouquet Papers*, 6:186–90.

55. Shy, *Toward Lexington*, 114.

56. Houlding, *Fit for Service*, 126.

57. Thomas Gage to Halifax, January 23, 1765, in Clarence Edwin Carter, ed., *The Correspondance of General Thomas Gage with the Secretaries of State, 1763–1775* (1931–1933) (reprint, Hamden, Conn.: Archon Books, 1969), 1:49.

58. Lewis Ourry to Henry Bouquet, January 17, 1761, *Bouquet Papers*, 5:253–54.

59. John Christie to Henry Bouquet, April 8, 1761, *Bouquet Papers*, 5:398.

60. Shy, *Toward Lexington*, 140–41.

61. For an excellent overview of wilderness warfare, see Ian K. Steele, *Warpaths: Invasions of North America* (New York: Oxford University Press, 1994).

62. George Croghan to Benjamin Franklin, February 25, 1766, *Johnson Papers*, 5:39.

63. William Johnson to Arthur Lee, February 28, 1771, NYCD 4:430–39.

64. William Johnson to George Croghan, April 8, 1763, *Johnson Papers*, 10:652.

2

Conspiracies

"Destroy Their Forts and Make Them Rue the Day"

I am clear that too much economy ought not to be thought of as yet with the Indians, if we expect to keep them in temper & maintain our posts—but it is not in my power to convince the General thereof.
—William Johnson to George Croghan

How it may end the Lord knows; but I assure you I am of the opinion that it will not be long before we have some broils with them.
—George Croghan to Henry Bouquet

Our suspicions of their plots . . . are mere bugbears.
—Jeffrey Amherst to William Johnson

The English treat us with much disrespect. . . . They have possessed themselves of our country. It is now in our power to dispossess them and recover it. . . . There is no time to be lost. Let us strike immediately.
—Kayashuta

Gone were the days when the Indians could play off the French and British against each other. Only the British now provided the ammunition and other products upon which Indians had grown dependent over the previous century and a half. To attack the British would be to bite the hand that fed them. Besides, with the Union Jack flying from forts in their midst, the Indians no longer had unassailable sanctuaries from which to raid British settlements. In the face of overwhelming British power, who would dare raise their war clubs?

But British arrogance, insensitivity, and exploitation quickly drove most

Indians to the breaking point. The ink was barely dry on Canada's surrender when the debate arose within each tribe whether or not to overthrow their new master. The British got plenty of word that rage was fueling conspiracies. It was not just friends in those villages who slipped into the forts to whisper warnings to commandants. At council after council the chiefs themselves cautioned the British that animosities were rapidly worsening and British policies were to blame.

More than any other tribe, the Seneca would provoke the 1763 Uprising. As early as November 1760, two months after Governor Vaudreuil had surrendered Canada, a Seneca council agreed to carry on the war against the British. Seneca head chief Kaendae dispatched Kayashuta and Teantoriance to carry red wampum belts to the western tribes urging them to attack the British. In doing so they broke with an earlier decision reached at the Onondaga council to keep peace.

Why did the Seneca alone favor war when the other Iroquois tribes insisted on peace? With Fort Niagara not far off the Seneca had traditionally tilted toward the French as strongly as the Mohawk at the Iroquois Longhouse's eastern end had favored the British. With an estimated 1,050 warriors, the Seneca could field more than half of the Six Nations fighting men. Thus they were strong enough to defy the Iroquois council. Still, why would they do so? The Seneca burned with anger at losses suffered during Fort Niagara's 1759 siege and perceived insults from Amherst during the 1760 campaign. They lusted for vengeance.[1]

During a half-year journey Kayashuta and Teantoriance called for war at councils with the Shawnee, Delaware, Mingo, Miami, Wea, Munsee, Kickapoo, Piankeshaw, Kaskaskia, Peoria, Cahokia, and Wyandot. Their mission must have been discouraging. Few warriors from those tribes showed any enthuisiasm for war. Those tribes had sided with the French and shared their defeat. Although bitter, the years of war had exhausted them with numerous deaths from battle and smallpox; for now most wanted only trade goods and peace.[2]

Nonetheless, the French surrender worried all the tribes. Ironically, the reputation British traders had before the French and Indian War changed dramatically afterward. Indians eagerly sought British goods from the the 1720s when Oswego was founded and traders began to circulate west of the Appalachians. The reason was that British goods were better made and lower priced than French goods. Throughout the war, the French had warned their allies that if the British won they would exploit and eventually exterminate the Indians. That is exactly what happened. Once the French surrendered, British traders took advantage of their new power to raise prices and insult native feelings. The Indians naturally grew ever more embittered against the British and nostalgic for the French.

Anger at what the British were doing to them was reason enough to resist. But a charismatic prophet emerged at that time to preach an inspiring tale of Indian regeneration and the destruction of white rule. The Delaware Neolin, whose name means "Enlightened," had long desired to commune with the Master of Life.[3] That wish was finally granted. During a dream he received a dazzling vision.

A voice told Neolin to set forth on that quest. He traveled for eight days through an unknown country until he reached a clearing where three trails met. After considering which path to take he chose the widest. He hiked it for half a day until he reached a fiery pit. He hurried back to the clearing and took a different path which led to yet another fiery pit. Finally, he took the third path which after a long day's hike led to a glistening white mountain. There a beautiful woman clad in white greeted him and told him he must strip off his clothes and then cross over. He climbed straight up the ice mountain's perpendicular face until he reached its summit. From there he saw three distant villages. He chose the most appealing one to visit but hesitated until a voice urged him to go forward. Awed by the village's beauty he stood before the gate until it mysteriously opened. A handsome man in white appeared, took his hand, and drew him before the Master of Life.

The Master of Life embraced Neolin, gave him a gold hat to sit upon, and then revealed the secret to salvation: "I am He who hath created the heavens and the earth. . . . Because I love you you must do what I say and love and not do what I hate." He warned against worshipping Manitou, an evil spirit. He called on husbands to have only one wife and love her for all their life together. Such European ways as the use of alcohol, firearms, and dress must be abandoned. Pray daily for goodness and salvation. The Indians must live as they did before the whites came to steal their country. All of this was very important to the Indians' salvation.

But the Master of Life's most vital message was: "This land where you dwell I have made for you and not for others. Whence comes it that you permit the Whites upon your lands? Can you not live without them. . . . Drive them out, make war upon them. . . . Send them back to the lands which I created for them and let them stay there. . . . Drive off your lands those dogs clothed in red who will do you nothing but harm." If the Indians purified themselves of their sins they would gain the moral power to drive the whites back across the ocean.

The Master of Life had revealed the path to Indian salvation to Neolin. Now he must carry that message back to his people and all Indians. And that is what he did. He left his village on the Cuyahoga River and spread his message throughout the region. Before excited crowds at one village after another he would illustrate his vision on parchments or paper. Heaven was above and earth below where the Indians dwelled. Dividing them was a triangle representing whites and Indian sins. Salvation depended on the Indians uniting, purifying themselves of their sins, and abandoning firearms and liquor. Only then could they drive off the whites and restore their lost world. As he preached, he wept continuously, accompanied by many who listened.

What inspired Neolin's message? His sermons combined his own visions with Native American beliefs and Christian motifs. Neolin also may have been partly inspired by the visit several years earlier of far western Indians who had no firearms or other European accoutrements. While he embraced some traditional practices like using bows and arrows, he spurned others like polygamy, war dances, and medicine-man rituals. Like many a religious leader, he made money from his preachings. He sold his charts for one buckskin or two doeskins each.

Neolin was not the only prophet who arose at this time. In 1762, perhaps influenced by Neolin, an Onondaga preached a similar vision of spiritual renaissance. Unfortunately, his name was unrecorded. Given first Onondaga neutrality and then British alliance during Amherst's War, he must have preached nonviolence and even then was not very influential.[4]

The British were not oblivious to rumors of Seneca war envoys, the Delaware prophet, and other conspiracies. Indeed, from 1760 to 1763, British officials received so many warnings from so many sources that most officials became inured to them, the "cry wolf" syndrome. At first the frontier commanders would place their troops under alert. But when no attack occurred, repeatedly, the officers and soldiers alike lowered their guards.

As early as December 1760, the British received their first warning that danger lurked beneath the tranquil surface of their new empire. The word came from an Ottawa who had just returned from the Illinois country. There he attended a council held by Fort de Chartres' commander, Captain Villiers, who presented a warbelt and urged the Indians to join the Cherokee in their struggle against British rule. Speaking for the others, one chief rejected the challenge, arguing that the French "always said the English was old women and could not fight, but we now know better. They have beat you everywhere and are your masters. So Father we will think for ourselves & listen no more to anything you say to us. Here they returned the war belt & broke up the council without saying a word more, or waiting to hear anything the commandant would say to them. And in a few days the Indians was all set off a hunting."[5]

The fact that the Indians so swiftly dismissed the call for war reinforced the British perception that all was well in the west. It was not surprising that the French tried to stir up trouble. Such calls for war might well persist until the Union Jack flew over every fort in New France. Fortunately, those appeals fell on deaf ears, or so it seemed.

The British had their own complaints against the Indians. The worst festering issue was their retention of prisoners taken during the war and even earlier. By some reports the Shawnee and Delaware had 150 and 100 captives, respectively. They retained those prisoners for two reasons. The Ohio tribes did not trust the British. Holding hostages might deter a British attack or economic sanctions. But perhaps more importantly, most of the whites held by the Indians had been adopted into those tribes. The Indians could not bear to give up their loved ones. Many of the whites among them felt the same, especially those captured in childhood.[6]

These sentiments emerged clearly during a council at Fort Pitt from March 1 to 3, 1761. Deputy Indian Superintendent George Croghan tried to convince those tribes to return their prisoners. He distributed presents to soften their hearts. The chiefs promised to do so. But rumor had it that the tribes would retain their hostages as future bargaining chips or replacements for loved ones. Not only did they mistrust the British, the Shawnee and Delaware were quietly conspiring with other tribes against their new masters.[7]

In western Pennsylvania, a series of incidents threatened to plunge the frontier into war even before the conspiracy was launched. On May 29, 1761, a Mingo party camped near Fort Le Boeuf was suspected of stealing twelve horses. Soldiers caught up with the Mingo. They found none of the fort's horses but confiscated some from the Mingo herd anyway. The Mingo followed the soldiers to Fort Le Boeuf and demanded from Lieutenant Guy Townsend that he return their horses. The officer refused. Shots were exchanged. A bullet killed a horse. Both sides retreated. Those Mingo would burn for vengeance.[8]

Not long after, a fatal incident occurred near Fort Ligonier when two Mingo approached four unarmed soldiers guarding the horse herd. The Mingo seized the horses and threatened the soldiers with death if they resisted. The soldiers ran back to the fort and the Mingo galloped off. A pursuit was organized and soon caught up to the Mingo. Shots were fired. One Mingo died and the other escaped.[9]

The death of an Indian, even one stealing a horse, could spark a conflagration. When Colonel Henry Bouquet at Fort Pitt heard of the death he called in the local chiefs for a council on June 29. Bouquet denounced the horse stealings and warned the chiefs that they must control their hotheaded young men. But he also promised them justice if any whites did them wrong. To reinforce that promise he presided over a court of inquiry on the Fort Ligonier incident that same day. The inquiry absolved the soldiers of any wrongdoing in killing the Mingo.[10]

Tensions rose steadily. Although Amherst contemptuously dismissed any reports of Indian plots, he did finally accept Johnson's arguments that a diplomatic offensive was necessary to alleviate the animosities. In May 1761, he authorized the superintendent to organize councils with all the tribes during the summer, culminating in a Grand Council at Detroit. He also ordered two ships built on Lake Erie to intimidate the Indians, supply the distant forts, and explore the upper Great Lakes.[11]

Johnson plunged into preparations for his mission. The success of any Indian council depended on many things, none more so than the amount and type of gifts dispensed by the host. Johnson carefully calculated what he would need and proposed to Amherst a budget for 1,845 pounds. The general rejected the budget and ordered the superintendent to pare his expenses to 1,000 pounds. Johnson reluctantly but politely agreed to do so. But the forced cutback in expenses was not critical. By overestimating expenses and then charging for vital goods that were not covered by the 1,000-pound budget, he could get enough presents to the Indians to quell their amimosities, at least for a while.[12]

Johnson asked Amherst to accompany the expedition, arguing that the general's august presence would reinforce any agreements forged with the tribes. Amherst was clearly uninterested in leaving the comforts of New York City for a nearly 2,000-mile round-trip wilderness journey. He replied that "it is not yet determined but I shall have the pleasure of accompanying you. Which I should be very glad to do, if time would but permit me. If I should not be able to go, you may be assured I will furnish you with the necessary orders for receiving every assistance you can want."[13] Johnson's invitation may have been another of his clever ploys. He undoubtedly guessed that Amherst would find some excuse not to go, and then feel compelled to make up for it by giving Johnson what amounted to a blank check for "assistance" en route. As Amherst would discover to his regret, Johnson would include in that assistance extra goods to be distributed among the Indians.

It was not until June 22, 1761 that Amherst ordered Major Henry Gladwin to lead 300 troops of the 80th Light Infantry to accompany Johnson, while leaving behind 100 troops of that regiment to defend Fort William Augustus and Oswegatchie. En route, Gladwin would pick up ten 4-pounders, fourteen swivels, and appropriate ammunition at Oswego. At Niagara wagons would transport his troops, guns, and supplies around the portage to Fort Schlosser where the two warships were being constructed. He would arm the *Michigan* with six 4-pounders and eight swivels, and the Huron with four 4-pounders and six swivels. He would collect enough whaleboats and bateaux to convoy his troops and Johnson's delegation to Detroit; if the warships were finished they too would accompany his expedition. From Detroit an expedition would be launched to occupy all the posts of the upper Great Lakes. He would also establish a fort at Sandusky near the Wyandot village. Upon finishing his mission Gladwin would return to Fort William Augustus.[14]

Eventually, Amherst got around to assigning an escort for Johnson. Orders were sent to Captain William Walters to pick 41 New York provincial troops and lead them to Johnson Hall. On July 5, Johnson, his escort, their supplies, and the Indian gifts were packed into bateaux and embarked up the Mohawk River. Progress from Johnson Hall to Oswego would be slowed by low water in the creeks and rivers.[15]

Johnson took advantage of the delay by meeting with Oneida and Tuscarora chiefs at German Flats on July 7. He had called them to discuss a murder one of them committed while drunk. The murderer had long before fled and was rumored to be in the Ohio country. The chiefs promised to deliver him when he was found, then presented their own demands. Several years earlier a man named Smith had murdered two of their people. The chiefs called for justice. Johnson promised he would have Smith tracked down. Speaking on behalf of the entire Six Nations, the chiefs then asked Johnson to restrain settlers from taking their lands and complained about how prices for goods had soared since the war, while ammunition was especially scarce. Johnson agreed to alleviate these problems and then distributed some presents to mollify their anger. The Indian Superintendent would receive the same litany of grievances at every council on his journey and he would address them with the same promises and gifts.[16]

As Johnson embarked on his peace offensive, the Indian plot thickened. By early June, Kayashuta and Teantoriance reached the Wyandot village at Sandusky. They sent word to the Detroit tribes to journey down to Sandusky for a Grand Council. But those tribes rejected the request and invited the Seneca to visit them at the Huron village across the river from Detroit. The Seneca agreed. Meanwhile, they counciled with the Wyandot and some visiting Shawnee on June 10, 1761.[17]

Rumors of the conspiracy trickled in to Captain Donald Campbell at Detroit. He reported, on June 1, 1761, that "I am obliged to mount a strong guard to do duty in this large Fort and besides . . . I had some hints given me of the discontent of the Indians which I am glad to report is turned out to nothing."[18] A week later he wrote that that the Recollet priest Father Simple Bocquet revealed that the "Indians were never more disposed against us here at Detroit but at last he prevailed on them to come here . . . [and] they are peaceably enclined at present."[19] Two days later he reported that the "Six Nations . . . have sent belts of wampum and deputys to all the Indians from Nova Scotia to the Illinois to take up the hatchet against the English. . . . Their project is . . . to surprise Niagara and Fort Pitt and cut off the communications everywhere. . . . I have put my fort in the best posture of Defense I can & shall take all methods to prevent a surprise."[20]

Campbell fired off warning letters to Amherst, Bouquet, Fort Presque Isle's Captain Gavin, and Fort Niagara's Major Hugh Walter. He also put his own troops on alert, shored up Fort Detroit's defenses, and dispatched Indian trader James Hambach with 50 men in five bateaux to withdraw the Sandusky traders and their goods to Fort Detroit. For now, all he could do was wait.[21]

Campbell gathered chiefs from the four Detroit tribes and announced that he knew all about the conspiracy. He then demanded to know the chiefs' intentions. They declared their loyalty and promised to reject the Seneca warbelt. Campbell seems to have rewarded their allegiance with rum. When the Seneca deputies arrived at the Huron village on June 14, they had to cool their heels for three days while those Indians enjoyed a drinking binge.

By June 17, the liquor had run out and a council convened. Displaying a large red belt, Teantoriance appealed to the Huron, Ottawa, Chippewa, and Potawatomi to join their eastern brothers in revolt against the British. But the local tribes asked him to make his same appeal before Captain Campbell. Surprisingly, the Seneca agreed but apparently only after they made one more private appeal to the Detroit tribes.[22]

The council opened at the Huron village on July 3. Teantoriance and Kayashuta presented three small belts, 20 strings, and a large red belt of wampum "termed the war hatchet, and addressing themselves particularly to the Wyandots, made the following speech: 'As you are the leading nation here you have only to say the word the others will follow your example. We invite you by this to cut off the English at Fort Detroit, to which if you agree it will give us the greatest joy & pleasure. . . . We will return to our nation and endeavor to do the same with the garrisons at Niagara and Fort Pitt. The English treat us with much [dis]respect. Their behavior toward us gives us the greatest [reason] to believe they intend to cut us off entirely. They have pos[sessed] themselves of our country. It is now in our power to [destroy?] them and recover it, if we will only embrace the opportunity [before] they have time to assemble . . . and fortify themselves. There is no time to be lost. Let us strike immediately. Our warriors are already prepared & impatiently await till they hear from you.' "[23]

As etiquette demanded, the Detroit tribes could not reply until the next day. When the council opened on July 4, Campbell, his officers, and leading Canadians were seated in the circle with chiefs of the six tribes speaking on behalf of the Detroit tribes. Huron Chief Teata not only firmly rejected the call for war but handed over the warbelt to Campbell. The Seneca were humiliated. Campbell then spoke to the council through his interpreter Pierre LaButte. He thanked the chiefs for their honesty and friendship, and promised them that he would take care of his Indian brothers. He ended by warning that if the Indians "proceed in their designs against the English it will terminate in their utter ruin and destruction."[24]

When the council reconvened on July 5, Teantoriance spoke. Thoroughly humbled by his failure to ignite a revolt, he promised that upon his return home he would call on the Iroquois to join with William Johnson in a council in which all Indian grievances would be aired. But most importantly, he swore that "the English had now opened his eyes . . . he would bury all bad thoughts and forget the injuries done against them by the English . . . and would recommend to [the Six Nations] in the most ardent manner to lay aside all thoughts of war and live in peace."[25]

The relief of Campbell and his men upon hearing the Seneca's promises can be imagined. The exposed conspiracy had died before their eyes. But Campbell warned his superiors that the continued loyalty of the Detroit tribes had a price: "The Indians have constant demands on me and think themselves entitled to all the favours that we can bestow upon them, for their good behavior in this last affair."[26] Amherst would refuse to pay that price.

The Senecas' diplomatic mission was not yet over. They traveled through Ohio to speak at various councils whose words remain hidden from history. They emerged at Fort Pitt to council on July 27 with Colonel Henry Bouquet, George Croghan, and the local chiefs. Kayashuta and Teantoriance repeated their Detroit peace message—they presented the familiar litany of complaints but denied rumors that they were part of any conspiracy against the British. Bouquet and Croghan knew the Indians were lying but accepted their promises and rewarded them with some gifts and platitudes. Both men were confident that by merely exposing British suspicions those Indians involved in the plot would abandon it. Bouquet concluded that "whatever turn our Indian affairs may take it is almost certain that we shall be quiet for some time."[27]

Bouquet was not the only commander who felt that exposing the plot would destroy it. Amherst and all the commanders and Indian agents shared that belief. An uprising's success depended on surprise. Without surprise it was not worth trying. The Indians and British alike understood this.[28]

Nonetheless, when Bouquet and the other frontier commanders had first learned of the conspiracy, most took steps to reinforce their forts and relations with the local tribes. Bouquet, for example, organized the 120 civilian men around Fort Pitt into two militia companies which would post guards in the vicinity. He ordered the fort's weaker walls and ramparts shored up. But the smaller posts did not have local British populations from which to organize militias to supplement their meager garrisons. The survival of those forts ultimately depended on the mingled good will, respect, and fear of the local Indians. Those sentiments would soon evaporate.[29]

While most commanders fortified when they learned of the plot, many Pennsylvanian frontier settlers fled. At Fort Bedford Lieutenant Ourry noted that the "country people have been so much alarmed by the report that the Indians had infested the roads . . . that the scattered inhabitants have fled with their best effects to Carlisle & Fort Loudoun & elsewhere."[30] Unfortunately, the uprising's failure to appear would afflict many of those same people with the "cry wolf" syndrome. In 1763, hundreds would stay at their farms and be slaughtered.

Throughout the first half of 1761, Amherst had categorically rejected any rumors of an Indian conspiracy "which seem to me to be so very wild that I cannot give credit to them."[31] When Campbell sent him proof of that conpiracy Amherst typically reinterpreted it to reinforce his belief that it did not exist. A conspiracy was not real if it would evaporate with a simple exposure, now was it? Over the next two years the commander in chief would continue to deny such warnings and even early reports of attacks in the summer of 1763. He rejected any suggestions by Johnson and others that generosity strengthened and stingyness weakened Indian loyalties. Amherst did "not doubt but all the nations will complain of not having powder sufficient; but I am for giving it to them with as sparing a hand as possible."[32]

Meanwhile, Amherst decided that the Indians must be further cowed with military power rather than placated with more presents, trade, and kind words. In July the general announced to Johnson that troops would build a blockhouse near the Wyandot village at Sandusky Bay. Johnson politely criticized that plan "which I fancy will not be agreeable to the Indians."[33] Amherst's decision to do so makes no strategic, diplomatic, or financial sense. A fort there would cost a considerable amount to build and maintain, and would be at best redundant given the proximity of Forts Detroit and Miami. The Wyandot living there did not want it and would demand a small fortune of gifts if Amherst insisted that it be built.

Dismissing Johnson's protests, Amherst insisted that "a post at that place is absolutely necesary, not only for the . . . purposes of keeping up communications, but also to keep the Canadians in proper subjection; I must and will therefore say that they will have one at that place." Fearing this would inflame the Indian conspiracy, the general insisted that "the discovery of the disaffected & the overthrow of their machinations . . . never gave me a moment's concern, as I know their incapacity of attempting anything serious, and that if they were rash enough to venture upon any ill design, I had it in my power not only to frustrate them, but to punish the delinquents with entire destruction, which I am firmly resolved on, whenever any of them give me cause; but I am hopeful they never will."[34]

What explains Amherst's confident belligerency? Reinforcing his utter contempt for Indians as warriors and humans, British troops had just defeated the Cherokee uprising which had begun in December 1759. The general believed that "from this example the Indians may be convinced that we have it in our power to reduce them to reason."[35]

Amherst ordered Bouquet to implement his decision. On August 12, Bouquet passed on that command to Lieutenant Elias Meyer, who set forth the next day with 33 troops overland to Sandusky and there to build a blockhouse. Upon their arrival Captain Campbell would send them supplies from Detroit. Meyer and his troops finished hiking the 202-mile trail to Sandusky on August 31. The lieutenant selected a site, set his men to work felling trees, and dispatched a messenger to Detroit to bring back sawyers, tools, and supplies.[36]

Johnson meanwhile had finally arrived at Fort Niagara on July 24. Over the next three weeks he met with delegations of Onondaga, Tuscarora, Oneida, Chippewa, and Mississauga, all of whom insisted that they were dedicated to peace. Nonetheless, he discovered "an universal jealousy and uneasiness . . . amongst . . . every nation on account of the hasty steps they look upon it we are taking towards getting possession of their several countrys."[37] And the Seneca had haughtily rejected Johnson's summons to the Niagara council. Johnson chastized the Indians for even contemplating a conspiracy "so villainous & treacherous in its nature."[38] He praised the western Indians for revealing the conspiracy and called on the assembled chiefs to show similar loyalty. He then sent a belt to the Seneca chiefs to join him at the Detroit council or be considered Britain's enemy. In all, the Niagara council exposed the conspiracy and eased some tensions. But the underlying problems remained unresolved.

After the council broke up, Gladwin and his 400 troops were the first to depart. On August 14, they marched from Fort Niagara to Fort Schlosser where they would embark on bateaux for the long row to Detroit. High winds and waves on Lake Erie delayed his departure until August 17. On August 19, Johnson left Fort Niagara escorted by 60 troops of the 60th, a delegation of chiefs, and some merchants. At Fort Schlosser they set forth in a flotilla of thirteen heavily laden bateaux.[39]

Johnson had set in motion a two-pronged peace offensive. While he slowly journied directly from Johnson Hall toward Detroit, his deputy George Croghan headed there by a far more circuitous route. He had started not with his July 27 council with Bouquet, the Seneca, and local chiefs at Fort Pitt, but a month earlier at Albany where he counciled with Canadian Iroquois on June 28, 1761. The council went well. Croghan's words and gifts returned those Indians to Canada in "good humour." He then traveled to the Fort Pitt council. Upon the council's conclusion he sent out runners to various tribes to meet him at Delaware Chief Beaver's village. There he elicited several protests of innocence and promises of peace from that region's tribes. For his final council en route to Detroit, Croghan stopped at the Wyandot village at Sandusky. There he engaged in the most ticklish negotiations of all—he was to convince the Wyandot to allow the British to build a fort on their land. When the Wyandot angrily protested, Croghan apologized and explained that he was simply following General Amherst's orders. They agreed to defer a decision until Johnson himself arrived later that summer. After distributing gifts, Croghan departed for Detroit, which he reached on August 16. There he met on August 20 and 21 with the Potawatomi, Ottawa, Huron, Chippewa, and Delaware chiefs to forge understandings before the Grand Council with Johnson. In all, his whirlwind diplomatic tour had accomplished most of its missions.[40]

It would be another two weeks before the army expedition arrived. On September 1, Gladwin and his troops set foot at Detroit. The major did not make a triumphal entrance. Some fever, probably malaria, forced Gladwin to bed. There he would remain for several months. Johnson and his escort disembarked on September 3.

Although Johnson was physically healthy he was filled with dread. En route he had received a letter from Amherst that threatened to destroy his mission. The general condemned the traditional policy of "purchasing the good behavior of Indians by presents, the more they get the more they ask, and yet are never satisfied . . . I think it much better to avoid all presents in the future, since that will oblige them to supply themselves by barter & of course keep them more constantly employed by means of which they will have less time to concert or carry into execution any schemes prejudicial to His Majesty's interest; and to abolish entirely every kind of apprehension on that account, the keeping them scarce of ammunition . . . since nothing can be so impolitic as to furnish them with the means of accomplishing the evil which is so much dreaded."[41] Johnson resolved to ignore the advice.

After a series of preliminary meetings, Johnson convened the council on September 9, 1761, in the fields just beyond Fort Detroit's walls. Rarely before had delegations from so many tribes gathered there. The 500 Indians came from various bands of Wyandot, Chippewa, Ottawa, Potawatomi, Kickapoo, Miami, Delaware, Shawnee, Mohican, Mohawk, Oneida, and, most importantly, the Seneca.

As he who had called the council, Johnson was the first to speak. He did so with the full power of his double authority as Indian Superintendent and Iroquois Chief Warraghiyagey. He promised to address their grievances if they returned their prisoners and stolen horses. Croghan repeated the same promises when he spoke at length that afternoon.

During the following days Huron Chief Anaiasa, Ottawa Chief Macate-pilesis, and other chiefs rose to complain of the high prices for trade goods and dearth of powder, shot, and muskets. Hunting and war demanded the same stealthy skills. To varying extents, each tribe had suffered losses of their finest men from battle and smallpox epidemics during the war. Now, more than usual, the Indians needed supplies in order to survive. Each tribe was trapped in a vicious cycle—it lacked both munitions and hunters in order to take the skins with which to buy munitions. The Indians desperately needed credit, something the French had given but which the British traders were at first understandably reluctant to offer. Muskets broke. The Indians lacked the skills, equipment, and parts to fix them. They requested gun-smiths to live among them. Finally, the Indians demanded that rum be sold to them and annual councils be convened where mountains of presents would be generously distributed.

Johnson eventually agreed to fulfill most of these demands. He promised them that only traders licensed by himself or Croghan would be allowed in Indian territory. Prices for all goods were strictly regulated. In addition, Indians could have their muskets repaired free of charge by gunsmiths at the forts. Credit, however, depended on each trader, who would be more likely to extend it if the recipient was likely to repay the loan. Such trust took time to nurture. A wampum belt was exchanged with each promise. The only Indian demands that Johnson refused were rum sales and annual councils with generous gifts. Adding icing to the cake, Johnson ended the conference with a feast of roasted oxen and the distribution of 6,000 pounds' worth of presents, of which 4,400 pounds were from the Crown and much of the balance from his own pocket. In doing so Johnson had disobeyed Amherst's order not to bribe the Indians into obedience but subdue them with fear.

As for rumors of war, Macatepilesis admitted that "such bad birds have been amongst us, but we should look upon ourselves as a very unhappy people if we payed any attention to such disturbers of peace whom we shall always despise for attempting to put such even thoughts into our ears, who are all determined as one Man to hold fast by the Convant Chain forever."[42] He then said, "if you would know who this bird is, cast your eyes to Kayashunta." Such confessions of temptation and declarations of loyalty were music to British ears.

An indignant Kayashuta was allowed later to address the council. Astonishingly, he not only denied brandishing the warbelt but even being present at such rallies. Either he or hundreds of witnesses were lying. Johnson did not press the point. Instead he expressed his hope that Kayashuta was "as innocent as he pretended." He then turned his back on Kayashuta and announced he would distribute gifts the next day. Privately, he later warned Kayashuta that he could "easily have persuaded many of the western and other nations to fall upon them & revenge our quarrel, they being easily inflamed against the Senecas." He then "condoled the death of a young Seneca killed at Venango, by covering his grave (after the Indian custom) with a black shroud &c after which they departed."[43] Here Johnson displays his mastery of Indian diplomacy and psychology, alternating the roles of the stern and the forgiving Great Father.

With the council over, Johnson then issued very strict trade regulations for Fort Detroit and all other posts that set prices, forbade sharing rum with the Indians, and imposed uniform weights and measures. As for the fixed prices, of the two standard currencies, three buckskins equaled two beaver plews. One large beaver or two small buckskins could buy a large white blanket, a fine ruffled shirt, gingham dress, or a pound of vermillion. A scalping knife or jew's harp could be had for a small raccoon or two muskrat skins. A pound of gunpowder, silk handkerchief, or three bars of lead demanded a beaver or doeskin. And so the list went. It was hoped that these rules would curtail the worst cheating of Indians and the animosities it inflamed.[44]

It was not all work and no play for Johnson during his two weeks at Fort Detroit. On September 6, Captain Campbell held a ball where Johnson "opened the ball with Mademoiselle Cuire—a fine girl. We danced until five o'clock the next morning." Johnson threw his own ball on September 15 where everyone "danced the whole night until 7 o'clock in the morning, when all parted very much pleased and happy." That "fine girl" with whom Johnson danced the night away was actually Angelique Cuillerier dit Beaubien, the 26-year-old unmarried daughter of prominent merchant Antoine Cuillerier, whom Pontiac would tap as Fort Detroit's leader when he destroyed the British, and the niece of Captain Belestre, her father's half brother.

Johnson must have made quite an impression. With a wink, Campbell wrote Johnson that Angelique "never neglects an opportunity of asking about the general; what, says she, is there no Indian council to be held here this summer—I think by her talk Sir William had promised to return to Detroit. She desired that I would present you her best compliments."[45] Apparently, she kept pining for the Indian Superintendent. Major Gladwin passed on a similar message. In his reply, Johnson assured Gladwin that "I have not forgotten the powerful effect of the charms of the Lady who honors me with a place in her remembrances, & should be very happy in any opportunity which might offer of paying her my devoirs."[46]

On September 17, Johnson and Croghan embarked with troops for Sandusky Bay to win permission from the Wyandot to build a fort there. Odinghquanooron (Big Jaw) and the other chiefs grudgingly agreed. All but fifteen men were left with Lieutenant Elias Meyer to finish their work.[47]

The two Indian agents and their respective escorts then parted company, with each to parley with the tribes on his way home. Johnson continued down Lakes Erie and Ontario and then overland to Johnson Hall in the Mohawk valley. Croghan headed overland through Ohio to Fort Pitt.

In all, Johnson was pleased with what his diplomatic mission had accomplished. The Indian complaints were all legitimate and had been, to varying degrees, alleviated. The feasts and presents had dampened the British reputation for greed. Outside the general council in their talks with each tribe's leaders, Johnson and Croghan tried to widen the traditional distrust between the eastern and western Indians. They especially played on the long-standing fear and resentment of the Great Lakes Indians toward the Seneca and other Iroquois. The diplomacy had allowed the British to occupy the Great Lakes forts and even build a new post at Sandusky. In all, Johnson could not be more pleased. He boasted to Amherst that he had "left the western Indians extremely well disposed towards the English and I am of the opinion that matters are settled on so stable a foundation there that unless greatly irritated . . . they will never break the peace."[48] Johnson's assessment was uncharacteristically and tragically wrong.

Even while the Detroit council unfolded, the British asserted their power over the upper Great Lakes. On September 9, Gladwin's second in command, Captain Henry Balfour of the 80th Light Infantry, led from Fort Detroit a 120-man expedition that would garrison posts Michilimackinac under Lieutenant William Leslye on September 28; La Baye, renamed Edward Augustus under Ensign James Gorell on October 12; and St. Joseph under Ensign Francis Schlosser on November 9. Balfour then marched overland back to Detroit. It was an epic trip. Meanwhile Ensign Robert Holmes led troops to Fort Miami to replace Lieutenant Butler and his rangers. It was not until November 6, 1761 that Captain Campbell dispatched Lieutenant Edward Jenkins and his men to occupy Fort Ouiatenon. By late November, Lieutenant Elias Meyer and his troops had completed their blockhouse on Sandusky Bay.[49]

The British hold over the Great Lakes seemed secure. By the end of 1761, British troops had occupied all the French forts except Fort La Pointe on Madeline Island and Sault Sainte Marie. The Union Jack now flew over twelve western forts: Pitt, Niagara, Presque Isle, Venango, Le Boeuf, Detroit, Miami, Sandusky, Ouiatenon, Michilimackinac, St. Joseph, and Edward Augustus. British forces in the upper Great Lakes included Captain Campbell's 79 troops at Detroit, Lieutenant Leslye's 26 troops at Michilimackinac, Lieutenant Gorell's 16 troops at Fort La Baye, Ensign Holmes' 17 troops at Fort Miami, Ensign Schlosser's 10 troops at Fort St. Joseph, Lieutenant Jenkins' 20 troops at Fort Ouiatenon, and Elias Meyer's 33 troops at Fort Sandusky. Most officers and troops were from the first battalion of the 60th Royal Americans. Some commanders would be replaced over the next year and a half before the uprising broke. The chief concern was provisions. At Detroit the troops had to stretch 38 barrels of flour, 39 of pork, and 1 of rice, along with 15 firkins of butter, 20 bushels of Indian corn, and 16 head of cattle for the next half year until the spring supplies arrived. The other upper Great Lakes posts faced similar shortages. The situation, however, was not dire. Each post's garrison could supplement their stores by trade with the local tribes.[50]

Otherwise, all seemed well. Each fort's commander had exacted from the Canadians their muskets and loyalty oaths. Business rapidly expanded among the British, Canadians, and Indians. Relations with the Canadians seemed as manageable and profitable as those with the Indians. That conspiracy scare aside, everything seemed to be going so well. The British Empire was pushing steadily toward the Mississippi River while encountering no more than scattered resentment and idle talk of resistance.

It was up to merchants to reap the riches of empire. Trade sometimes followed, sometimes preceded the flag. Conquest could bring fortunes to those courageous and well-heeled enough to buy canoe loads of goods, hire men, and paddle to the upper Great Lakes. The Indians across that vast region were starved for munitions and other European products upon which they had grown dependent. During the war, furs had piled up in their lodges as the British fleet captured ever more French supply ships heading to Canada. There was a catch to the easy riches for British merchants intrepid enough to reach that region. The French had taught those Great Lakes Indians to hate and war against the British. Most villages had lost loved ones in the distant lands near Lake George, western Pennsylvania, or Niagara. They might leap at any chance at vengeance by capturing and torturing a stray British merchant. Others would be incensed that the British had conquered Canada and would soon try to plant the Union Jack in their village. Although the British merchants would hire Canadian paddlers and guides, that might not guarantee their safety. The local Canadian merchants would certainly resent the carpetbaggers and try to stir Indian jealousy against them literally to "kill off the opposition." Any British merchant who beached his canoes would have to reckon with the chance he might die a gruesome, prolonged death.

Those risks were well-known. But they did not deter some men eager for wealth and adventure. In the summer of 1761, Henry Bostwick and Alexander Henry independently managed to wrangle passes to travel to the upper Great Lakes even though British Indian agents had not signed any treaties with the tribes of that region.[51] After being told repeatedly that the Indians would kill him as soon as he set foot at Michilimackinac, Henry disguised himself as a Canadian with breechcloth, "a shirt hanging loose, a molton or blanket coat, and a large red milled worsted cap. The next thing was to smear my face and hands with dirt and grease; and this done I took the place of one of my men, and when Indians approached, used the paddle with as much skill as I possessed . . . my skill enabled me to pass several canoes without attracting the smallest notice."[52]

The news that the British had conquered Canada profoundly disturbed the Chippewa. Shortly after reaching Michilimackinac, Henry was brought before Chippewa Chief Minivavana who was "six feet in height, and had in his contenance an indescribable mixture of good and evil."[53] Although Minivavana would allow Henry to live and even stay, he offered a chilling assessment of the British victory: "Englishman, we are informed that our Father, the King of France, is old and infirm; and that being fatigued with making war upon your nation, he is fallen asleep. During his sleep you have taken advantage of him and possessed yourselves of Canada. But his nap is almost at an end. I think I hear already stirring and inquiring for his children, the Indians; and when he does awake, what must become of you? He will destroy you utterly."[54]

While the French king would remain asleep, the "irritation" Johnson warned about would come and Amherst would provide it. Making promises, of course, is easier than fulfilling them. Peace depended on the British willingness and ability to fulfill their promises. Overshadowing Johnson's diplomacy was Amherst's policy of denying the Indians all that had been promised them. Johnson had applied bandages to gaping wounds. Amherst would soon rip off those bandages by insisting on policies he believed restrained both his administrative costs and the Indians. Instead, Amherst's "containment policy" would provoke a war that cost the British Crown and its empire far more in money, lives, and foregone opportunities than if Johnson's "appeasement policy" had been generously applied.

Amherst was obsessed with expenses. He castigated Johnson for spending twice as much as the general had allocated, along with similar cost overruns by Croghan and another agent, John Butler. He insisted that "we must deal more sparingly for the future, for the now tranquil state of the country and the good regulations you have put the trade under, I can see very little reason for bribing the Indians or buying their good behavior, since they have no enemy to molest them, but, on the contrary, every encouragement & protection they can desire for their trade."[55]

Amherst's policy appalled the Indian agents. They countered that periodic Indian councils and gifts, though costly, averted a far more devastating, tragic, and expensive war. George Croghan explained that "the British and French colonies since . . . first settling America has adopted the Indian customs and manners by indulging them in treaties and renewing friendships making them large presents which I fear won't be so easy to break them of as the General may imagine."[56]

Most experienced frontier officers feared that Amherst's policies could provoke the very war they wished to avoid. Subordinates dared not write their commander in chief of such worries. But they did communicate with each other. Captain Campbell, Detroit's commander, wrote to Colonel Henry Bouquet at Fort Pitt that "everything is now quiet, tho I am certain that if the Indians knew General Amherst's sentiments about keeping them short of powder it would be impossible to keep them in temper." He then asked Bouquet to send him some powder so he could distribute it among the Indians for their winter hunt which "would be doing a good thing, tho it is against the general's orders." He later wrote Bouquet that the Indians had departed for their winter hunt and so things should be peaceful until spring. Meanwhile he hoped that Amherst "will change his present way of thinking with regard to Indian affairs. As I am of the opinion if they were supplied with ammunition it would prevent their doing mischief."[57] Campbell's hope would be severely misplaced.

Although he was safely back at Fort William Augustus, Major Henry Gladwin continued to seek any intelligence on Indian intentions. He passed on alarming rumors of circulating warbelts, intrigues by Jesuit priests and Canadians, French and Spanish fleets and armies, and an aborted conspiracy to assassinate Sir William Johnson at the Detroit council last autumn. An incredulous Amherst wrote Johnson to ask if he could verify any of Gladwin's alarming reports. Johnson had indeed heard similar rumors of various conspiracies, but had no way of assessing the credibility of any. Without concrete proof, Amherst happily dismissed conspiracy rumors as fantasies.[58]

At Fort Pitt, Croghan heard tell of discontent among the Mingo and their cousins the Seneca. He warned Johnson that "the Senecas are a very bad people, proud & mischevous and look upon themselves as the absolute Lords . . . I am of opinion they will make some disturbance tho all the other nations this way behave extremely well at present but the Senecas seem ripe for some mischief."[59]

Word that Spain had allied with France heightened fears of an imminent

Indian uprising: "The Indians are a good deal elevated on the news of a Spanish war and daily reports spread amongst them that the French and Spanish are soon to retake Quebec . . . they only want a good opportunity to fall upon us if they had encouragement from an enemy." Amherst contemptuously dismissed such warnings. He insisted that the "commanding officers at the posts . . . have nothing to fear from the Indians, while they keep a proper look out, and prevent their getting too much ammunition."[60] The Indian Superintendents, their agents, and all fort commanders would observe the strictest economy. And that was final.[61]

It was not just Amherst's policies that riled the Indians. They suffered insults, threats, and thefts from all sides. Squatters enraged the Indians as much as cheating traders. Bouquet issued a proclamation at Fort Pitt and other forts in the region to preserve "peace and a good understanding with the Indians, to avoid giving them any just cause of complaint, this is therefore to forbid any of His Majesty's Subjects to settle or hunt to the west of the Allegheny Mountains on any pretense whatsoever."[62] Indeed, colonials could only travel west with a pass or trade license issued by General Amherst or the governor. But that sensible edict was never enforced. Neither army officers nor provincial governors wanted to deploy their troops against American colonists, even when the lawbreakers threatened to provoke an Indian uprising.

Bouquet was just as aware of the destructive effects of selling alcohol to Indians. On March 1, 1762, he issued an order that because the "use of rum and of all strong liquors is destructive to the Indians and attended with the most pernicious consquences, all Indian traders and others are expressly forbid to carry, sell, or give strong liquor to the Indians, and the officers commanding this Department are strictly to adhere to this order."[63]

Rage swollen by cheating and squatting was exacerbated by British racism. Most British soldiers and civilians did not hide their utter contempt for Indians. Bullies tend to be cowards at heart, projecting their own insecurities on their victims. Johnson recognized this and noted the irony that "gentlemen of any rank or sense should give themselves airs now in talking so slightly of Indians, who before would fly before a handfull of them, nay perhaps would do the same now if put to the trial. Those are the kind of people whom the Indians would have least to dread from if ever they were to engage, for brave men would not talk so idely or inconsistently."[64]

Amherst could dismiss the warnings of his subordinates. But when Whitehall wrote he had to ponder their words and orders carefully. Johnson's reports of an Indian conspiracy and the reasons for it had worried Whitehall. The ministers agreed with Johnson that the "primary cause of discontent" is the "cruelty and injustice with which they had been treated with respect to their hunting grounds, in open violation of those solemn compacts by which they had yield to the dominion but not the property of those lands."

The king and his ministers had been "awakened to a proper sense of the injustice and bad policy of such a conduct towards the Indians."[65]

Lord Egremont, the secretary of state for the Southern Department, informed Amherst that "His Majesty's interests may be promoted by treating the Indians upon the same principles of humanity and proper indulgence. . . . The Indians are disgusted & their minds alienated from His Majesty's Government by the shamefull manner in which business is transacted between them and our traders, the latter making no scruple of using every low trick and artifice to overreach and cheat those unguarded ignorant people in their dealings with them, while the French by a different conduct, and worthy of our immitation, deservedly gain their confidence."[66]

An act followed that awareness. On December 9, 1761, King George III issued instructions to the colonial governors that forbade them "to pass any grant or grants to any persons whatever of any lands within or adjacent to the territories possessed or occupied by the . . . Indians or the property possession of which has at any time been reserved or claimed by them."[67] Only licensed traders would be allowed in Indian country. Those officials who disobeyed the edict would be dismissed. That edict seemed straightforward enough. But it did not address previous land treaties and was widely ignored in future negotiations.

Johnson received a copy of the Royal Instructions in spring 1762 and immediately used them to bolster his diplomacy. He did all he could to repair the damage wreaked by Amherst's policies. A superintendent's work was a constant round of councils, both grand and small. Johnson gathered chiefs of the Onondaga, Oneida, and Tuscarora at his home from January 23 to 29, 1762, to address lingering disputes over land, prices, and crimes. On February 25, he met with Mohican chiefs. His deputy at Montreal, Daniel Claus, met with Indians on March 15 and then traveled to Johnson Hall to report directly to Johnson. Oneida chiefs passed the pipe with Johnson at his home on April 9 and 10, followed by Cayuga on April 17, and finally Onondaga, Tuscarora, more Cayuga, and, most importantly, Seneca, from April 20 to 28. At all of these councils little more than grievances and promises could be exchanged from either side.[68]

There was only so much that the Indian Superintendent and his agents could do. In early April word spread that a Shawnee war party had murdered four whites on the Virginia frontier. Many worried that this was the first Indian blow in an all-out war. Croghan investigated and concluded that the murders were not "a national thing but rather a kind of robbery committed by some straggling Indians."[69] The Shawnee chiefs explained that the murderers thought the whites were Cherokee and attacked them during the night. The chiefs "were prodigious uneasy at this accident and declare they will deliver up the men who committed the murder."[70] Although the murders would escape justice, Croghan was encouraged that the Shawnee were contrite rather than defiant over the tragedy. It was a sign that either they were not part of any conspiracy or doing all they could to cover one up.

One of the worst open wounds on the frontier was the Wyoming valley of the upper Susquehanna River where Connecticut squatters employed by the Susquehanna Company enraged Indians and Pennsylvanians alike. William Johnson wrote to Connecticut governor Thomas Fitch with a warning that an Indian war would explode on the frontier if he did not restrain the Susquehanna Company. To Johnson's irritation, Fitch did not reply directly but instead wrote to Amherst. Meanwhile, 44 Susquehanna Indians arrived at Johnson Hall for a council from May 3 to 6, during which they complained bitterly about the Connecticut squatters. Johnson distributed gifts and sympathy, and encouraged them to attend a council at Easton, Pennsylvania later that summer, which would be devoted to resolving that dispute. On June 8, 1762, Fitch did issue a proclamation warning people not to enter those lands. Strangely, he would not inform Amherst of his action until the middle of July. The general promptly wrote of the news to the superintendent and also reported that he had received a letter from Pennsylvania governor James Hamilton acknowledging that he had read the proclamation and was satisfied the issue was resolved. Although Johnson, Amherst, and Hamilton breathed a collective sigh of relief, the conflict was far from over.[71]

With hopes that he had helped stamp out that most recent blaze on the frontier, Johnson traveled to Easton, Pennsylvania to put out another land dispute that had smoldered for decades. The Easton council opened on June 18, 1762, with the Delaware led by Chief Teedyuscung, William Johnson, George Croghan, Governor Hamilton, and even two of Pennsylvania's proprietors, Richard Peters and Hamilton Chew. The council was supposed to resolve the lingering animosities from the Walking Purchase of 1737, a notoriously blatant land fraud. Israel Pemberton headed the Quaker delegation which championed the cheated Delaware. Most Pennsylvanians argued that the Walking Purchase was legitimate. Whitehall had ordered Johnson to sort out and resolve the mess.

Few councils in Johnson's career were more rancorous. Coached by Pemberton, Teedyuscung loudly protested the Walking Purchase and accused Johnson and the others of upholding that fraud. Throughout the council Teedyuscung raised all sorts of substantive and procedural points. Pemberton himself interrupted and refused to desist. Johnson was in a delicate position. Although sympathetic to the Delaware, many of the documents that could have supported their case were missing; Johnson had to rule on the evidence. He also hoped to reduce the Quaker influence among the Delaware. But he did not want to alienate those Indians.

Some deal must have been struck behind the scenes between Johnson and Teedyuscung. On June 27, after a long, rambling speech, Teedyuscung abruptly announced that "I did not come to put my hand in your purse or to get clothing. I give up the land to you and the White people." That decision was codified in treaty the next day. Johnson distributed gifts and the council broke up.[72]

The Easton council exhausted Johnson's always-precarious health. He went home and sent his deputy, George Croghan, on to the follow-up council at Lancaster, which convened from August 11 to 29. Five-hundred fifty-seven Indians attended including Seneca, Cayuga, Onondaga, Oneida, Tuscarora, Shawnee, Delaware, Nanticoke, Sapony, Munsee, Kickapoo, Ouiatenon, and Miami. The Lancaster council too was about land, but about new rather than old acquistions. Once again the Quakers championed the Indians' cause and distributed about 8,000 pounds among their charges. Contrary to the Board of Trade's orders, Pennsylvania's representatives, including Croghan, sought to purchase land from those tribes on the Susquehanna River's west branch, ostensibly for a trading post that could better serve the Indians. They also wanted to survey that river to see how far it was navigable. The Indians flatly rejected those requests. They did, however, release about 30 prisoners, but they demanded that Fort Augusta be abandoned. This Governor Hamilton rejected, although privately he conceded that the troops might be withdrawn and only traders lodged there. Despite these differences, the envoys did sign the Treaty of Lancaster, which papered over the disputes.[73]

The seemingly successful conclusion of the Easton and Lancaster councils reinforced Amherst's belief that the Indians posed no threat to British rule. Reports of Indians' complaints from distant forts continued to drop on his desk. But he dismissed the Indian protests as "groundless, for I suspect what they call ill treatment is only necessary checks which the commanding officers are obliged to give them in their drunken frolicks."[74]

Two such "drunken frolics" almost ended in tragedy at Fort Schuyler, which protected German Flats in the lower Mohawk valley. In mid-July a drunken brawl broke out when sutler Sarah Montour rolled out a wine barrel before some Oneida to entice them into selling her some land. The Oneida were soon quite drunk but refused to sell. Instead, they demanded more alcohol. When that was refused they broke into a store and stole a barrel of rum. Then they tried to climb into Fort Schuyler but were scared off by the sentries. Fortunately, no one was harmed in that riot. An indignant Amherst announced that he would have supported the sergeant had he "ordered the garrison to fire on the Indians if they had persisted in getting over the stockade, and killed some of them."[75]

Another scare occurred on July 31, 1762, when an express reached Johnson that Indians were attacking German Flats. Johnson promptly ordered the militia and Mohawk mustered, and rode at their head through the night to the rescue. Upon reaching German Flats they discovered to their relief that peace was restored. "On a strict enquiry into the affair," Johnson found "it was occasioned by a drunken Indian stripping of his cloathes, swimming across the Mohawk River in order to buy more rum at a tipling house a mile distant from where he lives and on entering the house, a couple of little girls who were left in charge of it got frightened at the sight of the naked Indian (tho without any arms) run out and came to a number of people mowing wheat, crying out that there were Indians naked in the house on which these timorous people who had often experienced Indian cruelty (without further enquiry) run away to the river, which they crossed and frightened all the people on the other side who immediately spread the alarm as far as Conajoharee with this addition, that the settlement was destroyed, on receipt of which one of my officers dispatched an express to me."[76]

The incident left Johnson relieved, irritated, and bemused. He convened a council with the Oneida on August 11 and 12, 1762, to settle the two affairs. The Oneida apologized and requested that no more rum be sold to them.[77]

Absurd incidents like the German Flats brawl or naked Indian, and the mistaken tragic murder of four whites by Shawnee earlier that summer led many frontier settlers, traders, soldiers, and Indian agents to lower their guard. They became innured to too many alarms "crying wolf."

Not so Johnson, who became convinced that the frontier teetered at the brink of war. Its causes were clear. Ever since the conquest he had warned the commander in chief that denying the Indians the goods that they needed to survive would provoke a war. Unable to pry open Amherst's trapped mind, he increasingly went over his head. In August 1762, he warned the Board of Trade that "the Indians are not only very uneasy, but jealous of our growing power which the enemy (to engage them more firmly in their interest) had always represented would prove their destruction, as we should hem them in and in the end extirpate them." That French prediction, of course, would tragically come true. He went on to contrast how the French and British treated the Indians, with the former showering indulgences and the latter contempt upon them. Johnson then argued that "we who always fell short of the enemy in presents and kindnesses to them, may become too premature in a sudden retrenchment of some yet necessary expences." If cutbacks were truly needed then make them gradually so that the Indians may be gently weaned of their dependence on European goods. That was the best means of securing British interests, "namely a quiet possession of our distant posts, and an increase of settlements on the back parts of the country so as within a few years to have a well settled frontier, in itself strong enough to repel any sudden attempt from the Indians." Now the frontier was largely defenseless with its isolated, undermanned forts and scattered settlements. Given the cutback policy an Indian war was increasingly likely that would cost the empire a fortune in lost lives, property, and finance. That disaster could be avoided through generous "presents and kindnesses."[78]

Yet a council at Johnson Hall on August 22 seemed to indicate that the

Seneca, at least, were calmer than before. A Seneca sachem arrived with a message from his tribe promising that they remained dedicated to peace. They thanked Johnson for sending them a blacksmith to repair their muskets and other equipment. They also requested some rum for medicinal purposes and blankets to warm them during the winter. Along with the requested gifts, Johnson sent his compliments to the Seneca for their good will.[79]

Johnson followed up that council by immediately sending out runners with word for an even larger one. From September 8 through 14, chiefs from all six Iroquois bands gathered at Johnson Hall. Aside from the usual rituals, complaints, and promises there was an intriquing exchange between the unnamed Onondaga chief and Johnson over religion. The chief revealed that the Great Spirit had recently revealed to an Onondaga that he was angry to see "the white people squabbling and fighting for these lands which he gave the Indians . . . and would, although their numbers were ever so great, punish them if they did not desist."[80]

This was a direct challenge that Johnson had to crush with diplomatic finesse. It was not only a question of whose God was superior, but who was therefore justified to rule over the land. Johnson dismissed the Indians' "romantic notions, custom of dreaming, and seeing visions [which] however usual amongst you cannot but appear in a very ridiculous light to white people who will consider it only as a scheme set on foot by some designing persons to answer their purposes; and I hope you cannot but be convinced that the Divine Being is satisfied with the justice of our cause from the great successes with which he has crowned the British arms."[81] Thus did might make Divine right.

Relations with the Detroit tribes were also unraveling. But in August 1762, an excellent officer would arrive to take command of that vital post. Major Henry Gladwin had been a lieutenant in the 48th regiment in 1755 when he accompanied General Braddock to North America. He caught a musket ball in his arm during Braddock's disastrous defeat at the Monongahela on July 9, 1755. He was promoted to captain that December. In 1758 he transferred to the 80th Light Infantry regiment that Colonel Thomas Gage was organizing. Gage rewarded Gladwin's abilities by thrice naming him temporary major for special assignments. In August 1760, Gladwin received his first independent command after Amherst's army captured Fort Levis. Amherst renamed the fort William Augustus and placed Gladwin in charge. In December 1760, Gladwin was formally promoted to major. The major's only apparent weakness was a recurring bout with malaria which plagued him, especially when he was stressed. He was sent to Detroit three times, but had to return to Fort William Augustus the first two times when his malaria flared in autumn 1761 and summer 1762. Having finally established himself at Detroit, Gladwin would soon have his hands full. Rumors soon reached his ear of a conspiracy among the local tribes led by the Ottawa war chief Pontiac.

Pontiac does not clearly enter history until late 1762 when he converted to Neolin's teaching and used it to whip up passions against the British.[82] Pontiac's role, if any, in the earlier conspiracies is unknown. But after entering history he overshadowed all other chiefs during the war in how the British viewed and wrote about him.

What kind of man was Pontiac? He was in his mid-forties when the revolt exploded in 1763. For the previous two decades he had most likely warred most years against either the British or southern tribes. What is certain is that by late 1762 he had risen to become war chief of the Detroit Ottawa band. As for his early years, his contemporaries whose views were recorded differ over when or where he was born, who his parents were, what he looked like, or even what his name meant. They agree on one thing—Pontiac was an extraordinary leader.

Not everyone admired him. The anonymous author of *Journal of Pontiac's Conspiracy* calls him "a proud, vindictive, war-like, and easily offended man . . . whose only bravery lies in the treachery he is able to inspire by his sauve exterior."[83] No one who knew Pontiac would dispute that.

Yet many of the British who got to know Pontiac not only believed he was a great leader but acquired a grudging respect and even affection for him. In May 1765, Lieutenant Alexander Fraser wrote that Pontiac was "the most sensible man among all the Nations and the most humane Indian I ever saw. He was as careful of me and my men as if we were his own children, and has saved my life twice since I came here.[84] Croghan found Pontiac "a shrewd sensible Indian of few words, and commands more respect amongst these nations than any Indian I ever saw could do amongst his own tribe."[85] An exasperated but intrigued Thomas Gage argued that Pontiac "should be gained in our interest or knocked in the head. He has great abilities but his savage cruelty destroys the regard we should otherwise have for him."[86] Gage saw Pontiac "not only as a savage possessed of the most refined cunning and treachery natural to the Indians, but as a person of extraordinary abilities. He . . . keeps two secretarys, one to write for him and the other to read the letters he receives, and he manages them so as to keep each of them ignorant of what is transacted by the other."[87]

Pontiac was popularly believed then and now to be a decisive, ruthless leader. Ironically, he would change from one of the fiercest advocates of war with Britain to one of the staunchest advocates of peace. At crucial times he hovered Hamlet-like in indecision over whether to pursue war or peace with the British.

Until late 1762, the Detroit tribes were cold to the Seneca warbelts. Pontiac changed all that. Having fought valiantly for years against the British, their conquest of Canada deeply embittered him. Then Neolin's teachings and the Seneca war cries had uplifted him like hundreds of other Indians. Pontiac was committed to leading the destruction of Detroit and its satellite forts. First he had to rally his own village to that cause. As a great war chief and orator he soon inspired his warriors to follow him. Next he would convince the Potawatomi. He did so by intimidating their chief, "Ninivois, a weak and easily influenced man; and knowing that Pontiac was his superior chief and treacherous, he and his whole tribe joined him."[88]

The Huron would be more difficult to convince. French missionaries had converted them nearly a century and a half earlier and retained enormous power over the Huron. During the Seven Years' War the priests had urged the Huron to war against the British. With the British conquest, however, the priests cautioned their charges to live at peace with their new masters. Pontiac's entreaties split the tribe between the majority war faction led by Takay and a minority peace faction led by Teata.

In early September, Pontiac convened a huge Indian council among the Great Lakes tribes at the Ottawa village near Detroit. With the Ottawa were Huron, Chippewa, and Potawatomi. Runners carried warbelts to the Miami, Ouiatenon, Kickapoo, and Piankeshaw, and Shawnee, and perhaps the Delaware and Iroquois as well. Other councils followed. Those chiefs eager for war held smaller councils in the scattered villages across the region. Hopeful rumors spread of a French army gathering at New Orleans to join the Indians for a spring attack. Pontiac used a bizarre meteorological phenomenon around Detroit on October 5, 1762 to reinforce his call that the time had come to sweep the British from their land. The thick cloudy skies opened up a deluge of black, sulphurous-smelling rain. Pontiac spread word of the event to distant villages and called for yet another council. That council convened in November at Fish Island not far from Detroit. Delegations of Huron, Wyandot, Ottawa, Potawatomi, Chippewa, Mississauga, Miami, Shawnee, and Delaware debated whether to raise the war hatchet. All the tribes rallied around Pontiac except for the Huron who split over the war call. Chief Takay's Detroit Huron and Chief Odinghquanooron's Sandusky Wyandot agreed to join the attack while Teata's Huron and Orontony's Wyandot opted for a troubled peace. Runners carried warbelts to all the villages throughout that vast region with word to assemble for a final council where the Ecorse River flowed into the Detroit River around mid-April 1763, the month of the Green Moon.

Word of the councils first reached Gladwin at Detroit and Croghan at Fort Pitt in late September. On September 28, less than two weeks after the secret council, a loyal Indian informed Croghan that it had taken place. Two days later that news was confirmed by three Iroquois. Alarmed, Croghan sent word to Amherst and Johnson.[89]

Croghan's intelligence was corroborated by another warning, which came from even farther afield. Earlier in 1762, Amherst had asked Captain Thomas Hutchins to organize and head an expedition to the upper Great Lakes to explore and map that region. Hutchins was a good choice. He had joined the Second Pennsylvania Regiment as an ensign in 1756, was promoted to lieutenant the following year, and served as one of General John Forbes' supply officers in the campaign which took Fort Duquesne in 1758. In 1761 he joined the 60th Royal Americans and served as an aide to Colonel Bouquet. While his administrative skills were formidable, he proved to be a brilliant cartographer.

When Hutchins returned in late September he provided more than accurate maps of the region. Croghan passed on Hutchins' report to Johnson: the Indians "were disappointed in their expectation that I had presents for them; and as the French have always accustomed themselves, both in times of peace and during the late war, to make these people great presents three or four times a year and always allowed them a sufficient quantity of ammunition at the posts, they think it very strange that this custom should be so immediately broken off by the English, and the traders not allowed even to take so much ammunition with them as enable those Indians to kill game sufficient for the support of their families."[90]

In October 1762, George Croghan dispatched Alexander McKee to the Shawnee, Delaware, and Mingo of the upper Ohio and Muskingum Rivers to gain intelligence of their intentions and try to mollify them with presents and promises. McKee set out from Fort Pitt on October 12. He met various Indians along his route including a 20-man Shawnee war party with "a Cherokee prisoner and a scalp, and as their principal warrior was dead and most of their party sick, they requested I would write back to Fort Pitt in order to get a doctor to view their sick." During his six-week journey McKee counciled with a half dozen village chiefs, gained the release of four prisoners, and, most importantly, learned that last spring the Delaware and Seneca had tried to rally the other tribes into an uprising against the British by circulating a large warbelt with a bloody hatchet. Only the Shawnee had joined the Delaware and Seneca, but even those three tribes were divided over whether or not to go to war. McKee safely returned to Fort Pitt on November 31, 1762 and the word was soon passed to Amherst and Johnson.[91]

A crisis erupted on the frontier in November when two Kanestio Seneca gruesomely murdered two white men near Fort Niagara. The news incensed Amherst, who was "determined that the murderers shall be delivered up or I will give immediate orders for the march of a body of men to take revenge on the nation or village to which they belong."[92] Amherst risked an enormous stake for bringing two murderers to justice. If they could not be found, Amherst would either have to back down or mobilize troops and supplies for a campaign, an expensive undertaking that might provoke an Indian war.

Johnson, of course, was stuck with the thankless task of sorting out the mess so the murderers would be apprehended and an Indian war and loss of British prestige averted. But Johnson had already made plans for a different trip. He sent his nephew, Guy Johnson, through the Iroquois League to discuss the murder and other issues. Fortunately, he cautioned Guy not to make any extravagant threats. Johnson counciled with the Oneida on November 30 and sachems of all six Iroquois bands at Onondaga on December 4, 5, and 7. He promised that white settlers would be restrained and their other grievances resolved. He also informed them that the French and Spanish were about to make peace with Britain that permanently transferred their territory east of the Mississippi River. He also demanded that the Kanastio Seneca surrender the murder suspects from their village. Finally, he warned them to remain at peace. The Iroquois would have the winter to ponder the weight of those demands and promises.[93]

Amidst these rumors of pending war, British power expanded briefly. Sault St. Marie is 90 miles north of Michilimackinac where the waters of Lakes Superior and Huron mingle. It was a small post with a stockade enclosing four cabins. A Chippewa village with 50 warriors stood nearby. Jean Baptiste Cadotte was the local Canadian merchant. Alexander Henry had recently joined him. The British army did not occupy Fort Sault Sainte Marie until September 19, 1762, when Lieutenant John Jamet arrived with five soldiers of the 60th Royal Americans from the garrison at Fort Michilimackinac.

Jamet would have little time to enjoy his first independent command. Tragedy struck the post on December 10. A fire broke out in a wattle and daub chimney of the barracks and spread to the commander's cabin, trapping Jamet inside. There he would have burned to death had not Henry burst through the flames and dragged him to safety. Within minutes a keg of gunpowder exploded flaming logs throughout the compound. All but Cadotte's cabin was destroyed. Without supplies, Jamet chose to send his troops across the straits to Michilimackinac before ice clogged the passage. They survived that perilous trip and arrived at Michilimackinac a few days later. Jamet, however, was so badly burned that he could not be moved and remained at Sault St. Marie to recover. Two months later, Jamet, Henry, Cadotte, two Canadians, and two Indians set forth across the ice for Michilimackinac. They almost perished from fatigue and starvation but finally made it. They could not know that they had escaped from a fire into a frying pan.

As 1762 ended, many wondered whether the new year would bring war or peace. There were signs that the smoldering crisis might abate. A common theme had run through the dozens of councils held that year. The chiefs reluctantly admitted exchanging warbelts and plans for an uprising. Not that they wanted war, but they felt provoked against their will into raising the tomahawk. The Indians almost universally feared that the British were preparing to destroy them as a race by first denying them essential arms, munitions, and other goods upon which their lives depended. Meanwhile, the British demanded that the Indians surrender their only bargaining chips, prisoners. It was assumed that the British would attack as soon as the last prisoner was returned and the Indians could no longer defend themselves. This terror united tribes historically split by war and animosities. Canadian propaganda fed these native perceptions. So far a fragile peace persisted, but if one or more tribes were courageous enough to revolt against British rule, the rest would likely follow to avenge years of insults and deprivations. However, resume the supply of essential goods, the chiefs asserted, and the enthusiasm for war would evaporate. That very confession of conspiracy undercut its imminent fulfillment. An uprising seemed unlikely if its leaders were willing to admit that the tribes were seriously considering it. And the crisis's solution was so simple. Just giving the Indians what they needed not only alleviated their plight but clearly advanced British economic and military interests as well. The trouble was that any attempts by William Johnson, George Croghan, and other Indian experts to convince Amherst of his policy's folly only prompted his ever more vigorous defense of it.

Despite the crisis, some tribes were willing to make concessions to the British beyond merely confessing that they contemplated war. In mid-December the Shawnee brought in some prisoners to Fort Pitt and promised more in the spring. Most Great Lakes tribes swore their love for the British. The Iroquois seemed more intent to attack the distant Cherokee than adjacent British settlers. If Amherst ruled out appeasing the Indians with gifts, government agents could still divert native rage by encouraging wars against one another.[94]

Yet those who best knew the Indians were bleakly pessimistic about whether the brittle peace would hold. As Croghan put it to Bouquet, the Indians "never intended to make war on the English but say it's full time for them to prepare to defend themselves & their country from us. . . . They interpret the General's frugality in lessening the expense of presents in a design of revenging. . . . How it may end the Lord knows; but I assure you I am of opinion it will not be long before we shall have some broils with them."[95] He was even more blunt with Johnson: "I am of the opinion we should soon have an Indian war. . . . If the Senecas, Delawares, & Shawnees should break with us it will end in a general war with all the western nations."[96] Bouquet for one agreed that war was likely but thought it would be limited: "the discovery of a pretended new conspiracy of the Senecas, Delawares, and Shawaneses to strike us, but the Western Indians having refused to join them their intentions must prove abortive."[97] But whether they believed that the war would be limited or general, nearly all high officers and officials thought one was inevitable. Everyone, that is, except Sir Jeffrey Amherst.

As the tribes conspired to war against the British Empire, another war ended. The Treaty of Paris was signed by representatives of France, England, and Spain on February 10, 1763. Versailles had abandoned all of its North American empire but for two tiny islands, Pierre and St. Miquelon, near southern Newfoundland which served as shelters for fishermen. Like a wishbone, New France was torn asunder at the Mississippi. Britain took all lands east of that river except for New Orleans. Spain took New Orleans and all lands west of the Mississippi. Spain traded East Florida to Britain for the return of Cuba which the British had captured in August 1762. France now could not legally aid an Indian uprising in North America even if it had the resources and will to do so, which it did not in any case. As for the Canadians and Louisianans now living in the British Empire, the Treaty of Paris gave them eighteen months to decide whether or not to leave with their possessions. Those who chose to remain chose to become British subjects.

The French did manage to insert one twist into the treaty. Although France had lost its North American empire, thanks to the negotiating skills of Foreign Minister Etienne de Stainville, duc de Choiseul, it won a minor victory at the diplomatic table. Choiseul accepted Whitehall's demand that British subjects be free of duties and restrictions on the Mississippi River. But he convinced the British that the river split into two above New Orleans and insisted that the British confine themselves to the eastern Iberville River and Lakes Maurepas and Pontchartrain route, which bypassed New Orleans. The British agreed. That route, however, was a chimera. It was too shallow for boats half the year and clogged with fallen trees all year. The British would not know of that unpleasant reality until they tried to ascend that route later in 1764.

The problem now for Whitehall was what to do with the new lands. Or, as Lord Egremont put it, the king now had "to fix his Royal attention upon the next important object of securing to His subjects & extending the enjoyment of the advantages which peace has procured." That entailed determining for the new lands what new governments should be established, what military forces would be sufficient, and what contributions the colonists should make for underwriting that civil and military administration. The purpose of that new government was to preserve peace with the Indians and promote prosperity for merchants trading in those lands.[98]

Thus did Britain's North American defenders and inhabitants have reason to be optimistic as the new year opened. The French threat to the American colonies, which had persisted through nearly a century and a half and five wars, was destroyed. The British Empire now stretched to the Mississippi River. The pent-up energies and ambitions of thousands of Americans eager for trade and land but confined east of the Appalachian Mountain chain were ready to jump that barrier and spread across the new realm. All that prevented them from doing so were the Indian tribes scattered across the region and British law.

Yet war clouds were steadily thickening. On the uprising's eve, many of the forts received advanced warnings that it was coming. At Fort Pitt on January 30, 1763, Captain Ecuyer interrogated a Shawnee chief, probably Red Hawk, on the warbelts which had circulated the previous year. The chief admitted that each tribe had debated whether or not to seize the war hatchet but were too divided to initiate one at that time. He warned Ecuyer that "all the Indian nations are very jealous of the English, they see you have a great many forts in this country and you are not so kind to them as they expected. The French were very generous to the Indians and always gave them clothing, and power, and lead in plenty, but you do that Brother, and that is what makes the Indians so uneasy in their minds. This I assure you is the true cause of all this jealousy."[99]

Indian agent Alexander McKee counciled with the Shawnee at their village at the mouth of the Scioto River on February 11, and told them that the French had agreed to surrender North America, a decision that would soon be formalized by treaty. He called on them to release all their white prisoners. That information and demand sparked a debate among the Shawnee. On February 26, they met with McKee and angrily denounced the transfer of their lands from France to Britain. They would retain their prisoners as bargaining chips. Although McKee did not receive an explicit warning, it was clear that the Shawnee were primed and ready for war.[100]

Six weeks later on March 30, 1763, Fort Miami commander Ensign Robert Holmes learned that a red warbelt had appeared in the nearby Miami village. He promptly called a council, announced his discovery, and demanded that the belt and an explanation be delivered to him. Holmes recalled that "after a long & troublesome spell with them, I obtained the belt. . . . This affair is very timely stopt."[101] In handing Holmes the belt, a Miami chief, probably Little Turtle (Michikiniqua) explained that "we were all to rise and put the English to death all about this place, and those at the other places. . . . We desire you to send this [belt] down to your General and George Croghan. . . . For our part we will be still and take no more notice of their mischief."[102] The Indians contemplated war because they believed the British "mean to make slaves of them by taking so many posts in their country, and that they had better attempt something now to recover their liberty, than wait till we were better established."[103] The chief then ended with this revealing statement: "If we had ever so much a mind to kill the English there is always some discovery made before we can accomplish our design."[104] So it was fear of failing to take an alerted fort rather than sentiment that kept Miami scalping knives sheathed, for now. Holmes sent the warning to Gladwin at Detroit.

Around the same time Lieutenant Edward Jenkins, Fort Ouiatenon's commander, also received warning of the pending attack and sent Gladwin a similar report: "The Canadians here are enternally telling lies to the Indians and . . . told the Indians a few days ago that we should all be prisoners in a short time (showing them when the corn was a foot high) that there was a great [French] army to come from the Mississippi, and that they were to have a great number of Indians with them. . . . They would soon take Detroit and these small posts, and then they would take Quebec, Montreal, & go into our own Country."[105]

George Croghan received a more muted warning from friendly Indians in April and forwarded the intelligence to Johnson. News that France had ceded its land to Britain had exacerbated all the other Indian grievances. As a result, the Indians "seem a good deal sulky of late and appear more unwilling to bring in the prisoners than formerly."[106] Croghan tried to alleviate the rising Indian anger at a council from April 16 to 24. The Indians would leave "very much dissatisfied" despite having consumed "17,000 pounds, half flour and half beef."[107] Captain Ecuyer blamed Croghan for being far too generous to the Indians. But it seems he was not allowed to be generous enough.[108]

The persistence of such rumors and the impossibility of a French army ascending the Mississippi caused otherwise conscientious officers like Jenkins to dismiss such reports as idle Canadian bravado, annoying but harmless. The real harm to British interests from the Canadians was economic. Jenkins complained that the Indians prefer to trade with the Canadians despite paying higher prices. Thus on the eve of the uprising, the British received warnings that tended to relax rather than stiffen their guard.

On April 4, Gladwin convened an officers' council to discuss the reports from Holmes and Jenkins. They agreed to tighten security, forward the warnings to Amherst, and keep their ears open to other rumors. It was all that they could do, for now.

Amherst's response to these latest warnings was typical. Arrogance and ignorance made him dismiss those Cassandras no matter how experienced and high placed they might be. The general's obstinate pride was astonishing. It seemed the more warnings he received that his policy was leading to disaster the deeper he dug in his heels on the issue. On April 3, 1763, he haughtily replied to Johnson that "the Indians, I see, continue their old way of reasoning. . . . Our suspicions of their plots . . . are mere bugbears. . . . As the war . . . is now over I cannot see any reason for supplying the Indians with provisions; for I am convinced they will never think of providing for their families by hunting if they can support them by begging provisions from us."[109] The debate over public welfare to the poor and dependent is not new! The general insisted that "I cannot think the Indians have it in their power to execute anything serious against us while we continue to be on our guard."[110]

On the fifteenth day of the Green Moon month, or April 27, 1763 in the Western calender, 460 Ottawa, Huron, and Potawatomi warriors, along with several Canadians, gathered at the Ottawa village on the banks of the Ecorse River only six miles from Detroit. After they had crowded into a circle, Pontiac stood and held up a warbelt. He claimed that the French king himself had sent him the belt and a plea to overthrow British rule. The Ottawa Chief then reminded them of all the insults and exploitations they had suffered under British rule. As anger swelled among the warriors, he recited Neolin's vision of meeting with the Master of Life who had admonished them to purify themselves and drive the whites back across the ocean.

Finally, Pontiac promised that he and his men would soon take Fort Detroit. It was only a matter of striking at the right time.[111]

Incredibly, no word of that vast gathering reached British ears at Fort Detroit despite all the drumming, singing, and comings and goings. The first blood would flow less than two weeks after that council fire was extinquished.

NOTES

1. Enumeration of Indians within Northern Department, November 18, 1763, in E. B. O'Callaghan and Berthold Fernow, eds., *Documents Relative to the Colonial History of the State of New York* (hereafter cited as NYCD), 15 vols. (Albany, N.Y.: Weed, Parsons, and Co., 1856–1887), 7:582–84. For an undocumented argument that the Seneca were angry at the British for not allowing them to sack Fort Niagara in 1759 or Fort Levis in 1760, and refused them presents, see Howard H. Peckham, *Pontiac and the Indian Uprising* (1947) (reprint, Chicago: University of Chicago Press, 1961), 73–75.

2. George Croghan provides the best account of the Seneca conspiracy. See Nicolas B. Wainwright, ed., Journal of "George Croghan, 1759–1763," *Pennsylvania Magazine of History and Biography*, 71 (1947), 411.

3. The best account of Neolin's vision was recounted by Pontiac and recorded in Milo Milton Quaife, ed., *The Siege of Detroit in 1763: The Journal of Pontiac's Conspiracy and John Rutherford's Narrative of a Captivity* (Chicago: Lakeside Press, 1958), 8–18. See also Anthony F. C. Wallace, *The Death and Rebirth of the Seneca* (New York: Alfred A. Knopf, 1970), 117–21.

4. Wallace, *Death and Rebirth*, 121.

5. Indian Intelligence, December 1760, in James Sullivan and A. C. Flick, eds., *The Papers of William Johnson* (hereafter cited as *Johnson Papers*), 14 vols. (Albany: State University of New York, 1921–1965), 3:336–37.

6. Henry Bouquet to Robert Monckton, July 24, 1761, in Sylvester K. Stevens, Donald H. Kent, Autumn L. Leonard, Louis M. Waddell, and John Totteham, eds., *The Papers of Henry Bouquet* (hereafter cited as *Bouquet Papers*), 6 vols. (Harrisburg: Pennsylvania Historical and Museum Commission, 1972–1994), 5:654–55.

7. Croghan Fort Pitt Conference, March 1–3, 1761, *Bouquet Papers*, 5:324–26.

8. Gavin Cochrane to Henry Bouquet, June 1, 1761, *Bouquet Papers*, 5:518–21; Guy Townsend to Henry Bouquet, June 1, 1761, ibid., 5:521–22.

9. Ward Speech to Six Nations, June 28, 1761, *Bouquet Papers*, 5:558–59.

10. Bouquet Speech to Indians, June 29, 1761, *Bouquet Papers*, 5:592, 590–92; Court of Inquiry, June 29, 1761, ibid., 5:594–96; Henry Bouquet to Robert Monckton, May 4, 1761, ibid., 5:459.

11. Jeffrey Amherst to William Johnson, May 30, 1761, *Johnson Papers*, 10:274–75.

12. Goods for Indian Presents, June 7, 1761, *Johnson Papers*, 10:278–79; Jeffrey Amherst to William Johnson, June 11, 1761, ibid., 10:284–86; William Johnson to Jeffrey Amherst, June 12, 1761, ibid., 10:286–87; Jeffrey Amherst to William John-

son, June 24, 1761, ibid., 10:297; William Johnson to Jeffrey Amherst, June 28, 1761, ibid., 10:306.

13. Jeffrey Amherst to William Johnson, June 15, 1761, *Johnson Papers*, 10:289.

14. Amherst's Instructions to Henry Gladwin, June 22, 1761, *Johnson Papers*, 10:293–96.

15. For the best account of Johnson's diplomatic journey, see Niagara and Detroit Proceedings, July–September 1761, *Johnson Papers*, 3:428–503; Jeffrey Amherst to William Walters, June 24, 1761, ibid., 10:299–300; William Johnson to Jeffrey Amherst, June 27, 1761, ibid., 10:300–302.

16. William Johnson to Jeffrey Amherst, July 7, 1761, *Johnson Papers*, 10:312–13.

17. Report of an Indian Council, June 18, 1761, *Bouquet Papers*, 5:561–65.

18. Donald Campbell to Henry Bouquet, June 1, 1761, *Bouquet Papers*, 5:490–93.

19. Donald Campbell to Henry Bouquet, June 8, 1761, *Bouquet Papers*, 5:533.

20. Donald Campbell to Henry Bouquet, June 17, 1761, *Bouquet Papers*, 5:560–61; Donald Campbell to Henry Bouquet, June 27, 1761, ibid., 11:582–83.

21. Donald Campbell to William Walters, June 17, 1761, *Johnson Papers*, 3:405, 405–6.

22. Donald Campbell to Henry Bouquet, June 21, 1761, *Bouquet Papers*, 5:569.

23. James Sterling to John Duncan, July 8, 1761, Sterling letterbook, William L. Clements Library, Ann Arbor, Mich. (hereafter cited as CL), Report of Indian Council Near Detroit, July 3–5, 1761, *Bouquet Papers*, 5:648, 647–50.

24. Report of Indian Council Near Detroit, July 3–5, 1761, *Bouquet Papers*, 5:649.

25. Ibid., Donald Campbell to Henry Bouquet, July 7, 22, 1761, *Bouquet Papers*, 5:618–21, 646–47; William Johnson to Daniel Claus, August 9, 1761, *Johnson Papers*, 10:323–25.

26. Donald Campbell to Henry Bouquet, July 22, 1761, *Bouquet Papers*, 5:646.

27. Henry Bouquet to Robert Monckton, July 27, 1761, *Bouquet Papers*, 5:660; Bouquet speech to Indians, July 27, 1761, ibid., 5:660–61; Croghan, Uneasiness of Iroquois, July 27, 1761, ibid., 5:644–65.

28. Henry Bouquet to Donald Campbell, June 30, 1761, *Bouquet Papers*, 5:596–97; Robert Monckton to Henry Bouquet, July 13, 1761, ibid., 5:632–33.

29. Henry Bouquet to Donald Campbell, June 30, 1761, *Bouquet Papers*, 5:596–97; Henry Bouquet to Robert Monckton, June 30, 1761, ibid., 5:598–600; Militia List, Fort Pitt, June 30, 1761, ibid., 5:606–9; Henry Bouquet to Donald Campbell, July 9, 1761, ibid., 5:621–23; Gavin Cochrance to Henry Bouquet, July 9, 1761, ibid., 5:623–25.

30. Lewis Ourry to Henry Bouquet, July 13, 1761, *Bouquet Papers*, 5:633.

31. Jeffrey Amherst to William Johnson, July 8, 1761, *Johnson Papers*, 4:505.

32. Jeffrey Amherst to William Johnson, July 11, 1761, *Johnson Papers*, 3:507, 506–7; William Johnson to Jeffrey Amherst, July 24, 1761, ibid., 3:510–13.

33. William Johnson to George Croghan, July 26, 1761, *Johnson Papers*, 10:319; William Johnson to Jeffrey Amherst, July 29, 1761, ibid., 10:322.

34. Jeffrey Amherst to William Johnson, August 9, 1761, *Johnson Papers*, 3:516, 514–16.

35. Jeffrey Amherst to William Johnson, *Johnson Papers*, 4:517, 516–17.

36. Henry Bouquet to Elias Meyer, August 12, 1761, *Bouquet Papers*, 5:691–92; Elias Meyer to Henry Bouquet, September 1, 1761, ibid., 5:725–28.

37. William Johnson to Jeffrey Amherst, July 29, 1761, *Johnson Papers*, 10:321; William Johnson to Daniel Claus, August 9, 1761, ibid., 10:324–26.

38. Niagara and Detroit Proceedings, July–September 1761, *Johnson Papers*, 3: 464, 428–503.

39. Johnson Journal to Detroit, August 19, 1761, *Johnson Papers*, 8:241; William Walters to Henry Bouquet, August 24, 1761, *Bouquet Papers*, 5:718–20; William Johnson to Jeffrey Amherst, August 19, 1761, *Johnson Papers*, 3:521–22.

40. Indian Conference, June 28, 1761, *Johnson Papers*, 10:306; Jeffrey Amherst to William Johnson, June 29, 1761, ibid., 10:307–8; George Croghan to William Johnson, July 25, 1761, ibid., 10:316–18; William Johnson to George Croghan, July 26, 1761, ibid., 10:319–20.

41. Jeffrey Amherst to William Johnson, August 9, 1761, *Johnson Papers*, 3:514–16.

42. Niagara and Detroit Proceedings, July–September 1761, *Johnson Papers*, 4: 488.

43. Ibid., 3:492, 493.

44. Regulation for the Indian Trade at Fort Stanwix, February 1762, *Johnson Papers*, 10:389–91; William Johnson to Henry Bouquet, September 18, 1761, *Bouquet Papers*, 5:761; Indian Regulations at Fort Pitt, September 18, 1761, ibid., 5: 762–63; To Officers at Western Posts, September 16, 1761, *Johnson Papers*, 3:527–28; William Johnson to Henry Bouquet, Prices for Indian Goods, September 18, 1761, ibid., 3:529–30; Trade Regulation at Fort Pitt, ibid., 3:530–33; Trade Regulation at Sandusky, ibid., 3:533–35.

45. Donald Campbell to William Johnson, June 9, 1762, *Johnson Papers*, 3:757–59.

46. William Johnson to Henry Gladwin, April 8, 1763, *Johnson Papers*, 4:81, 80–81.

47. Indian Conference, September 25 to October 3, 1761, *Johnson Papers*, 10: 325–29; Donald Campbell to Henry Bouquet, September 17, 1761, *Bouquet Papers*, 5:75–58; Elias Meyer to Henry Bouquet, September 24, 30, October 12, 22, 1761, ibid., 5:777–80, 787–89, 818–20, 833–37; Donald Campbell to Elias Meyer, October 5, 1761, ibid., 5:820–21.

48. William Johnson to Jeffrey Amherst, November 5, 1761, *Johnson Papers*, 10: 330.

49. Donald Campbell to Henry Bouquet, October 12, 1761, *Bouquet Papers*, 5: 815–17; Donald Campbell to Jeffrey Amherst, November 8, 1761, ibid., 6:28–29; Henry Balfour's Conference with Indians, September 29, 1761, *Johnson Papers*, 3: 537–45.

50. Return of Garrisons at Detroit and Dependent Forts, November 8, 1761, *Bouquet Papers*, 6:30; Return of Provisions in Store at Detroit, November 8, 1761, ibid., 6:31.

51. For a literary and historical classic which captures the nature of the trade and times, see Milo Milton Quaife, ed., *Alexander Henry's Travels and Adventures in the Years 1760–1776* (Chicago: Lakeside Press, 1921).

52. Ibid., 35.

53. Ibid., 42–43.

54. Ibid., 43–44.

55. Jeffrey Amherst to William Johnson, December 26, 1761, *Johnson Papers*, 10:347–48; Jeffrey Amherst to William Johnson, December 30, 1761, ibid., 3:597–98; Jeffrey Amherst to William Johnson, January 16, 1762, ibid., 10:353–55.

56. George Croghan to Henry Bouquet, March 27, 1762, *Bouquet Papers*, 6:69, 68–70.

57. Donald Campbell to Henry Bouquet, November 30, 1761, *Bouquet Papers*, 6:48.

58. Henry Gladwin to Jeffrey Amherst, February 4, 24, 25, March 5, April 4, 5, 1762, *Johnson Papers*, 10:380–81, 384–85, 385–86, 392–94, 422–24, 424–25; Jeffrey Amherst to William Johnson, March 17, 1762, ibid., 10:399–400; William Johnson to Jeffrey Amherst, March 20, 1762, ibid., 10:404–6; Jeffrey Amherst to William Johnson, March 21, 1762, ibid., 10:406–7; Jeffrey Amherst to William Johnson April 11, 1762., ibid., 3:678–79; William Johnson to Jeffrey Amherst, May 16, 26, 1762, ibid., 3:741–42, 744–45.

59. George Croghan to William Johnson, March 31, 1761, *Johnson Papers*, 3:663–64.

60. Jeffrey Amherst to Henry Bouquet, May 2, 1762, *Bouquet Papers*, 6:82, 81–83.

61. William Johnson to George Croghan, January 8, 1762, *Bouquet Papers*, 6:70–71.

62. Bouquet Proclamation, October 31, 1761, *Bouquet Papers*, 5:844; Henry Bouquet to James Livingston, October 31, 1761, ibid., 5:847.

63. Bouquet, General Order, March 1, 1762, *Bouquet Papers*, 6:49–50.

64. William Johnson to Daniel Claus, February 9, 1762, *Johnson Papers*, 3:629, 629–30.

65. Order of the King in Council on a Report of the Lords of Trade, November 23, 1761, NYCD 7:473, 472–76.

66. Lord Egremont to Jeffrey Amherst, *Johnson Papers*, 3:588.

67. Lords of Trade to the King, Draft Instructions for Governors, December 2, 1761, NYCD 7:478, 477–79.

68. Journal of Indian Affairs, January 23–29, February 25, 1761, *Johnson Papers*, 10:356–71, 386–88; Conference with Canasadaga Indians, March 15, 1762, ibid., 10:398–400; Journal of Indian Affairs, March 24–30, April 9–10, 14–17, 20, 1762, ibid., 10:409–15, 428–29, 431–32, 436–38; Six Nations Proceedings, April 21 to 28, 1762, ibid., 3:690–715.

69. George Croghan to Jeffrey Amherst, May 10, 1762, *Johnson Papers*, 10:452; William Johnson to George Croghan, April 17, 1762, ibid., 10:432–33; William Johnson to Jeffrey Amherst, April 17, 1762, ibid., 10:433–36; Jeffrey Amherst to William Johnson, May 30, 1762, ibid., 10:458–59.

70. Croghan Journal, May 21, 1762, *Johnson Papers*, 10:456–57.

71. William Johnson to Thomas Fitch, March 30, 1762, *Johnson Papers*, 10:416–17; Thomas Fitch to Susquehanna Company, June 8, 1762, ibid., 3:756–57; Journal of Indian Affairs, May 3–6, 1762, ibid., 10:442–49; Jeffrey Amherst to William Johnson, July 18, 1762, ibid., 10:473–74.

72. Meeting at Easton with Delawares, June 18 to 28, 1761, *Johnson Papers*, 3:785, 760–91; William Johnson to Pennsylvania Commissioners, June 2, 1762, ibid., 10:465–66; John Morton and Others, June 22, 1762, ibid., 3:794–99; Richard Pe-

ters and Others, June 24, 28, 1762, ibid., 3:799–811, 812–18; William Johnson to Lords of Trade, August 1, 1762, ibid., 3:837–51.

73. Minutes of the Treaty of Lancaster, August 1762, *Johnson Papers*, 10:498–99; George Croghan to William Johnson, September 4, 1762, ibid., 3:873–75; Lancaster Council minutes, August 11 to 29, 1762, in *Minutes of the Provincial Council of Pennyslvania* (1852) (reprint, New York: AMS Press, 1968, 8:721–74.

74. Jeffrey Amherst to William Johnson, July 6, 1762, *Johnson Papers*, 3:824–25.

75. Jeffrey Amherst to Thomas Baugh, August 1, 1762, *Johnson Papers*, 3:835; Thomas Baugh to Jeffrey Amherst, July 20, 1762, ibid., 3:831.

76. William Johnson to William Winepress, August 4, 1762, *Johnson Papers*, 3:855–56.

77. William Johnson to Jeffrey Amherst, August 1, 1762, *Johnson Papers*, 10:477–78; Indian Conference, August 11–12, 1762, ibid., 10:480–83.

78. William Johnson to Lords of Trade, August 20, 1762, *Johnson Papers*, 3:866–67, 865–69.

79. Indian Conference, August 22, 1762, *Johnson Papers*, 10:490–92.

80. Indian Conference, September 8–10, 1762, *Johnson Papers*, 10:505–6, 500–508.

81. Indian Conference, September 13–14, 1762, *Johnson Papers*, 10:511, 509–18; Extract from Journal on Indian Affairs, September 15, 1762, ibid., 10:518–19.

82. For various views of Pontiac, see Peckham, *Pontiac and the Indian Uprising*, 15–20, 28–29; Alan Eckert, *Wilderness War* (1969) (reprint, New York: Bantam, 1980), 714–15; Wallace, *Death and Rebirth*, 121.

83. Quaife, *The Siege of Detroit*, 3.

84. Alexander Fraser to William Johnson, May 18, 1765, *Johnson Papers*, 11:743.

85. George Croghan to Murray, Illinois Historical Collections, 11:31–32.

86. Thomas Gage to William Johnson, July 2, 1764, *Johnson Papers*, 11:250.

87. Thomas Gage to Lord Halifax, April 14, 1764, Gage papers, CL, 1:25–26.

88. Quaife, *The Siege of Detroit*, 5.

89. Indian Intelligence, September 28, 1762, *Johnson Papers*, 10:534–35.

90. Croghan to Johnson, December 8, 1762, Journal and Report of Thomas Hutchins, April 4, to September 24, 1762, *Johnson Papers*, 10:521–29.

91. Journal of Alexander McKee, October 12 to November 27, 1762, ibid., 10:576, 576–80; Instruction for Alexander McKee, October 5, 1762, ibid., 10:546–48.

92. Jeffrey Amherst to William Johnson, November 21, 1762, *Johnson Papers*, 4:942, 941–42.

93. Indian Proceedings, November 21 to December 8, 1762, *Johnson Papers*, 10:583–96; William Johnson to Jeffrey Amherst, December 7, 1762, ibid., 4:961–63.

94. Francis Fauquier to the Six Nation Chiefs, December 1762, *Johnson Papers*, 10:10:604–5.

95. George Croghan to Henry Bouquet, December 10, 1762, *Johnson Papers*, 10:596–98.

96. George Croghan to William Johnson, December 10, 1762, *Johnson Papers*, 4:965, 964–66.

97. Henry Bouquet to Jeffrey Amherst, December 12, 1762, *Bouquet Papers*, 6: 139.

98. Lord Egremont to Lords of Trade, May 5, 1763, NYCD 7:519, 519–22.

99. Indian Intelligence at Fort Pitt, January 30, 1763, *Bouquet Papers*, 6:156, 155–56.

100. Alexander McKee to George Croghan, April 12, 1763, *Bouquet Papers*, 6: 180–82.

101. Document 2 of Holmes, March 30, 1763, *Johnson Papers*, 4:96.

102. Robert Holmes, Copy of Miami Chief Speech Made Winter 1762, Recorded March 30, 1763, *Bouquet Papers*, 6:171.

103. Document 1 of Holmes, April 20, 1763, *Johnson Papers*, 4:95.

104. Robert Holmes, Copy of Miami Chief Speech Made Winter 1762, Recorded March 30, 1763, *Bouquet Papers*, 6:171.

105. Edward Jenkins to Henry Gladwin, March 28, 1763, *Johnson Papers*, 10: 640–41.

106. George Croghan to William Johnson, April 24, 1763, *Johnson Papers*, 10: 659–60.

107. Simeon Ecuyer to Henry Bouquet, April 23, 1763, *Bouquet Papers*, 6:176– 79.

108. McKee, Indian Council at Fort Pitt, April 16, 1763, *Bouquet Papers*, 6:182– 86.

109. Jeffrey Amherst to William Johnson, April 3, 1763, *Johnson Papers*, 10:648– 49.

110. Jeffrey Amherst to William Johnson, May 29, 1763, *Johnson Papers*, 4:99, 98–100.

111. Quaife, *The Siege of Detroit*, 14–15, 6–18.

3

Attacks

"And Drive These Britons Hence Like Frightened Deer"

They would not dare to anger us for before a regular army the Indians
are helpless.

—Sir Jeffrey Amherst

I know the Indians cannot long persevere. They are a rash, inconsistent
people and inclined to mischief and will never consider consequences
though it may lead to their ruin.

—George Croghan

All the nations who are our brothers attack—why should we not attack
too? Are we not men like them? . . . What do we fear? It is time.

—Pontiac

Fort Detroit was the key bastion of British power in the upper Great Lakes.[1]
For that the British could thank the French who founded Detroit in 1719
at one of the most strategic sites in North America. The Detroit River flows
southwest from Lake St. Clair, Lake Huron's drainage, and then south into
Lake Erie. Fort Detroit was sited on the northwest bank where the river
begins to angle south.

The fort was a rectangular palisade whose walls rose a dozen feet and
were backed by packed earth ramparts seven feet high from which troops
could level their muskets at the surrounding fields. Two blockhouses anchored each corner of the wall along the river while another blockhouse
stood at the north wall's center. About 150 yards beyond the north wall
two blockhouses were placed within musket fire of each other. Three cannon

defended the fort; a 3-pounder on the north wall and two 6-pounders along with three cohorn mortars on the parade ground to be conveyed where they were needed. Only the north wall had no gate. The east and west gates opened onto a road which paralleled the river while the south gate faced the river. Within the palisade, barracks, storehouses, shops, and perhaps 70 houses crowded the four parallel streets running east to west, with Rue St. Joseph the northern most followed by Rue St. Jacque, Rue St. Anne, and Rue St. Louis. Only one north-south street linked those streets and the walls. The Chemin du Ronde was a lane running along the four inside walls. A small square surrounded three sides of St. Anne's church beside the east wall. A 120-foot square garden near the southeast bastion supplied the troops with vegetables. The council house and headquarters also stood near the east wall. Soldiers and settlers lived together in the fort.

The ground beneath the fort rose nearly 30 feet from the riverside to the north wall; the slope gave observers 900 yards away on the south shore a partial view inside the fort. Still the fort was well beyond musket if not cannon shot from that side. No wharf existed. Ships anchored a dozen yards from shore. Supplies and troops had to be transferred from the ships to bateaux which were then ground ashore along a marshy beach.

Surrounded by farms rather than forest, Fort Detroit was not an isolated wilderness clearing. Farms crowded the river for five miles on either side of the fort. Most farms had narrow fronts on the water for 400 to 800 feet but then extended for several miles inland. The earth was usually tilled only several hundred yards from the river's edge. Nearly 800 Canadians lived in or near Detroit when the British conquerors arrived; over the next three years newcomers swelled that population to well over 1,000.

Then there were the Indians. Three villages bracketed Fort Detroit. Two miles downstream a Potawatomi village with 150 warriors stood on the north shore. Directly opposite the river's south shore lay a Huron village with 250 warriors. Pontiac's Ottawa village with 300 warriors was about two miles upstream on the south shore. The Mississauga Chippewa band of 320 warriors lived in several villages near Lake St. Clair and along the Thames River. Shortly before and during the siege ever more of those men would set up their lodges at Pontiac's village.[2]

Could the Indians take Detroit? Possibly. But they could do so only by treachery or siege, not a direct assault. Although Fort Detroit seemed formidable from afar, in May 1763 it lacked enough troops to crush an unexpected attack from within or enough supplies to withstand a prolonged siege. The garrison numbered about 100 men who included a skeleton company of Queen's Rangers and two companies of the 60th Royal Americans.[3] In a fight around 40 armed traders could back up the regulars. Those troops and traders would be stretched thin along the walls. Even thinner would be the rations, should the Indians attempt a prolonged siege. The storehouses only held a few weeks' worth of food and powder. But few among the

British expected any Indian danger as the month of May opened. The annual spring convoy was expected within a week or two to refill the fort's warehouses.

Only a portion of those supplies would be consumed by Fort Detroit's garrison. Fort Detroit served as the trans-shipment point for five other western posts. Should Fort Detroit be cut off from supplies, those other forts would wither on their respective vines. Yet few would have imagined that happening. In addition to the scores of bateaux and whaleboats which linked Fort Detroit with the other posts, there were two sailing ships, the 80-ton, six-cannon sloop *Michigan*, and the smaller, six-cannon schooner *Huron*. Besides, Indian warfare was innocent of direct assaults or prolonged sieges against forts. Although troubled by the growing unrest and rumors of conspiracy, Detroit's troops and officers alike felt secure.

On May 1, Pontiac and 50 Ottawa appeared before the east gate. They carried pipes and tobacco pouches. Only a few had knives in their belts. All were unpainted. No other Indians were on the plain around the fort. Pontiac declared their intention to dance the calumet before Major Gladwin as a gesture of friendship. His real intention was espionage. If Fort Detroit was to be overrun, he and his men had to ferret out its strengths and weaknesses.

Gladwin suspected as much. At first he refused to open the gates to them. It was an extremely risky decision, one that stunned Captain Donald Campbell and interpreter Pierre LaButte who vigorously protested it. To spurn the annual friendship renewal ceremony to be conducted by the Ottawa's war chief was tantamount to severing relations if not outright declaring war. Gladwin countered that the risk of keeping them out was less dangerous than letting them in. Who among the British knew what they truly intended? But the arguments of Campbell and LaButte finally prevailed.

While Pontiac and 30 men performed the calumet dance before the commander's house, ten others scattered among the houses to count troops and weaknesses. When the dance ended, Gladwin offered his thanks and sent them away with presents of bread, tobacco, and beer. Before departing, Pontiac informed the major that he would bring all of his people to visit in a few days. Upon returning to his village, Pontiac sent runners to the Huron and Potawatomi to share his intelligence with them and ask that they join his plans. A consensus was reached that a council would be held at the Potawatomi village in four days.

The peaceful encounter allayed Gladwin's suspicions. On May 2, he ordered Lieutenant Charles Robertson to lead an expedition to chart Lake St. Clair's waters. If they were deep enough then Fort Michilimackinac and the other forts could be supplied by schooner rather than bateaux. Robertson's expedition departed later that day. Crammed into one bateau were Robertson, six soldiers, the trader John Rutherford, and two sailors; an adventurer, Sir Robert Danvers, and his Indian boy slave accompanied the expedition in a canoe.

At the Potawatomi village on May 5, Pontiac held a council to forge a consensus for war. All of the women had been sent from the village to prevent any leaks while sentinels were posted to prevent anyone from approaching the council. Besides Pontiac, Macatepilesis represented the Ottawa, Chief Washee the Potawatomi, Chiefs Perwash and Wasson the Chippewa, and Chief Takay the Huron. Pontiac rose to urge them to unite in rebellion against the British: "It is important for us, my brothers, to exterminate from our lands this nation which seeks only to destroy us . . . All the nations who are our brothers attack them—why should we not attack? Are we not men like them? Have I not shown you the wampum belts which I received from our Great Father, the Frenchman? He tells us to strike them—why do we not listen to his words? What do we fear? It is time."[4] Pontiac then announced that he had sent warbelts to the Chippewa at Michilimakinac, the Ottawa at L'Arbre Croche, and the rest of the Thames River Mississauga. The chiefs agreed on war and a strategy for taking Detroit. Runners were dispatched to the other tribes with word that the Detroit Indians would soon attack.

The plan for taking Fort Detroit was ingenious. Pontiac and 60 warriors would enter the fort carrying tomahawks, knives, and muskets with their barrels sawn short beneath their blankets. Following them, hundreds of other men and women would also carry hidden weapons. At a signal the Ottawa would slaughter the troops. While the Ottawa prepared to capture the fort, the Chippewa, Potawatomi, and Huron would intercept any boats approaching Detroit from up- or downriver.

But the first blow would fall elsewhere. While Pontiac prepared his men for the surprise attack, Chief Perwash's warriors set off after Robertson's expedition and lay in wait for it at a Chippewa village not far from Lake St. Clair. On the morning of May 6, Robertson and his men were rowing near where the Pine River flows into Lake St. Clair when they spotted a camp of Canadians who were building a sawmill. Robertson ordered his men to head for shore to deliver some flour for those men. Somehow the Canadians had learned of the ambush and "begged us with tears in their eyes for God's sake to return."[5]

Robertson dismissed the warning. He believed that resolution would cow any Indian into passivity and that, anyway, the Indians would not dare to attack in broad daylight. He would be tragically wrong on both counts.

The expedition continued upstream. The current was so strong that the rowers hugged the west bank where the water's force was weaker. That was also the bank on which Perwash and his village waited six miles upstream where the Huron River flows into Lake St. Clair. When the bateau was spotted, three or four hundred Indians surged to the bank to try to entice the British ashore. Men waved furs for trade; women made lewd gestures for a different sort of business; they all demanded bread and tobacco. Danvers ground his canoe ashore and stepped out with his pipe held high.

When the bateau came abreast of the village, about 60 yards from shore, the women suddenly ran off and the warriors opened fire. A shot hit Robertson in the left side; he ordered his men to row off. Shots killed him and two other soldiers. Screaming war cries, the Chippewa jumped into their canoes and paddled furiously toward the bateau. The survivors were too terrified to fire and cowered below the gunwhales. The Indians boarded and forced the troops to row to the village. There some Chippewa scalped and mutilated Robertson and the two dead soldiers; others claimed the survivors as captives; still others plundered the bateau.

What happened to Danvers? During the confusion he had leapt back into his canoe and paddled for the far shore. After seizing the bateau the Chippewa called on Danvers to return and promised they would not hurt him. Danvers refused but hesitated in mid-stream. That was his mistake. Two Indians leveled their muskets and fired. A shot flung him dead into the river; he was quickly fished out and mutilated. The boy was captured.

Those lucky enough to claim a prisoner bound him and dragged him off to their lodge. The Chippewa celebrated that afternoon and into the night by gulping down the captured rum and dancing continuously. Someone skinned Robertson's arm, dried the skin, and sewed it into a tobacco pouch. The meat of the lieutenant's body was roasted and devoured. The Chippewa tried to force their captives to cannibalize Robertson, assuring them that "Englishman's flesh is very good to eat."[6] Most refused.

Rutherford pretended he was happy to become a Chippewa and noted that "by this behavior I fared in many respects better than those prisoners who appeared sullen and displeased with their situation, some of them suffered death on that account." He also observed the social leveling and bonding effects of captivity: "It gives inexpressible pleasure to meet one of our countrymen when in a foreign country; judge how much more so when in captivity with a nation of savages of a different color from ourselves. Happy was I to meet and converse with these poor fellows, who a little before I would not suffer to speak to me without the usual marks of respect from an inferior to a superior. Here there was no distinction."[7] Rutherford would survive. He was later taken down to the Chippewa camp near Detroit, escaped, and eventually wrote a stirring, insightful account of his horrifying experiences.

Fate was kinder to Fort Detroit's garrison. On May 6, Gladwin received at least one and probably two warnings. Had the mysterious informant kept his or her tongue, Pontiac's plot most likely would have succeeded. Although Gladwin kept his promise to protect the informant's identity, to sow mistrust he did tell Pontiac that the whistleblower was an Indian. To Amherst, Gladwin merely wrote that "I was luckily informed the night before."

Who told? There are several prime suspects.[8] One possibilty was a disaffected Ottawa named Mahiganne. A more romantic suspect is an Indian woman named Catherine who is given three possible personas. In one she is Gladwin's beautiful, young Chippewa lover who is beaten by Pontiac and later dies from a fall or push into a boiling kettle of maple sap. She is also described as a "straggler among the private soldiers" or an elderly woman who suffers the same fate from Pontiac and the maple-sap kettle but is uninvolved with Gladwin. There are other possibilities. One is the daughter of interpreter Pierre LaButte who, while visiting the Ottawa village, witnessed the Indians sawing short their muskets and told her father who passed on the information to Jacques Duperon Baby who in turn told Gladwin. Another is the Canadian Thomas Gouin who sent Jacques Chavin to warn Captain Campbell who then told Gladwin. Three others include the adopted Chippewa William Tucker, an Indian slave, and Angelique Cuillerier who told her lover the merchant James Sterling. Who of these was the most likely informant? Probably Baby. Gladwin may well have tried to protect him by later telling Pontiac that an Indian had leaked word of the sneak attack.[9]

Regardless, Gladwin faced a cruel decision. If he simply barred Pontiac and his warriors the next day he feared the insult might give the Indians the excuse to attack Robertson's expedition, the supply convoy from Fort Niagara, another from Fort Michilimackinac, and any British traders in the vicinity. Yet if he allowed Pontiac and his Ottawa into the fort they might massacre the garrison. He finally decided it was best to present as bold and decisive a face as possible to the Indians.

The major took an enormous risk. On the morning of May 7 he had his troops under arms and dispersed at key positions throughout the fort. Around ten o'clock Pontiac, his subchiefs Chavinon, Greton, Macatepilesis, Mukeeta, and Waubinema, and about 50 warriors appeared walking toward the fort. Campbell and LaButte met Pontiac and his men outside the fort and escorted them inside and through the lanes to Gladwin's headquarters. When Pontiac and his men entered, they found themselves surrounded at every turn by soldiers with muskets loaded and bayoneted. Traders too were armed and silently watching. Throughout the morning nearly 300 other Ottawa men and women strolled into the fort. They came ostensibly for trade, though all the merchant shops were locked up. The Indians stoically awaited Pontiac's signal for the attack. It never came.

Hays explained what happened: "we saw from their behavior & from reports that they were not well intentioned, upon which the commandant took such precautions that when they entered the fort, though they were by the nearest accounts about three hundred and armed with knives, tomahawks, & a great many guns cut short and hid under their blankets, they were so much surprised to see our disposition that they would scarcely sit down to council."[10]

Pontiac and his men were ushered before Gladwin in the council house. All along Gladwin and Pontiac pretended nothing was amiss. They performed each act of the council with all the protocol demanded. Gladwin and his officers listened intently to Pontiac's speech. As he spoke, Pontiac held aloft a wampum belt, white on one side and green on the other. If he turned the green side up or screamed a war whoop his men would instantly attack.[11]

Instead, Pontiac proclaimed his surprise "at this unusual step thou hast taken to have all the soldiers under arms and that the young chiefs are not at council as formerly. We would be very glad to know the reason for this, for we imagine some bad bird has given thee ill news of us, which we advise thee not to believe, my brother, the Indians, who have been always in perfect friendship with their brothers, the English."[12]

In his reply Gladwin sidestepped Pontiac's questions and instead emphasized the importance of peace between the British and Indians. He then distributed bread, tobacco, and six suits of clothes to Pontiac and his chiefs. The council broke up. Pontiac, his chiefs and warriors angrily strode from the fort followed by several hundred other Indians.

The role of fate or chance weighs heavily in all human endeavors, most dramatically in war. Gladwin took an enormous gamble in allowing into Fort Detroit over 300 Indians, more than two and a half times his own garrison that day. Had Pontiac uttered his war cry rather than stalked angrily away, history might well remember Gladwin as a fool rather than a hero, ranking him with George Armstrong Custer as a commander whose ego, arrogance, ignorance, and thirst for glory got his men killed. And the war's subsequent course would have been dramatically different as well.

Fortunately Gladwin did not compound that foolish act with another. Detroit most assuredly would have fallen had Gladwin ordered Pontiac and the other chiefs arrested. Their war whoops would have signaled the 300 warriors crowded around the fort's soldiers to attack. Although scores of Indians would have died, they most likely would have wiped out the garrison. Later that day Gladwin did, however, order seized two Potawatomi, Chiefs Winnemac and Nontenee, who had come into the fort to council. Those men would become valuable bargaining chips.

Pontiac was severely criticized when he failed to launch the attack. He defended his inaction: "Did not you see them all under arms? Then you must have lost some men." "Yes," says they, "but we should not have minded the loss of ten or twelve men, which would have ben the most. It is more vexing to us to think those dogs are yet alive in the fort."[13]

His followers felt Pontiac had lost his nerve at the most crucial moment. Time was essential if the fort was to be taken. The longer Pontiac hesitated, the more likely word would reach Gladwin of attacks elsewhere. Once that happened the charade of peace would end. All Indians would be barred from the fort and thus would lose their best chance of taking it.

Pontiac and his followers took out their rage on an old Chippewa woman named Catherine whom they suspected of warning Gladwin. Around six o'clock that evening a party of Ottawa dragged her before Detroit and demanded from Gladwin whether she was the "bad bird." Gladwin denied it but admitted the informant was among them. When the Ottawa returned to their village Pontiac struck her three times in the head and the village surrounded her and screamed for her death. But finally she was released.[14]

The next afternoon around five o'clock on May 8, Pontiac, accompanied by the Ottawa Chiefs Macatepilesis, Chavinon, and Breton, appeared before the gate and asked for another council with Gladwin. The four chiefs were soon seated before the major. Pontiac presented a calumet to Gladwin as a symbol of his desire for peace. He then said he and his men would return the next day to smoke it with Gladwin. The major replied that he would smoke with the chiefs but not with all the warriors. Gladwin would be strongly criticized for not seizing Pontiac and his chiefs at this point. If so the uprising around Detroit might well have sputtered out. After all, he had taken the two Potawatomi. Why not the uprising's leader?

After Pontiac withdrew he called on the Ottawa, Potawatomi, and Huron, along with the Canadians, to gather outside Fort Detroit's walls for a game of lacrosse. The hope was to accustom the garrison to large numbers of warriors and other Indians just beyond the fort.

The charade continued. Around eleven o'clock on May 9, Detroit's defenders watched as 56 canoes each with seven or eight warriors crossed the river from Pontiac's to the fort. Pontiac led over 400 Ottawa, Huron, and Potawatomi up to the fort's gate where Campbell met them. Pontiac demanded that he and all his followers be allowed into the fort to council with Gladwin. Campbell conveyed Gladwin's order that only Pontiac and no more than 60 of his men would be brought before him; the rest of the Indians must remain outside the walls. Pontiac protested that all the Indians wished to smell the smoke of the peace pipe. After conferring with Gladwin, Campbell said the major would allow all the Indians inside but only in small groups one at a time. After mulling this parry, Pontiac and his followers surged away.

This latest setback crumbled Pontiac's prestige a bit more. Blood must be shed to refire the enthusiasm and commitment of the tribes. The trouble was that any possibility of a surprise had clearly been lost. A direct attack on the fort had little chance of success. The only option was to kill any British in the area and cut off Fort Detroit from any relief. Brandishing his tomahawk, Pontiac danced and chanted the war song. The others joined him. When the dance ended warriors scattered across the countryside around Fort Detroit to butcher any British they could find.

One raiding party slaughtered Mrs. Edgar Trumball and her two sons at their home a half mile inland from Detroit. Another paddled over to Hog Island (Isle aux Cochons) where the garrison's 24 head of cattle grazed. The Indians murdered Sergeant James Fisher, his wife, one of his children, a soldier, and a Canadian, and captured a servant, a soldier, and Fisher's three daughters. The Indians would enjoy a massive feast off the slaughtered cattle. Other Indians began sniping at Fort Detroit and the schooner *Huron*.

Meanwhile, a Huron war party headed to Turkey or Fighting Island downstream from Fort Detroit to intercept that long-awaited British supply convoy. Pontiac moved his entire village across the river to Parent's Creek, a mile and a half upstream from Fort Detroit. Perwash and his Chippewa appeared later that day with the scalps and prisoners of Robertson's party. They set up their lodges alongside Pontiac's people.

Pontiac got a Canadian, Peter Desnoyers, to approach the fort under a white flag to explain that the Indians had killed nineteen British, including Robertson and his men. Gladwin then dispatched his interpreter Pierre LaButte to visit Pontiac with the warning that he put down his tomahawk or risk the destruction of his people. It was all that the major could do.

The situation for Gladwin, his troops, and the British civilians was grim. Hundreds of Indian warriors had cut them off from the outside world. It would take months before word could get to Amherst so that he could organize a relief army, and those troops could reach Fort Detroit. With only a few weeks of provisions Fort Detroit would most likely have been starved into submission long before then, if a massed Indian assault did not overrun it first. The only hope lay in the arrival of the spring supply convoy. But it would most likely be captured as it neared Fort Detroit. Then all would be lost. The British could only pray that the Indians would quickly lose heart at the prolonged siege and grudgingly accept peace. After all, history had never recorded a case of Indians having the patience to starve out a fort. Would that record soon change?

Meanwhile, the garrison and civilians just had to sit tight and keep constant vigilance. Gladwin ordered the gates shut. Throughout the fort, tubs and barrels of water were distributed to allow fires to be extinquished. The two ships were anchored so that their guns could rake any assault on the east and west walls. All soldiers and armed traders were split into two watches which relievd each other every six hours along those long walls.

The following day, May 10, Indians crept up to several homes and outbuildings only 100 yards from the north wall. The exchange of shots wounded five soldiers and three Indians. The 3-pounder on the north wall was fired with red-hot nails toward those houses. Several hits sparked a conflagration that destroyed the refuge.

When the snipers fled, Gladwin dispatched Pierre LaButte again to ask Pontiac to restore peace. Prominent Canadians Jean Baptiste Chapeton and Jacques Godfroy sought and received permission to join LaButte. Pontiac seemed receptive and asked that Captain Donald Campbell, whom he had known during his two-and-a-half-year stint as Detroit's commander, come to the Indian village for a peace council.

Not all of the Detroit Indians supported Pontiac. While the Canadian delegation met with Pontiac, Chief Teata and a small group of Huron approached the fort's west gate and asked to council with Gladwin. The major let them enter. The interpreter Jacques St. Martin explained that Teata wished to assure Gladwin that he and his followers wanted peace but that most of the Huron under Chief Takay had joined Pontiac. The major reassured Teata that his good conduct would be amply rewarded.

Why did Teata and his people stay neutral? The most important reason seems to have been the influence of their priest Father Pierre Potier. Although he may have couched his pleas to his minions in "turn the other cheek" ethics, hardnosed realism was probably more important. He understood what was beyond the comprehension of any upper Great Lakes Indian—the British Empire was the mightiest on earth and would eventually crush any resistance to its expansion.

The Huron had no sooner left when the Canadians returned with Pontiac's demand that Campbell join him in council. LaButte handed over a letter from the Canadians promising that the captain would be returned safely to the fort after the council. Gladwin called his officers to a meeting to debate Pontiac's demand. A consensus was reached that talks might just bring a truce to the fighting and if nothing else would at least buy a bit more time for the garrison. But the mission was perilous. Gladwin would not order Campbell to undertake it. Not only Campbell but Lieutenant George McDougall bravely volunteered.

The two officers strode out under a truce flag to meet with Pontiac and his chiefs at Antoine Cuillerier's home. Cuilierier was the former French commandant's brother-in-law and Pontiac had appointed him Detroit's new leader. Clad in his laced hat and coat, Cuillerier sat at the table's head throughout the talks. With LaButte translating, Pontiac announced his terms—the British were to abandon Fort Detroit, the two warships, and their arms and supplies; they would be escorted east by the Indians; and they must promise never to return. The demands were as filled with irony as with hope—the British had just imposed the same peace on the French.

When Campbell rejected the demands, Pontiac interned the two officers in the home of Jacques Baptiste Meloche. Although at first unbound, they were closely watched. LaButte brought word of their seizure to Gladwin, along with Pontiac's terms that Campbell had jotted down. Gladwin despaired at this latest calamity. He finally sent word that he completely rejected Pontiac's demands and would agree to nothing unless Campbell and McDougall were released. This Pontiac angrily refused to do. Instead, Pontiac vented his rage by allowing two messengers from Fort St. Joseph, whom the Potawatomi had caught that day, to be tortured to death.

At this crucial time an unlikely British savoir appeared. No man did more to rescue Fort Detroit than Canadian Jacques Duperon Baby. That same night he and his men smuggled supplies from his home across the river to the *Huron* anchored offshore. In subsequent nights they eventually managed to bring two months' worth of supplies to the fort. Now Gladwin and his men need merely remain vigilant until help arrived.

On the morning of May 11, "the Indians gave their usual Whoop and five or six hundred attacked the fort on all quarters—indeed! some of them behaved extremely well, advanced very boldly in an open plain, exposed to all our fire, and came within sixty yards of the fort, but upon having three men killed and above a dozen wounded, they retired as briskly."[15] The Indians would never again try that tactic. Instead, they crept behind outlying buildings, fences, and natural cover, and sniped at the fort.

The firing stopped around seven o'clock when LaButte appeared before the fort with a message from Pontiac. The surrender demand was almost identical to his previous message except for one curious addition: the Ottawa chief wanted trader James Rankin to give him his black slave. Gladwin called his officers together to discuss the terms. Gladwin again rejected Pontiac's terms and demanded that Campbell and McDougall be immediately released. Night brought an end to the negotiations.

That same day Pontiac and his Ottawa Chiefs Macatepilesis, Breton, Chavinon, and his nephew visited the Canadian settlers and augmented their warriors' own meager munition supplies by ordering the Canadians to hand over all their powder, shot, and guns.[16] He split the supplies into three large allotments and one smaller one. The larger piles went to his Ottawa, Chief Sanpear's Chippewa, and Chief Washee's Potawatomi, along with a portion for the smaller contingent of Chief Takay's Huron.

Pontiac and four chiefs then met with Teata and issued a chilling demand—either join their Indian brothers or die under their scalping knives. But he also promised that all warriors would reap a bloody harvest of scalps, plunder, glory, and freedom from arrogant British rule. Against Pontiac's stick and carrot arguments, Father Potier could only plead with his congregation to hew to the pacifism of Jesus. Teata agreed to discuss the issue with his men, but only the next day after mass for the Feast of the Assumption.

On May 12, Teata fulfilled his promise to join his band to the uprising. After mass he assembled his warriors and explained: "My brothers, you see as well as we do the risks that we are running . . . we have nothing else to do but to side either with our brothers, the Ottawas and Potawatomis, or else abandon our wives and children—a rash thing to do. We would hardly get started to leave before the Ottawas and Potawatomis and even those of our own nation would fall upon us and kill our wives and children. . . . We do not know what the designs of the Master of Life toward us may be. Is it He who inspires our brothers, the Ottawas, to make war? If it is not He who commands it, He will well be able to make his desires known and we shall yet be able to withdraw without being stained by the blood of the English. Let us do what our brothers demand of us, and spare not."[17] Fear of Pontiac rather than hatred for the British had clearly forced the decision. The Huron warriors paddled across the river to join Pontiac and the other tribes.

Despite these reinforcements, the stalemate at the fort dragged on. The

Potawatomi under Ninivois and the Huron led by Takay and Teata approached Detroit from the west and Pontiac and his Ottawa from the east. The Indians crept toward the fort through the sparse cover and fired at glimpses of soldiers behind the palisade. Likewise, the soldiers leveled their muskets through the loopholes and squeezed their triggers when they thought they had a good shot. Red-hot spikes wired together were shot from the 3-pounder and ignited two hay-filled barns, prompting the snipers within to scurry to safety. The warships fired throughout the day. The shooting ended around seven o'clock that evening. So far it was much safer to be inside than outside the fort. Among that day's casualties were as many as four dead and ten wounded Indians, of whom a cannon shot broke one man's thigh and the other's arm. Two soldiers were also wounded, one in the fort and the other on a warship. Gladwin honored Pontiac's request for a cease-fire to carry off their casualties.[18]

The Indians did not reappear at their positions the following morning. Gladwin ordered Captain Joseph Hopkins who commanded an Independent Ranger company of hardened frontiersmen to lead a sortie of 40 volunteers to burn any buildings within musket shot of the fort's west side. The troops swarmed out and quickly fired all but two houses. After Hopkins and his men safely returned, Gladwin immediately dispatched Lieutenant Jehu Hay of the 60th Royal Americans and 30 volunteers to burn two houses and stables on the fort's north side. Despite the fires, no Indians appeared.

Where were they? Pontiac and the chiefs were counciling with Campbell and McDougall. Pontiac repeated his demand that the British abandon Fort Detroit and return east. Campbell wrote down the demand which was carried to the fort. Gladwin replied that his king had entrusted him with Detroit and he would defend it to his death, if need be. Angered by this latest rebuff, Pontiac called on the warriors to resume their sniping. But without cover the Indians could not approach the fort closely enough to do any damage.

The Indians did score an important victory that day, however. Takay's Huron ambushed a five-bateau supply convoy led by Abraham Chapman and William Rackman. They enticed the merchants ashore by claiming they had some deerskins to trade. The Huron released the Canadian boatmen but tortured Rackman to a hideous death and gave Chapman to the Potawatomi for a similar fate. Chapman was tied to a stake and the wood at his feet fired. He begged for a drink. A warrior handed him a bowl of scalding water. Chapman scalded his mouth when he sipped it and angrily threw it in the warrior's face. The Potawatomi were so astonished by this act that they declared him insane, untied, and adopted him.

Among the loot were 30 kegs of rum and seventeen barrels of gunpowder, enough to sustain the siege for months. The Huron women, fearing their men would commit crazy acts in the orgy that would follow, stove in all the kegs except an eight-gallon barrel which a warrior managed to carry away and secrete in the woods. Learning of the capture, Pontiac immediately conceived a plan. He withdrew the snipers from around the fort and had Gerrieu St. Louis carry word to the fort of the convoy's fate and a drunken Indian victory debauch that night. He hoped that Gladwin would launch a sortie to recapture or destroy the gunpowder, which had been spirited away across the river to safety. Gladwin would take that bait three days later.

The next morning, on May 14, a sergeant led 20 volunteers to burn two houses which sheltered snipers. Pontiac and his followers then suffered another disappointment. Teata and his Huron left the siege when Father Pothier refused to administer sacraments unless they remained neutral. Although Pontiac and others must have angrily considered murdering the priest, they dared not do so. Instead, he gathered his chiefs and the leading Canadians at Jean Baptiste Meloche's home where Campbell and McDougall were interned. Pontiac demanded that the Canadians join the revolt. The Canadians protested that they had declared a loyalty oath to the British king and could not break it. The war was endangering their livelihoods and lives. They asked Pontiac for peace. Pontiac declared that for now he would neither insist that the Canadians join the revolt nor would he accept peace. The war would continue.

On May 15, Lieutenant Hay led 40 volunteers to burn the last house within musket shot of the fort, Pierre LaButte's home, only 100 feet from the east gate. They not only destroyed that house but cut down his orchard and its fence and dragged those trees and posts into the river. Gladwin ordered embrasures sawn on either side of the west gate and had the two 6-pounders placed there so that their fire could sweep the approaching road.

Although, thanks to Jacques Duperon Baby's midnight smuggling the garrison had enough food, it was running low on gunpowder. At an officer's meeting Gladwin called for volunteers to sail the schooner *Michigan* downriver that night, anchor off St. Louis' house, wade ashore, and seize the gunpowder supposedly stored there. Captain Joseph Hopkins stepped forward. From the ranks he was able to encourage 25 soldiers to join him, along with three traders, Ceasar Cormick, James Sterling, and John Watkins.

Even if all the Indians had fallen into a drunken stupor the mission would have been nearly impossible to pull off. The current might carry the *Michigan* downstream but there was no guarantee that when they needed to return the winds would be there to push them up the current. Even riskier was to land that tiny force in the teeth of hundreds of Indians. And not just their lives were at stake. At the first burst of gunfire the Indians would most likely tomahawk their remaining captives.

Some whim of nature saved the expedition from certain massacre. Halfway to the Huron village there arose a southern wind so powerful that the *Michigan* stopped dead in the water. The *Michigan*'s captain, Jacob Newman, informed Captain Hopkins that the winds made it impossible for them to continue. Hopkins reluctantly agreed to return to Fort Detroit. As they did so musket fire erupted from the shore. Only then did the volunteers realize how close they had come to death.

But the *Michigan* was not yet out of danger. It ran aground five-eighths of a mile below Detroit and 20 feet from shore. The schooner remained stuck there for much of May 16 as Indian snipers splintered its side. Finally, Newman ordered a boat launched with an anchor aboard. The anchor was dropped 200 upstream. Men grasped the chain wheel and strained to turn it. Fortunately, the anchor held and pulled the *Michigan* off the sandbar. By late afternoon the *Michigan* was safely anchored once again behind Detroit.

That same day, 60 miles as the crow flies south, another attack would occur. Fort Sandusky held Ensign Christopher Pauli and fifteen soldiers along with twelve traders. They were completely oblivious to the siege of Detroit. Within days of the uprising, Pontiac's envoys reached Chief Odinghquanooron, known by the British as "Big Jaw," and his Wyandot village with 200 warriors near Fort Sandusky.[19] On May 16, Big Jaw, the Ottawa envoys, and the Wyandot warriors appeared at Fort Sandusky's gate with a request for a council. Pauli allowed the chief, three Wyandot, and three Ottawa to enter his headquarters. Meanwhile, the other warriors scattered throughout the fort so that a group hovered near every soldier or trader. Suddenly, the chiefs seized Pauli; their war cries caused the warriors to murder the troops and traders. With gleeful shouts of triumph the warriors hauled away the supplies and 27 scalps. They then burned empty Fort Sandusky to the ground.

Only Pauli was spared. The Ottawa took him and much needed munitions by canoe to Fort Detroit. There Pauli would run the gauntlet. He might well have died beneath the blows of hundreds of screaming Indians had not a woman whose husband was killed in the siege claimed him as a slave.[20]

To the relief of Detroit's defenders and the frustrations of its besiegers, nearly all the Canadians sat on the fence as the hostilities unfolded. Although Pontiac repeatedly urged them to join their Indian "liberators," the Canadians nervously demurred by citing the loyalty oaths they had made to the British king. Some Canadians did promise they would join the rebellion when a French army appeared, an extremely unlikely event as all knew. Tensions rose between the Indians and Canadians as the warriors seized food, gunpowder, and other supplies from the farmers and traders. In response to Canadian complaints, Pontiac instituted a system whereby any supplies could only be taken with a promissory note signed with his totem, the otter. Those supplies would then be stored at Jean Baptiste Meloche's home and distributed as needed to the tribes.

Pontiac faced a challenge. Enthusiasm was ebbing and he had to shore it up with a fiery speech and promises. At a council between the leading chiefs and Canadians on May 18, Pontiac announced that he was writing a letter to Fort de Chartres' commander, Captain Pierre Joseph Neyon de Villiers, calling for French help against Detroit. What he did not admit was that what the Indians needed was someone skilled in siege warfare. Only French regular officers had those skills. Pontiac dictated a letter to Villiers explaining the uprising and requesting help. Chippewa Chief Wasson dictated his own letter to Villiers expressing his people's determination to drive out the British.

One final letter remained to be written. Pontiac asked the Canadians to back the Indians' plea with their own. Although the Canadians bowed to Pontiac's demand, if the chief were literate he might have objected to their message: "We are obliged to submit to what the Indians exact from us. The English are blocked up. . . . We cannot express to you our perplexity. . . . God alone can prevent our becoming the victims of the English and the savages. . . . We look upon you as protectors and mediators who would be willing to employ themselves efficaciously to pacify two contending parties who threaten us with an unexampled destruction."[21] Jacques Godefroy, Mini Chene, Philippe Beauban, Maurice Chauvin, and Pierre Descomptes Labadie would join an Ottawa delegation in conveying the letters to Fort de Chartres. En route they would present wampum belts at those tribes neighboring Forts Miami and Ouiatenon to spur them into attacking the British.

Meanwhile, Detroit's defenders witnessed events that mingled hope with despair. The next two days passed quietly. The Indians were encouraged on May 21 when Mississauga Chief Sekahos of the Grand River Chippewa band led 120 warriors into Pontiac's village. They would soon see action.

That same day Huron Chief Takay sent their interpreter, Jacques St. Martin, into the fort with a message that they wanted peace. Pontiac had forced them to fight. Takay's followers would gladly release their prisoners and pay for the goods they stole if the British would forgive them with a peace treaty. Gladwin promised to assure General Amherst of their good behavior as long as they continued to practice it.

Later that day Gladwin entrusted two missions to the *Michigan*'s captain Jacob Newman. First he would pilot the *Michigan* to the Detroit River mouth to await the supply convoy's arrival and warn them of the danger lying just upstream. If the convoy did not arrive before June 6 he was then to sail immediately east across Lake Erie for Fort Schlosser which guarded the portage leading around Niagara Falls and down to Fort Niagara. He was to deliver three dispatches to Fort Niagara's commander, Major John Wilkins. In his letter to Wilkins, Gladwin explained thoroughly the situation at Fort Detroit and advised him to warn all the other frontier forts as well as forward his other letters to Lieutenant Colonel Jeffry Amherst, the general's nephew, at New York, and the other to Captain Simeon Ecuyer at Fort Pitt.

Despite Pontiac's promises and attempts to impose order on his requisi-

tions, the Canadians continued to complain that the Indians were indiscrim-
inately looting their possessions. A delegation of fifteen leading Canadians
visited Pontiac on May 25 to ask for another council. Pontiac promptly
dispatched runners to the other chiefs who arrived later that day.

When all were assembled, a Canadian spokesman rose to proclaim: "My
brothers, you seem surprised to see us. We have come here only to renew
the ancient alliance which our fathers made with you, and which you are
today destroying by bringing death upon us. . . . When you enter our homes
you enter with the tomahawk raised as if you intended to kill us while begging for food. Have we ever refused you at any time when you have asked
us? You do not speak to us any more like brothers, but like masters, and
you treat us as we treat our slaves."[22] He then reminded the chiefs that "we
are all brothers and the children of your Great Father, the King of France.
You are expecting him back, you say. When he returns to supply your needs,
as he has already done, and sees that you have killed us and taken all that
we were preserving for him, what will he say to you? Do you think he will
give you presents to cover up the wrong you have done us? On the contrary
he will regard you as rebellious children."[23]

Concerned that he was losing Canadian support, Pontiac tried to reassure
them that "we have never planned to do you any injury or harm. . . . I am
making war upon the English; it is for you, my brothers, as well as us."[24]
He then turned to the chiefs and chastised them for not curbing their men's
looting. But he also admonished the Canadians to be more generous to
their liberators who had fought loyally for the French. The council ended
with compromises made by both sides. The chiefs promised to be more
respectful while the Canadians allowed the Indian women to plant corn in
fallow fields. The council seems to have alleviated some of the worsening
tensions between the Canadians and Indians.

That same day it would be Fort St. Joseph's turn to fall. The fort stood
on the short St. Joseph River draining into Lake Michigan's southeast corner
and guarded the portage leading over to the Kankakee River which joined
the Illinois River. The garrison included Ensign Francis Schlosser and sixteen
troops. Nearby were two villages, one Potawatomi with 200 warriors led by
Chief Kioqua and the other with 150 Ottawa.[25]

Chief Washee and his Detroit Potawatomi warriors arrived on May 25 to
announce that the uprising had begun and the time had come to attack Fort
Joseph. To Washee's disappointment, Kioqua explained that his people's
grievances with the British did not warrant spilling blood. The Detroit Potawatomi alone would have to attack. A Canadian slipped away and informed
Schlosser of the danger. Minutes later Washee and his men appeared before
the fort gate and demanded a council. Schlosser decided to appeal to the
Canadians for help and had them assembled in his headquarters. Apparently,
he did not order his troops to be under arms and at the ready. As Schlosser
spoke with the Canadians, groups of Potawatomi knotted themselves around

each soldier or group of soldiers in the fort. At a signal they either seized or murdered the redcoats; only Schlosser and three privates were spared. Canadian Louison Chevalie hid two British traders, James Hambach and Richard Winston at his home. The Potawatomi discovered them there four days later and took them captive.[26]

On May 26, scouts reported to Pontiac that the *Michigan* remained anchored at the Detroit River mouth. Pontiac devised a plan to pursue and capture it. Soon several hundred warriors scrambled into canoes and dug their paddles deep into the river current. Pontiac was in the lead canoe with his prisoner, Captain Donald Campbell, whom he hoped to use as a human shield and bargaining chip.

One can only imagine the agonizing thoughts tormenting Campbell as the canoe fleet surged downsteam. He faced the harshest of moral dilemmas. Pontiac warned him he would be killed if he could not convince Captain Newman to surrender. Should he save his life if it meant his countrymen would be captured and most likely fiendishly tortured to death? Would his life be worth living if he did so? Or should he sacrifice himself by warning Newman and his crew to escape? And by the time he got within hailing distance, would it be too late for the sailors to raise their anchor and set sail?

That evening the Indians' canoe fleet caught up to the *Michigan* where it had anchored at Grosse Island's south end to await the supply convoy. The Indians hovered just beyond effective musket range. By the time Pontiac's canoe had come within shouting distance of the *Michigan*, Campbell had chosen to put duty first. He shouted to Newman to weigh anchor and flee. Newman promptly did so. The Indians paddled furiously in pursuit. Shots were exchanged. A bullet killed a Potawatomi in one of the lead canoes. The pursuit died with him. The *Michigan* gradually diminished in sight until its crew trimmed its sails far out into Lake Erie. There it rocked at anchor. The Indian canoe fleet turned and headed back upstream to Detroit. The reason why the *Michigan* stopped would badger Pontiac until finally he understood. As for Campbell, Pontiac still needed him alive, for now. Though he was supposed to wait until June 6 for the supply flotilla, Captain Newman ordered his men to set sail on May 26.

Fort Miami sat astride the strategic junction where the St. Mary's and St. Joseph's Rivers join to form the Maumee River which flows into Lake Erie, and the head of the portage leading over to the Little Wabash River, which drains into the Wabash River and then the Ohio River. For New France this was the most direct route between Canada and Louisiana. Ensign Robert Holmes and eleven troops guarded Fort Miami. Unlike most of his fellow western fort commanders, Holmes took the rumors of war seriously. On May 23, a Canadian arrived and told Holmes that he had heard cannon fire coming from Detroit; he assumed the fort was under attack. Holmes ordered his troops to remain inside Fort Miami and busy themselves making cartridges. Ironically, he would violate his own precautions.

Near the fort was a Miami village with 230 warriors led by Chief Cold Foot.[27] He and some of his men had attended Pontiac's war councils and were awaiting word that the time had come to sweep the British from their land. That word was on the way.

The third week of May the delegation of five Canadians and an Ottawa war party were en route to Chief Cold Foot's village to urge him to assault Fort Miami. They spied four British paddling down the Maumee River in canoes loaded with peltry and supplies bound for Detroit; three were traders and one, Private Robert Lawton of the 60th, was carrying dispatches from Ensign Holmes to Major Gladwin. The Canadians quickly told the Indians "to hide themselves in the wood close by until they would entice the English ashore; then hailing them to come and smoke a pipe and get the news, they came ashore and sat down."[28] The Canadians and Ottawa seized the men. Three of the Canadians, Philippe Beauban, Maurice Chauvin, and Pierre Descomptes Labadie, along with some of the Ottawa turned back to Detroit with some of the loot while Mini Chene, Jacques Godefroy, and the rest of the Ottawa war party hurried on with their captives.

The Miami and Ottawa concocted a clever means to take the fort. Holmes was enticed out of the fort by his Indian mistress, who claimed another woman was sick and needed to be bled. Holmes was shot as he approached the cabin 300 yards from the fort. Hearing the two gunshots in the direction Holmes had gone, Sergeant Wesley Williams foolishly dashed out of the fort to investigate. Indians tackled and captured him. The leaderless privates managed to slam the fort's gate shut and mount the walls. The Ottawa among the Indians forced the captive trader John Welsh to demand the fort's surrender. The suddenness of the murders, the sight of their ensign's mutilated body, and Welsh's promises that they would not be harmed prompted the nine terrified soldiers to hastily give up. The Indians and the Canadians swarmed into the fort. As the Indians looted, Chene and Godefroy tore down the Union Jack and hoisted the Fleur de Lis in its place. Cold Foot retained four of the captives while the others were hurried off to Detroit. Godefroy, Chene, and most of the Ottawa then continued on toward Fort de Chartres with their letters pleading for help. On the way they would pass one more British fort.[29]

Fort Ouiatenon overlooked the Wabash River roughly midway on the route between Vincennes and Fort Miami. Lieutenant Edward Jenkins commanded the garrison of 20 men. Nearby were four villages of 180 Kickapoo warriors, 90 Mascouten, 100 Piankeshaw, and 200 Wawiaghtono.[30]

The Ottawa and Canadian delegation reached Fort Ouiatenon's vicinity on the evening of May 31 and promptly sent out runners for a council. After the local chiefs and many warriors had gathered, the Ottawa presented their warbelt and demanded that Fort Ouiatenon be captured. Relations between the garrison and local Indians had been reasonably good and at first the chiefs resisted the Ottawa pressure. But the fear of vengeance by the northern Indians eventually forced the local chiefs to agree reluctantly to seize the fort.

Two local Canadians, Alexander Maisonville and one Lorain, convinced the Indians to take the fort nonviolently. Together they devised a strategy that avoided killing anyone, at least initially. On the morning of June 1 they called on Lieutenant Jenkins to council in their village on urgent business. When Jenkins appeared they seized him, then captured other soldiers who for various reasons were outside the fort. The victorious Indians then appeared before the fort and demanded that its few defenders surrender or be killed. The troops promptly gave up. As they interned the soldiers in Canadian and Indian homes, the local leaders "say they are very sorry, but that they were obliged to do it by the other nations."[31] Jenkins wrote Gladwin a letter explaining his garrison's fate; the Lorain carried the letter to Detroit.

A month later the Indians herded Jenkins and his men to Fort de Chartres where they were eventually sent down the Mississippi River to New Orleans. There they caught a ship to New York. Compared to the fate of their comrades in the other frontier forts, Jenkins and his men were lucky indeed.

Runners from Pontiac spread the news among the Shawnee and Delaware in the Tuscarora River region that the time had come to revolt. At that time a party of thirteen traders was camped near the Delaware village where Sandy Creek joins the Tuscarora River. Delaware Chief Shingass had mixed feelings about attacking the traders, several of whom were his friends. On May 27 he and his warriors forced the traders to surrender their arms and goods in return for leaving their land. The refugees filed east toward Fort Pitt. En route they ran into another trader who joined their flight. Most Delaware were as eager to attack the British as Shingass was reluctant to do so. Two days later, near the Beaver River's mouth, a war party led by Delaware Chief Pitweowa caught up to them. The Indians slaughtered eleven traders while three escaped into the thick brush.[32]

Pitweowa led his Delaware and Mingo warriors south of Fort Pitt. On May 27 they slaughtered the settlement of William Clapham, killing him, one of his men, two women, and a ten-year-old girl. Unsatiated, the war party hurried on to Fort Pitt where two days later they killed two of three soldiers cutting wood at the sawmill on the Allegheny River. The third fled to the fort and raised the alarm. Fort Pitt's commander, Captain Simeon Ecuyer, ordered word sent to those living in the cabins scattered in the countryside around Fort Pitt. Soon the civilians had packed into Fort Pitt. There they watched in rage as smoke billowed from their cabins as the warriors looted and burned. Among those destroyed was George Croghan's home. While the Delaware and Mingo could rejoice over their scalps and plunder, they had lost all chance of taking Fort Pitt by surprise.[33]

Within days the three traders who had survived the ambush straggled into the fort. Other settlers and traders appeared with similar stories of warning or death. Ecuyer sent messages down the chain of forts and settlements across Pennsylvania. In an extended report to Colonel Henry Bouquet, he wrote that "I see that the uprising is general. I tremble for our posts. I believe from our reports that we are surrounded by Indians. I am neglecting nothing to give them a good reception, and I believe we shall be attacked tomorrow. Everybody is at work and I do not sleep; but I tremble lest my messenger should be cut off."[34]

Ecuyer tried to delay that attack. He invited the local Delaware chiefs to a council on May 29. He condemned the recent murders and called on the Delaware to lay down their tomahawks and go home. His speech seems to have had little effect.[35]

Meanwhile, he set his men to work strengthening Fort Pitt's defenses. There was much to do. Although, during Major General John Stanwix's tenure as commander from August 1758 to March 1760, Fort Pitt had begun to be transformed from a ramshackle palisade into a fortress, it had remained in a deplorable state. Stanwix's chief engineer, Captain Harry Gordon, oversaw the construction of the ditch, earthworks, and the mounting of artillery on the walls. But serious problems lingered. Fort Pitt's strategic location at the confluence where the Allegheny and Monongahela Rivers form the Ohio was both a strength and weakness. Spring floods regularly inundated Fort Pitt, undermining walls, soaking provisions and gunpowder, and turning the grounds into a swamp. Recent floods had undermined and destroyed the walls on the two river sides. The parapet stretching across the triangle of land between the Monongahela and Allegheny Rivers was poorly constructed and rotting.

Since Ecuyer had arrived to command Fort Pitt in January 1763, he had done all he could to strengthen its defenses. The parapet was reinforced and raised with new logs. Two ovens and a forge were built. When the first attacks occurred Ecuyer ordered the lower town demolished and its lumber brought into the fort; the upper town was burned. Barrels of earth were placed atop the fort's walls. A fire engine was constructed to douse any conflagrations. Open beaver traps were mounted on the walls each night and iron crow-foots were scattered in the ditches.[36]

The fort had ample troops, cannon, and supplies. Crowding Fort Pitt were 540 mouths to feed, including 338 men, 104 women, and 106 children. Of 289 armed men, 145 were from the 60th regiment's 1st battalion, 125 were militia, and 19 were royal gunners. The militia were split between two companies commanded by Major William Trent. Three companies rotated on the walls day and night. At two o'clock in the morning all the troops mounted the walls and waited until daybreak. Of cannon there were six 12-pounders and ten 6-pounders, of howitzers 2 eight-inchers and 2 five-and-a-half inchers, of mortars 1 eight-incher, 2 royal, 12 cohorn, and 3 patternors, along with two iron swivels. Twenty gunners manned those pieces. In addition, there were 433 muskets, 10,000 cartridges, and 4,456 pounds of gunpowder. Of provisions Fort Pitt held 119,051 pounds of flour, 285 barrels of salt beef, 2,314 pounds in the smokehouse, and three oxen, 54 barrels of salt pork, 5 hogs, 3 sheep, 259 barrels of salt sheep, and 468 pounds of rice. Unlike the Detroit's defenders, those at Fort Pitt did not worry about being starved out.[37]

As for Fort Pitt's commander, Simeon Ecuyer was from French Switzerland. He was born in August 1720 in the canton of Vaud. During his early military career he served successively in three foreign regiments of the Dutch army. In 1741 he joined the Sturler Regiment of Berne, and was promoted to sergeant in 1743. In 1748 he transferred to the Grafenried Regiment of Berne where he rose to adjutant, ensign, and finally lieutenant before the regiment was disbanded in 1751. Ecuyer then enlisted in a Brunswick regiment where he remained until he heeded the call of officers for the Royal Americans regiment. He was commissioned an ensign on January 25, 1756, a captain lieutenant on February 14, 1760, and captain on April 27, 1760. Ecuyer was a brave, energetic, and resourceful commander. As will be seen, he could also be ruthless.

If the supply convoy then slowly rowing along Lake Erie's north shore were safely to reach Fort Detroit, the siege would most likely be broken. Lieutenant Abraham Cuyler commanded the eighteen large bateaux with 139 barrels of supplies aboard and 96 men, of which 76 were Queen's Rangers and eighteen of the 60th Royal Americans. They were ignorant of the Indian uprising and thus took no extra precautions when they landed and camped each night.

On the evening of May 28 they reached Pine (Pelee) Point 25 miles from the Detroit River mouth and dragged their boats onto the shore. That point was a standard camping spot well-known to all. It was also an ideal place for an ambush. As the troops set up camp, a man and boy wandered down the beach to gather fire wood. Indians burst from the foliage to grab the boy and chased the man who shouted for help. With their surprise lost, Mississauga Chief Sekahos, Ottawa Chief Mehemah, and about 200 warriors charged from the woods screaming, firing, and slashing warclubs. Some troops snatched up muskets and fired; others fled toward the boats. Within minutes most had been shot or hacked to death. The survivors scrambled into five bateaux and rowed hard into the lake. A musket ball hit Cuyler in his right chest but somehow he dragged himself aboard one of the boats. The Indians packed into other bateaux and pursued. They caught up to three of the bateaux and forced the troops to surrender. Cuyler's bateau was one of the two whose crew were able to hoist sails and escape. In all, the Indians killed or captured 61 troops and took sixteen boats filled with supplies desperately needed by the besiegers and besieged alike at Detroit.

Cuyler ordered his men to set sail and oar for Fort Sandusky south across Lake Erie. Late that night they landed exhausted on Kelly's Island. Two of the wounded had died during the night and were buried ashore. The troops holed up there until noon the next day and then resumed their flight. The sight of Fort Sandusky's charred ruins must have renewed their terror. Assuming that Detroit was also taken, Cuyler ordered his men to head east. Their odyssey would end on June 6 when they reached Fort Niagara[38]

Meanwhile, Detroit's siege, such as it was, sputtered on. The Indians sniped at the fort but rarely hit any defenders. Ammunition and enthusiasm among the Indians were dwindling. Gladwin kept up an active defense. On May 25 he ordered a barricade built to shield those going to the river from snipers posted in two lime-kilns downstream. On May 28, Lieutenant Hay led 20 men to destroy an Indian breastwork 135 yards from the west gate. That same day news and booty arrived from a victory, which boosted Indian spirits. A war party strode into Pontiac's village with Sergeant Patrick Shaw, nineteen troops, and a woman, in two bateaux. That expedition had been returning to Fort Detroit from a supply mission to Fort Michilimackinac when it was captured on the St. Clair River.

Two days later, on May 30, eight of Cuyler's captured bateaux filled with Indians, captive soldiers, and supplies appeared rowing up the Detroit River. But the Indian elation was marred by an unexpected event. As the flotilla neared the Indians on shore, the four captives aboard one boat "seized on two Indians, and threw them overboard. Unluckily, one of the soldiers was brought overboard by one of the Indians who tomahawked [him] . . . Another soldier laid hold of an oar and struck the Indian upon the head of which wound he is since dead. There remained but three soldiers, of which two were wounded, and although fifty Indians were on the bank not sixty yards distant, firing upon them," they reached Detroit.[39]

The captives aboard the other bateaux were dragged ashore. There the Indians split them into three groups. The Indians forced one group to "strip naked, and other Indians then discharged their arrows into all parts of their bodies. Sometimes these poor unfortunates tried to pull back or lie down on the ground to avoid some arrow, but the Indians who were near made them get up by beating them with clubs and their fists. . . . the poor victims had to keep standing till they fell dead in their tracks, and then those who had not engaged in killing fell upon the dead bodies and hacked them to pieces, cooked them, and feasted upon them. Some they treated with different cruelty, slashing them alive with gun-flints, stabbing them with spears, cutting off their hands and feet and letting them bathe in their own blood and die in agony; others were bound to stakes and burned by children in a slow fire."[40]

The Indians then tossed the mutilated bodies into the river to float past Fort Detroit. That grisly sight and knowledge that nearly all of Cuyler's supply bateaux had been captured and the guards wiped out was a severe blow to the garrison's morale.

The capture of dozens of rum barrels allowed the Indians to lose themselves in a vast drunken orgy that lasted several days. That spree kept nearly all the Indians in their villages either guzzling, passed out, or nursing hangovers. Apparently, none witnessed a suicidal charge against Detroit on May 31. The rum inspired delusions of invincibility in two warriors who dashed toward the fort. The sentries leveled their muskets and fired. Two lead balls smashed through the body of one Indian who dragged himself off several hundred yards before he died. A shot smashed through the other's right eye and exited his jaw, while two buck shots tore through his back. The soldiers dragged him into the fort where he lay exposed to derision and curiosity until he died and was buried.

The following day two soldiers and a trader took advantage of the debauch by struggling free of their bondage, and slipped away to the fort; the next day another soldier escaped from the Ottawa camp. They reported that Saginaw Chippewa Chief Wasson had arrived with 200 more warriors. A council of chiefs agreed to shift the strategy from sniping to cutting off Detroit's approaches. On June 2, after the three-day orgy of drunkenness and mayhem had ended, Pontiac sent east a 250-man war party led by Ottawa subchiefs Breton, Chauvinon, and Miniwaby to capture Forts Presque Isle, Le Boeuf, and Venango, leading from Lake Erie to the Allegheny River. This reduction of strength was somewhat offset a few days later when the rest of the warriors of the Mississauga Chippewa band arrived. Now Detroit was surrounded by as many as 870 warriors, including Pontiac's 250 Ottawa, Chief Wasson's 250 Chippewa, Chief Ninivois' 150 Potawatomi, Chief Sekahos' 170 Mississauga, Chief Takay's 50 Huron, and Chief Odinghquanooron's several score Wyandot, with perhaps more on the way.[41]

Until this time, Fort Michilimackinac's garrison (250 miles north by canoe) was oblivious to the carnage and terror ravaging Detroit and elsewhere. Commanding the straits between Lakes Michigan and Huron, Fort Michilimackinac was a trade magnate for a vast region. Lieutenant William Leslye and 28 troops had manned the fort since they arrived on September 28, 1761, with Captain Henry Balfour's expedition of 120 troops to secure the upper Great Lakes. Captain George Etherington took over command in 1762. The accidental destruction of Fort Sault Sainte Marie by fire on December 10, 1762 brought Fort Michilimackinac's garrison up to 35 troops when Lieutenant John Jamet and his troops later took refuge there.

The fort was surrounded by Canadians and Indians. About 300 Canadians lived in the small hamlet or on farms nearby. A Chippewa village with 400 warriors was near the fort. An Ottawa village with 250 warriors stood at L'Abre Croche 20 miles west.[42]

Although Etherington, since he had arrived, had heard the rumors and received warnings of Indian conspiracies from Gladwin, he dismissed them. He had heard so many unrealized reports that he assumed all were groundless. Regardless, he believed his garrison was strong enough to repulse any attack. Like most British commanders with limited frontier experience, he disparaged Indian fighting skills.

The most recent warning had arrived on May 2 when a Canadian named Laurent Ducharme informed Etherington that an attack was being planned. Etherington not only rejected the notion as a ruse to get the British to pack up and leave, he "threatened to send the next person who should bring a story of the same kind to Detroit."[43] On May 30, he reinforced his belief that all was fine during a council with Chippewa Chiefs Minivavana and Matchekewis, and several Sauk chiefs. They pledged eternal friendship between the British and Indians. Indeed, the chiefs informed Etherington that in a few days when all the men from different tribes arrived they would celebrate their friendship with a massive game of lacrosse just outside the fort.

On the morning of June 2, several hundred Chippewa and 70 visiting Sauk warriors gathered in the meadow just outside the fort to watch 20 armed with lacrosse sticks from each nation face off in the center. Most of the soldiers mingled with the Indians or watched from the palisade. Captain Etherington and Lieutenant Leslye were among the crowd on the sidelines; officer of the day Lieutenant John Jamet most likely watched from the parapet. Perhaps few among the British noticed that groups of Indian women wrapped in blankets sidled up beside them inside and outside the fort.

The game began. All eyes watched the ball as it was tossed back and forth among the players. For hours cheers or laments burst from the crowd as the ball shifted between the Chippewa and Sauk. Then around noon at some signal a player suddenly hurled the ball over the fort's wall and all the players and many of the spectators dashed inside. Some Indians seized Etherington and Leslye. Women pulled warclubs and sawn-off muskets from beneath their blankets. Warriors grabbed them and hacked and shot the soldiers. Jamet was among those killed outright along with fifteen troops and the merchant John Tracey. Etherington, Leslye, and the rest of the garrison along with the traders Ezekiel Solomon, Henry Bostwick, and a recent arrival named Samuels were captured and interned in the fort.

Only the trader Alexander Henry initially escaped. He was in his house when the massacre began. From his window he watched in horror as the "dead were scalped and mangled; the dying were writhing and shrieking under the unsatiated knife and tomahawk; and from the bodies of some, ripped open, their butchers were drinking the blood, scooped up in the hollow of joined hands and quaffed amid shouts of rage and victory."[44]

Knowing the Indians would soon be after him, he slipped out the back and into his neighbor's house. Shocked and frightened, Charles Michel Langlade ordered him to leave. He reluctantly did so but an Indian slave beckoned him back and locked him in the garret. Indians meanwhile vainly searched Henry's home. They then barged into Langlade's home and demanded that they be allowed to search it. Langlade agreed. The Indians actually looked through the dark garret but Henry had hidden under some baskets. Langlade's wife later found out about Henry and alerted her husband. Langlade grudgingly agreed to continue sheltering him. The next day, on June 3, the Chippewa learned Henry was hiding there and ordered Langlade to surrender him; Langlade complied. Pure chance had saved Henry from murder the previous day; it intervened a second time. The subchief Wenniway was about to tomahawk Henry when he had a second thought—he would adopt the white man to replace his brother Musinigon who was killed during the French and Indian War. Wenniway even allowed him to remain in Langlade's home so that no drunken Indians could seize, torture, and kill him. Henry was almost killed a third time when an Indian who owed him money enticed him from Langlade's house and into the woods. Henry broke free and ran to the fort where he was allowed to stay with Etherington and the other survivors.

Astonishingly, the Chippewa had left the survivors unguarded in the fort. This presented them with a tempting but cruel choice. The officers and Henry "proposed to Major Etherington to make an effort for regaining . . . the fort and maintaining it against the Indians. The Jesuit missionary was consulted . . . but he discouraged us by . . . the merciless treatment which we must expect from the Indians should they regain their superiority."[45] The British reluctantly chose to await their fate.

Father de Jaunay, the Jesuit priest, and Charles Langlade did all they could to soften Chippewa passions and ensure safety for the captives. Despite the Canadians' efforts, five of the prisoners would later be tortured to death. But the fate of the survivors could have been worse. They would be saved from the Chippewa by Father de Jaunay, friendly Canadians, the Ottawa, and even more distant tribes.[46]

While the defenders and refugees at Fort Pitt were safe, hundreds of settlers elsewhere across Pennsylvania west of the Susquehanna River would soon be slaughtered. Most of that region was still wilderness broken by scattered pockets of hamlets and farms. During the recent war, hostile Indians had killed or driven off over 1,000 settlers. With the war's end several thousand survivors and others in search of land, opportunity, and "elbow room" had reappeared. Word of the Indian uprising stampeded most of them back east once again or into the forts guarding the supply line from Harris Ferry to Pittsburgh. But many would not reach safety.

Lieutenant Archibald Blane commanded Fort Ligonier, which was located 45 miles southeast of Fort Pitt. On June 2, a war party of Shawnee and Delaware opened fire on Fort Ligonier from the woods, but the range was so far that Blane did not even bother ordering his men to return fire at the mostly invisible foe. Instead, he had his troops send them "three cheers . . . But as they still continued their popping upon the side next the town I sent the Sergeant of the Royal Americans with a proper detachment to fire the houses, which effectively disappointed them in their plan."[47]

Forty miles east of Fort Ligonier was Fort Bedford, commanded by Captain Lewis Ourry. He had only twelve troops to defend that fort. He soon received reinforcements. As the word of the Indian uprising rapidly spread, refugees streamed into Fort Bedford. Ourry organized the men into militia companies. As of June 2 he had 155 militia under arms with more expected once word of the uprising reached the more distant settlements and farms. Ourry was an energetic, able commander but unable to stem the outflow of settlers back to their homes when no attack followed the initial panic. By mid-June Ourry's command was once again reduced to his twelve Royal Americans. The stress was burying Ourry: "Since the alarm I never lie down till about twelve, and am walking about the fort between two and three in the morning, turning out the guards and sending out patrols before I suffer the gates to be opened . . . My greatest difficulty is to keep my militia from straggling in twos and threes to their dear plantations, thereby exposing themselves to be scalped, and weakening my garrison . . . I shall use all means to prevail on them to stay until some troops come up, I long to see my Indian scouts come in with intelligence, but I long more to hear the Grenadier's March, and see some more redcoats."[48]

Ourry soon got his wish for reinforcements, although they were hardly grenadiers. Another massacre sent the civilians scrambling back to its shelter: "Some scalps taken at Dennings Creek yesterday and today some families murdered and houses burnt have restored me my militia . . . two or three other families are missing, and the houses are seen in flames. The people are all flocking in again." Another day "while the country men were on drill on the parade here three Indians attempted to seize two small girls close to the fort; but they were . . . driven off by a volley. This has greatly added to the panic of the people . . . With difficulty I can restrain them from murdering the Indian prisoners."[49]

Captain Ecuyer's warning to Forts Venango, Le Boeuf, and Presque Isle never got through; Indians fired on the messengers and they fled back to Fort Pitt. The first inkling any of those troops had of the uprising appeared with Lieutenant Abraham Cuyler and his two bateaux filled with exhausted men at Fort Presque Isle on June 3. The fort's commander, Ensign John Christie, sent a messenger to the commanders at Venango and Le Boeuf. He also talked Cuyler into detaching six of his troops before setting off for Fort Niagara on June 4. Christie and 27 soldiers now guarded Fort Presque Isle. More bad news arrived on June 8 when the *Michigan* sailed past and its captain, Jacob Newman, told of Detroit's siege.

Fort Presque Isle was an important way station on routes leading from Forts Niagara and Pitt to Fort Detroit and beyond. The fort appeared strong with its large blockhouse but was poorly positioned. It was built on a small bluff overlooking Lake Erie. There was little likelihood of an attack from that quarter. A creek ran along much of the fort's other side. But the creek's high far bank and woods could shelter attackers.

Christie did what he could to strengthen the defense. Extra boards were nailed to the blockhouse doors and sentry box. Sod was packed on roof-towns to render them fireproof; water barrels were hauled atop the block-house and gutters extended to the roofs of the other buildings so that any fire might be extinguished. Having done all that the defenders could do nothing more than wait and hope.

On June 3, the rider got through with Christie's warning to Ensign George Price and his fifteen men at Fort Le Boeuf and Lieutenant Francis Gordon and his sixteen men at Fort Venango. Gordon was a classic example of someone with cognitive dissonance or the power of one's preconceptions to reject contrary evidence. Although he received Christie's warning a week before Fort Venango was attacked, he refused to believe he was vulnerable. Reality would soon intrude on that delusion.

On June 13, about 50 Shawnee and Delaware led by Seneca Chief Kayashuta approached the fort. Having counciled with Kayashuta many times before, Gordon led him and fourteen other headmen into his headquarters while the other warriors dispersed within the fort. Suddenly, the chiefs seized Gordon and uttered war cries. The Indians outside immediately began hacking and shooting any soldiers nearby. Within seconds all fifteen troops were dead.

Gordon was briefly spared for two reasons. One was that he could write. Kayashuta dictated a letter to him. In a trembling hand Gordon wrote down the list of Indian grievances that Kayashuta recited. Among the complaints were the persistence of British forts on Indian land long after the French had been defeated, and the lack of gunpowder. With the letter done the warriors had only one use left for Gordon; they tortured him to death. Then, with the fort looted and burned, they stalked north. Surprisingly, they by-passed ill-defended Fort Le Boeuf and headed on toward Presque Isle. They had a rendezvous to make.

On June 19, Kayashuta and his Seneca had joined with around 250 Chippewa, Ottawa, Huron, and Mississauga led by the Mississauga Sekahos and the Ottawa Breton and Miniwaby, just west of Fort Presque Isle on Lake Erie's shore. Although heartened as they exchanged news of successful attacks, they were to meet with bitter disappointment the next morning.

At dawn on June 20, when the Indians surged out of the woods and dashed toward the fort, Ensign Christie and his 27 troops massed in the blockhouse were ready. Musket fire kept the Indians at bay. Some warriors did manage to reach a ditch 50 or so feet from the fort, from which they could fire relatively protected. Other Indians scrambled over the walls, sheltered behind the buildings, and fired up at the blockhouse. Elsewhere around the fort the Indians dragged logs into piles as rough breastworks.

Yet they could get no closer. Fire-arrows shot at the blockhouse were quickly doused. The musket fire slackened except for sporadic shots.

Miraculously, a rescue seemed imminent. The *Michigan* had reached Fort Schlosser, was loaded with supplies and troops, and was returning toward Detroit on June 20 when its men heard the gunfire from Fort Presque Isle. Captain Jacob Newman ordered his sailors to anchor the *Michigan* a couple of miles from shore. Newman did not dare sail to the fort for fear that the Indians would embark in their canoe fleet and overwhelm the *Michigan*. Yet he and Lieutenant Cuyler hesitated to sail off and leave the fort to its fate.

The defenders had survived the first day of siege. None of the men had suffered more than flesh wounds. There was plenty of food and ammunition. Yet they faced a crisis. Most of their barreled water had been used to drown the fires. The well sat between the blockhouse and the other buildings occupied by the Indians. Christie ordered his men to dig a well beneath the blockhouse.

The Indians resumed their firing on June 21. Around noon they set fire to Christie's headquarters beside the blockhouse. The flames began licking up the side of the defenders' bastion itself. Christie ordered half his troops to level their muskets toward the Indian positions while the other half burst out of the blockhouse and formed a bucket brigade from the well to the fire. They soon extinquished the flames and retreated into the charred blockhouse. Had the Indians rushed the bucket brigade they would have likely killed most of them. But they squandered that decisive moment. When Newman and Cuyler saw the defenders successfully douse the flames, they agreed that the *Michigan* should sail on to Detroit. The spirits of Christie and his men must have plummeted as the *Michigan* disappeared into the western horizon.

That night an Indian called out in French that if the defenders surrendered they would be allowed to leave safely but if they resisted they would be slaughtered. Christie said he would answer that offer the next day after discussing the matter with his men. The debate among them raged far into the night. If they surrendered, could the Indians' word be trusted that they would be released unharmed? But if they fought on and were overrun every one among them would surely be killed. It was finally agreed that two volunteers would be sent into the Indian camp to hear their specific terms and access their strength and temper. If the odds looked overwhelming then the volunteers would signal Christie to join them for a formal surrender.

What the two men saw on the morning of June 23 convinced them that further resistance was futile. Around the fort the Indians had prepared to rain the blockhouse with scores of pitch drenched fire-arrows; hundreds of Indians would then rush the survivors as they stumbled from the conflagration. If the soldiers surrendered, the Indians promised that they would be allowed to retire unmolested to Fort Niagara or Fort Pitt. The volunteers signaled Christie to join them. After listening to the chiefs' promises, Christie agreed to give up the fort.

As his troops laid down their muskets and emerged warily from the blockhouse, the Indians charged, imprisoned them, and ransacked the fort. Incredibly, two troops managed to escape. David Smart and Benjamin Grey dashed down the ditch to the creek and into the woods. The tribes split up the loot and prisoners among themselves and dispersed to their distant villages. The Huron took Christie, four soldiers, and a sergeant's wife while the rest of the prisoners were split among the other tribes.[50]

News of Presque Isle's surrender infuriated Colonel Henry Bouquet: "Humanity makes me hope that Christie is dead, as his scandalous capitulation for a post of that consequence & so impregnable to savages deserves the most severe punishment."[51]

Fort Le Boeuf would be the last to fall. Upon receiving Christie's message, Ensign George Price and his thirteen troops had shored up the fort's defenses. Then all they could do was nervously await their fate. It came on June 18.

That morning five Seneca appeared in the clearing before the fort. Corporal Jacob Fisher went out to talk with them. They asked to council with Price. The ensign allowed them to approach the gate after they left their muskets stacked; their knives and tomahawks remained in their belts. While his troops manned the ramparts, Price met them at the open gate. The Seneca claimed that they were on the warpath against the Cherokee and demanded munitions. When Price refused they then asked to spend the night outside the fort. He agreed. A Seneca ran off into the woods. He soon emerged followed by around 30 other warriors. Alarmed, Price and Fisher jumped back into the fort and slammed the gate shut behind them. The Seneca crowded around the palisade and demanded a kettle. Price refused. The Indians scattered beyond musket shot. Some broke into a storehouse 100 feet from the fort and began knocking out loopholes. Despite these belligerent actions Price ordered his men to desist firing. He still hoped that bloodshed could be avoided through firmness.

Toward evening the Indians discharged muskets and fire-arrows at the fort. The blockhouse roof was soon ablaze. The troops tried to douse the flames but quickly ran out of water. The only hope was to try to break through the Indian lines and escape into the dark woods. Price ordered five troops to keep firing while the rest, one by one, squeezed out through a small window at the blockhouse's back and reached the woods. Finally, the troops inside followed. Price led his troops toward Fort Venango.

They stumbled through the forest all night. Six troops somehow got separated in the darkness, thick woods, and hills. At dawn Price and his remaining twelve men discovered that they were nowhere near Fort Venango. They had circled the woods around Fort Le Boeuf. Only chance had prevented them from running into the Indians in the dark. Daylight revealed the way south. Late that night they reached Venango's butchered bodies and charred remnants. Their terror and exhaustion can only be imagined. The only choice now was to try to make Fort Pitt, 80 miles down a trail infested with Indians. Price would lead seven men to Fort Pitt; six fell out along the way.[52]

By mid-June the Indian uprising had proven brilliantly successful. They deployed various strategies to overrun seven forts—Michilimackinac, Joseph, Ouiatenon, Miami, Sandusky, Presque Isle, and Venango, and took sixteen of Lieutenant Cuyler's eighteen supply bateaux. Forts Edward Augustus and Lyttleton would soon be abandoned. Indians continued to besiege Fort Detroit and harass Forts Pitt, Bedford, Ligonier, and Loudoun. While suffering few losses, they had killed or captured several hundred soldiers, traders, and settlers. The uprising had destroyed nearly the entire British Empire west of the Appalachians.

Yet the Indian success was not complete. Forts Detroit, Pitt, and those near Niagara still held out. Not all Indians had seized the warbelt. Although under enormous pressure by Pontiac, Teata and his Huron faction had remained neutral. Most importantly, the Iroquois League had refused to join the rebellion, though most Seneca led by Kayashuta participated in attacks, and nearly all of the Canadians remained loyal.

Those Canadians living near the posts were trapped in a terrible dilemma between their forced loyalty to the British Crown and their life under the shadow of Indian scalping knives. Although Indian warriors were more immediately threatening, the Canadians understood that British power could ultimately crush any rebellion.

When the uprising broke out most Canadians chose to remain passive onlookers, grudgingly yielding to the requisition demands of either side but refusing to fight. Likewise the Catholic priests proselytizing among the Indians faced the same dilemma. Well aware that any Indian victories would be fleeting and followed by a crushing British retaliation, they urged their charges to remain at peace. While the handful of Canadians who sided with the Indians had no appreciable effect on the war, one man among those few who joined the British had a crucial role in Fort Detroit's survival. It was Jacques Duperon Baby, who smuggled enough supplies to Fort Detroit to allow it to survive a siege that dragged on for months. Most likely it was also Baby who warned Gladwin of Pontiac's plan and thus enabled him to thwart it.

Still, the Indians had achieved a series of dazzling victories. What explains them? The western posts were at best days and sometimes a week or more hard paddle or hike from the nearest neighbor. Communication among them was irregular at best. Weeks could pass before a trader, Indian party, or supply convoy came in with the latest news. When the lakes froze over and snow buried the forest those posts were cut off from the world beyond.

The isolation of the posts partially explains the uprising's initial success.

For weeks commanders in the other posts would remain oblivious to the attack that opened against Fort Detroit on May 8, 1763. In each of those posts the uprising would be announced with war shrieks, a flurry of musket shots and hatchets thudding into skulls, and the screams of dying soldiers.

Yet British arrogance was more important than isolation in explaining the capture of those nine posts, the ambush of supply convoys, and the slaughter of several hundred of His Majesty's soldiers and civilians in the early summer of 1763. Each post commander dismissed warnings from Canadians, British traders, and Indians that an uprising was imminent. "The savages wouldn't dare," sneered the commanders and most of their underlings. Most responsible for that attitude and the policy of squeezing the Indians, upon which it was based, was their commander, Sir Jeffrey Amherst.

Ironically, while mayhem blood-soaked the frontier, the commander in chief of His Majesty's forces in North America was reassuring his Indian Superintendent that all was well. On May 29, Amherst wrote Johnson that he "cannot think the Indians have it in their power to execute anything serious against us while we continue to be on our guard."[53]

That delusion would soon end.

NOTES

1. For excellent descriptions, see Donald Campbell to Henry Bouquet, December 11, 1760, in Syvester K. Stevens, Donald H. Kent, Autumn L. Leonard, Louis M. Waddell, and John Totteham, eds., *The Papers of Henry Bouquet* (hereafter cited as *Bouquet Papers*), 6 vols. (Harrisburg: Pennsylvania Historical and Museum Commission, 1972–1994), 5:170–72; Donald Campbell to Henry Bouquet, March 10, 1761, ibid., 5:340–341.

The best accounts of Detroit's siege include: Milo Milton Quaife, ed., *The Siege of Detroit in 1763: The Journal of Pontiac's Conspiracy and John Rutherford's Narrative of a Captivity* (Chicago: Lakeside Press, 1958); Franklin B. Hough, ed., *Diary of the Siege of Detroit in the War with Pontiac. Also a Narrative of the Principal Events of the Siege by Major Robert Rogers; A Plan for Conducting Indian Affairs by Colonel Bradstreet; and other Authentick Documents, never before printed* (Albany, N.Y.: J. Munsell, 1860); Jehu Hay's diary, William L. Clements Library, Ann Arbor, Mich. (hereafter cited as CL); James McDonald to George Croghan, July 12, 1763, in James Sullivan and A. C. Flick, eds., *The Papers of William Johnson* (hereafter cited as *Johnson Papers*), 14 vols. (Albany: State University of New York, 1921–1965), 10: 736–45.

The following account of the siege has been drawn mostly from those sources. Differences among the accounts are noted in footnotes.

Ironically, the siege's most comprehensive story, "The Journal of Pontiac's Conspiracy," is anonymous. For discussions of possible authors see Quaife, "Historical Introduction," "Preface," and "Translator's Preface," in *The Siege of Detroit*, xxiv–xxviii, xli–xliv, xlv–lv. Former notary and sub-intendent under the French regime Robert Navarre is the most likely author. In Hay's diary he is constantly in contact with the fort, either sending messages or visiting while staying in the Canadian town or visiting Indian councils.

For other good primary accounts summarizing many of the actions, see George Price to Henry Bouquet, June 26, 1763, *Bouquet Papers*, 6:266–67; Robert Rogers manuscript, John Porteous journals, John Porteous to parents, November 20, 1763, in Burton Collection, Detroit Public Library (hereafter BC).

2. Enumeration of Indians with Northern Department, November 18, 1763, in E. B. O'Callaghan and Berthold Fernow, eds., *Documents Relative to the Colonial History of the State of New York* (hereafter cited as NYCD), 15 vols. (Albany, N.Y.: Weed, Parsons, and Co., 1856–1887), 7:582–84.

3. The official strength in August 1762 was 1 captain, 2 lieutenants, 1 ensign, 4 sergeants, 4 corporals, 2 drummers, and 100 privates. Jeffrey Amherst to Henry Gladwin, August 19, 1762, Amherst collection, Library of Congress, Washington, D.C., microfilm, B-2664. But accounts of the fort's garrison varied: 130 troops, 40 traders (Quaife, *The Siege of Detroit*, 36); 120 troops and traders (Franklin B. Hough, ed., *Lieutenant John Hay, Diary of the Siege of Detroit in the War with Pontiac* [hereafter cited as *Hay Diary*] [Albany, N.Y.: J. Munsell, 1860], 4); 100 troops and traders (Sterling letterbook, CL).

4. Quaife, *The Siege of Detroit*, 22–23.

5. Ibid., 223.

6. Ibid., 229.

7. Ibid., 235.

8. For discussions of who that mysterious informant might have been, see Francis Parkman, *The Conspiracy of Pontiac: And the Indian War After the Conquest of Canada* (1851) (reprint, Lincoln: University of Nebraska Press, 1994), 1:219–22; Helen Humphrey, "The Identity of Major Gladwin's Informant," *Mississippi Valley Historical Review* 21 (1934), 341, 358, 359; Howard Peckham, *Pontiac and the Indian Uprising* (1947) (reprint, Chicago: University of Chicago Press, 1961), 121–25; Allan W. Eckert, *The Conquerors: A Narrative* (1970) (reprint, New York: Bantam, 1981), 786–87.

9. John Price to Henry Bouquet, June 26, 1763, *Bouquet Papers*, 6:266–67.

10. Hough, *Hay Diary*, 2.

11. For accounts that identified the war whoop as the signal see Quaife, *The Siege of Detroit*, 29. For the green wampum, see John Porteus journals, BC.

12. John Porteous journals.

13. Quaife, *The Seige of Detroit*, 29–30.

14. Ibid., 30.

15. James McDonald to George Croghan, July 12, 1763, *Johnson Papers*, 10:740.

16. Strangely, although Pontiac's nephew would be present at crucial events over the next five years, no one seems to have recorded his name.

17. Quaife, *The Siege of Detroit*, 64.

18. These are Lieutenant Jehu Hay's figures in Hough, *Hay Diary*, 6; the anonymous author believed that several were killed and wounded on the warships. Quaife, *The Siege of Detroit*, 66.

19. Enumeration of Indians within Northern Department, November 18, 1763, NYCD 7:582–84.

20. Court of Enquiry held by order of Major Henry Gladwin to enquire into the

manner of the taking of the Forts Sandusky, St. Joseph, Miamis, and Presque Isle, Detroit July 6, 1763, *Johnson Papers*, 10:730.

21. Canadian Letter to Villiers, May 18, 1763, Michigan Pioneer Collection 27: 644–45.

22. Quaife, *The Siege of Detroit*, 96.

23. Ibid., 97.

24. Ibid., 96.

25. Enumeration of Indians within Northern Department, November 18, 1763, NYCD 7:582–84.

26. Richard Winston to Detroit Merchants, June 19, 1763, *Johnson Papers*, 10: 715; Court of Inquiry, July 6, 1763, ibid., 10:731; Hough, *Hay Diary*, 25.

27. Enumeration of Indians within Northern Department, November 18, 1763, NYCD 7:582–84.

28. Declaration, June 11, 1763, *Johnson Papers*, 10:692–94.

29. Court of Inquiry, July 6, 1763, *Johnson Papers*, 10:731–32; Hough, *Hay Diary*, 22, 26; Declaration made to Ceasar Cormick and the Therein Named Witnesses, at Detroit, June 11, 1763, Michigan Pioneer and Historical Society, 27:632–33; Proceedings of a Court of Inquiry Held by Major Gladwin's Order, December 20, 1763, ibid., 27:657–58; Court of Inquiry of Depositions of Persons Taken by Savages in Summer of 1763, Detroit, February 21, 1764, ibid., 27:660–63.

30. Enumeration of Indians within Northern Department, November 18, 1763, NYCD 7:582–84.

31. Edward Jenkins to Henry Gladwin, May 29, 1763, *Johnson Papers*, 10:690–91; Edward Jenkins to Henry Gladwin, June 1, July 29, 1763, Michigan Pioneer and Historical Society, 27:635–36, 633–34.

32. Indian Intelligence, May 27, 1763, *Johnson Papers*, 10:685–88. According to one unlikely version, Shingas single-handedly stole all the men's muskets to avoid both the deaths of his friends among them Dexter Calhoun, and his fellow Indians, should the traders resist.

33. Simeon Ecuyer to Henry Bouquet, May 29, 1763, *Bouquet Papers*, 6:192–93.

34. Simeon Ecuyer to Henry Bouquet, May 30, 1763, *Bouquet Papers*, 6:194–96.

35. Ecuyer Speech to Indians, May 29, 1763, *Bouquet Papers*, 6:196–97.

36. Simeon Ecuyer to Henry Bouquet, June 2, 16, 1763, *Bouquet Papers*, 6:200–204, 228–33.

37. Fort Pitt Strength Return, June 26, 1763, *Bouquet Papers*, 6:264; Fort Pitt Ordnance, January 24, 1763, ibid., 6:150–51; Return of Artillery Detachment, January 24, 1763, ibid., 6:152; Fort Pitt Provisions, January 26, 1763, ibid., 6:153; Jeffrey Amherst to Henry Bouquet, April 3, 1763, ibid., 6:173.

38. Simeon Ecuyer to Henry Bouquet, June 16, 1763, *Bouquet Papers*, 6:231, 228–33; Jean Baptiste de Couange to William Johnson, June 6, 1763, *Johnson Papers*, 4:137–38; John Clarence Webster, ed., *The Journal of Jeffrey Amherst, Recording the Military Career of General Amherst in America from 1758 to 1763* (Chicago: Ryerson Press, 1931), 306–7.

39. James McDonald to George Croghan, July 12, 1763, *Johnson Papers*, 10:742.

40. Quaife, *The Siege of Detroit*, 114.

41. Ibid., 128–29.

42. Enumeration of Indians within Northern Department, November 18, 1763, NYCD 7:582–84.

43. Quoted in Alexander Henry's brilliant, fascinating memoir from which much of the following account is taken. Milo Milton Quaife, ed., *Alexander Henry's Travels and Adventures in the Years 1760–1776* (Chicago: Lakeside Press, 1921), 72.

44. Quaife, *Henry's Travels*, 82.

45. Ibid., 92.

46. George Etherington to Henry Gladwin, June 12, 1763, *Johnson Papers*, 10: 694–97; George Etherington to Henry Gladwin, July 18, 1763, Michigan Pioneer and Historical Society 27:631–32, 639; Hough, *Hay Diary*, 299–301.

47. Archibald Blane to Henry Bouquet, June 2, 1763, *Bouquet Papers*, 6:206–7.

48. Lewis Ourry to Jeffrey Amherst, June 17, 10, 1763, *Bouquet Papers*, 6:250, 249–50, 246–48.

49. Louis Ourry to Henry Bouquet, June 2, 1763, Bouquet collection, Library of Congress, Washington, D.C., microfilm, A-1068.

50. Court of Inquiry, July 6, 1763, *Johnson Papers*, 10:732; Jeffrey Amherst to William Johnson, July 7, 1763, ibid., 10:733; Court of Inquiry, July 10, 1763, ibid., 10:734–36; John Christie to Henry Bouquet, July 10, 1763, *Bouquet Papers*, 6:301–3; John Price to Henry Bouquet, June 26, 1763, ibid., 6:266–67; Simeon Ecuyer to Henry Bouquet, June 26, 1763, ibid., 6:258–60.

51. Henry Bouquet to Lewis Ourry, July 4, 1763, *Bouquet Papers*, 6:296, 296–98. See also Court of Enquiry Held by Order of Major Gladwin to Enquire into the Manner of the Taking of Presqu'isle, Detroit, July 10, 1763, Michigan Pioneer and Historical Society, 27:638–39; Proceedings of a Court of Inquiry Held by Major Gladwin's Order, December 20, 1763, ibid., 27:658–59.

52. John Price to Henry Bouquet, June 26, 1763, *Bouquet Papers*, 6:266–67.

53. Jeffrey Amherst to William Johnson, May 29, 1763, *Johnson Papers*, 10:688–90.

4

Counterattacks

"Big with Their Victories"

Brethern those lands are yours as well as ours. God gave them to us to
live upon. Before the white people shall settle them for nothing, we will
sprinkle the leaves with their blood or die every man of us in the attempt.
                                         —Seneca to Shawnee and Delaware

I find the affair of the Indians appears to be more general than I had
once apprehended.
                                              —Sir Jeffrey Amherst

I long to hear the Grenadier's March, and see some redcoats.
                                   —Captain Ourry at besieged Fort Bedford

I wish they would take a notion to make an assualt, even should there
be 5,000, for the more they have, the more we shall kill.
                                           —Captain Simeon Ecuyer

It took over a month for the first word of the uprising to travel from the
frontier to General Jeffrey Amherst at his New York City headquarters. On
June 5 he received reports from Captain Simeon Ecuyer detailing the attacks
throughout western Pennsylvania and elsewhere, followed the next day by
similar news from Colonel Henry Bouquet. Typically, Amherst dismissed
the reports: "I am persuaded that this alarm will end in nothing more than
a rash attempt of what the Senecas have been threatening and we have heard
of for some time past."[1] Doomsdayers had cried wolf once too many times
for the general.

Amherst certainly hoped the attacks were merely local minor incidents.

He had few troops to spare for the frontier. Canada's conquest in September 1760 had not ended the war with France. The war had not only dragged on for nearly two and a half more years, it had widened. Spain openly joined France in January 1762. The Spanish would regret their decision. Whitehall immediately ordered the fleet to scour the seas of Spanish shipping and planned expeditions to take Spain's colonies in the Caribbean and elsewhere. Most of the troops in North America were earmarked for an attack on Havana, Cuba. In August 1762, the British did take Havana and with it the rest of the Cuba. But that victory came at a terrible price—5,000 troops dead, mostly of tropical diseases. Although the war was now over, most of the survivors remained stationed in Cuba and other Caribbean islands. Thus was North America stripped of all but a thin skeleton of troops just when an Indian war engulfed its newly won western empire.

What could Amherst do? The Indian Superintendent, William Johnson, was on the Connecticut shore seeking relief from his various physical ailments. Only his deputy, George Croghan, was in the field at Carlisle, Pennsylvania. Amherst wrote Croghan asking him to investigate the reports of disturbances. He also asked Bouquet at Philadelphia for his advice. Finally, to his credit and despite his doubts, Amherst did promptly order Major John Campbell of the 42nd to ready the light companies of the 17th, 42nd, and 77th regiments, based on Staten Island, for possible movement. Having done all that, he could only await further reports and hope for the best. Those reports soon arrived.

Ever more gruesome reports of slaughtered settlers and besieged forts reached Amherst's desk. By June 12, Amherst was forced to admit that "it would seem that the affair is more general than I had once apprehended."[2] Still he "cannot entertain a thought that they have been able to cut off the garrison of Detroit, or any of the posts where officers are stationed." In all, he found the reputed Indian attacks "extremely inconvenient at this time."[3]

Amherst ordered Major Campbell to march the light companies of the 42nd and 77th regiments to Bouquet at Philadelphia. Bouquet welcomed the news. Once those troops arrived he was prepared to act decisively. He wrote Amherst that "We are yet too much in the dark to form a plan but if things are as represented I propose to march these two companies to Fort Pitt, with a convoy of flour, sheep, and some powder, . . . and, in escorting back the horses and drivers, clear the forts of all useless people and leave sufficient garrisons on the communications to keep it clear and open to further supplies." He had strong views on just what kind of civilian soldiers could best fight Indians: "The panic appears general on the frontiers, which will soon be deserted. Should these provinces raise troops . . . they would . . . be of more service if formed into ranging companies composed of hunters and woodsmen . . . [R]eject the rabble too commonly received, which occasions great expense in pay and provisions without doing any service."[4] The colonel clearly understood the nature of frontier warfare.

The colonel offered Amherst some additional sound advice: "I beg you . . . to take into consideration whether the blockhouses at Venango and Le Boeuf ought not to be abandoned, and their small garrisons when disengaged sent to Fort Pitt or Presqu'Isle."[5] Indeed that would have been a wise decision had it been possible to get messengers to those forts in time. Alas, the fate of those troops was sealed when Bouquet fired off his letter. Regardless, Amherst would characteristically reject the advice: "The abandoning of any posts, at a time when the Indians are committing hostilities, must be attended with the worst of circumstances . . . as such a step would give the Indians room to imagine themselves more formidable than they really are."[6]

Nonetheless, by June 16 Amherst's fog of delusions began to clear. On that day he received word of Cuyler's disaster. Perhaps the warnings he had been receiving for years were more than unfounded fears. What if an Indian uprising did threaten to overrun Britain's just-conquered western empire? Amherst would be blamed. Yet he was still unwilling to face the horrors that had been inflicted on his troops and frontier civilians, horrors that he could have prevented had he followed the advice of more knowledgeable subordinates. As for the report that Indians had wiped out 63 of Lieutenant Abraham Cuyler's 96 troops and captured 16 of 18 supply-laden bateaux, Amherst offered this gem of understatement over an attack which "obliged him to return to Niagara with (I am sorry to say) too few of his men."[7] No matter how much he tried to downplay the attacks, they deeply frustrated him. He swore he would "bring certain & inevitable ruin on the whole race of the Indians, that are so rash . . . & perverse in this pernicious behavior."

The latest news did prod Amherst into another flurry of actions. He ordered his aide, Lieutenant James Dalyell, to Albany to scrape up any troops available, mostly the understrength 17th regiment along with Major Robert Rogers and any available rangers, and lead them west for Detroit's relief. Amherst ordered the rest of the 42nd and 77th to assemble on Staten Island should Bouquet need them. He recalled Major Campbell to command those troops while the two light companies proceeded to Philadelphia under Captain James Robertson of the 77th. On June 18, he dispatched the 42nd to Philadelphia but retained the 77th, whose ranks had been nearly destroyed by tropical disease at Havana. After scraping up some reinforcements for the 77th, Amherst sent it on to Philadelphia on June 24. Thus did a nascent strategy for crushing the uprising emerge. Dalyell's force would move directly to Detroit via the Great Lakes while Bouquet's would march overland across Pennsylvania reopening the road to Fort Pitt.

Yet, Amherst whined that "it is extremely inconvenient to be sending these corps away when I am in hourly expectation of receiving from England the alottment for all the troops, but I however think it necessary to be prepared for the worst the Indians can do, who in the dispersed situation of the troops may do mischief. Indeed they always may unless there were many more troops." The general awaited instructions from government head William Pitt detailing the disposition of regiments in the Western Hemisphere. The uprising, of course, rendered moot any dispositions imposed by Whitehall. As commander in chief, Amherst's first duty was to crush the uprising with any means possible. But somehow Amherst could not grasp even that simple point. Instead, as late as June 17, he was still obsessed with "recommending the utmost economy & frugality to be observed, & you must provide everything in the most reasonable manner you can, transmitting to me the accounts."[8]

It was not until June 21 when he received Gladwin's report that Detroit was besieged that Amherst could no longer deny that an Indian war had engulfed the frontier. He quickly penned a reply, mostly words approving Gladwin's actions and assuring him that help was on the way. Amherst forwarded the letter to Dalyell at Albany. Dalyell would hand Amherst's letter to Gladwin, providing that he and his men could survive the Indian gauntlet along the Great Lakes and especially at Detroit. Amherst also wrote General Thomas Gage at Montreal, Colonel Henry Bouquet at Philadelphia, and army quartermaster Colonel John Bradstreet, ordering each to prepare their respective men and supplies to embark on campaigns against the Indians. He asked Pennsylvania governor James Hamilton to convene the assembly to deal with the frontier violence in that province. Finally, he called on his commanders to summarily execute any Indians responsible for depredations. Writing of Gladwin's council with Pontiac at Detroit in early May, Amherst expressed his "regret" that the chiefs "were not instantly put to Death." In the future "I cannot but wish that whenever we have any of the savage barbarians in our power, who have in so treacherous a way committed barbarities on our people, a quick retaliation may be made without the least exception or hesitation."[9]

If Amherst now was forced by the mounting evidence to agree that an Indian uprising had broken out which threatened to destroy Britain's newly won empire, he remained in a state of deep denial over its cause. To Governor Hamilton he wrote that "what has stirred them up to this I know not, unless it has been owing to a war belt which was sent some time ago."[10] It was not until June 26 that he bothered to write of the affair to Lord Egremont, the Secretary of State for the Southern Department whose duties included North America. Amherst expressed how "difficult" it was, "my Lord, to account any causes that can have induced these barbarians to this perfidious attempt."[11]

Was Amherst really so dense or was he simply engaging in crude dissembling? After all, for years Indian experts like Sir William Johnson and others had warned Amherst that his policies would lead to tragedy. Arrogance led Amherst to persist in those policies. Cowardice prevented him from manfully accepting responsibility for the ensuing disaster. That was as clear to his informed contemporaries as it is to scholars today. Yet, to his last breath, Amherst clung to the notion that he was right and all others wrong.

Amherst was as oblivious to the plight of the civilians who had settled on the frontier. He castigates "the behavior of the inhabitants in so rashly throwing themselves into the power of the Indians, without the least hesitation or resolution to defend themselves which, is indeed very unaccountable and attended with bad consequences, as it encourages the savages to repeat their attempts."[12]

Meanwhile, the Indians expanded their raids across Pennsylvania's frontier. Ever more dead littered the road from Carlisle to Fort Pitt, and the valleys leading west from the Susquehanna River. War parties picked off messengers, fleeing settlers, those who dared to stay on their land, and soldiers at Forts Ligonier, Loudoun, Bedford, and Pitt. Refugee camps of terrified, enraged settlers mushroomed outside the forts or towns further east. Sickness, malnutrition, poverty, and despair afflicted the wretched inhabitants.

Bizarrely, amidst these attacks a civil war loomed over the Wyoming valley of the upper Susquehanna River. The Connecticut settlers who had arrived in 1762 had fouled British relations with the Iroquois and Delaware as well as squatted on land claimed by Pennsylvania. The Indians had demanded that those settlers leave and asked for help from Indian Superintendent William Johnson, and Pennsylvania Governor James Hamilton. Warnings those two officials sent to the trespassers were ignored. Connecticut governor Thomas Fitch himself issued a proclamation forbidding any of that province's subjects to settle in the Wyoming valley.

Yet, despite all these warnings, during spring 1763 other families actually settled in the Wyoming valley. More were readying themselves for the journey. By autumn the Susquehanna Company hoped to have 300 to 400 people settled there, a population too large for the army or Indians to drive off, or so they hoped.

On May 28 and 30, 1763, as those people built homes and tilled fields, Governor Fitch counciled with Iroquois envoys at Hartford over his colony's squatters. He insisted that his government "has not given any orders for any such settlement. We are no ways concerned in that matter. Only as friends to you have [we] endeavored to prevent the people from going to settle those lands. . . . And lately I received orders from the King, our common Father, commanding me to use my authority and influence to prevent these people from attempting to settle on those lands till the matter should be laid before the King."[13]

Meanwhile, Governor Hamilton issued his own proclamation on June 2, 1763, demanding that the squatters depart immediately. He authorized Colonel James Burd and Indian agent Thomas McKee to evict the squatters. Their expedition left Fort Augusta on June 7, warned off the settlers, and returned by June 18. It is not clear whether the warrants, militia, and threat of Bird and McKee or reports of the Indian uprising were more important. Regardless, the settlers fled back to Connecticut. Ironically, while Indian raiders were slaughtering settlers elsewhere along the frontier, one of the most blatant group of squatters got away without suffering a scratch.[14]

Indian war parties skulked around and sniped at Fort Pitt. On June 15 a militia man foolish enough to wander off from a hay cutting detachment was killed. That night some Indians crept up to the fort's garden and fired at the livestock in their pen. On June 22, Indians slipped up to the horse herd grazing outside Fort Pitt and drove it off while others shot down the cattle herd. Musket shots killed one militia man and wounded another. Captain Ecuyer ordered a howitzer and two cannon trained on three Indians in the open; the shots killed one of them. Throughout these trials Ecuyer's enthusiasm never waned: "I wish they would take a notion to make an assault, even should there be 5,000, for the more they have, the more we shall kill."[15]

On June 24, the Delaware Chief Kitchi, or Turtle's Heart, appeared at the fort's gate and asked to speak with Captain Ecuyer. When Ecuyer appeared with his interpreter Alexander McKee, Kitchi informed him that hostile Indians had wiped out Forts Presque Isle, Venango, and Le Boeuf. He then warned Ecuyer that a huge Indian army was approaching Fort Pitt and would destroy it as well. He pledged his undying friendship to the British and promised his warriors would protect the British if they abandoned Fort Pitt and retreated east.

Whether Kitchi was sincere in his promises is unclear. Although Ecuyer replied to Kitchi with all the correct forms of Indian etiquette, the captain was being anything but kind. After diplomatically demurring from surrendering his fort, Ecuyer sent Kitchi away with two blankets and a hankerchief. Those "gifts" that Kitchi carried away had covered the bodies of two soldiers who had just died from smallpox. Ecuyer fervently hoped that the smallpox would spread among the coalition of warriors besieging the fort and, ideally, their near or distant villages. His hopes were realized. That summer and into the fall that invisible but deadly ally would burn through the Ohio valley tribes and beyond, killing hundreds. As such, no one man may have done more to weaken the Indian revolt than Captain Simeon Ecuyer.[16]

If Ecuyer ever had second thoughts about the morality of his act, they likely disappeared on June 26 when Ensign George Price led his eight troops into Fort Pitt. Miraculously, those men had survived an eight-day, 80-mile trek from Fort Le Boeuf without encountering a single Indian. Price confirmed what had been feared for weeks. Indians had taken Forts Venango and Le Boeuf and most likely Presque Isle as well. Hours later Fort Presque Isle's fate would be confirmed when privates David Smart and Benjamin Grey stumbled through Fort Pitt's gate. They were the only troops who had escaped.[17]

Indians harassed the other forts eastward. On June 21, a war party nearly wiped out much of Fort Ligonier's garrison. The post's commander, Lieutenant Archibald Blane, believed only a few Indians infested the woods. When four warriors displayed themselves in the clearing just beyond musket shot and shouted taunts, Blane ordered fifteen troops to chase them down. It was a classic Indian ambush. The four dashed into the woods followed by the troops who ran into the musket fire of 100 charging warriors. An intervening bog and poor marksmanship spoiled what might have been an Indian victory. The soldiers sprinted back to the fort's safety. The enraged Indians crept up and peppered the fort with shots but did not dare charge. By the day's end all the gunfire caused only one casualty—a soldier suffered a slight wound.[18]

A hornet's nest of warriors buzzed around Fort Bedford. The garrison's beleaguered Captain Lewis Ourry recorded one typical day's terror: "whilst the militia was under arms on the parade near Bedford house fronting the creek two little girls fetching their cows just on the opposite bank were within 30 yards of being taken by 3 Indians, but being discovered by the men such a volley immediately fell upon them that they [fled] . . . I believe one was wounded the ball went thro' the girls hair."[19]

There were some excellent woodsmen among Bedford's militia. Ourry sent out a lieutenant and twelve men disguised as Indians who scouted 40 miles without catching up to any raiders. He sent another scouting party of 18 men toward Fort Pitt. On July 1, 20 Indians attacked a mowing party within sight of Fort Bedford, and killed three men. Upon hearing the musket fire, Ourry ordered fourteen troops to rescue the fleeing mowers. But the Indians pursued and routed the troops and mowers, killing three more men.[20]

The stress on the surviving post commanders and their troops was horrendous. The sight of the mutilated, blackened, bloated bodies of soldiers and civilians, the smoke billowing from nearby burning homes and fields, the war cries, taunts, musket shots, and fire-arrows raining from the surrounding woods, the reports of other forts fallen and messengers murdered, the dwindling supplies, the sense of being cut off, trapped, perhaps abandoned in a wilderness filled with hostile "savages" bent on destroying all the British, the inability to strike back, the utter helplessness of it all filled those men with the deepest dread, pessimism, and fatalism.

That incessant strain pushed Fort Bedford's commander, Lieutenant Archibald Blane, to the breaking point. Learning that the Indians had wiped out Forts Presque Isle, Venango, and Le Boeuf, Blane nearly panicked. To Captain Ourry at Fort Ligonier he scribbled off a letter describing his Hamlet-like indecision over whether immediately to march east with his garrison to safety or simply wait and surrender to the first large Indian force that appeared in the clearing before his fort. An alarmed Ourry fired back to Blane an order to sit tight and hold out, help was on its way.[21]

Bouquet "shivered when" he learned of Blane's intention: "Death and infamy would have been the reward he could expect instead of the honor he has obtained in his prudence, courage, and resolution."[22] The colonel did not flinch on the battlefield and expected the same fortitude from his brother officers: "I hope that the conduct of those who remain will be worthy of men of honor, who know how to meet death with firmness if their duty & the service of their country require it."[23]

War brought out the savagery in most of its participants. The uprising's horrors enraged Bouquet. He was eager and confident that his force would "fully enable me to crush the little opposition they may dare to offer along the road, and secure that part of the country against all their future attempts." Fort Pitt's relief was merely the first stage of a campaign to destroy the Indians for all time. He eagerly awaited Amherst's orders for "us to act in conjunction with the rest of your forces to extirpate that vermin, from a country they have forfeited and, with it, all claim to the rights of humanity." Bouquet vitriolically denounced any notion of using friendly Indians as allies: "I would rather choose the liberty to kill any savage that may come in our way than to be perpetually doubtful whether they were friends or foes."[24] Circumstances would later force him to change his opinion.

Not suprisingly, Amherst agreed fully with his subordinate's methods for quelling the uprising. To Bouquet he wrote of "your sentiments agreeing exactly with my own regarding the treatment the savages deserve from us. A proper spirit exerted now may be the happy means of preserving the lives of many of his Majesty's subjects thereafter. . . . I wish to hear of no prisoners, should any of the villains be met with arms."[25]

With a Biblical wrath Amherst demanded an eye for an eye or genocide for genocide. He encouraged Gladwin to take "immediate and total vengeance upon all Indians in every encounter . . . and that no mercy whatever be shown to these perfidious barbarians. They must be destroyed utterly as an example for any others who might hope to follow the pattern they have set."[26]

In this, of course, Amherst was right. Britain's imperial prestige was imperiled. Although a policy of generosity toward the Indians could have prevented the war, now that it had erupted only the harshest retaliation could best deter future uprisings and restore a fear of British omnipotence. But were any means justified to that end? Amherst certainly thought so. In a July 7 letter he asked Bouquet, "could it not be contrived to send the small pox among those disaffected tribes of Indians? We must, on this occasion, use every stratagem in our power to reduce them."[27]

Bouquet eagerly seized the suggestion, writing that "I will try to innoculate the bastards with some blankets that may fall in their hands, and take care not to get the disease myself."[28] He also related to Amherst another strategy for destroying Indians. A former Pennsylvania assemblyman and commissioner named John Hughes wrote Colonel Bouquet a long letter detailing his idea for hunting down the Indians with dogs. He concluded that "500 men with 500 dogs would be much more dreadful to 2000 Indians than an army of some thousand of brave men in the regular way."[29] The only catch was where to find enough trained hunting dogs. Only England could supply the number demanded for that grand a hunt.

An excited Amherst replied to both strategies in a July 16 letter. Bouquet should "try to innoculate the Indians by means of blankets, as well as to try every other method that can serve to extirpate this excrable race. I should be very glad your scheme for hunting them down by dogs could take effect but England is at too great a distance to think of that at present."[30]

Although many motives lay behind such a fierce desire to exterminate the Indians, the desire to avenge the atrocities and suffering they inflicted was probably uppermost. Bouquet agonized that "the list of people known to be killed . . . increases very fast every hour. The desolation of so many families reduced to the last extremities of want & misery; the despair of those who have lost their parents, relations & friends, with the cries of distracted women & children who fill the streets form a scene of horror painful to humanity & impossible to describe."[31] Of course, any Indian could have expressed the same despair when describing the effects of British warfare on his people.

Settlers vented their hatred on Indians, often Christian, living in their midst. Despite having hundreds of troops at his command, Bouquet almost failed to protect eight Indian captives, two men, two women, and four children: "It was with the utmost difficulty I could prevail with the enraged multitude not to massacre them. I don't think them very safe in the gaol. They cannot be released as they would be torn to pieces by our people."[32] Those Indians survived. Other Indians in "protective" custody would not be so lucky.

When he was not contemplating exterminating the Indians with germ warfare and other means, Amherst spent most of his time trying to scrape up all available troops and dispatch them to Forts Detroit or Pitt. Unfortunately, there were just not enough regular troops left in North America to crush the rebellion.

On July 17, Amherst finally received Pitt's orders for the disposition of regiments in the Western Hemisphere. Of 20 regiments assigned to the New World, only the 17th, 42nd, 44th, 45th, and the 60th's two battalions were then in North America. That was a thin red line indeed to protect such a vast empire. Pitt would send from the Caribbean to North America the 15th, 27th, 28th, 40th, and 46th. But those reinforcements would be skeletons of the proud regiments that had sailed to the Caribbean a year or so earlier. Tropical diseases ravaged their ranks. Some of those regiments would be assigned to West Florida. On July 29, five of those regiments arrived at New York. Amherst made a bizarre choice in dispersing them. During an Indian war he sent four of the five to safe havens—the 15th and 27th to

Quebec, the 28th to Montreal, and the 40th to Nova Scotia. He did send the newly arrived 46th along with the 31st to Albany to refit and then possibly head west. Apparently, he still believed that not only regulars alone, but the lone regiments posted on the frontier, would be sufficient to crush the uprising.[33]

Provincial troops from any beleaguered colony might have been quickly raised if Amherst had promised those legislatures that the Crown would supply all the necessary pay and provisions. But Amherst's overweening arrogance made him reject that notion: "I cannot say I approve of raising any of the country people for that service, for I have a very poor opinion of them in time of danger, being persuaded that they seldom can be depended on."[34]

Nor would Amherst accept Johnson's advice that Indian allies could most swiftly and inexpensively defeat the rebels. Johnson called for organizing the Stockbridge Indians into ranger companies, and turning the Canadian Indians against the Great Lakes tribes and the Cherokee and Catawba against the Ohio valley tribes. He asserted that the Stockbridge Indians had performed well as an independent ranger company during the last war while the Canadian Indians had repeatedly bloodied the British. Both the Stockbridge and Canadian Indians could ably serve British efforts in the current struggle. Besides, given how war was meshed within their cultures, those Indians who did not fight with the British might well be tempted to fight against them for scalps, plunder, and prestige among their people.

Amherst dismissed the idea that "anything could be done by employing Indians in fighting against one another."[35] In defense of his position he cited his own 1759 and 1760 campaigns when the Indian "allies" had done nothing more than eat up supplies, complain when they were forbidden to torture prisoners to death, and finally stormed off in a huff over perceived slights. The Indians who served in those campaigns, of course, had a different story to tell of Amherst's arrogance and insensitivity. As for Stockbridge rangers, Amherst crushed the request: "I would on no account whatever think of engaging the Stockbridge Indians. I know them to be a worthless tribe; and I really cannot say I approve of employing any of the Canadian Indians. All I ask of them is to remain quiet."[36] Johnson was forced to disband them.

Although reality would eventually force Amherst to reverse his policy, why would he initially reject the idea of raising ranger, provincial, or Indian contingents? After all, those troops had proven their worth in many a previous battle. The explanation is simple—snobbery, racism, and pigheadedness or cognitive dissonance, as psychologists label it. Just as Amherst still clung to the belief that a harsh policy toward the Indians would subject them, despite all the evidence that the policy had been disastrous, he just as fervently insisted that only regulars could defeat the Indians on the battlefield. The notion of enlisting provincials to fight Indians was bad enough, but to rely on Indian allies deeply offended the general's belief in British military and racial superiority. History, of course, revealed those beliefs as utter nonsense. But true believers never permit reality to confound their imaginary worlds.

Yet something had to be done and quickly. Each letter from a field officer revealed that the disaster was worsening. On July 31, Amherst received word that Chief Wasson had tortured and murdered Lieutenant Donald Campbell. The news incensed Amherst. Regular troops had to be raised from any source. That same day he authorized Captain Valentine Gardiner to press recently discharged troops to rejoin the army for one last campaign. Gardiner soon netted nearly 100 men for his company. The motivation for those volunteers went beyond appeals to patriotism and the miserable army pay. Amherst told Gardiner that "I personally shall pay 100 pounds sterling to the man who shall kill the chief of the Chippewas who butchered Captain Campbell."[37]

Those troops would not just serve to fulfill Amherst's vendetta against Chief Wasson. Amherst ordered them and his other troops to put to the sword all Indians in their path to Detroit: "the Senecas and the Indians of the Lakes are to be treated not as a generous enemy, but as the vilest race of beings that ever infested the earth, and whose riddance from it must be esteemed a meritous act, for the good of mankind. You will, therefore, take no prisoners, but put to death all that fall into your hands of the nations who have so unjustly and cruelly committed depredations."[38] The uprising was no longer just another imperial war but a Manichean struggle between Good and Evil.

With each report of the latest bloody disaster to reach Amherst, his reluctance to use provincial troops weakened. By July he was hounding the provincial governors to raise as many troops as possible.

Pennsylvania's assembly convened on July 4, 1763. Two days later, after a vigorous debate, it voted to raise 700 troops, wagon transport, and supplies. Frontier veteran Lieutenant Colonel George Armstrong was appointed to command them. Despite this promising start, there was a catch. The assembly's Quaker majority refused to authorize funding for the troops and forbade them to march against the Indians, with regulars, or beyond the province's borders. The militia's sole role was to guard farmers as they harvested their crops and reinforce the garrison at Fort Augusta. No financial relief was provided for the thousands of refugees. Governor James Hamilton apologized to Colonel Bouquet for the limited help but admitted he could do no more for now.[39]

Amherst pleaded with Hamilton to pay for Pennsylvania's troops and their provisions, and order them to join Bouquet in his march to relieve Fort Pitt. Hamilton could only mutter his regrets. Not even Amherst's personal envoy to Pennsylvania's assembly could squeeze more help from those legislators. Colonel James Robertson "found all my pleading vain, and believe Cicero's would have been so. I never saw any men so determined in the right as these people are in this absurdly wrong resolve."[40]

Learning of this latest frustration, Amherst declared that the legislators' behavior came from "their supineness and timidity, which seem to spring from an obstinacy peculiar to themselves."[41] Bouquet was just as enraged that the politicians fiddled while the people and their homes literally burned. To Amherst he declared his hope "that we shall be able to save that infatuated people from destruction in spite of all their endeavors to defeat your vigorous measures. I meet everywhere with the same backwardness, even among the most exposed of the inhabitants, which makes everything move on heavily and is disgusting to the last degree."[42]

It would be nearly six weeks before Bouquet could muster enough troops and supplies to march west. Fortunately, George Croghan was already on the frontier when the uprising broke out. Responding with his usual energy and decisiveness, he gathered 25 men and sent them to reoccupy abandoned Fort Lyttleton, and had the supplies stored at out-of-the-way Fort Loudoun transported to beleaguered Fort Bedford. The arrival of the near-legendary Croghan on June 14 with those supplies at Fort Bedford quelled much of the panic among the civilians.

While Croghan brought some measure of calm to those portions of the frontier he reached, a fire opened on him from his rear. The uprising rekindled a long conflict between the Quakers who dominated Pennsylvania's assembly and Croghan. For the Quakers, Croghan had become a "bête noire" who was blamed for sparking the rebellion by founding settlements on Indian lands. That charge was partially true; every frontier settlement inflamed Indian passions, Croghan's no more than dozens of others. The originators of this charge were two speculators, William Peters and Daniel Clark, who had the misfortune to buy 30,000 acres of wilderness from Croghan just before the uprising exploded.

The uprising had financially damaged not just Clark and Peters, but hundreds of settlers and frontier speculators; several hundred of those settlers would lose their lives. The rebellion would cost Croghan himself a small fortune, including his plantation Croghan Hall on the Allegheny, whose total assets were valued at 2,000 pounds; the 2,500 pounds he had invested with the murdered Colonel Clapman; and hundreds of more pounds worth of supplies he distributed to needy settlers and soldiers.[43]

When Bouquet raised the charges made against Croghan, he replied: "As for what the Quakers accuse me of, it is of little concern to me, as I know from whence it stems. Perhaps somehow their eyes will be opened to what they are doing. I wish the Quakers might find that their interfering with Indian affairs may have done more hurt to His Majesty's Indian interest— and given them a greater dislike to his troops—than any settlement."[44] Just how had the Quakers interfered? Since Pennsylvania's founding in 1683, mostly by siding with the Indians in disputes with the white settlers and traders who sought their land and wealth. Were they wrong to do so?

The Indian raids continued to ravage the frontier. In mid-July a Shawnee war party systematically murdered its way through the Juniata valley, first killing four settlers at William White's house and killing another two and wounding four at Robert Campbell's house on Tuscarora Creek. They then ambushed a dozen militia who pursued them, killing six; the survivors fled. The Shawnee murdered four more settlers in Sherman valley before satiating their rage.

Pennsylvania's frontier was the worst hit but settlers elsewhere suffered as well. In July a Shawnee war party led by Chiefs Hokolesqua (or Cornstalk) and Pucksinwah slaughtered the six-member Filty Yokum and seven-member Frederick Lea families in the Great Kanawha River valley. They swept over into the Greenbriar valley where then attacked Archibald Glendenin's fortified post in which settlers had holed up; all the men were killed and the women and children taken. Finally, they attacked isolated homesteads in the Jackson River valley before heading home.

That same month Major Thomas Livingstone, Fort Cumberland's commander, breathlessly reported that on July 13 "the Indians fired upon six men shocking wheat . . . & killed one man, but was prevented scalping him by one man firing on them as they ran up. On the 14th 5 Indians fired upon 16 men as they were sitting, standing, & lying under a large tree . . . & wounded one man, but on being fired at by the white men who wounded one or more of them . . . they immediately ran off & were pursued but could not overtake them. . . . On July 15 Major Welder was going to a house of his . . . with 3 men & several women, the Indians to the amount of 20 or upwards rushed on them from a rising ground, which being heard by them at the house they immediately ran to their assistance & met them & the Indians . . . on which the Indians instantly fired on them & killed Major Welder, the party of white men returned their fire, killed one of them dead on the spot & wounded several more (as appears by the great quantity of blood left in the field & on the tracts)."[45]

Although only the western-most of the six Iroquois tribes, the Seneca, had joined the uprising, New York's frontier settlers feared the others would soon join the attacks. In mid-July a panic occurred at Goshen, New York. The discharge of hunters' muskets in the surrounding area was feared to be an Indian attack. Over 500 families fled the area.

In the upper Great Lakes, as the British mustered their forces the Indian alliance slowly unraveled. At Michilimackinac, though repeatedly implored in the weeks leading up to the attack to do so, the Ottawa had refused to join the Chippewa and Sac in the uprising. Learning of the successful attack, the Ottawa paddled over from their village at L'Arbre Croche 20 miles away to demand an equal share of the loot and all the prisoners. The Chippewa rejected the demand. Relations between the two tribes strained to the breaking point. The trouble reached a crisis on June 4 when Ottawa subchief Okinochumake and his men seized four prisoners from the Chippewa, installed themselves in Fort Michilimackinac, and repeated their demand. The two bands tried to resolve their differences in a council at Michilimackinac on June 5 and 6. Chippewa Chief Minivavana finally agreed to hand over fifteen of the prisoners including the officers Etherington and Leslye, and traders Bostwick and Salomon; the Chippewa retained Henry, Samuels, and four privates. The Chippewa promptly butchered their captives one by one. Henry would experience one more miraculous escape. His Chippewa friend Wawatam ransomed him; Henry was spirited away with his ears ringing from the screams of the other captives as they died from excruciating pain.

As the thrill of mass murder, looting, torture, and drunkenness wore off, the Chippewa leaders mulled the possible consquences of what they had done. The British would seek vengeance, that was nearly certain. The Indians could defeat the British in battle and even drive them away. But for how long? British power would eventually extend through the Great Lakes back to Michilimackinac itself.

In early June, the Chippewa decided to abandon their village near the fort and erect a new one on Mackinac Island a half dozen miles away. There they might be less vulnerable should a wrathful British army return. Around the same time they rejected a delegation from Pontiac asking them to join the siege of Detroit. The Chippewa just wanted to be left alone.

Meanwhile, upon receiving his prisoners, Okinochumake did not immediately make for the Ottawa village at L'Arbre Croche. Instead he camped on the Michilimackinac Straits' south shore, sent word of what he had accomplished to Chief Mackinac, and awaited instructions. While doing so something remarkable happened. Two canoes appeared laden with goods and paddled by Canadians working for a British employer. Undoubtedly alarmed, they had passed abandoned Fort Michilimackinac and the Chippewa village and continued on toward their destination, Fort Edward Augustus. The mystery of the deserted fort and village was resolved upon reaching Okinochumake's camp.

Captain Etherington acted boldly. He confiscated the goods in the name of the British government from the startled Canadians, promising them that the Crown would amply compensate them. He then magnanimously handed over those goods to Okinochumake, promising that much more would flow to the Ottawa if they continued to treat their guests well and remained at peace. Okinochumake accepted the gift along with Etherington's request that his letters be forwarded to Lieutenant James Gorell at Fort Edward Augustus and Gladwin at Detroit. Etherington ordered Gorell to abandon his fort and bring his men to the protection of the Ottawa at L'Arbre Croche. Father de Jaunay, the Jesuit missionary to the Chippewa, agreed to carry Etherington's letter to Gladwin. He was accompanied by seven Ottawa and eight Chippewa led by Kinonchamek, Chief Minivavana's son.[46]

Fort Edward Augustus, the former French Fort La Baye, was built at Green Bay's southern end at the Fox River mouth and thus controlled the portage leading over to the Wisconsin River, which in turn fed the Mississippi River at the Indian market town of Prairie de Chien. Near Fort Edward Augustus were villages of Winnebago, Menominee, Sauk, and Fox. Lieutenant James Gorell commanded the seventeen-man garrison. He and his men remained blissfully ignorant of the horrors afflicting the eastern forts. Gorell was well aware, however, of the Indian sufferings from the lack of gunpowder and gifts, and high prices for the few goods available. Nonetheless, he had managed to maintain good relations with the Indians.[47]

Then three L'Arbre Croche Ottawa arrived with Etherington's letter. Gorell boldly tried to cap any potential explosion among the local Indians by addressing their complaints at a council that day. Several hundred showed up including Chief Oshkosh and his Menominee, Chief Taychee and his Winnebago, Chief Osa and his Sauk, along with Fox and a Dakota chief named Sahagi. To them Gorell announced the massacre at Michilimackinac, the freeing of Etherington and some of his men by the Ottawa, and his orders to lead his troops east to assist in retaking the fort. He emphasized that he was only temporarily leaving Fort Edward Augustus and asked them to take care of it for him while he was gone. He sweetened his request by promising to distribute as gifts all the goods in the fort, including gunpowder and lead, that he and his troops did not need on their journey. In doing so, he directly disobeyed Amherst's orders. Gorell reckoned it was better to face his commander's wrath than that of the Indians.

The Indian reaction was mixed. The Menominee and Winnebago were inclined to remain at peace and guard the fort. The Sauk and Fox chiefs called for attacking the British. When they did so, Dakota Chief Sahagi warned that his people would retaliate against the Sauk and Fox, which stifled their threats. Gorell and his troops were free to leave. They did so on June 21, escorted by 90 Menominee led by Chief Oshkosh.

On June 30, Lieutenant James Gorell, his troops, and their Menominee escort pulled their canoes ashore before the Ottawa village on L'Arbre Croche. Captain Etherington and his surviving troops gave them a joyous welcome. The next step was for the troops to paddle east on the long journey to safety. The worst obstacle would be the Chippewa village at Mackinac Island 20 miles away. The day after the Gorell party's arrival, Ottawa chief Okinochumake led an Ottawa delegation to council with Minivavana's Chippewa. The Chippewa finally agreed to allow the British to pass in safety. Fifty-four Ottawa and 30 Indians from other tribes would escort them to Montreal. Two men whose wounds remained serious would have to be left behind.

On August 6, Captain George Etherington, Lieutenant James Gorell, their troops, and their Ottawa escort safely reached Montreal. Until then the situation on the upper Great Lakes was opaque. A disaster had evidently occurred but its murky extent could not be illuminated beyond the alarming and often conflicting rumors. Upon debriefing Etherington and his officers, Montreal's governor General Thomas Gage understood the full horror of what had transpired. Still, that some tribes had resisted the call for war was encouraging. Sensitive diplomacy could entice more tribes from the warpath. But first the ties with friendly tribes had to be cemented.

Gage convened a council from August 9 to 11, 1763. The Indian envoys included the L'Arbre Croche Ottawa and other Indians from various upper Great Lakes tribes who so far had remained neutral and had accompanied Etherington. The chiefs expressed their desire to remain at peace with the British. Gage in turn embraced the peace chiefs and castigated those others who had joined the uprising. He called on the chiefs to "unanimously resolve not to let this breach of faith pass unpunished, but cheerfully and cordially join us in chastising those base and perfidious nations who delight in nothing but mischief and devastation."[48] Only by allying openly with the British could those tribes "regain your former credit" which had been besmirched by association with the hostile tribes. Gage's best argument was to inform the Indians that France had accepted peace and relinquished its North American empire. The Indians were British subjects whether they wanted to be or not. The French could no longer save the Indians.

Although the chiefs rejected warring against their Indian brothers, they did agree to carry Gage's message to the hostile chiefs at Detroit and Michilimackinac. In gratitude Gage filled their canoes with gifts before they departed. Doing so, of course, violated Amherst's order but Gage was willing to take the heat. Indian loyalty could not be coerced, it had to be bought. Perhaps all the deaths, destruction, and expense of crushing the Indian uprising would finally open the commander in chief's eyes to that reality. Pleased with Gage's generosity, the Indians shoved off from shore for the paddle back to their distant homes.

Meanwhile, the siege dragged on at Detroit. Unable to take the fort by assault, the Indians could only try to cut it off from all supplies or reinforcements. Yet Fort Detroit was never completely shut off. Information flowed remarkably freely between the defenders and sympathetic Canadians and Indians who slipped within the walls at night. The most reliable sources continued to be Jacques Duperon Baby and Jacques St. Martin. An anonymous word soon spread about which Canadians had abetted Pontiac. On June 11, Deputy Commissioner Samuel Fleming and merchants James Sterling and Ceasar Cormick declared in writing to Major Gladwin that Mini Chene, Jacques Godefroy, Philippe Beauban, Maurice Chavin, and Pierre Decompts Labadie had helped lead Indian attacks against Fort Miami and the trader John Welsh, and were trying to stir similar attacks elsewhere.[49]

On June 12, Potawatomi Chief Washee appeared under a flag of truce and asked to speak with Gladwin. Washee blamed Pontiac for all the troubles and offered to trade his captives, Ensign Schlosser and three soldiers, for

Potawatomi Chief Winnemac, held hostage in the fort. Gladwin refused. The reason remains obscure. He probably hoped for a better deal in which all the British prisoners would be released. But he had also learned that Washee, despite his contrary claims, had led the attack on Fort Joseph. He might well have bluntly pointed this out to Washee, thus scuttling the deal. Regardless, Gladwin castigated Washee, demanding if the Potawatomi "were the slaves of Pondiac, at which they hung their heads; he then told them . . . that they would see in the end that the Ottawas would kill Pondiac for bringing them into such an undertaking, for that they and everyone who joined heartily with them, would be ruined; as they would forfeit their lands and be deprived of all the necessaries of life."[50]

Gladwin's tough stand worked. Three days later, on June 15, Washee was back in the fort counciling with Gladwin. He brought along Ensign Francis Schlosser and three privates, two from Fort Joseph and one from Fort Miami, for which he demanded the release of the highly esteemed Chief Winnemac, or "Big Ears," and No-Kaming, whom the Potawatomi despised as a "rogue." No-Kaming's reputation was well earned. It was he who convinced Gladwin to release him while retaining his trump bargaining card Winnemac. Gladwin insisted that Winnemac would be freed only if all the British prisoners were returned. Washee reluctantly agreed to the major's deal. He handed over the four soldiers for the Potawatomi. As for returning the other prisoners, he first had to seek a consensus among his people and the other tribes.[51]

The next day Washee returned, accompanied by two other Potawatomi chiefs and two Mississauga chiefs, including Mindoghquay. They were ushered into the council house. There the pipe was passed, speeches made, and wampum exchanged. Washee reasserted that the Potawatomi knew nothing of the war until it started and blamed Pontiac for it. Mindoghquay proclaimed his people too wanted peace. Gladwin expressed his satisfaction but said he was unauthorized to negotiate a formal peace treaty. He asked the chiefs to bury the hatchet and encourage the other, still-belligerent tribes to do the same.

Gladwin received a surprising visitor on June 18. Father de Jaunay asked to meet him. He was accompanied by seven Michilimackinac Chippewa, including Chief Minivavana's son, Kinonchamek, and eight L'Arbre Croche Ottawa. It was only then that Gladwin learned of Michilimackinac's fall and Etherington's plan to retreat to Montreal with the remnants of his command as soon as Lieutenant Gorell and his seventeen troops from Fort Edward Augustus joined him. Detroit was now the westernmost bastion of the British Empire. With supplies and morale dwindling, how long could it hold out?

Father de Jaunay did offer some hope. Many Indians were losing enthusiasm for the uprising. Rifts were widening in their councils. Even many of those who wished to fight on bristled at Pontiac's strategy and haughty demeanor. The Canadians also resented Pontiac's command that the Indians freely take their ammunition and devour their crops and livestock, along with the fear he might turn his followers against them. His mission complete, the priest then set off for L'Arbre Croche with his Ottawa escort and a verbal message from Gladwin to Etherington approving his actions, and to Langlade authorizing him to command the fort until further orders, an ironic request for the man who had led many a bloody attack on the British.

Pontiac sought to honor Kinonchamek on June 19 by convening a council of all the tribes, including two canoes filled with Shawnee and Delaware who arrived just that morning. Knowing how the northern Chippewa had taken Michilimackinac so easily, all were eager to hear Kinonchamek's words. His speech would astonish them.

The rifts Father de Jaunay had observed were much in evidence. Kinonchamek was among the dissenters. After boasting of his people's brilliant strategy for taking Michilimackinac, he derided Pontiac's ineffective siege of Detroit, the bullying of the Canadians, and the cannibalizing of the prisoners. Staring at Pontiac, he proclaimed: "We have learned at home, my brothers, that you are waging war very differently from us. Like you, we have undertaken to chase the English out of our territory and we have succeeded. And we did it without glutting ourselves with their blood after we had taken them, as you have done. . . . We did not do any harm to the French, as you are doing. . . . But as for thee . . . after having brought them to thy camp thou hast killed them, and drunk their blood, and eaten their flesh. . . . Moreover, in making war upon the English thou hast made war upon the French by killing their stock and devouring their provisions."[52] Shawnee Chief Plukkemotah then rose to echo Kinonchamek's criticisms.

How did Pontiac react to these charges? He "was like a child surprised in some fault with no excuse to give, and he did not know what to say."[53] With that council his stature diminished noticeably, especially when his failure to take Detroit was contrasted with the triumphs elsewhere. Within a day after the council, word arrived that warriors had taken Forts Presque Isle, Venango, and Le Boeuf. Among the local Indians pride or the fear of shame animated their struggle to take Detroit.

But Pontiac and his warriors could only harass rather than besiege Detroit. The musket fire was sporadic at best. Days passed when no shots exploded. When they did, few hit anyone. But morale in the fort was sinking. Jacques Duperon Baby brought the grim word that the Indians had captured and destroyed Forts Presque Isle, Venango, and Le Boeuf. Detroit was cut off, now a lone, tiny island in a wilderness ruled by hostile Indians. Had the *Michigan* ever reached Fort Niagara with word of their plight? If so, where were the desperately needed reinforcements and supplies? If not, what fate had the *Michigan* met? And what would be their own?

The *Michigan* was on its way. But since mid-June adverse winds had kept it anchored at the Detroit River mouth for nearly a week. Along with its

Captain Jacob Newman and Lieutenant Abraham Cuyler, it held 40 troops, eleven sailors, and a month's worth of supplies for the fort. If the *Michigan* reached Detroit, Pontiac's siege was as good as broken. Learning of its presence, Pontiac sent several hundred warriors to Turkey Island's southern tip. Smaller islands clogged the waters between there and the eastern shore. The main channel lay on the west in the half-mile of river across to Grosse Island's north end.

In early evening on June 22, the winds shifted. Newman ordered the anchor weighed, sails dropped, and the *Michigan* pointed upstream. As the *Michigan* lumbered slowly up the narrowing river, Cuyler ordered his troops to load their muskets and take cover. The Indians on Turkey Island had watched the *Michigan*'s slow progress with growing excitement. They crouched beside their canoes hidden in the brush waiting for the signal to attack. By the time the *Michigan* reached Turkey Island's southern tip, twilight was darkening the earth. Just then the wind died.

Unaware of the danger lurking just a few hundred yards away, Newman ordered the anchor dropped. Waiting there seemed the best decision. Although drifting back to more open waters might be safer, it would be tricky to get there in the dark, and though the river was wide, the channel was narrow and twisty. The *Michigan* could run aground or, even worse, splinter its hull against a sharp upturned rock. Besides, the men's morale, already tense from a week of tedious waiting on the cramped boat, would plunge with yet another retreat downstream. They were armed and primed to reach Detroit's safety. There was no sign of Indians. Newman would order the sails spread as soon as the winds revived.

Eager for scalps and plunder, the Indians played their hand too soon. Before the night grew pitch dark they dragged their canoes from the brush into the river and began a furious paddle toward the *Michigan*. On the *Michigan* a lookout spotted the dark shadows of canoes flitting ever closer across the dark waters. Cuyler ordered his men to mass on that side, make ready, and aim; Newman did the same with his gun crews. As the canoes got within musket range, an order was yelled to "Fire!" The volley of 50 muskets and roar of the cannon must have terrified the Indians. Even in the dark, balls killed fourteen and wounded as many. As the troops loaded and fired at will, the Indians could reply only with a sporadic fire from their canoes, always an awkward place to reload. Within minutes the Indians had paddled back out of range. The *Michigan* was safe for now.

But the wind did not revive. At dawn Newman ordered the *Michigan* taken downstream again to the mouth of the Detroit River. There they would wait another six days until a strong southern wind would again fill their sails.

The *Michigan*'s proximity remained unknown to Detroit's defenders. To strengthen his defense and troops' morale, Gladwin kept launching sorties against the enemy. At four in the morning on June 26, Captain Joseph

Hopkins led 24 troops to search a house 500 yards from the fort, which two Indians had been seen to enter the previous evening. They did not find the Indians but did round up two sows with their litters, and herded those squealing pigs back to the fort.

Later that morning Pontiac attended mass at the Huron mission. Then, perhaps in an attempt to outshine the priest, he had poles tied on either side of three chairs. As he sat in one and warriors in the other two, he forced the Canadians to carry them through the surrounding villages and farms to demand that the settlers give up yet more supplies and munitions to the Indians or face grave consequences. When they did so he gave them a receipt with his sign, the otter, scratched on birchbark.

The following day, Major Gladwin received a letter from Pontiac. Its contents were interpreted by Canadian Laurence Gamelin and written by the captive Captain Donald Campbell. The unsurprising message was to surrender now and return unharmed to the east, or die. The major replied by refusing any talk of surrender unless the hostages Captain Donald Campbell and Lieutenant George McDougall were returned.

Relief was not far off. On June 28, six days after the *Michigan*'s first aborted attempt to push up the Detroit River, a south wind finally rose. Captain Newman immediately ordered the sails unfurled and the anchor lifted. Discouraged by their failed canoe assault on the *Michigan*, the Indians did not try another. Instead, they peppered the boat with musket shot from the wooded shores of Grosse and Turkey Islands. Five troops suffered wounds during the agonizingly slow gauntlet upstream. Then the wind died when the *Michigan* was just off the mouth of the Rouge River. The reinforcements endured another two nights and a day of waiting on the cramped boat. Fortunately, they were beyond musket range. A new wind arose early on June 30. Musket fire erupted from the Huron village just below Fort Detroit. Newman ordered his gunners to return fire on the village. At a cost of four privates and a sergeant wounded, the *Michigan* lumbered past and dropped anchor at Detroit that afternoon. Its deck and hull disgorged 150 barrels of supplies and 40 reinforcements, including 22 troops from the 30th regiment and 28 rangers. The fresh provisions and gunpowder would enable the fort to hold out for months; the reinforced garrison should be able to drive off even the most determined massed assault. Only folly could doom Detroit now.

On July 2, four refugees reached Fort Detroit's safety. Lieutenant George McDougall, a recently captured trader named Abraham Van Eps, and two others had escaped from their prison in the loosely guarded Meloche house and slipped through during the night the nearly two miles to the fort. Fearing that his girth and nearsightedness would slow the others and increase the likelihood of recapture, Captain Donald Campbell, the other prisoner, had elected to remain. It must have been an excruciatingly miserable decision to make. Once the Ottawa found that four of their five hostages had disappeared, they were likely to torture to death the fifth.

Although Pontiac was furious to learn that two hostages had escaped, he did not split open Captain Campbell's skull with a hatchet or permit anyone else to do so. As the only remaining hostage, Campbell's importance as a bargaining chip grew. That status saved him. But perhaps, also, Pontiac's rage was softened by the successful council he had held with the Canadians the previous night.

At the council Pontiac had warned the Canadians to join the uprising or die with the British. He then threw a warbelt at their feet and demanded they pick it up: "If your are French, accept this war belt for yourselves or your young men; if you are English we declare war upon you."[54]

The demand imposed a terrible quandary for the Canadians. A spokesman rose with a copy of the Treaty of Paris by which France had split its North American empire between Britain and Spain. He patiently explained to Pontiac and the other chiefs that after the conquest the British had forced the Canadians to swear an oath of allegiance to the English Crown. Joining the Indian uprising would have been an act of rebellion. Captured rebels were punished with death. But the vital need to remain loyal if passive subjects of King George III became even more imperative now that a peace treaty had been signed between France and Britain. He explained that under the Treaty of Paris, France granted its empire east of the Mississippi River and south of Hudson Bay, among other territories, to Britain. There was no hope now for a French army to rescue the Canadians and Indians from British domination.

This may have been the Indians' first knowledge of the Treaty of Paris. If so it was a terrible blow to their morale and cohesion. Those Indians who had been lukewarm about the uprising all along now had an excuse to lay aside their hatchets. Even those most determined to wipe out the British must have paused and wondered if all hope was lost.

Just when the Indian uprising might have suffered a mortal wound, a Canadian named Zacharias Cicotte saved it. He snatched up the warbelt and shouted that all brave Canadians would die with the Indians against the British oppressors. A score or more other Canadians leapt to their feet and joined him. Those men promised to rally others who had not attended the council.

The volunteers shielded Pontiac from his own self-imposed terrible dilemma. Had no Canadians joined he would have had to act on his threat or lose face before them and the chiefs. Although the Indians had stripped the Canadians of most of their ammunition, enough remained hidden to allow them to defend themselves, and any attack on the Canadians would have immediately driven them into the arms of the British. But, with a token Canadian force openly at his side, Pontiac could spare the lives of the others and thus avoid simultaneously fighting on two fronts.

Gladwin soon learned of the council. A delegation of mostly older Canadians visited him to insist that most in their community remained loyal to Britain despite their own public neutrality and the aid given to the Indians by a handful of malcontents whom they refused to name. The major, in turn, said he understood their frightful dilemma and would not demand a more open show of support.

Those Canadians who had openly joined the Indians were soon known to Detroit's defenders. The merchant James Sterling angrily declared that "the Indians are supported & prompted on by the rascally French settlement all around us; I know enough to hang a dozen of them, & I am sure that all the rest except three or four merit at least transportation."[55]

Worried that the renegade Canadians might tip the balance, Gladwin ordered new defense measures. Guards on the parapet were tripled. The weak parts of the wall were shored up. A systematic search was begun for rumored copies of the gate keys which a sympathizer would use to open the fort during an attack. A week later three keys were found buried behind the silversmith Pierre Barth's house; Barth himself had slipped away before the discovery. A proclamation was issued to the Canadians permitting those afraid of Indian retaliation to shelter in the fort. Several score families would eventually cram into the fort, swelling the defenders' ranks along with those of potential spies and traitors. Gladwin's two most helpful informants, Jacques Duperon Baby and Jacques St. Martin, were among the refugees. James Sterling volunteered to organize 40 Canadians into a militia company.

Pontiac had blundered badly when he threatened the neutral Canadians. More important than the extra muskets they raised, the Canadians in the fort neutralized the power of those who had joined the Indians. The renegades' fight was against the British, not their fellow Canadians. They protested to Pontiac that they would not participate in any attack on their relatives and neighbors.

That reluctance was witnessed by two hostages imprisoned in Jules St. Bernard's home, the trader John Rutherford and Ensign Christopher Pauli. The house was a meeting place on the night of July 3 for those Canadians who longed to rid their land of the British, including Baptiste and Francois Meloche, Pierre Barth, Baptiste Campeau, Louisan Denter, and Sancho Obeigo. Rutherford was asked to translate a text of the Treaty of Paris. Still hesitant to believe that their king had abandoned them, those Canadians agreed to continue to aid the Indians in any way short of an all-out attack on the fort.

They expressed that support later that night when Pontiac arrived accompanied by the translator Pierre LaButte and another Canadian named Jadeau. When Jadeau learned of the Treaty of Paris he tried to argue with Pontiac that the Indian cause was lost and they should try to negotiate the best possible terms with Gladwin. If those arguments were having any effect on Pontiac, LaButte's incensed reaction counteracted them. LaButte rebuked Jadeau, snatched up a copy of the treaty, and tossed it into the fire. Although Pontiac was naturally heartened by LaButte's action and the proclaimed support of the other Canadians, the meeting must have reinforced his own nagging doubts about whether the uprising could ever succeed. In later explaining his version of what happened that night to Gladwin, Jadeau said that LaButte, speaking for Antoine Cuillerier, asked Pontiac to spare the life of Captain Joseph Hopkins in the fort, claiming "he is one of us."[56] Pontiac promised to do so if possible during the fighting.

Was Hopkins really a spy? Or did some dispute between him and Jadeau provoke an unwarranted accusation? The record is hazy. Hopkins personally led many sorties against the enemy. His credentials seemed impeccable. But he was later sent back east under a cloud which the surviving documents do not explain. Shortly after the war he turned his back on Britain and joined the French army. He would later play a role in Robert Rogers' alleged treachery at Fort Michilimackinac. Thus it is not inconceivable that he was a double agent amidst Detroit's siege.

The next attack at Detroit would be launched by the British rather than the Indians. At daybreak on July 4, Gladwin ordered Lieutenant Jehu Hay to lead a sortie of 30 troops to Jacques Duperon Baby's house, seize ammunition stored there, and destroy nearby Indian breastworks. Hay and his men covered the 400 yards between the fort and Baby's house with no resistance. As they worked frantically to gather the munitions and tear down the breastwork, a score of Indians and several Canadians crept up to another nearby barricade and opened fire. Seeing that Hay and his men were pinned down, Gladwin ordered Captain Joseph Hopkins to lead 40 troops, including about ten Canadians, to the rescue. Caught between Hopkins' charging troops and the musket fire from Hay's men, the Indians fled. Hopkins called on his men to pursue. The redcoats killed one Indian and wounded two others. Weeks of pent-up rage exploded in Private Frederick Dann; he scalped and mutilated the dead Indian. The combined force of Hopkins and Hay returned triumphantly to the fort; only one man was wounded. Although they would not learn of it until later, the butchered Indian was Tewalee, the nephew of Chippewa Chief Wasson. That death would lead to another, even more gruesome.

An enraged Wasson and his people surged toward Pontiac's camp. Wasson denounced Pontiac as "the cause of all their ill luck, that he caused them to enter into the war, and did nothing himself, that he was very brave in taking a loaf of bread or a beef from a Frenchman who made no resistance, but it was him who had all the men killed and wounded every day." He then bitterly demanded, "My brother I am fond of this carrion flesh which thou guardest. I wish some in my turn—give it to me."[57] When word reached Campbell, Pauli, and Rutherford in St. Bernard's house that the Chippewa would likely avenge themselves on all the hostages, they weighed the survival odds of staying or making a run for it. The fort was nearly three miles away. Campbell admitted he was too fat and nearsighted to sprint that distance in broad daylight through hundreds of Indians; if he stayed put he might be spared. Rutherford also opted to remain. Pauli aimed to die trying. He suddenly dashed out of the house toward the fort. Astonishingly, he made it.

Pontiac gave in to Wasson's demand that he surrender Campbell, ordering Francois Meloche to turn him over to the Chippewa. Wasson gleefully tortured Campbell to death and even then was not done. He tore out and ate Campbell's heart. After hacking off the head and limbs, he tossed the torso into the river. The body floated downstream to the fort's watergate where it bobbed until it was dragged ashore and buried.

Fate was kinder to Rutherford. Wasson forced Pontiac to surrender him as well. But Wasson's butchery of Campbell satisfied his bloodlust. He then alleviated some of the sorrow at his son's death by adopting Rutherford. He became so fond of the amiable and fearless Englishman that he offered him the pick of his three beautiful daughters. Rutherford feigned interest to gain Wasson's trust and await a chance to escape.[58]

Gladwin was determined to avenge Campbell's murder. On July 7 he ordered the *Michigan*, packed with Hopkins' rangers and Pauli, to sail upstream toward Pontiac's camp. Although all fled unhurt as the first of 50 cannon shots exploded among their huts, Pontiac moved his village three miles inland up Parent's Creek and behind a large swamp called the Grand Marais. Now it was Pontiac's turn to seek vengeance. He vowed to destroy the *Michigan*. The question was, how?

That same day a delegation of Potawatomi received permission to council with Gladwin. The chiefs told the major that they were against the war and to end it would trade all their prisoners and stolen merchandise for Chief Winnemac and peace. This was an extraordinary offer. A Huron delegation arrived the next day with the same excuse and offer. Gladwin had the chance to collapse Pontiac's fraying alliance right then and there. To his credit, he took it.

There was, however, a catch. Not all the British prisoners could be immediately released. Many had been adopted by families who had lost loved ones. It would take considerable persuasion and presents to convince them to give up their new family members. Yet two days later the first arrived when Huron Chief Teata brought in nine prisoners including Ensign John Christie, five privates, a trader, and a woman and child. On July 12, Potawatomi Chiefs Washee and Errant brought in three more soldiers. Six days later they handed over seven soldiers and three traders. Having shown good faith they asked Gladwin to reciprocate. He was about to release Chief Winnemac when Abraham Chapman revealed that the Potawatomi had other captives in their village. Then Lieutenant McDougall noticed an Ottawa in the Potawatomi delegation. Gladwin ordered the Ottawa seized and denounced the Potawatomi for allowing a spy in their midst. He would refuse to return Chief Winnemac until all the prisoners were delivered.

Canadians continued to flee to Detroit. Fortunately, many brought with them their own provisions. A few had enough to sell to the garrison. On July 8 the trader Charles Maisonville brought downriver five piroques or dugout canoes filled with munitions and other supplies, an important boost to the fort's stores.

Pontiac sought vengeance for the *Michigan*'s attack on his village. Four bateaux captured from Lieutenant Cuyler were lashed together and packed with tinder and pitch. On the dark night of July 9, Pontiac, warriors, and several Canadians embarked in canoes and guided the raft downstream toward the *Michigan*. The raft was fired and set adrift on the strong current. The sailors on the *Michigan* desperately tried to weigh the bow anchor and cut the stern cable. They succeeded in shifting the *Michigan* enough so that the fire raft glided by crackling and spitting flames. [59]

The failure was the latest blow to Pontiac's prestige. Yet he had no choice but to try again. He did so two nights later. The idea was to send down one bateau and if the *Michigan* was pulled aside to then dispatch the other directly at it. The first was lighted and set adrift. Captain Newman and his crew again sidestepped the fire raft by slipping one cable and hauling on the other. The guncrews meanwhile opened fire upriver toward the canoes convoying the second fire raft. The Indians paddled away, abandoning the unlighted raft. Several bateaux of troops led by Captain Joseph Hopkins hooked the raft and towed it to the fort.

This latest failure compounded questions and resentments over Pontiac's leadership. Those Canadians who supported the uprising encouraged Pontiac by giving him fake letters from the French king praising the great chief and promising that a French army would soon arrive. This hope was seemingly confirmed on July 22 when an Abenaki reached Pontiac's camp with word that the eastern tribes were all in revolt and a French fleet and army had arrived in the St. Lawrence River to retake Canada. The Abenaki was either lying or seriously misinformed. Neither claim was true. But it stiffened the resolve of Pontiac and his followers. Unable to break the deadlock with Detroit, Pontiac dispatched a delegation with a warbelt to the Shawnee and Delaware villages of the upper Ohio valley with the message that he would soon arrive with a war party to lead them against Fort Pitt. That strategy too would be thwarted.

Meanwhile, he set his men and Canadians to work building yet another fire raft, this one so large that it could not be evaded. Planks were nailed over six bateau. But the craft was too unwieldy and kept breaking apart. Getting word of the effort, on July 24 Gladwin ordered two bateaux with their sides reinforced with oak planking and swivels mounted on the bow to ascend the river and bombard the rafts. Ottawa fired on the bateaux; a bullet grazed one soldier's head. A swivel blast wounded two Indians, one in the arm and the other in the thigh; the latter died a few days later. The troops in the bateaux could not locate the raft and they finally rowed back to Detroit. That search was the last straw for the Indians. They abandoned the project as impractical.

So far, Detroit's defenders had thwarted every attempt to weaken or destroy them. In the following two days James Sterling offered these assessments: "the siege continues here as formerly tho we are not so much harassed as at the beginning, having burned & destroyed all the houses, fences, gardens, & that were within 200 yards of the fort; not only so but our garrison is much stronger than it was, & the enemy weaker at present, tho there are vast numbers of the northern Indians expected every day. Also the Indians from Miamis, Ouiatenon, the Hurons & Potawatomis after having quit hostilities for some time, are going to recommence & join the enemy . . . Major Gladwin . . . cannot be sufficiently recommended for his courage & merit. Yesterday I bribed a Frenchman to help Mr. Rutherford to make his escape, & in my next hope to have the pleasure of informing you of his safe arrival." As for supplies, "we have at present plenty of provisions, ammunition . . . which we always repay with double interest" from the Canadians.[60]

Those northern reinforcements arrived as Sterling penned those words. On July 25 a delegation of 70 Michilimackinac Chippewa led by Chief Matchekewis reached Pontiac's village. Although the arrival cheered the Indians, the news that the L'Arbre Croche Ottawa not only remained neutral but had set Etherington and Gorell free was disturbing. A council opened between the Detroit chiefs and the newcomers to decide on their next steps. A damper descended on the council when Jacques Godefroy and Mini Chene arrived from Fort de Chartres where they had received a cool reception from the commander, Major Neyon de Villiers. Although Villiers did accept the prisoners they brought and lauded the uprising, he could give the Indians no help and warned the Canadians to remain strictly neutral. He had not received word that the peace negotiations among France, Britain, and Spain had resulted in a treaty, but he had to assume that that had occurred or would occur. Chene and Godefroy explained this at a chief's council near Detroit on July 26.

An even nastier surprise would soon arrive. A large relief force was nearing Detroit. Its commander, Captain James Dalyell, was eager for action. He had long wanted to make a glorious name for himself but until now lacked the chance. It was not for want of trying. In January 1756, he had bought a lieutenancy in the newly formed 60th Royal Americans regiment. Although the four battalions of that regiment would eventually fight on nearly every front during the war, Dalyell got tired of waiting. In December 1757, he jumped at a chance to be promoted to captain in the 80th Light Infantry regiment that General Thomas Gage was organizing. Once again he would have to wait impatiently as a regiment was formed and then given a role in an army on campaign. Although the 80th was supposed to replace the rangers as light infantry, Amherst continued to rely on Rogers and his men. The 80th played no more than a supporting role in Amherst's 1759 and 1760 campaigns. By the war's end, though Dalyell was trained in wilderness fighting, he had been little more than a bystander. In September 1760, with Canada conquered, he joined the 1st regiment. His loyalty and energy soon attracted the attention of General Amherst who tapped Dalyell to be his aide. For the next three years Dalyell served at Amherst's side. The general mistook Dalyell's faithfulness for competence. It was for that reason that he bypassed senior officers to hand his captain such an important mission.

Dalyell was determined to excel in his first independent command. He soon ran into a series of frustrations. At Albany it took longer than he expected to muster supplies and the companies of the 55th and 60th regiments, along with Major Robert Rogers and 20 New York volunteers. He finally arrived at Fort Niagara on July 6 with 220 troops. There, citing Amherst's orders, he demanded that Major John Wilkins give him all that garrison's troops of the 80th regiment. Wilkins refused, pointing out that those orders said that Fort Niagara should provide only what troops it could spare. Dalyell persisted, arguing that as Amherst's aide he knew the general's mind and had his unlimited support. The major timidly gave in to the captain. With two companies of the 80th added to his command, Dalyell embarked on Lake Erie with 280 troops for Detroit's relief.

Much more important than the number of soldiers with Dalyell was the presence of one man, Major Robert Rogers. No man on either side in the late war had proved more more daring, inexhaustible, and effective a guerrilla leader. Yet, when he was mustered out in late 1760, five years of nearly constant deprivation, exertion, fear, and duties had taken their toll. Gunshot wounds and disease had aged Rogers beyond his 32 years. The three following years of peace and home cooking from his wife Betsy had thickened his waist. Yet his mastery of wilderness warfare remained intact, even if his fire for wielding it had dwindled. When Amherst's orders arrived for him to join Dalyell, Rogers had no choice but to obey. His enthusiasm for the undertaking withered further with the humiliation of serving under a captain with little experience of wilderness war. Amherst's disdain for colonials and especially frontiersmen was well-known; Dalyell shared that disdain. He would haughtily reject Rogers' advice. The result would be disaster.

The long row along Lake Erie's southern shore was emotionally as well as physically gruelling. On July 15 they paused at Fort Presque Isle's charred ruins and bones, and on July 26 at those of Fort Sandusky. Would they find the same destruction and death at Detroit? And the same fate?

Undaunted, Dalyell ordered his flotilla to row toward Chief Odinghquanooron's Wyandot village three miles distant. The Wyandot could not muster enough warriors to resist the British. They gathered their possessions and disappeared into the forest. Dalyell sent his troops ashore to burn the village and corn fields. He then reembarked his men and they headed toward Detroit.

During the night of July 28 and 29, Dalyell's troops pulled extra hard at their oars for the homestretch of river just below Detroit. They passed the Potawatomi village without being detected through the dark and fog. They pulled abreast of the Huron village about dawn. Someone spotted them and yelled an alarm. Scores of warriors ran down to the shore and opened fire. Hearing the gunfire and hoping it was a relief expedition, Major Gladwin dispatched Captain Hopkins and 20 troops in a bateau to escort in whoever was on the river. As the expedition plowed its way up the stiff current, musket balls wounded fifteen men, two of whom later died. But every bateau survived that gauntlet of fire and ground ashore near the fort to the garrison's cheers in the early morning light. The fresh troops and supplies should have made Detroit impregnable to the Indian coalition slowly unravelling around it; that is, as long as those troops were deployed prudently.

But Captain Dalyell was impatient for glory. He had no sooner met with Gladwin than he raised the notion of attacking the Indians. The major deferred a decision until a formal officers' council the next day. On July 30, Dalyell again insisted that a vigorous attack could crush the uprising and referred to Amherst's orders giving him full authority to do so. The captain further argued that if an attack were not launched immediately Pontiac and his followers would escape. The major countered that given the thousand or so warriors among the three villages, any British attack on one would be cut off and destroyed as the Indians converged from all directions. What the captain proposed was folly, madness even. But Dalyell made it clear that His Majesty's Commander in Chief for North America fully supported an offensive. Like Wilkins, Gladwin felt he had no choice but to give in to this junior officer with the general's ear.

Given the distance of the villages from Detroit, a surprise attack even at night would be most unlikely. Some Indians were nearly always lurking just beyond musket shot and would spread the alarm shortly after the expedition cleared the fort's gate. But any possibility of surprise died when the Canadian interpreter Pierre LaButte passed on word of the planned attack to Pierre Barth who slipped out of the fort to Pontiac's camp.

Pontiac devised an ingenious strategy for defeating and perhaps destroying Dalyell's attack. At a council on July 30 the assembled Ottawa, Chippewa, Huron, and Potawatomi chiefs, despite their wide-ranging degrees of enthusiasm for Pontiac and the uprising, rallied once again to his latest plan. He gave an important role to the Huron who, along with the Potawatomi, were the coalition's most reluctant allies. The Huron village was the only one visible to the garrison. The Huron would abandon their village, load up their canoes, and paddle downriver. Once out of sight they would beach their canoes. While the women and children set up a makeshift camp the warriors would slip back to the woods near their homes. The hope was that

Gladwin would order a sortie to cross the river and burn the seemingly abandoned Huron village. If so, the Huron could ambush and cut off those troops. But Pontiac considered that scenario unlikely. The most important reason for sending off the Huron was to lead the British to believe that the coalition was breaking up and provoke them into an even hastier attack on Pontiac's camp.

The sight of the departing Huron had the desired effect on the British, especially Dalyell. He was more determined than ever to catch Pontiac before he escaped. And indeed a portion of Pontiac's village was leaving. The women and children gathered their possessions and hurried away to a safe position a few miles away. Pontiac split his warriors into two groups and deployed them on either side of the bridge spanning Parent's Creek, just upstream from its confluence with the Detroit River, over which a British force marching from the fort toward his camp would pass. The larger group of about 250 warriors scattered among the fences, buildings, and trees across Maurice Chauvin's farm between the fort and the bridge. Those warriors, accompanied by Pontiac, would tensely watch the shadows of redcoats marching past through the dark. Once the 150 or so Indians north of the bridge around Baptiste Meloche's farm opened fire and pinned down the British, Pontiac would lead his warriors screaming and firing against their rear. After nightfall every warrior was in place.

They did not have long to wait. Dalyell had also split his 247 troops into two. Around 2:30 A.M. on the morning of July 31, the larger force marched out of Fort Detroit along the mile and a half of road leading to Parent's Creek and Pontiac's village upstream. With Jacques St. Martin and Jacques Duperon Baby acting as guides, Lieutenant Archibald Brown and 25 troops from the 55th formed an advanced guard followed by Dalyell and Captain Robert Gray with the rest of the 55th, along with Major Rogers and his rangers. The troops marched two abreast, which stretched out the column for nearly 100 yards. Meanwhile, Captain James Grant and his 80th and Lieutenant Diedrick Brehm and his 60th clambered into bateaux and rowed as quietly as possible upstream. Beside the swivel gun in each bateau's prow crouched a soldier with a lighted punk ready to open fire when ordered.

As the troops on the road neared the bridge the command was instructed to form into six abreast. The advanced guard was halfway across the bridge when the Indians opened fire into their packed ranks. Bullets wounded Brown and struck down several of his men. Dalyell ordered the troops to return fire through the dark split briefly by muzzle flashes and war whoops. Astonishingly, some troops charged across the bridge and took cover.

When the Indians at the bridge opened fire, Pontiac's men deployed around Chauvin's farm immediately leveled their muskets toward Grant's troops bringing up the rear and squeezed their triggers. Grant ordered his troops to wheel and return the fire. Dalyell ordered Grant and Rogers to lead their rangers to Jacques Campeau's nearby house to secure the British left flank and rear. A bullet clipped Dalyell's thigh. The Indians continued to snipe at the dark forms shifting through the night but did not attack. The bateaux hovered offshore; the officers aboard held their troops' fire for fear of hitting their own men. Wounded and some dead were dragged to the river. The bateaux were rowed ashore to take them aboard.

The firing continued sporadically until dawn. Dalyell ordered his troops to retreat but the firing from Pontiac's warriors around Chauvin's farm pinned down the redcoats. Dalyell rose to lead his men in a charge. One bullet ploughed into his skull and two splintered his chest. Gray assumed command and shouted for his troops to follow. The redcoats rushed the Indians, who scattered. Rogers and his rangers were cut off in Campeau's house. Gray ran down to the river and hollered for Brehm to open fire with his bateaux's swivel guns. He then ordered Ensign Christoper Pauli to form his 20 men across the road to cover Rogers' troops when they retreated. Rogers and his men burst from Campeau's house and rejoined the redcoats. By eight o'clock the remaining wounded were dragged onto the bateaux. With the Indians hovering just within musket range, the troops slowly fell back, using houses, fences, and orchard trees as cover. An hour later they reached the fort's safety.

Dalyell's attack had been a debacle. In all, the most accurate estimate of British casualties includes 23 dead and 38 wounded at what became known as the Battle of Bloody Run. Not surprisingly, the 55th, which advanced on land, suffered the most—18 men killed and 22 wounded. The two regiments afloat got off relatively lightly with the 60th losing one man killed and seven wounded, and the 80th two killed and three wounded. Despite being in the thick of the fighting, the rangers lost only two killed and one wounded; a trader's servant was also wounded. In what was to be the last of his 20 or so Indian fights, Major Robert Rogers escaped unscathed. As for Indian casualties, the best estimate is that musket balls killed only seven and wounded perhaps no more than a dozen.[61]

Dalyell, primed for glory, met an ignominious end. The Indians mutilated his body, disemboweled it, hacked off an arm, leg, and the head. They carried the head back to the Ottawa village where they proudly mounted it on a pole. They rubbed his bloody heart in the faces of the captives. Dalyell's folly, of course, was hardly unique in frontier warfare. He would join a parade of other commanders like Braddock, St. Clair, Harmar, Grattan, and Custer, to name the more prominent, who, bloated with ego, ignorance, and racism, would lead their men to disaster against the Indians.

Detroit had been relieved. Now it was Fort Pitt's turn. Militarily, no man would contribute more to the reassertion of British imperial power than Colonel Henry Bouquet. He would spearhead Fort Pitt's relief in 1763, winning the bloody battle of Bushy Run along the way, and a 1764 offensive into the Muskingum River valley, which forced that region's tribes to bury the hatchet. But those were only a few highlights of a life filled with professional triumphs and private anguish.[62]

Henry Bouquet had been a professional soldier all his adult life. At age 17 he joined a Swiss regiment which served with the Dutch republic. Later he transferred to another regiment which fought for the Kingdom of Sardinia during the War of Austrian Succession in northern Italy, where he won distinction for his bravery and leadership at the battle of Cony in 1744. In 1748 he returned to Holland to be promoted to lieutenant colonel of a new Swiss guard regiment formed there and serve as aide to William IV, the prince of Orange. During the years of peace from then until 1755, he studied military and natural science at the University of Leyden, toured the battlefields of France, Italy, the Netherlands, and Germany, and enjoyed the social and intellectual whirl at The Hague. But he longed for a field command and chance to prove his skills on the battlefield.

That chance came in 1755 when Whitehall announced that it was forming the 62nd (renumbered the 60th in 1757) Royal Americans to be composed of foreign and American officers. Bouquet was friends with Britain's ambassador to the Netherlands, Sir Frederick Yorke, who urged him to apply for a commission. Bouquet took Yorke's advice. On January 3, 1756, he was commissioned the lieutenant colonel of the first battalion of the 62nd Royal Americans. He arrived at Philadelphia in June 1756 and spent the summer recruiting among the Pennsylvanian Germans. In the autumn he assembled his battalion at Philadelphia where he experienced difficulties finding quarters for his troops. This would be the first of his confrontations with independent-minded colonial assemblies and peoples. Despite this conflict, his learning made him popular in Philadelphia's intellectual circles. In May 1757, he and his battalion were sent to Charlestown, South Carolina. A personality dispute with Governor William Henry Littleton marred that first independent command. In 1758 his battalion was returned to Pennsylvania to join General John Forbes' expedition against Fort Duquesne. Although Bouquet was second in command he took over most duties because of Forbes' illness. After the British marched into the smoldering ruins of an abandoned and torched Fort Duquesne in November 1758, Bouquet and his battalion remained to administer the region and prepare an expedition against French Forts Venango, Le Boeuf, and Presque Isle. The French abandoned those forts as well in 1760. Bouquet's troops occupied those forts without firing a shot. Amherst promoted Bouquet to full colonel on February 25, 1762.

Bouquet was 44 in 1763 and enduring a mid-life crisis. To a few close friends he expressed the fear that his career and life had deadended. Yet he saw no alternative: "if I should get rid of the continual occupation of a military life, I should of course feel a weariness of which I see nothing that would relieve me. We must have some object in view. What could be mine? I have no turn or capacity for agriculture or any kind of business. How could I spend my time in a manner satisfactory to myself or useful to others? From being a something I should fall to nothing, and become a sort of incumbrance in the Society."[63] Such was the lament of many a career officer.

Bouquet was a deeply lonely man of quiet passions and unrequited love. In a letter to the wife of his officer friend he admitted their friendship was "the only pleasure to me in a loneliness which never ends, and where I have exhausted all other resources."[64] He courted several women from afar through eloquent, melancholy letters. But those women refused to return his love. He thought he had engaged Anne Willing but she married another on February 18, 1762. He then wooed Peggy Oswald but she evaded his entreaties until his death. These words to a friend reflected his own disappointments: "Don't you see all the girls disappear one after another, as the stars below the horizon? And will you never consider that old age is at hand ready to invade you with all his comfortless train? . . . Who shall be the sacred depository of your most secret thought, the kind partaker of your joys and sorrows? Who, your friend, your counseller, your guide? but the wife of your bosom."[65] He then ended his letter by promising that "if I live to see more propitious skies I swear by the dear remembrance of my former loves that the first and sole business of my life shall be to exchange that ill fated title for the endearing name of husband."

Expressions of such deep existential angst are rare in early American life. Bouquet would soon have the chance to throw off that "quiet desperation." Despite his private agony, Bouquet was an outstanding choice to command the expedition. He hid his doubts and worries behind the mask of a true professional soldier. He performed all his duties with crisp efficiency, honesty, and good cheer. His successful campaigns during the Indian uprising would make him a hero.

Probably no one who served in North America during the 1750s and 1760s was a more learned and experienced student of military history than Henry Bouquet. He saw a clear parallel between the British and Roman Empires and their respective attempts to conquer "barbarians." He compared Britain's North American empire to the Roman Empire's Gaul, and the Indians to the Celts. He concluded that only Roman tactics could defeat the Indians. In battle, on the march, and at camp he would deploy his troops in tight, oblong formations that could offset "barbarian" hit-and-run or rushing horde tactics.

It was not until July 7 that Amherst sent Colonel Henry Bouquet formal orders to relieve Fort Pitt and then send troops north to reoccupy Fort Presque Isle.[66] Bouquet, however, had been preparing for a possible campaign ever since he first got word of the uprising. Carlisle was the campaign's base of operations. There Bouquet would assemble his troops, transport, and supplies before heading west to relieve Fort Pitt. The two light companies which formed Bouquet's advance guard reached Carlisle on June 28. By mid-July Bouquet had gathered at Carlisle 460 troops, including 214 of the 42nd Blackwatch Highlanders, about 150 of the 60th Royal Americans, 148 of the 77th Highlanders, and a depleted ranger company.[67]

Getting the troops from Philadelphia to Carlisle was easy enough; the roads ran mostly level through rich farmlands, where food was requisitioned. Getting them further proved to be much more difficult; the rutted trail twisted through mountainous wilderness. Lack of transport and provisions prevented Bouquet from marching forth immediately after his troops had gathered at Carlisle. He requisitioned supplies, wagons, livestock, and draft animals from local magistrates and his quartermaster in Philadelphia. By July 3 he had collected "all the flour in this county, 100 head of cattle, 200 sheep, and about 3000 weight of fine powder from the Indian traders. I expect the wagons & flour from Lancaster about the 8th."[68]

While Bouquet had amassed enough supplies, his army suffered a dearth of rangers to act as scouts and flankers. He offered extensive advice to Governor Hamilton about the need to raise ranger companies, abandon the indefensible sectors of the frontier, and the need to accumulate supplies.[69] He tried to recruit among the refugee camps that had sprouted around Carlisle but he found few willing to leave their families or Carlisle's relative safety. Another wave of terror had swept over the inhabitants when news arrived on July 3 that the Indians had destroyed Forts Presque Isle, Venango, and Le Boeuf. Since then messengers had arrived from the commanders of Forts Bedford, Ligonier, and Pitt who all pleaded for relief. Bouquet finally decided he would have to march with only a handful of rangers.

On July 18, Bouquet led his army from Carlisle toward Fort Pitt nearly 180 miles away. Lacking enough rangers, he tried deploying his Highlanders as scouts and flankers. Hearty as those troops were, the wilderness bewildered and terrified them. Bouquet wrote that "the highlanders lose themselves in the woods as soon as they got out of the road and cannot on that account be used as flankers."[70] En route he observed that "a general panick has seized this extensive country and made the inhabitants abandon their farms & their mills. . . . There appears to be few savages yet on these frontiers, but every tree is become an Indian for the terrified inhabitant."[71]

All the way from Carlisle to Fort Pitt, Bouquet marched and encamped his men in a rectangular formation with a 100-man reserve guarding the baggage in the center. Scouts would explore the forest and trail on all sides of the main body. Whenever the army approached a defile, scouts would hurry forward to investigate thoroughly the surrounding area. Only when that search ended was the march resumed. Should an attack occur the troops were immediately to face outward with bayonets bristling. Thus would the army react like a giant hedgehog. Light troops would lead any charge, followed by the line infantry. But they would advance no more than 200 yards before withdrawing into that hedgehog position around the baggage train. That tight security would prevent a disaster.

Bouquet feared that the Indians would destroy Forts Bedford and Ligonier before he could relieve them. To forestall that, he took a calculated but risky gamble. He hurried 30 crack troops of the 42nd Highlanders ahead of his slow-moving column to relieve those two forts. An Indian ambush would have wiped out those highlanders but none lurked along the road. On July 23 the highlanders reached Fort Bedford where Captain Ourry retained them two days to deter an expected attack. After Bouquet arrived with the main force on July 25 he dispatched them to Fort Ligonier. They arrived there on July 27 just as Indians were attacking that post. The unexpected reinforcements startled the attackers who gave way as the Highlanders rushed toward the fort. Bouquet rested his troops three days at Bedford where he managed to recruit 30 frontiersmen to act as scouts. On July 28 he pushed on toward Fort Ligonier where he arrived on August 2. From there it was 45 perilous miles to Fort Pitt.

Meanwhile, the siege of Fort Pitt sputtered on. Having looted and burned the surrounding farms and hamlets, the Indians lurked around, occasionally sniping at troops on the ramparts. Then, on July 15, the Indians tried to rush the fort but were driven off and the fire-arrows doused. The subsequent lull lasted until July 26 when a delegation of chiefs carrying a Union Jack approached the fort and asked to council. Ecuyer agreed and was soon seated with the Delaware Chiefs Shingass, Tessecumme, Grey Eyes, Winginum, Turtle's Heart, Captain John, Maumaullee, and Big Wolfe of the Shawnee. Speaking for the chiefs, Shingass promised that if the British abandoned Fort Pitt they could go unmolested, but if they stayed they would die. He then displayed the warbelt that Pontiac had sent him and explained that a huge war party of Detroit Indians would soon join the Delaware and Shawnee in wiping out Fort Pitt. In his reply, Ecuyer warned them to give up their struggle or they would be the ones to die. He swore that "we shall never abandon [Fort Pitt] as long as a white man lives in America."[72]

As soon as the chiefs returned from the fort, their men opened a barrage of musket shots, fire-arrows, and war cries. Despite all the noise, Ecuyer reported that the Indians "did us no harm; nobody killed, seven wounded, and I myself slightly. Their attack lasted five days and nights. We are certain of having killed or wounded twenty men without counting those we could not see. I permitted no one to fire without seeing his target, and as soon as they showed their noses were picked off like flies, for I have good marksmen. . . . Our men do marvelously, regulars and others; they are very good natured; they ask only to go out and fight. I am glad to have the honor of commanding such brave men . . . they shot burning arrows to set fire to our works but they could not reach our buildings, not even the rampart. Only two arrows came into the fort, one of which had the insolence to make free with my left leg."[73]

Then, on August 1, the Indians all mysteriously vanished. Runners had arrived with word that Bouquet's force was approaching. A council quickly agreed that those redcoats had to be ambushed and destroyed if the uprising was to succeed. And the best place for that was in one of the wooded, rocky complexes of hills that squeezed the road between Fort Pitt and Fort Ligonier.

To Fort Pitt's garrison the Indians' destination was not hard to guess. Captain Ecuyer sought to warn Bouquet that an Indian horde was on its way. On August 2 he dispatched a letter which noted "the siege was lifted a little time after noon yesterday and the Indians shortly thereafter were observed leaving with their baggage in the direction of Ligonier."[74]

Where was Bouquet? On August 4, after resting two days at Fort Ligonier, Bouquet led his troops on the rugged road through the forested, rocky hills to Fort Pitt, a grueling four-day march away. Three hundred and forty pack animals carried their supplies; a small cattle herd rendered fresh meat. They marched a dozen miles that first day.

On the second day, by one o'clock on August 5, the troops had marched seventeen miles and had reached Edge Hill, a mile from the waters of Bushy Run. It was there the Shawnee, Delaware, Mingo, and Huron attacked. As soon as the Indians opened fire on the advanced guard, Bouquet ordered the 42nd regiment's two light infantry companies to quickmarch to the front. Those troops "drove the enemy from the ambuscade & pursued them a good way. The savages returned to the attack and the fire being obstinate on our front and extending along our flanks, we made a general charge with the whole line to dislodge the savages from the heights, in which attempt we succeeded, without obtaining from it any decisive advantage, for as soon as they were driven from one post they appeared on another, till by continual reinforcements, they were at last able to surround us & attacked the convoy to our rear. This obliged us to march back to protect it. The action then became general and the savages exerted themselve with uncommon resolution."[75]

Bouquet deployed his men in a tight circle around the frenzied animals of his packtrain. The Indians crept or dodged forward from one tree or boulder to the next, firing at the troops. When a group of Indians neared, Bouquet had the nearest platoon drive them off with a bayonet charge. But parade ground tactics were suicidal in the forest and British casualties mounted steadily. Bushy Run teetered on becoming another Braddock's debacle.

Unlike Braddock, Bouquet allowed his troops to shelter behind boulders and fallen trees. And that is what saved him and his men from massacre. The firing lasted all that afternoon and into the evening. Ammunition on both sides began to run low. Nearly 60 redcoats lay dead or wounded. The wounded were dragged to the circle's center where flour sacks were heaped along with fallen trees and rocks into a makeshift barricade. Many of the packhorses were killed or crippled or had yanked free and bolted away through the forest; the drovers struggled to restrain the rest. The troops were exhausted from their seventeen-mile hike, the battle, and sheer terror. As bad was the worsening thirst. There was no water within their circle. A horde of Indians separated the troops from Bushy Run a half mile away.

The night ended the firing but the troops got little rest. Bouquet kept half on guard half the night to be relieved by the other half until morning. Those trying to sleep were startled by periodic war cries, alarms at the sounds of Indians creeping closer, and the fear that they would all die tomorrow.

Indian musket shots resumed with the dawn's light. One by one more soldiers died or gasped and thrashed from wounds. The soldiers fired back but hit few Indians; they had been trained to fire in the direction of troops massed in open fields, not at warriors dodging among trees and rocks or snaking forward along the ground. Bouquet's army was desperate: "Our troops were . . . extremely fatigued . . . and distressed to the last degree by a total want of water . . . the drivers, stupified by fear, hid themselves in the bushes or were incapable of hearing or obeying orders."[76] The Indians pressed ever closer, probing for a weak spot in the circle of troops. A rush that broke the circle would destroy their enemy and reap several hundred scalps, the packtrains' booty, and glorious stories to be told for generations.

Bouquet reckoned only a desperate gamble might save them. He called an officers' council and proposed that they allow just such a breakthrough. Part of the circle would give way in simulated panic. The Indians would dash in for the kill. But the fleeing soldiers would halt in the circle's center and turn to join the flanks in a murderous crossfire on the massed Indians. The officers agreed to the plan with varying degrees of enthusiasm or reluctance. The appropriate orders and explanations were then spread to the two light companies which would fall back to Major John Campbell, who commanded the 3rd Light Company and the 42nd regiment's grenadier company (which were hidden in a depression in the circle's center); those flank companies on the collapsed circle's horns whose troops would double up with half firing outward and the other half firing across the gap; and the rest of the troops on the circle's far side who would continue to hold.

Bouquet gave the order for two decoy companies to withdraw. The Indians took the bait and charged with war cries and brandished clubs, muskets, and hatchets. As the Indians neared the center the decoy companies turned while Campbell's men on their flank rose from cover. For a few horrifying seconds the Indians realized they had fallen into a trap. Then Campbell shouted a command to fire. The volleys tore through the Indians, killing and wounding several score. Bullets toppled others as they dashed back through the horns of the collapsed circle. Campbell ordered the four companies in the center to pursue and reclose the circle. The troops charged forward; gleefully bayoneting crippled warriors.

When the circle closed, about 60 Indians lay dead within it or around it. The trap and slaughter broke the Indians' spirit. They slipped away into the forest for the trek back to Fort Pitt and beyond. But the British victory was bought at a heavy cost—50 dead, 60 wounded, and 5 missing in two days of desperate fighting. With 29 killed and 35 wounded the 42nd Highlanders bore the brunt of the fighting. The 60th Royal Americans lost 7 killed and 5 wounded, the 77th Highlanders 6 killed and 12 wounded, and the rangers, volunteers, and drovers 8 men killed and 8 wounded. The British casualties were heavy but they could have been much worse.[77]

Bouquet gave orders to move forward to Bushy Run. The wounded were slung in litters. Those supplies that could not be hoisted upon the remaining packhorses were destroyed. Some Indians returned and sniped at the camp but they fled before a rush by the light companies. By late afternoon the troops had revived from the plentiful water, cooked food, and hope that the worst was behind them.

The colonel had nothing but praise for his men: "The behavior of the troops upon this occasion speaks for itself so strongly that for me to attempt their eulogium woud but detract from their merit." Their discipline held firm in battle and triumph alike: "Our brave men disdained so much to touch the dead body of a vanquished enemy, that scarce a scalp was taken except by the rangers and packhorse drivers."[78]

Four days later, on August 10, Bouquet's troops marched or were carried into Fort Pitt. After a day's rest Major Campbell and 400 troops returned to Fort Ligonier to convey there the settlers and wounded. Those troops would then return to Fort Pitt with supplies that had accumulated at Fort Ligonier. As always the shortage of draft animals and wagons limited the amount of supplies that could be carried at any one time.

Important as Bouquet's victory at Bushy Run and relief of Fort Pitt were, diplomatic rather than military battles would prove to be more important in quelling the Indian revolt. That was a reality that all of the Indian agents and an increasing number of British officers understood. When he first learned of the uprising in early June, William Johnson must have been tempted to remind Amherst of all the warnings he had given him over the previous years. Instead, typically, he threw himself into a diplomatic offensive.[79]

Johnson's immediate priority was to prevent the uprising from spreading. To that end he and his men pursued a two-stage diplomatic strategy with those tribes that had not yet raised their scalping knives. So far only the Seneca had joined the uprising. Johnson's first step was to ensure that the other five Iroquois tribes not only stayed neutral but enticed the Seneca from the warpath. He sent belts to the Iroquois council fire at Onondaga asking that the sachems discourage any warriors from joining the hostile tribes. Meanwhile, he gathered as many goods as possible, confident that Iroquois loyalty "may be purchased at a moderate expense."[80]

Throughout the summer the Indian Superintendent convened a series of councils at Johnson Hall. The challenge of keeping the Iroquois at peace demanded all of his formidable diplomatic skills. All along he promised both the carrots of gifts and satisfaction of Indian grievances to reward compliance, and sternly threatened the stick of destruction should the Iroquois choose war. He also appealed to their sense of honor by reminding them that the 1760 conquest treaty bound them to war against any tribes that revolted against British rule.

One of the most important councils was held with 340 Iroquois and envoys of other tribes at German Flats from July 18 to 20, 1763. Johnson listened patiently as the chiefs repeated the familiar bitter litany of complaints of British abuses, most of which he was impotent to redress. The Mohawk, for example, railed against the machinations of George Klock to steal their land and debauch their men with rum. Klock's chicaneries had persisted for years and not only Johnson but the New York Assembly was legally and politically powerless to stop it. Johnson was similarly helpless before other burning issues raised by the Iroquois. Nonetheless, by the council's end Johnson had managed to elicit a lukewarm commitment to peace. And so it went from one council to the next that summer whether it took place at Johnson Hall, Montreal, or Philadelphia.[81]

Diplomacy with British officials and settlers was nearly as important as with the Indians. Johnson spent considerable time trying to convince the Mohawk valley's settlers to stay put, that running might well provoke the Indian attack so much feared. Calm, firm resolution should keep in check any inclinations by the so far peaceful tribes to join in the plunder and scalping.

If this first diplomatic round succeeded, the next step was to enlist the neutral tribes into warring against the hostile tribes. Meanwhile, all British officers and Indian agents would use every contact with the hostile tribes to convince them to bury the hatchet.

By Indian standards the war so far had been incredibly successful—nine forts captured and burned, hundreds of scalps taken, scores of prisoners adopted or tortured, and tons of loot garnered and distributed, while British bullets had killed relatively few warriors. Nonetheless, with the relief of Forts Pitt and Detroit the initiative largely passed from the Indians to the British. The Indians were no longer capable of winning the war. At best they could win a favorable peace, and ever more Indians understood that.

Ammunition, food, and enthusiasm for the war were steadily diminishing. Copies of the Treaty of Paris had circulated and been translated, ending hopes that a French army would reinforce them. The question was increasingly raised, in lodges and councils alike, whether it was now time to quit while they were ahead. But enough chiefs and warriors retained the vision of further victories and eventual independence from Britain that the struggle continued.

NOTES

1. Jeffrey Amherst to Henry Bouquet, June 6, 1763, in Sylvester K. Stevens, Donald H. Kent, Autumn L. Leonard, Louis M. Waddell, and John Totteham, eds., *The Papers of Henry Bouquet* (hereafter cited as *Bouquet Papers*), 6 vols. (Harrisburg: Pennsylvania Historical and Museum Commission, 1972–1994), 6:209.

2. Jeffrey Amherst to William Johnson, June 12, 1763, in James Sullivan and A. C. Flick, eds., *The Papers of William Johnson* (hereafter cited as *Johnson Papers*), 14 vols. (Albany: State University of New York, 1921–1965), 4:138–39.

3. Jeffrey Amherst to Henry Bouquet, June 12, 1763, *Bouquet Papers*, 6:220.

4. Henry Bouquet to Jeffrey Amherst, June 16, 1763, *Bouquet Papers*, 6:225–26.

5. Ibid.

6. Jeffrey Amherst to Henry Bouquet, June 19, 1763, *Bouquet Papers*, 6:240, 239–41.

7. Jeffrey Amherst to William Johnson, June 16, 1763, *Johnson Papers*, 4:148, 148–49.

8. First quote in John Clarence Webster, ed., *The Journal of Jeffrey Amherst, Recording the Military Career of General Amherst in America from 1758 to 1763* (hereafter cited as *Amherst Journal*) (Chicago: Ryerson Press, 1931), 306; second quote in Jeffrey Amherst to [ ], June 17, 1763, Gage papers, William L. Clements Library, Ann Arbor, Mich. (hereafter cited as CL). For his troop movements, see Jeffrey Amherst to Henry Bouquet, June 16, 25, July 2, 1763, *Bouquet Papers*, 6: 227, 255–56, 283–84.

9. Jeffrey Amherst to Henry Bouquet, June 23, 1763 (undated but clear from the letter's words), Amherst collection, Library of Congress, Washington, D.C., microfilm, B-2664.

10. Jeffrey Amherst to James Hamilton, June 19, 1763, *Bouquet Papers*, 6:242.

11. Jeffrey Amherst to Lord Egremont, June 26, 1763, Amherst collection, microfilm, A-1826.

12. Ibid.

13. Hartford Indian Conference, May 30, 28, 1763, *Johnson Papers*, 4:128, 127–29, 123–27; Thomas Fitch to William Johnson, May 30, 1763, ibid., 4:130; Thomas McKee to William Johnson, June 2, 1763, ibid., 4:132. See also the Council between James Hamilton and Teedyuscung, November 19–20, 1762, in *Minutes of the Provincial Council of Pennsylvania* (herafter cited as MPCP) (1852) (reprint, New York: AMS Press, 1968), 9:6–9.

14. Thomas Mckee to William Johnson, June 2, 28, 1763, *Johnson Papers*, 4:132, 10:720; William Johnson Journal of Indian affairs, May 29 to June 29, 1763, ibid., 10:722; George Croghan to Henry Bouquet, June 8, 1763, *Bouquet Papers*, 6:210–11; James Hamilton Memorandum and Proclamation, June 2, 1763, MPCP 9:27–28; Instructions to James Burd and Thomas McKee, June 2, 1763, ibid., 9:29–30.

15. Simeon Ecuyer to Henry Bouquet, June 16, 1763, *Bouquet Papers*, 6:232, 228–33; Simeon Ecuyer to Henry Bouquet, June 26, 1763, ibid., 6:258–60.

16. Discourse between Delawares and Ecuyer, June 24, 1763, *Bouquet Papers*, 6: 261–63; See also Bernard Knollenberg, "General Amherst and Germ Warfare," *Mississippi Valley Historical Review* 41 (1954), 491.

17. Simeon Ecuyer to Henry Bouquet, June 26, 1763, *Bouquet Papers*, 6:258–60.

18. Archibald Blane to Henry Bouquet, June 28, 1763, *Bouquet Papers*, 6:268–69.

19. Lewis Ourry to Henry Bouquet, June 20, 1763, *Bouquet Papers*, 6:244, 243–44.

20. Lewis Ourry to Henry Bouquet, July 2, 1763, *Bouquet Papers*, 6:286–87.

21. Henry Bouquet to Lewis Ourry, July 4, 7, 1763, *Bouquet Papers*, 6:296, 296–98.

22. Henry Bouquet to Lewis Ourry, July 4, 7, 1763, *Bouquet Papers*, 6:296, 296–98.

23. Henry Bouquet to Lewis Ourry, July 7, 1763, *Bouquet Papers*, 6:296, 296–98.

24. Henry Bouquet to Jeffrey Amherst, June 25, 1763, Bouquet collection, Library of Congress, Washington, D.C., microfilm, A-1065.

25. Jeffrey Amherst to Henry Bouquet, June 29, 1763, Bouquet collection, microfilm, A-1065.

26. Jeffery Amherst to Henry Gladwin, July 3, 1763, Amherst collection, microfilm, B-2664.

27. Jeffrey Amherst to Henry Bouquet, July 7, 1763, *Bouquet Papers*, 6:301, 299–301.

28. Henry Bouquet to Jeffrey Amherst, July 13, 1763, Bouquet collection, microfilm, A-1065.

29. John Hughes to Henry Bouquet, July 11, 1763, *Bouquet Papers*, 6:305, 304–5.

30. Jeffrey Amherst to Henry Bouquet, July 16, 1763, *Bouquet Papers*, 6:315, 313–15.

31. Henry Bouquet to James Hamilton, July 13, 1763, *Bouquet Papers*, 6:307–8.

32. Ibid., *Bouquet Papers*, 6:308, 307–9.

33. Webster, *Amherst Journal*, 311–12, 314.

34. Jeffrey Amherst to William Johnson, August 14, 1763, *Johnson Papers*, 4; 188, 186–89.

35. Jeffrey Amherst to William Johnson, July 16, 1763, *Johnson Papers*, 4:172, 171–74.

36. Jeffrey Amherst to William Johnson, July 28, 1763, *Johnson Papers*, 10:764.

37. Jeffrey Amherst to Valentine Gardiner, July 31, 1763, Bouquet collection, microfilm, A-1065.

38. Ibid.

39. James Hamilton to Henry Bouquet, July 12, 1763, *Bouquet Papers*, 6:305–6.

40. James Robertson to Jeffrey Amherst, July 19, 1761, *Bouquet Papers*, 6:322; Jeffrey Bouquet to James Hamilton, July 16, 1763, *Bouquet Papers*, 6:315–16.

41. Jeffrey Amherst to Henry Bouquet, August 7, 1763, *Bouquet Papers*, 6:351, 350–52.

42. Henry Bouquet to Jeffrey Amherst, July 26, 1763, *Bouquet Papers*, 6:326, 325–26.

43. George Croghan to Henry Bouquet, June 11, 1763, *Bouquet Papers*, 6:218–19; Lewis Ourry to Henry Bouquet, June 17, 1763, ibid., 6:249–50; George Croghan to William Johnson, June 20, 1763, *Johnson Papers*, 6:252–53.

44. George Croghan to Henry Bouquet, June 17, 1763, Bouquet collection, microfilm, A-1065.

45. James Livingstone to Henry Bouquet, July 16, 1763, *Bouquet Papers*, 6:317–18.

46. George Etherington to Henry Gladwin, June 12, 1763, *Johnson Papers*, 10:692–94.

47. James Gorrell Journal, October 12, 1761 to June 14, 1763, *Johnson Papers*, 10:697–714. ˙

48. Indian Conference at Montreal, August 9–11, *Johnson Papers*, 10:785, 779–86; See also, Thomas Gage to William Johnson, August 12, 1763, ibid., 10:787–88; Canada Indians to Western Indians, August 25, 1763, ibid., 10:792–94.

49. Declaration at Detroit, June 11, 1763, Amherst collection, microfilm, B-2664.

50. Franklin B. Hough, ed., *Lieutenant Jehu Hay, Diary of the Siege of Detroit in the War with Pontiac* (Albany, N.Y.: J. Munsell, 1860), 24.

51. Milo Milton Quaife, ed., *The Siege of Detroit in 1763: The Journal of Pontiac's Conspiracy and John Rutherford's Narrative of a Captivity* (Chicago: Lakeside Press, 1958), 135–39.

52. Ibid., 143–44.

53. Ibid., 144.

54. Quaife, *The Siege of Detroit*, 161; Declaration of Jadeau to Major Gladwin and Captain Grant at Major Gladwin's house, December 24, 1763, Michigan Pioneer and Historical Society 27:656–57.

55. James Sterling to William MacAdams, August 7, 1763, Sterling letterbook, 109, CL.

56. Declaration of Jadeau to Gladwin, December 24, 1763, Gage papers, CL.

57. First quote from Hough, *Hay Diary*, 40–41; second quote from Quaife, *The Siege of Detroit*, 175. For details of Campbell's hideous death, see Proceedings of Enquiry Held by Order of Major Gladwin, at Detroit, August 9, 1763, Michigan Pioneer and Historical Society 27:639–43.

58. Quaife, *The Siege of Detroit*, 246–74.

59. Proceedings of Court of Inquiry Held at Detroit, October 1, 1763, Michigan Pioneer and Historical Society 27:650–52.

60. James Sterling to Duncan & Co., July 25, 1763, Sterling letterbook, 106–7, CL; James Sterling to Brother, July 26, 1763, Sterling letterbook, 107, CL.

61. Hough, *Hay Diary*, 54–57. Other accounts give slightly different figures: 59 killed and wounded in James Sterling to William McAdams, August 7, 1763, Sterling letterbook, 107, CL; Alexander Duncan to William Johnson, Account of July 31, 1763 Action, *Johnson Papers*, 10:762–66; James Sterling to Brother, August 7, 1763, Sterling letterbook, 108, CL; James Sterling to John Duncan & Co., August 7, 1763, Sterling letterbook, 110–11, CL; Webster, *Amherst Journal*, 320. For a secondhand account, see Jean Baptiste de Couange, August 24, 1763, *Johnson Papers*, 10:790–91.

62. Edward G. Williams, ed., *The Orderly Book of Colonel Henry Bouquet's Expedition against the Ohio Indians, 1764* (Pittsburgh: Mayer Press, 1960), 3–10.

63. Henry Bouquet to Anne Willing, January 15, 1761, *Bouquet Papers*, 5:250.

64. Henry Bouquet to Gually, October 18, 1761, *Bouquet Papers*, 5:827, 825–28.

65. Henry Bouquet to Alexander Lunan, Feburary 1762, *Bouquet Papers*, 6:48–49.

66. Jeffrey Amherst to Henry Bouquet, July 7, 1763, *Bouquet Papers*, 6:299–301.

67. Allan Campbell to Henry Bouquet, June 24, 1763, *Bouquet Papers*, 6:254–55; Henry Bouquet to Jeffrey Amherst, June 29, 1763, ibid., 270–71.

68. Henry Bouquet to Jeffrey Amherst, July 3, 1763, *Bouquet Papers*, 6:289, 288–89; Henry Bouquet to Lancaster County Magistrates, June 29, 1763, *Bouquet Papers*, 6:275; Henry Bouquet to Matthias Slough and Joseph Simon, June 29, 1763, ibid., 6:275–76; Henry Bouquet to William Plumstead and David Franks, July 19, 1763, ibid., 6:320–21.

69. Henry Bouquet to James Hamilton, July 1, 1763, *Bouquet Papers*, 6:279–81.

70. Henry Bouquet to Jeffrey Amherst, July 26, 1763, *Bouquet Papers*, 6:326, 325–26.

71. Henry Bouquet to Jeffrey Amherst, June 29, 1763, *Bouquet Papers*, 6:270–71.

72. Ecuyer Reply to Indians, July 27, 1763, ibid., 6:337, 336–37; Indian Speeches at Fort Pitt, July 26, 1763, *Bouquet Papers*, 6:333–36.

73. Simeon Ecuyer to Henry Bouquet, August 2, 1763, *Bouquet Papers*, 6:332–33, 330–33.

74. Simeon Ecuyer to Henry Bouquet, August 2, 1763, *Bouquet Papers*, 6:345–46.

75. Henry Bouquet to Jeffrey Amherst, August 5, 1763, *Bouquet Papers*, 6:339, 338–40.

76. Henry Bouquet to Jeffrey Amherst, August 6, 1763, *Bouquet Papers*, 6:343, 342–44.

77. Casualty Return at Bushy Run, August 6, 1763, *Bouquet Papers*, 6:354–46. How many Indians were killed or wounded? As always, accounts vary. Bouquet simply says "many." By one account there were only 110 Indians on the field, of which five were killed on the field and one died of his wounds. Journal of Indian Affairs, March 2, 1765, *Johnson Papers*, 11:618. Unfortunately, the true figure will remain a mystery.

78. Henry Bouquet to Jeffrey Amherst, August 6, 1763, *Bouquet Papers*, 6:343, 344.

79. William Johnson to Jeffrey Amherst, June 6, June 19, July 1, 8, 11, 30, August 4, 1763, in E. B. O'Callaghan and Berthold Fernow, eds., *Documents Relative to the Colonial History of the State of New York*, 15 vols. (Albany, N.Y.: Weed, Parsons, and Co., 1856–1887), 7:522–24, 524–25, 530–31, 531–32, 532–33, 533–34, 534–35.

80. William Johnson to Jeffrey Amherst, June 26, 1763, *Johnson Papers*, 10:717, 716–18.

81. Indian Conference, July 18–20, 1763, *Johnson Papers*, 10:746–53; William Johnson to Jeffrey Amherst, July 24, 1763, ibid., 10:754–59; Journal of Indian Affairs, July 4 to August 4, 1763, ibid., 10:766–76; William Johnson, Journal of Indian Affairs, May 29 to June 29, 1763, ibid., 10:720–26.

5

Stalemate

"Leave These Distant Lakes and Streams to Us"

Thou knowest the Master of Life. It is he who has put arms in our hands. And it is he who has ordered us to fight against the bad meat that would come to infect our lands.

—Pontiac

We have visibly brought upon us this Indian War by being too saving of a few presents to the savages which properly distributed would certainly have prevented it.

—Henry Bouquet to Thomas Gage

If your Excellency still intends to punish them . . . it may easily be done . . . simply by permitting a free sale of rum, which will destroy them more effectively than fire and sword.

—Major Henry Gladwin

If an Indian injures me, does it follow that I may revenge myself on all Indians?

—Benjamin Franklin

The bayonets, spears, lances on board her are dyed with Indian blood like axes in a slaughterhouse.

—James Sterling

Although expeditions had relieved Forts Detroit and Pitt the war was far from over. The first essential steps in a long march toward reconquering the British Empire had been taken. But those gains had to be consolidated. The tenuous communication and transportation links to distant forts needed to be strengthened until they were impregnable to Indian attempts to sever them. Only then could the British consider marching against the Indian villages and reestablishing their rule. That demanded enormous amounts of troops, transport, and supplies.

By late summer Detroit was no longer in danger of being starved into submission. Pontiac's defeat of Dalyell's attack briefly lifted Indian spirits but was hardly decisive. The stalemate dragged on. The Indians could not destroy the fort. The soldiers could not crush the Indians. That front's outcome would depend on supply and season rather than battle. The Indians could only replenish their munitions from captured bateaux or the cartridge boxes of dead redcoats. Although the Indians had intercepted some bateaux and delayed others, they were unable to capture or destroy the sailing ships. The *Huron* and *Michigan* brought in fresh supplies of munitions, provisions, and troops just when Detroit's defenders were down to their last biscuits and bullets. That summer and fall, as the fort's warehouses were gradually refilled and its ramparts packed with redcoats, time shifted to Britain's side. The Indians, meanwhile, were anxious to harvest their crops and then depart for the winter hunt. Short of powder and lead, they faced a long, bleak winter and uncertain spring.

On August 6, the *Huron* dropped anchor before Detroit and disgorged 80 barrels of provisions and 60 troops from the 17th and 44th regiments under the command of Lieutenant John Williams. The *Michigan* and *Huron* weighed anchor on August 13 for the long sail east. Aboard both boats were the fort's wounded and letters from Gladwin to Amherst detailing the Battle of Bloody Run and Detroit's plight.

Although Detroit was secure for now, with Dalyell's debacle still vivid in their minds, no one spoke seriously of trying another large-scale attack on an Indian village. Only when an overwhelming number of reinforcements arrived could they realistically consider going after Pontiac and his followers.

The British, however, did not just sit tight. Gladwin and his officers planned and executed several sorties. During the night of August 5, Captain James Grant led 50 troops out to occupy some houses from which the Indians approached to get within musket range of the fort. But the Indians got wind of the ambush and stayed away. Grant and his men retired to Detroit. On August 8, Captain Joseph Hopkins and 60 troops embarked in bateaux to raid the Huron village. But the bateaux became separated in the fog and when they finally gathered for an attack the village's warriors waited ashore eager for battle. Hopkins wisely aborted the attack. On August 20, Hopkins ventured another sortie, this time with 40 troops in the middle of the night to set up an ambush against the Potawatomi on the road they took to pester the fort with gunfire each day. But the troops were discovered and converging warriors forced them to beat a hasty retreat. On August 21, troops sortied against Indian sharpshooters 400 yards away. But the Indians scattered out of range, others surged to their sides, and they slipped forward to cut off the redcoats. The troops scurried back to Detroit. On August 23, Indian snipers posted in a distant house wounded three soldiers. Major Rogers led out a sortie but they disappeared. Rogers and his men spent the night deployed around the house in hopes of ambushing the Indians if they returned. The Indians stayed out of sight. On August 24, an officer, probably Hay, led 30 troops into the night to deploy around the homes of Brarrois and St. Martin. Indians wounded two of the men. These potentially lethal cat-and-mouse games produced few casualties on either side. They did, however, raise British morale and lower that of the Indians.

The "siege" dragged on. Various numbers of warriors from various tribes strode down toward the fort each day to fire at any defender careless enough to expose himself. The Indians were fine marksmen. Although handicapped by distance and inaccurate muskets they managed to wound seven soldiers in August. But the sniping posed no threat to Detroit's survival and merely used up the Indians' limited supplies of ammunition.

With an all-out assault on Detroit ruled out, the only other thing the Indians could do was to issue periodic demands that the British abandon Detroit. Gladwin received one such letter in French, allegedly dictated by Huron Chief Wasson on August 16. The threats in the letter enraged Gladwin, who replied: "If you have anything at all to say to me, come to the fort to say it in person under a flag of truce . . . the writer of another such letter can expect to be arrested and hanged at once."[1]

Although the siege did not threaten Detroit's survival, the constant sniping, crowded conditions, monotony, sporadic contacts with the east, and seeming endlessness of it all was a constant strain to its defenders. Tempers shortened. Depression showed among many, including its commander Major Henry Gladwin. Although he remained as outwardly in command as ever, he confessed to Johnson that "I came hither much against my will forseeing what would happen; I am brought into a scrape, and left in it; things are expected of me that cant be performed; I could wish I had quitted the service seven years ago, and that somebody else commanded here."[2]

Morale droped even further among the Indians. The victory glow of defeating Dalyell's attack soon faded. That attack and the sorties revealed the vulnerability of the villages. On August 18, Pontiac had his village moved to the mouth of the Rouge River south of Detroit. It was hoped that the new location would be more secure from British attacks and could intercept any bateaux or ships on the Detroit River. Neither hope was realized. The Rouge River camp proved vulnerable to bateaux raids while the *Huron* and *Michigan* sailed past far beyond musket shot.

On August 16, the *Huron* reached the harbor at Buffalo Creek near the mouth of the Niagara River; the *Michigan* would arrive the next day. Awaiting those vessels were Lieutenant John Montresor with dispatches to Gladwin from Amherst, Captain Edward Hope and 17 troops of the 17th regiment, and a small mountain of supplies. Their departure was delayed by word that two Iroqouis peace delegations would join them. It was not until August 26 that the *Michigan*'s Captain Jacob Newman ordered his men to weigh anchor. Aboard were Montresor, Hope, the troops, and a peace delegation led by Chief Daniel Oughnour. The *Huron*, captained by Walter Horsey, would follow two days later with six Mohawk led by subchief Aaron aboard. At Detroit those two delegations would try to convince the Indians there to give up the fight.

During the first day of sailing the *Michigan* was becalmed and then battered by a storm that drove it ashore at Catfish Creek, only fourteen miles from Buffalo Creek. As the *Michigan* broke up against the rocks, all hands managed to drag themselves to safety on land. Well aware that a large Seneca war party was lurking in the area, the officers had the troops build makeshift breastworks from planks and barrels salvaged from the *Michigan*. A sergeant was sent on the long hike to Buffalo Creek to seek help.

The sergeant made it. Word was passed on to Major Wilkins at Fort Niagara of the *Michigan*'s fate. Wilkins immediately gathered 100 troops and sent them to relieve the shipwrecked troops. They arrived on September 2. Anyone in the Catfish Creek camp who thought their ordeal was over would soon be proved wrong. The next day a war party attacked, killing a man who had strayed outside the breastwork and three troops inside. The troops snatched up their muskets and opened fire; a swivel mounted on the wall was touched off. The Indians retreated beyond range. Daniel Oughnour ventured out to parley with them. They would not reveal their identity but were most likely a Chippewa and Ottawa war party, reported lurking in the region. They lingered another day and then disappeared.[3]

In the following days the troops tried to patch up the *Michigan* but the sloop was wrecked beyond repair. On September 6, Hope and Montresor sent word to Wilkins of their failure and requested help. The officers put their men to work constructing a regular fort to protect themselves and the supplies they had managed to salvage. Other than that, all they could do was wait.

The *Huron* meanwhile had safely ridden out the storm and set sail on August 28. Far out on Lake Erie when it passed the site of the *Michigan*'s wreck, the *Huron*'s passengers would remain oblivious to its fate. In addition to the six Mohawk, the *Huron* carried an eleven-man crew and was crammed with 160 barrels of pork and 47 barrels of flour. Arriving at the Detroit River mouth on September 2, Captain Horsey granted a Mohawk request that they be put ashore so they could visit the villages on the way up to Detroit. That same day, two Canadians in a canoe paddled up to the *Huron* in hopes of selling vegetables to the crew. Horsey dashed their hopes for trade. The Canadians swiftly paddled to Pontiac's nearby Rouge River village with word that a poorly defended *Huron* was slowly sailing upriver. The wind finally died and Horsey was forced to drop anchor seven miles below Detroit in the narrow channel between Turkey Island and the west shore.

After dark, Pontiac led around 340 Ottawa and Chippewa warriors in 25 canoes toward the *Huron*. The crew spotted the Indians as they closed for the kill. A gunner managed to touch off a cannon whose ball soared harmlessly over the canoes. War screams and musket shots filled the air. The twelve men aboard fired down at the approaching canoes. Some Indians swarmed aboard the *Huron*'s bowsprit. The British and Indians desperately swung musket butts and tomahawks at each other. A ball struck Captain Horsey in the head killing him instantly. First Mate Ebenezer Jacobs took command and shouted for someone to fire the magazine. Adam Brown, a captive turned Indian, was among the attackers. When he heard Jacobs' order he shouted a warning to the other Indians. Those aboard the *Huron* hastily scrambled back into their canoes and the attackers drew back beyond musket shot. Jacobs ordered the cannon fired toward them. The Indians suffered 8 killed and 20 wounded, of whom 7 later died, and 60 muskets sunk from overturned canoes during the fight. Among the crew only Horsey and another man had died but 4 others were grievously wounded. It was astonishing that any had survived such seemingly overwhelming odds against them.

Although the wind refused to revive, the *Huron* did receive relief. Detroit's sentries had heard the cannon shots. Gladwin immediately ordered Captain Hopkins to embark with his company in four bateaux to row to the ship's rescue. The bateaux did not reach the schooner and returned the next morning on September 5. A wind rose shortly after dawn. The *Huron*'s crew spread sails. At 3:30 the schooner dropped anchor off the fort where stevedores offloaded 47 barrels of flour and 160 of pork. With a reinforced crew the *Huron* set sail on yet another supply run on September 8, only three days after reaching Detroit.

When the crews' tales were told, listeners deemed "the attack . . . the bravest ever known to be made by Indians & the defense, which as British subjects alone are capable. . . . The bayonets, spears, lances on board her are dyed with Indian blood like axes in a slaughterhouse."[4] More than hearty congratulations and awe greeted the five survivors. Gladwin was so impressed by their heroism that he dug into his own pocket and distributed 100 pounds sterling among them. When Amherst learned of the fight he had special medals stamped and given to each survivor and the families of those who died. The general also rewarded Gladwin's stalwart defense by naming him his deputy adjutant general and recommending to Secretary of War McEllis that he be promoted to lieutenant colonel.[5]

Meanwhile, Wilkins had received word from Catfish Creek that the *Michigan* was unsalvagable. He sent 240 troops in 23 bateaux to relieve the stranded troops, help dismantle the *Michigan*, and build rafts from the salvaged timbers upon which the supplies and troops could be conveyed back to Fort Schlosser. Just what purpose the supplies would serve there was not clear. And just how the troops were to accomplish their mission was equally foggy—Wilkins had sent them off without proper tools.

When all seemed at their most foolish, fortune graced the hapless troops. The *Huron* sailed into sight and was hailed forth. Aboard were all the necessary hammers and nails to salvage the *Michigan*. That done, the fort was abandoned and all the troops and 185 barrels of supplies were conveyed back to Fort Schlosser. There Montresor, Hope, a dozen troops, and as many supplies as possible were crammed aboard the *Huron* which sailed back toward Detroit, but not before learning of a horrifying disaster.

Although only the 25-mile-long Niagara River separates Lakes Ontario and Erie, it was no easy task getting from one to the other. Niagara's falls, rapids, and steep gorges along the river's heart demanded a long portage. All supplies, communications, and troops had to pass along a nine-mile trail leading from Fort Little Niagara south along the river's east side to Fort Schlosser. That long portage was largely flat, the only steep stretch being where it ran up the escarpment which cut from southeast to northwest across the region. The trail ran right alongside the gorge which dropped 200 feet to the rushing river below. From Fort Schlosser, rapids prevented ships from sailing on the upper Niagara River. Bateaux linked Fort Schlosser and the mouth of Buffalo Creek on Lake Erie, the nearest place where ships could safely anchor.

So far no war party had attacked troops and supplies traversing the long, vulnerable portage between Forts Little Niagara and Schlosser. That changed on September 14. Twenty-four mounted troops of the 80th regiment were escorting 30 afoot wagoneers back to Fort Little Niagara. They had just passed the portage's most spectacular segment around Niagara Falls and were now wearily hiking the stretch above the deep gorge where Devil's Hole, a huge whirlpool, swirled several hundred feet below. It was there while the British eyes were riveted on that awesome sight that the Indians attacked. At a signal 309 Seneca rose from the forest, fired, and charged. The British were trapped between the Indians and the steep cliff plunging down to the river. In minutes the Indians had killed 51 of the troops and wagoneers.

Only three survived. The detachment's commander, Sergeant William Stedman, was at the column's head when the attack opened. He whipped his horse into a gallop and managed to ride unscathed through the volley of musket shots. A wagoneer with a leg wound crept away during all the mayhem. The drummer boy Peter Matthews experienced the most terrifying escape of all. He lost his footing and hurtled off the cliff toward the whirlpool. He crashed through some tree branches and narrowly missed falling on boulders at the cliff's foot. The branches slowed his descent enough that his neck was not snapped when he hit the water. He swam ashore and hid among the rocks where he shook with cold and terror for hours until the relief expedition arrived.

The gunfire had echoed the mile and a half down the gorge to Fort Little Niagara. Captain Benjamin Johnston commanded that garrison, which consisted of two companies of the 80th Light Infantry regiment. He immediately called his troops to arms. Minutes later he was leading them double-quick up the steep portage trail. Before departing he sent word of his action to Major John Wilkins at Fort Niagara, another six miles down the trail.

That was the only sound decision Johnston made after the gunfire erupted. Everything else he did was pure folly. No scouts were sent ahead. The pace exhausted the troops. The Indians lay in wait for them just down the trail from where they had killed the others. Their fusilade killed many of the troops and the rush of warriors swinging tomahawks and clubs slaughtered nearly all the rest. In all, 75 troops died and only ten, six of whom were wounded, escaped into the forest. Johnston was among the dead.

After receiving Johnston's message, Wilkins left behind a skeleton garrison and quick-marched his 60th companies up the portage trail. At Fort Little Niagara he received word of the massacre and decided to sit tight until several companies of the 46th reached him. The reinforcements did not arrive until night. Wilkins and his troops cautiously marched up the trail the next morning. Satiated with their easy victories and wary of Wilkins' approach, the Indians melted away into the forest.

A couple of hours after setting off, Wilkins and his troops reached the massacre. The sight of scores of stripped, mutilated bodies of their countrymen must have at once terrified and infuriated the soldiers. The only survivor at the scene was the little drummer boy, Peter Matthews, who was helped back up the cliff. All Wilkins could do was to order the dead buried and then hurry his troops back to Fort Niagara before nightfall. In all, the Indians had killed 112 men in what became known as the Devil's Hole Massacre. Only one Indian was wounded in both ambushes. It would be their bloodiest victory of the war. With classic understatement, Amherst would describe the latest debacle as "an unfortunate affair."[6]

For weeks after the massacre, Seneca war parties haunted the woods around Forts Niagara, Little Niagara, Schlosser, and Buffalo Creek, sniping at the palisades and attacking soldiers collecting firewood or protecting teamsters transporting supplies. On October 12, about 50 Seneca charged the cattle guard in the meadows outside Fort Little Niagara and ran off eleven of sixteen oxen. On November 5, warriors captured a ten-man wood-cutting party within sight of Fort Little Niagara. As the fort's garrison watched in horror and fear, the Seneca gruesomely murdered eight men just beyond musket shot and then dragged off two others for the gauntlet and prolonged torture in their village. A lucky musket shot from the fort may have winged one of the Indians who was butchering a soldier "as he was seen to go off with the head in his hand."[7]

Danger lurked all along the frontier. From an Indian informant Bouquet learned in early September that a party of "800 western Indians in 80 canoes were gone toward Niagara to take the post at the carrying place and cut off all communications with the Detroit"; an Ottawa and Chippewa war party was lurking near Fort Presque Isle, and the Shawnee, Delaware, and Mingo were regrouping at their Muskingum River villages for another push against Fort Pitt.[8]

The closer to Fort Pitt the more dangerous the journey. Bouquet sent Captain Simeon Ecuyer back to Bedford with troops to convoy a supply train there to Fort Pitt. Along the way a war party attacked his rear guard, killing a driver and a horse. Just outside Bedford, Indians murdered two settlers and dragged off another. Ecuyer sent troops in pursuit. The patrol spotted six Indians but they disappeared into the forest.[9]

War parties stalked the frontier elsewhere. Shawnee, Delaware, and Mingo strode east deep into Pennsylvania to wipe out isolated farm families. But the pickings there were increasingly slim. Most settlers had either fled, been slaughtered, or were holed up in the forts. Although Pennsylvania's assembly had still not authorized the creation of a militia, many frontiersmen cited the sacred right of self-defense to ignore the law. Colonel George Armstrong gathered 300 militia in the Juniata valley on October 1 and led them against Delaware villages on the Susquehanna River's west branch. The inhabitants fled before the militia who could merely burn the empty lodges. By October 12, Armstrong's militia reached Fort Augusta and there mostly dispersed back to their homes. The Delaware retaliated with raids across Northampton County which killed eleven settlers. From there they slipped over into the Wyoming valley where 31 people from the Susquehanna Company remained. The war party slaughtered ten of them and captured the rest. Ironically, another war party was heading for Wyoming at the same time. Militia Major James Clayton had gathered 100 or so volunteers to chase off those squatters on Pennsylvania's territory. They must have viewed the carnage with mixed feelings.

That autumn the fighting was fierce on the Virginia frontier. There a party of 94 Shawnee that passed by in the spring to war against the Cherokee returned in the autumn to fall upon the settlements. A militia company of 30 men caught up with 23 of them, killing several and scattering the rest; 30 horses and four white prisoners were recovered. An account which may refer to the same or a completely different fight identified a party of Seneca returning from warring against the Cherokee. A Virginian ambush killed several and liberated two Cherokee. The Shawnee soon avenged those defeats. They ambushed a 60-man militia patrol and killed twelve, including its captains Moffat and Phillips, before disappearing into the forest. Colonel

Andrew Lewis led a pursuit of 150 militia who caught up to the Indians and killed six before the others escaped into a laurel thicket.[10]

Those aggressive and mostly successful troops were provincials, not regulars. Virtually everyone by now agreed that regulars alone could not quell the uprising. By mid-October Whitehall's ministers accepted that reality. They authorized the commander in chief and governors to raise provincial troops. Around that time Amherst had finally come grudgingly to that same conclusion. On October 30 he issued a request to several governors to raise troops the following spring for the summer campaigns, with quotas of 1,400 from New York, 600 from New Jersey, 1,000 from Pennsylvania, and 600 from Virginia.[11]

The governors dutifully put the measures before their respective legislatures. The lawmakers of each province studiously found excuses to limit, delay, or derail the proposal. New York's legislators, for instance, protested that no quotas were demanded of the New England provinces, which thus worsened their own burden. In the end, however, they voted to raise 300 troops to be deployed on the communication line between Albany and Oswego, in addition to the 173 troops New York already fielded at its frontier posts. The news of those petty squabbles would reinforce Amherst's prejudices against provincials.[12]

Pennsylvania's contributions were also controversial. General Jeffrey Amherst first wrote Governor James Hamilton on June 12 to express his hope that Pennylvania would aid the effort in crushing the rebellion. Hamilton laid the latter before his council and proposed a bill which would raise troops, supplies, transportation, and money. It was not until nearly a month later, on July 5, that the assembly convened and Hamilton called on those representatives to vote for his bill. After debating the issues, the assembly passed a bill which would raise 700 troops to be employed only to protect the farmers during harvest, and another bill that would contribute wagon transportation to the regular army. The legislatures neglected one key element of the troop bill—they refused to allocate any new money to implement it. They did, however, authorize 500 pounds for transportation. Then, admidst a war, the assembly adjourned until September 12, 1763.[13]

Hamilton raised the troops but the little money left in the province's coffers was soon exhausted. Hamilton appeared before the assembly when it reconvened and explain what he had done and request that the 700 troops, most of whom were stationed at Fort Augusta, be deployed until the hostilities had ended. He then asked the assembly to pay for the troops' wages, supplies, and other needs. The assembly mulled the proposal for the next two weeks and then rejected it on September 28. The tug-of-war continued for another month.[14]

The assembly incalcitrance incensed Amherst. On October 16, he wrote Hamilton "repeating my surprise at the infatuation of the people in your province, who tamely look on while their brethern are butchered by the savages when, without doubt it is in their power by exerting a proper spirit, not only to protect the settlements, but to punish any Indians that are hardy enough to disturb them."[15]

When Hamilton presented the assembly that letter, it enraged more than shamed them. On October 22, they delivered a message to Hamilton defending their actions and attacking Amherst. But that same day they passed three bills which regulated military pay, prohibited selling muskets and gunpowder to the Indians, and, mostly importantly, authorized 24,000 pounds for defense. Tensions may have eased somewhat when a new governor, John Penn, arrived on November 1. But the truce between the governor and assembly would not last long.[16]

Despite such contributions Amherst still harbored distrust and animosity toward provincial troops. In early November he bluntly rejected a request to raise three ranger companies augmented by Indian scouts, this one from Sir William Johnson himself. The general asserted that new troops were not needed since regular regiments would soon arrive from Pensacola and Halifax. Johnson was persistent. On November 10, he sent Amherst a memorandum arguing that the three ranger companies, augmented by "some trusty Indians," were essential to protecting the Mohawk River valley and communications lines to Oswego. His arguments were militarily impregnable. Such forces "will not only prevent our being surprised but will enable us to find out the enemy's haunts & places of retreat, their magazines, &c. and certainly intimidate the enemy as much as it will animate our troops who from frequent sustained by them begin to despair of success against such an enemy in the woods which should by all means be removed."[17]

Amherst ignored Johnson's memorandum. His bookkeeper mind was elsewhere, obsessed not in raising and deploying troops but in cutting costs. Bizarrely, he remained as obsessesd with "economy" as he was inspired by vengeance. He sent Johnson an excerpt of a letter penned by Lord Egremont before news of the uprising reached him. Whitehall called on the commander in chief to support financially any expenses by the Indian Superintendent to quell discontent among the tribes, as long as it did not exceed 1,000 pounds. It should have been obvious to all but the dullest mind that the uprising had rendered Egremont's financial limit irrelevant. Not so Amherst, who insisted that given Egremont's words, "I need not add anything on the subject of economy."[18] Although he seems to have vaguely understood that his policy of cutbacks had provoked the war, he clung to justifying those very policies. As late as September 30 he wrote Johnson that "the late defection of so many tribes, in my opinion, ought to lessen the expences in your Department."[19]

To such absurdities Johnson could only clench his teeth and politely keep trying to pry open Amherst's locked mind. He wrote a long letter repeating his arguments and finally asked, "it may appear to many people as a disagreeable circumstance to purchase their favor, but what can we do? Can we destroy them all? This certainly none will suppose."[20] But here Johnson was wrong. Amherst would happily have exterminated all Indians if he had the power to do so, whether from smallpox, dogs, or fusilades. And the general was by no means solitary in his hatreds.

Like any "great leader," Amherst tried to set a proper example. In May 1763, he had received orders from Whitehall to reduce several regiments. Unfortunately, the timing could not have been worse. Amherst received his orders just as the Indian uprising burst across the western empire. That did not stop Amherst, who certainly would have made a much better accountant than general. He was determined to obey those orders no matter how irrelevent they were amidst an unexpected war. Once expeditions had relieved Forts Pitt and Detroit by late summer, Amherst initiated the reductions.

Four regiments would be reduced or eliminated. The 77th Highlanders was among those on the chopping block; its healthy troops would be transferred to the 42nd Highlanders and the maimed and aged sent to Chelsea Hospital in London. The 42nd would be reduced to seven line companies, a light company, and a grenadier of 55 men each which would total no more than 500 troops. The 60th Royal Americans' 3rd and 4th battalions would also be erased and its troops transferred to the 1st and 2nd battalions. Three companies of the 60th would head to South Carolina to relieve there the three Independent Companies which would be disbanded. The 80th Light Infantry was scheduled for elimination but would serve a bit longer until a final peace treaty was signed. By eliminating the weak and strengthening the strong regiments the army was leaner and tougher. Yet even with the reductions and redeployments, the remaining regiments were undermanned. Desertions, diseases, detachments, and battle deaths had reduced six companies of the 60th's 1st battalion to only 298 men of their full complement of 430 troops in September 1763.[21] Other battalions were just as weak.

Amherst had received a second order designed to reduce expense which would be far more controversial than reducing those regiments. On September 22, 1763, he ordered a "stoppage" or deduction of four pence per day from every soldier's pay to defray food expenses; limited officers to one daily ration; and struck all wives and washwomen off the ration list. Although the reform affected every man in uniform, it hurt the poor privates the hardest. When this harsh policy was imposed, strikes and near mutinies broke out at Fort Pitt and other posts. The protests worked. On October 11, 1763, Amherst issued an order which reduced stoppage to two and a half pence. The grumblings persisted but less loudly.[22] The original and revised orders were transmitted by Sir Jeffrey's aide and younger brother William.

The reductions and stoppages may have pared expenses but they also devastated morale and discipline. No regiment suffered worse than the 60th. Bouquet requested that the 60th be withdrawn from their frontier posts to winter in the eastern cities. They had "been six years in the woods and their spirit is so much cast down. . . . If they are kept here another winter I forsee great desertion and the rest discouraged will be good for nothing."[23] Amherst rejected the request.

The troops were nearing the breaking point. Captain Simeon Ecuyer was appalled at his nearly mutinous troops: "I have served over 22 years but I have never seen such a tribe of rebels, bandits, and hamstringers, especially the grenadiers. I have been obliged, after all imaginable patience, to have two of them horsewhipped on the spot and without a court martial. One wanted to kill the sergeant and the other wanted to kill me. I was on the point of blowing his brains out but fear of killing or wounded several of those around us stopped me."[24]

Abysmal morale was not confined to the ranks. Even after Bouquet's army relieved the chain of forts across Pennsylvania to Fort Pitt, their commanders remained semi-isolated and assailed by Indian raiders. The punishing strain of fighting a wilderness war afflicted all those commanders to varying degrees, none more than Fort Ligonier's Lieutenant Archibald Blane. He wrote to Bouquet to "beg that I may not be left any longer in this forlorn way, for I can assure you the fatigue I have gone thro begins to get the better of me. I must beg you will appoint me. . . . a proper garrison."[25]

The strain of struggling to maintain order in his own ranks sapped the exhilaration Captain Ecuyer experienced fighting Indians. He implored Bouquet to "in the name of God let me retire into the country. . . . Besides I am not feeling very well and I do not know whether I will be in condition to go up again with this convoy."[26] Ailments afflicted Ecuyer, as much psychological as physical: "I have a severe cold and fever every night, stomach trouble, and a headache, with an abscess on the spot where I was wounded at Quebec which causes me unbearable agonies."[27] Bouquet denied Ecuyer permission to take leave and ordered him to return to Fort Pitt. Nonplussed, the captain continued east.

News of Ecuyer's "French leave" enraged Bouquet who demanded that he "explain how you found yourself in Philadelphia when your duty and your orders called you from Bedford to Fort Pitt. You must prove that under pretext of a disability (which the results have made to seem slight enough) one can leave a convoy that one is escorting in time of war, and in an enemy country and that without any pretext at all, one can leave his corps, not only without permission but directly contrary to the precise orders of his commander."[28] A vital principle was at stake. After all, many a private had been shot for much less. Officers set the example for their troops. If an officer deserted could his troops be blamed for following? Ecuyer eventually rejoined the 60th, but his jaunt had tarnished a reputation once lifted high by the captain's vigorous defense of Fort Pitt.

With typical ill-logic, Amherst rejected the best means to chop expenses after the war. Many of the smaller posts were expensive to maintain during peace and easily destroyed during war. Why not, Johnson suggested, eliminate them and consolidate British power at a few strategic posts like Detroit, Michilimackinac, Pitt, and Niagara? Amherst admitted that "before the insurrection I had some thoughts of demolishing the small posts but now I am determined not to give up a single post. . . . I see no right the Indians have to make such a demand; but on the contrary, are for their security, as well as ours: Such as have been destroyed in the upper country shall be reestablished, I hope never to be subject to the same fate."[29] And that was the end of it, at least for the general.

By the time Amherst departed America in late 1763, never to return, nearly all knowledgeable British subjects in the colonies thoroughly despised him. Those who understood Indians had warned for years that Amherst's policies would lead to disaster. After the uprising began, ever more civilians and soldiers living on the frontier realized that Amherst was responsible. Traders and settlers, of course, could freely flee. Soldiers who opted out of the fight were called deserters and could be shot or lashed 1,000 times if caught. Officers and civilian employees of His Majesty's government might try to resign subject to the permission of the commander in chief for North America.

Amherst's bluster about exterminating Indians was well-known, but derided by his troops and civilians alike. At Detroit, the merchant James Sterling remarked sarcastically that "the English nation is happy in having a general that despises the Indians, but would be much more so if he had put these out posts in a condition to do the same."[30]

For years Johnson had displayed admirable restraint in bowing as Amherst disdained one sensible idea after another. But the general's inane policies had driven one key man to the breaking point. George Croghan's diplomatic and military efforts, not just in 1763 but over the preceding decades, had exhausted him financially and psychologically. Offended and disgusted by Amherst's policies and their blood-soaked results, the deputy Indian agent had tried hard to avoid any association with them. He had refused to accompany Bouquet's expedition to Fort Pitt. Instead he had journeyed to Johnson Hall to seek a leave of absence from the Indian Superintendent. Although sympathetic, Johnson had denied the request with the claim that Croghan needed Amherst's approval.

So Croghan headed down the Hudson with his request and dispatches from Johnson to Amherst's New York headquarters. On September 26, 1763, he wrote to General Amherst requesting leave to journey to London to petition Parliament for compensation for 16,000 pounds currency he lost in the last war.[31] Croghan then appeared before Amherst shortly after his letter arrived. Amherst coldcocked Croghan's request, arguing that "he would as soon a battalion going home as parting with me."[32] Amherst's "flumery" enraged rather than soothed the tough frontiersman. A "warm dispute" exploded. Amherst "absolutely refused to comply with his request as . . . if his presence ever was of any consequence in the Department he filled, it certainly is so at this present time."[33] Croghan stormed out. The next day he sent Amherst a letter of resignation. Amherst rejected his resignation letter as well, although he admitted the decision was up to Croghan's boss, Sir William Johnson. Croghan returned to Johnson Hall.[34]

Was the season too late to strike a blow against the Indian villages? Certainly not at Detroit where Dalyell's disastrous attempt haunted the garrison and its commander. What about Bouquet at Fort Pitt? Surely he matched Dalyell's zeal but was far more prudent. Bouquet not only rejected any notion of moving against the Ohio Indians, but deemed it impossible even to fulfill the second part of Amherst's orders that he reoccupy Fort Presque Isle. This late in the summer the Allegheny River was too low for bateaux while Indians infested the forested banks. Even his Indian messenger, Andrew, was turned back on that route with Bouquet's letter for any British forces on Lake Erie.[35]

So Bouquet deemed the campaign season over. Leaving a company of the 60th and three companies of the 42nd at Fort Pitt under the command of Captain William Grant, he ordered most of his troops and the released prisoners to withdraw across Pennsylvania. One company of the 42nd was left at Fort Ligonier, another at Bedford, while three would winter at Carlisle. The expedition's unused supplies were stored with each garrison. The provincials were dismissed at Fort Loudoun. Bouquet himself spent the autumn and early winter at Fort Pitt supervising its reconstruction and the buildup of supplies there for the spring campaign. When he completed his work, Bouquet would leave on January 21, 1764 for an inspection of each link in the chain of forts leading back to Philadelphia.[36]

These dispositions conflicted with Amherst's plans. The general intended that the reoccupation of Britain's western empire would rest largely on two regiments. The 42nd would occupy the upper Great Lakes posts while the 60th would guard the string of Pennsylvania posts. To accomplish that, Amherst ordered the scattered detachments of the 60th in the Great Lakes withdrawn to Fort Pitt and replaced them with troops of the 42nd. But the 42nd's companies were scattered at forts across Pennsylvania while the 60th was even more split up with companies there and at Great Lakes posts. Those regiments would not be tangled and reunited any time soon. Amherst designated two regiments to be posted behind those two forward regiments, the 80th Light Infantry and depleted 46th which arrived from Havana in early August. Those reserve regiments would occupy Forts William Augustus, Ontario, and Niagara. Other regiments followed the 46th from Havana, but were even less combat-ready. Disease had reduced them to skeletons of the strength they had sailed away with to the Caribbean the previous years. Any campaign in the new year would have to make do with the regiments already on the frontier. They could expect no more significant reinforcements.[37]

Despite the withdrawals of the regular troops, there was still a chance to strike the Ohio villages. But provincials would have to do the job. In mid-August, as the regulars trudged down the long road from Fort Pitt to their respective winter quarters, reinforcements unexpectedly arrived. On August 19, Colonel Adam Stephens reached Fort Bedford with 98 Virginia volunteers, having along the way "been very successful in Virginia & Maryland in overtaking & routing several gangs of savages, killing & scalping some Indians, and stripping them of much of their booty, scalps, prisoners, & horses."[38]

Bouquet recognized that those hardened frontiersmen might go where regulars could not easily tread. Perhaps more than any other regular officer, he understood the difficulties that regulars faced in a wilderness campaign. He tried to convey that reality to Amherst through several letters. In one he argued that "without a certain number of woodsmen I cannot think it advisable to employ regulars in the woods against savages, as they cannot produce any intelligence and are open to continual surprises. Nor can they pursue at any distance this enemy when they have routed them, and should they have misfortune to be defeated the whole would be destroyed if at above one day's march from a fort."[39]

Alas, snobbery, ignorance, and economy ruled Amherst when it came to provincial troops. Until his last day in America their use remained repugnant to him. He would only reluctantly deploy those already raised and ready to go. Learning of the arrival of Stephens and his men, Amherst wrote asking that they march on to attack the Shawnee villages on the Ohio River. He promised that Captain Lewis Ourry at Bedford and Colonel Bouquet at Fort Pitt would supply all the provisions they needed to accomplish their mission.[40]

This was an extraordinary request. Opportunity prompted Amherst briefly to swallow his false pride. The trouble was that he was sending them on a suicide mission. As tough and skilled as those frontiersmen were, they would be rowing into a hornets' nest if they descended the Ohio River by bateaux to raid those Shawnee villages. Did that matter to Amherst? If he was at all dimly aware of the danger he seems to have thought the provincials expendable.

Nonetheless, Stephens at first enthusiastically agreed. Rejecting the river route as too dangerous, he marched his troops back to Winchester to prepare for an overland expedition. There he laid in supplies and reinforcements. But as the season advanced and passions cooled, the impossibility of that mission became ever more obvious. Not only had Stephens only 94 volunteers and few provisions, but he could get neither Amherst nor the Virginia Assembly to agree to pay for the expedition. Stephens asserted and Bouquet agreed that he would need at least 1,000 troops to successfully advance, attack, and withdraw. Bouquet wrote Amherst explaining that without a decision on funding the campaign would have to be postponed until the spring. Amherst could do nothing. On November 7, Stephens informed Bouquet that "there is no hope of executing your favorite plan this season."[41] On November 19, Bouquet actually received permission from the commander in chief to charge Stephens' expedition to the Crown. But by then the chance was lost, as winter descended along the Appalachian frontier. The delay had most likely prevented a disaster.

The British could not win the war militarily; at best they could only deploy the army to stave off defeat. The war could only be won and the empire regained diplomatically. During the late summer and into the autumn, British officials scored important victories on four widely dispersed diplomatic fronts.

From the first news of the uprising the fear that the northern tribes would destroy all before them and invade the eastern settlements mingled with a related fear—the southern tribes would join the war and stretch British military power to the snapping point. Rumors spread that the Creek and Choctaw were exchanging warbelts. If they scored victories the Cherokee and other southern tribes might join them. The commander-in-chief then would have to divert vital troops, supplies, and money from the northern campaigns and ask all the provincial assemblies to raise forces for the common defense. Extracting troops and taxes from the provincial assemblies was as tedious as pulling teeth.

The man most responsible for preventing that was John Stuart, the Indian Superintendent for the Southern Department. Like his northern counterpart, Stuart followed a two-stage strategy of first ensuring the tribes' neutrality and then eliciting their alliance against the hostile tribes. To those ends he convened dozens of councils with various chiefs and sent his agents throughout the southern tribes with gifts and promises. By December 1763, Stuart could reassure Johnson that for now all was quiet on the southern front.[42]

Stuart had scored a resounding diplomatic victory at the 1763 Augusta Congress. On November 5, 1763, 800 Chicksaw, Choctaw, Cherokee, Creek, and Catawba gathered at Augusta, Georgia, while their chiefs met with governors Thomas Boone of South Carolina, Arthur Dobbs of North Carolina, Francis Fauquier of Virginia, Henry Ellis of Georgia, and Stuart. On November 10, after five days of wrangling, those representatives signed a friendship treaty which settled the Georgia boundary, provided for delineating the frontier along all the southern colonies, and established trade rules to curb abuses by merchants. British promises were further sweetened with the distribution of 5,000 pounds worth of gifts. Stuart's successful diplomacy would enable the commander-in-chief to pursue the northern war without worrying about his southern flank.[43]

Negotiations with Indians were time-consuming and tedious under the best of circumstances. But during a war, with limited gifts to bestow, even the most skilled of diplomats might well have felt like Sisyphus. Yet despite the provocative news of one Indian victory after another throughout the summer, Sir William Johnson had managed to keep five of the six Iroquois tribes from taking the warpath. Only the Seneca had joined the rebellion.

Amherst's belligerence threatened to destroy the delicate peace Johnson had managed to forge with the Iroquois. Despite all contrary evidence, Amherst persisted in his belief that only genocide would quell the rebellion. He ordered Bouquet to treat the enemy as "the vilest race of beings that ever infested the earth, and whose riddance from it must be for the good of mankind."[44] If the Iroquois League learned that the Seneca would suffer "riddance," they might well join their brothers in a fight to the death against the British. Johnson managed to dismiss any such rumors of Amherst's intentions.

Johnson received Indian delegations of varying sizes and powers throughout late summer and the autumn. But the most potentially important council was convened with 320 members of the Iroquois tribes and seven Canadian tribes at Johnson Hall, from September 7 to 10. Of those invited only the Seneca refused to attend. In previous councils that summer Johnson had succeeded in shoring up Iroquois loyalty to Britain. Now the superintendent aimed to carry that professed loyalty one vital step further. Holding aloft a warbelt and tomahawk, he called on the Iroquois to join the British in warring against their enemies.[45]

The reaction varied from muted to hostile. The entire Seneca tribe along with other Iroquois warriors eager for glory had joined the uprising. Joining the British would pit Iroquois against Iroquois. At most the Iroquois would send emissaries to the hostile tribes requesting that they accept peace. The Iroquois could and would do no more.[46]

All along, Johnson got no rest from the continual stream of Indians counciling with him at his home on the Mohawk valley. But, exhausting and stressful as it was, his diplomacy was succeeding. After keeping all of the New York tribes except the Seneca on the fence throughout the summer and fall, he began to entice them down onto the British side during the winter. By December 23, 1763, he could report that the Iroquois had agreed to restrain their Seneca brothers and war against the Shawnee and Delaware in the spring.[47]

As Johnson tried to forge an Indian alliance, Pontiac's fragile coalition at Detroit steadily unraveled. The *Huron* crew's bloody repulse of his attack had further degraded his already diminished prestige. Then, on September 9, 70 St. Joseph Potawatomi, led by Chiefs Washee and Kioqua arrived at Detroit to negotiate a separate peace with Gladwin. Although the major was not authorized to sign an official treaty, he promised them that no harm would come to them if they simply returned to their village and buried their hatchets. Kioqua and 40 Potawatomi did so on September 13; Washee left with the rest on September 19. Pontiac and those Indians still enthusiastic for war dared do nothing to impede the Potawatomi. That same day Ottawa Chief Manitou and most of that band's warriors also deserted Pontiac. Demoralizing as these defections were, the worst blow was yet to come.

It was not until September 24 that an official copy of the Treaty of Paris and its accompanying instructions from Versailles reached the hands of Fort de Chartres' commander, Major Pierre Joseph Neyon de Villiers. Although he had not openly aided the uprising, he had turned a blind eye to the efforts of others who did so. Now it was his humiliating duty to inform all the French and Indian inhabitants of the upper Mississippi valley and Great Lakes that the rumors of France's defeat and surrender of its North American empire were true. On September 27, he issued a proclamation which allowed every inhabitant to choose which crown he would live under. Those who wished to remain east of the Mississippi River would become British subjects, those west of the Mississippi would join the Spanish Empire. If neither of those choices was appealing, the settler could return to France or one of its remaining colonies elsewhere. Villiers dispatched Cadet DeQuindre, accompanied by Jean la Davarette and two Indians to carry word to the Miami, Kickapoo, Mascouten, and finally to Pontiac and the other Detroit Indians that they abandon their struggle and accept peace with Britain.[48]

With the stream of defections from Pontiac the siege of Detroit had all but ended. At best 100 or more warriors remained committed to the uprising in the surrounding villages. But their ammunition and enthusiasm were mostly spent. War parties now rarely hovered about the fort sniping at anyone who exposed himself on the parapet. As autumn colored the forest leaves and days grew cooler and shorter they all worried about how their families would survive the winter without provisions from the fort and enough powder and shot for hunting. Most of those Canadians who had joined the uprising that summer now quietly kept away; fearing British reprisals, many had fled with their families to upper Mississippi valley settlements. Worst of all, smallpox was now spreading misery and death around Detroit. Captain Ecuyer's gift of infected blankets had proved to be even more grimly effective than he had imagined.

The peace delegation of six Mohawk led by subchief Aaron had provided a fig-leaf for those exhausted by the struggle. The Iroquois League may have held a mere shadow of its former power, but still commanded a grudging fear and respect among most other Indians. Five of the six Iroquois tribes had collectively urged their western brothers to bury the hatchet. Aaron reached Detroit on October 7 to reveal how demoralized the hostiles were and just how the Indian conspiracy had unfolded earlier that year.[49]

By early October nearly all the chiefs had appeared under truce flags beneath Detroit's wall to request a council with Gladwin. The major would greet them with the same message—the British Empire was indomitable; the warriors must give up their uprising and await the Indian Superintendent's arrival for a formal peace council and treaty.

Yet a sporadic danger lingered for Detroit's defenders. The restless troops and civilians risked all when they stretched their legs between the fort and surrounding Canadian hamlets and farms. On September 30, two Ottawa killed Sergeant Bertram Fisher as he carried a message to Jacques St. Martin. Then on October 1, Gladwin ordered troops to embark into a bateau to pursue a Canadian in a canoe in mid-river who appeared to be spying on the fort. The troops raced after the suspect who paddled to the river's far shore and disappeared into the woods. When the bateau neared his abandoned canoe two Indians rose and fired. A soldier slumped dead in the bateau. The Indians vanished.

The most serious scrape occurred on October 2. Around 10 o'clock that morning Lieutenant Diedrick Brehm departed with his troops in four bateaux. Their mission was to reconnoitre an island at the mouth of Lake St. Clair to see if wood could be brought off. Four miles from the fort, Indians began to fire from shore. Three times they tried to pursue in a bateau but were driven off by British fire. The British bateaux continued to forge upstrem. At the upper end of Hog Island, nineteen canoes and bateaux filled with Indians appeared on the river. Bullets killed one soldier and wounded three others. Lieutenant Jehu Hay recalled that "they were still pushing on with great bravery, all open to our fire, making a great hallooing; at length Lieutenant Brehm got a good shot at one of them with a four pounder charged with grape, at about forty or fifty yards distance which he so disabled that, out of fifteen or sixteen that were in it, we could not see but two that paddled." Word would later filter back to Detroit that that giant shotgun blast of grape had killed three and wounded seven Chippewa. The Indians swiftly paddled to "shore, some on one side of the river and some on the other, and cried two death halloos. We then rowed up and down in the same part of the river, and called to them to put off again, that we were waiting for them; but they then became very quiet, and did not halloo as in the beginning, and chose rather to fire a few straggling shots from shore than attempt coming off again. Then, finding it was too late to proceed, we returned to the fort."[50] James Sterling was in that fight. He recalled that "we gave a good drubbing to the Indians last Sunday in four of our new row gallies which they attacked with twenty-five canoes, but were beat off with considerable loss. I myself fired above a hundred shot during that engagement which began a little after 12 and lasted till 4 in the afternoon."[51]

The *Huron* arrived with its fourteen troops and 185 barrels of provisions at Detroit on October 3. Until then the hope was that enough troops would arrive to allow an offensive that could crush the rebellion that autumn. That hope now evaporated. The sight of such few reinforcements was disheartening enough to the defenders, but news of the *Michigan*'s destruction and the Devil's Hole disaster was a severe blow to morale. The nearly 500 soldiers and civilians crammed into Fort Detroit turned bitter faces toward a long winter of isolation, short rations, monotony, and fear.

The *Huron* was swiftly unloaded. Detroit's wounded were carried aboard. The *Huron* set sail the next day. The hope was that it could safely reach

Buffalo Creek and return filled with supplies and troops once or perhaps twice more before ice clogged Lake Erie.

By mid-October nearly all the Detroit Indians had had enough. On October 8, 100 Miami arrived to join the siege, but when they learned that the alliance was breaking up half turned and headed for home. On October 11, 12, and 13, Mississauga Chief Wabbicomigot negotiated with Gladwin over peace terms. Chippewa Chief Wasson and three subchiefs along with the Potawatomi joined the talks on October 14. By October 17, Gladwin could report that "the enemy sued for peace in a very submissive manner." He made them no promises but suggested that General Amherst might accept their peace offer if "the hostility ceased and they dispersed to their hunting grounds."[52]

Pontiac was not yet among the peace chiefs. On October 20 he convened a council which he hoped would rekindle the uprising's dying flames. The chiefs who attended did their best to douse whatever embers remained. Within days the Huron, Potawatomi, Chippewa, and almost all of the Ottawa abandoned their villages for their winter hunt. Only Pontiac and 100 followers remained.

The final blow to Pontiac's conspiracy arrived on October 30 with Cadet DeQuindre's delegation that had left Fort de Chartres on September 27. DeQuindre explained to Pontiac that the Indians not only would receive no French help but that they must immediately lay down their arms and accept British rule. He then read Villiers' eloquent, poignant eulogy to New France: "My Dear Children . . . I promised to communicate to you the news . . . Open your ears so that it may penetrate even to the bottom of your hearts. The great day has come at last, whereupon it has pleased the Master of Life to inspire the Great King of the French and him of the English, to make Peace between them, sorry to see the blood of men spilt so long. It is for this reason that they have ordered all their chiefs and warriors to lay down their arms . . . What joy you will have in seeing the French and English smoking with the same pipe and eating out of the same spoon and finally living like brethern. You will see the roads free, the lakes and rivers unstopped. Ammunition and merchandise will abound in your villages. Your women and children will be clothed as well as you. . . . Forget, then, my Dear Children, all the evil talks. May the wind carry off like dust all those which have proceeded out of evil mouths. . . . The French are free even as you. They change the land when the King orders it. He has not given yours; he has only ceded those which he had amongst you in order to avoid war for the future, and that you may always enjoy tranquility and have abundance of merchandise in your villages. . . . Leave off then, my Dear Children, from spilling the blood of your brethern, the English. Our hearts are now but one. You cannot at present strike the one without having the other for your enemy also. If you continue you will have no supplies. . . . I bid you all farewell and recommend you to respect always the French among you.

... I pray the Master of Life to enter into your hearts."[53] The British could not have drafted a better appeal for peace.

That was the final blow. Pontiac finally gave up. On October 31 he dictated to DeQuindre a letter for Major Gladwin which read: "My Brother: The word which my Father has sent me to make peace I have accepted. All my young men have buried their hatchets. I think that you will forget the bad things that have occurred for some time past. Likewise I shall forget what you may have done to me, in order to think of nothing but good. I, the Chippewas, the Hurons, we come to speak with you when you ask us. Give us an answer. I am sending this council to you in order that you may see it. If you are as kind as I, you will make me a reply. I wish you a good day."[54]

DeQuindre hurried to Detroit with that astonishing letter to Gladwin. Pontiac's "Brother" was willing to forgive if not forget: "If I had started this war, I would make peace; but it was you who started it, you must await the wishes of the general thereupon. I am not master but I shall acquaint the general of your present peaceable inclinations, and that you desire to live in peace. Thus if you conduct yourselves well in the future, as soon as the general is convinced of this, I have no doubt that everything will be well. When I shall receive his reply I shall inform you. I wish you good evening."[55]

Were the promises of peace by Pontiac and the other chiefs genuine? That "peace" was really just a truce. No issues were negotiated let alone solved when the chiefs came before Gladwin. They were eager to replenish their ammunition and begin their winter hunt. The cease-fire was a good way to save face when they inevitably would turn their backs on the "siege." The stalemate may have exhausted their patience and most of their ammunition, but the war's causes lingered. If those were not addressed the Indians would be ready to resume war in the spring if they got their hands on more powder and shot.

Gladwin had no illusion that the Indians had agreed to anything more than an armed truce. Yet that truce could be developed into the foundations for a general peace. It all depended on British policies. He sent word of the collapse of the Detroit siege to the Ohio valley Indians with a trusted Huron named Andrew. He then sent letters to the commander in chief calling for more conciliatory policies with the Indians.[56]

Three years on the frontier had rendered Gladwin a hardnosed realist when it came to Indians and British interests in the western empire. He rejected both Amherst's vitriolic bullying and Quaker sentimentality as each a self-defeating basis for policy. The only policy which served British interests was firm, fair dealings with the Indians. Amherst's policies had pushed the Indians into a war that cost the British Empire heavily in blood and treasury.

Throughout October and November the Indians had steadily dispersed from their Detroit villages for their distant winter hunting grounds. By mid-November Pontiac's Ottawa village split into two and both halves fled Detroit for the relative safety of the Maumee River. Pontiac's followers constructed their longhouses and cleared fields eighteen miles from Lake Erie and six miles above the first rapids. His village included 22 or 23 "cabins" of Ottawa and six of Chippewa. The rest erected a village of five or six lodges fifteen miles upriver from Pontiac's band.[57]

At Detroit, the British and Canadians alike revelled in the siege's breakup and news of the Treaty of Paris. Canadians once again were free to trade openly with Detroit's defenders. Gladwin quickly bought up on credit surplus crops from the Canadians. Within days Fort Detroit's warehouses were filled with enough food to last the winter. The truce also gave Gladwin a chance to retaliate against any rebels among the Canadians.

How many Canadians had joined the uprising? Surprisingly few, considering their recent subjection to British rule and the influx of American merchants who ate away their business. By one official count, of the nearly 1,000 Canadians living around Detroit only thirteen aided the Indians by carrying messages or arms. Of these men, two, Jacques Godefroy and Mini Chene, were captured at Detroit. What were the charges? In breaking their loyalty oath to Britain they had committed treason, a capital crime.

This put Major Gladwin in a ticklish spot. Both men were popular Canadian leaders. Executing them would martyrize them and perhaps inspire other Canadians to vengeance. Yet not dealing with the rebels firmly might encourage others into the field. Claiming he lacked the legal authority to try those men, he asked the commander in chief for instructions and powers. He would receive the power to court-martial the accused. Still he hesitated and eventually extradited the two for trial at Fort Niagara. There they were released after pledging to aid the British.[58]

Having conducted a brilliant active defense of Fort Detroit for nearly six months, Gladwin hoped that one of the supply ships would bring papers from Amherst recalling him to a less stressful command. Gladwin was exhausted. To Bouquet he admitted that "I am heartily wearied of my command and I have signified the same to . . . Amherst. I hope I shall be relieved soon. If not I intend to quit the service for I would not choose to be any longer exposed to the villainy and treachery of the settlement and Indians."[59]

Meanwhile, what had become of the promised relief force? It was on its way, with Major John Wilkins in command. In October, Amherst had ordered him to leave skeleton garrisons at the Niagara forts and head west with the remainder to Detroit. Wilkins was an unfortunate choice for such an important and dangerous mission. He had served in North America for eight years ever since he purchased a captain's commission in the 55th regiment on December 30, 1755. There he served until June 23, 1762, when he bought a major's commission with the 60th Royal Americans. Shortly thereafter he was named Fort Niagara's commander. The best that could be said about his career to date was that it was decidedly mediocre. Wilkins tended to procrastinate, especially when Indians were reported lurking in the nearby woods.

With reinforcements sent by Amherst, Wilkins marched with 600 troops across the carrying place from Fort Niagara around the falls. On October 20 his troops embarked at Fort Schlosser and began the hard row up the Niagara River rapids and into Lake Erie. The last two bateaux were passing into the lake when about 80 or 90 Indians rose from the bushes and trees along shore and opened fire. The sudden fusilade killed an officer, a sergeant, and six troops, and wounded two other officers and nine troops. Officers ordered troops on shore to pursue the Indians but they easily escaped. The attack spooked Wilkins who ordered his bateaux to return to Fort Schlosser.[60]

Wilkins was torn between the danger from Indians and the late season, and his duty to relieve Detroit. He finally reembarked his expedition on November 5 for the long row to Detroit. Hoping to make up for lost time, he took a foolish gamble. Rather than hug the Canadian shore he ordered his flotilla to head straight across Lake Erie from one jutting peninsula to the next. The flotilla managed to safely cross the 65-mile stretch from Buffalo Creek to Long Point. There they rested briefly before attempting the 85-mile leg to Pine Point. On November 7, a storm hit them just as they neared land. The torrential rains, winds, and waves consumed 16 bateaux, 71 men, 52 supply barrels, one 6-pounder, and nearly all their ammunition. Thirty boats were saved but they contained only 25 days of rations and five cartridges per soldier. As the survivors huddled shivering and cursing on shore their officers made the only logical decision. Without supplies or more than a handful of rounds each they would have to return to Niagara.[61]

On November 11, two friendly Huron arrived at Fort Detroit with a message from Wilkins hidden in the false bottom of a powderhorn. Wilkins wrote of the disastrous storm and decision to return to Niagara. Detroit could expect no relief before spring. That news may have been a disappointment for Gladwin but was, if anything, a blessing for the garrison. Fort Detroit's dimensions and supplies were too limited to have accommodated Wilkins' expedition. Indeed, given the uprising's collapse, Gladwin reckoned he needed only half of the nearly 500 troops crowding Fort Detroit. Retaining 212 of the best troops, on November 20 he sent off 240 troops in nineteen bateaux commanded by Major Robert Rogers and accompanied by Lieutenant John Montresor with dispatches back to Niagara. The flotilla reached Fort Niagara without incident a week later on November 27.[62]

Now all that remained was enduring the long, dreary winter. For Gladwin a silver lining brightened that prospect. Amherst had promoted him to lieutenant colonel and deputy adjutant general on September 17, 1763. But it would be another year before he could enjoy his new status. He would not leave Detroit until August 31, 1764.

During the winter Gladwin received another message from Fort de Chartres. Villiers assured Gladwin that he remained committed to peace. But he also blamed British traders for slandering the French with false accusations that they incited the Indians to war. As proof he offered Lieutenant Edward Jenkins who was captured at Fort Ouiatenon and ransomed by Villiers. After residing four months at Fort de Chartres, Jenkins was sent down the Mississippi to New Orleans where he would embark on a ship back to the British colonies. Villiers insisted that once Jenkins returned home he would vindicate the French.[63] If Villiers was sincere, the truce might continue through the spring and eventually be codified by treaty.

But the year's bloodshed was not done. Hundreds and perhaps over 2,000 Pennsylvanians had been slaughtered. Hundreds more had been dragged away into captivity in distant villages. Charred farms and hamlets littered the frontier. The survivors lusted for vengeance.

Impotent to strike back against their enemies, some Pennsylvanians would vent their rage on the innocent. There were three Moravian Indian communities in Pennsylvania: Wyalusing near the Wyoming valley and Wequetank and Nain near Lehigh. Each was dedicated to the Moravian beliefs in God, hard work, and pacifism. The Conestoga Indian community was equally peaceful and prosperous though not Moravian. Greedy Pennsylvanians had long coveted the land and wealth of those four communities; the war gave them the opportunity to steal and murder. The excuse would be rumors that those Christians supplied hostile Indians with guns, powder, shelter, and intelligence.

An attempt to massacre the Wequetank Moravian Indians on the night of October 10 literally misfired. A storm soaked the mob's gunpowder. The would-be murderers dispersed to their homes. Learning of their brush with death, the Indians fled with their missionary, Bernard Grube, to Nazareth, another Moravian town. They had been lucky. That luck would not hold.

Pennsylvania's assembly reacted with uncommon swiftness to the reports that plots were afoot to massacre the peaceful Indians in their midst. It was decided that the Moravian Indians would be disarmed and collected under the province's protection. Word was sent to their villages. Those people gathered their valuables and set off for the long walk to Philadelphia. In every town along the way they ran a gauntlet of hatred. At Germantown a mob would have attacked them had a hastily formed armed escort not restrained it. The procession of 140 Moravians reached Philadelphia on November 11. There another mob greeted them with stones and jeers. The Moravians were supposed to be housed in the city's barracks but the soldiers angrily barred their entry. A group of Quakers finally rescued the wretches and took them to Providence Island where they were housed in some decrepit abandoned buildings.

Not all of Pennsylvania's peaceful Indians made it to relative safety. The Conestoga Indians lived in a town of the same name a half dozen miles from Lancaster on the Susquehanna River's east bank. The Conestoga were a shard of the once powerful Susquehanna, who had been all but destroyed by the British and Iroquois in the 1670s. Now only 22 men, women, and children remained and they threatened no one. That made them an easy target.

On December 11, a Conestoga named Bill Soc walked into Lancaster to get his pipe fixed. Abraham Newcomer, the gunsmith, angrily refused to serve him. Harsh words were exchanged and Soc left. True or not, word spread that Soc had threatened Newcomer. That was just what a bully named Matthew Smith in nearby Paxton needed to hear. Smith gathered five like-minded terrorists and rode for Conestoga on the night of December 12. They scouted the sleeping town and then returned to Paxton for reinforcements. The alarm was called. Fifty-seven armed men rallied. The mob reached Conestoga early on December 14. Of the 22 Conestoga, two were not in one of the seven cabins at the time and fourteen, including Bill Soc, escaped into the dark. The "Paxton Boys" brutally murdered and scalped three men, two women, and a child.

When friendly neighbors heard of the massacre they brought the grieving, terrified survivors into protective custody at Sheriff John Hay's jail or work house in Lancaster. Word of the vicious crime reached Philadelphia. On December 19, Governor John Penn asked the assembly to issue a warrant and reward for the murderers' arrest. When the legislators failed to act immediately, Penn issued a proclamation on December 22 explaining the crime and asking the citizens to bring those murderers to justice.

Meanwhile, the "Paxton Boys" resolved to finish the job. On the morning of December 27, a mob numbering around 100 galloped into Lancaster. They surrounded the jail, burst inside, and methodically began murdering the Conestoga in their cells. Sheriff John Hays and assistant Felix Donnelly pleaded with them to stop but to no avail. Within minutes every Conestoga man, woman, and child was dead and scalped.

Penn again asked the assembly to issue a reward for the arrest of the murderers. On January 2, 1764, the assembly did so, authorizing a 200 pounds reward. No one ever claimed it. That same day the assembly also decided that given the swelling hatred against all Indians it could no longer protect the Moravians interned on Providence Island. Perhaps the expense of feeding them had grown too onerous as well. The Assembly voted to send them to Sir William Johnson's care in New York. Two days later, on January 5, a company of the 42nd that was marching to New York, agreed to escort the Indians. Those troops herded the Moravians on a terrifying journey through a guantlet of jeers, threats, and thrown stones all the way to Perth Amboy on the New Jersey coast. There the Indians awaited shipment up the Hudson River. On January 11, an express arrived from New

York Governor Cadwaller Colden. Pennsylvania's Assembly had not bothered to inform him of their decision, let alone seek his permission. Colden forbade the Moravians from touching New York soil. Three companies of the 60th under Captain Schlosser were heading to Philadelphia and would escort the Moravians back. Exhausted and bewildered, they arrived at Philadelpia on January 24.

Fortunately, the Indians would be better protected when they returned than before they left. On December 31, Penn asked his assembly to grant him the military authority to deal with the civil disruptions and wrote to Gage asking for troops. The assembly agreed. Philadelphians organized themselves into six companies of foot, two of horse, and one of artillery. On January 6, 1764, General Thomas Gage sent orders for three companies of the 42nd Highlanders under Captain William Murray at Carlisle and shortly thereafter three companies of the 60th Royal Americans under Captain Schlosser at New York to march to Philadelphia and be placed under Governor Penn's command. Those regular and provincial troops would soon be needed.

Gage was politically astute. To Captain Schlosser of the Royal Artillery Regiment in Philadelphia, he warned that "if you find that the country people shall persist in coming to Philadelphia to murder those Indians, you will be careful that the proper magistrate is present with the troops, to read the riot act, and give the orders to fire. The governor's verbal order to you is not sufficient. I doubt not that you will govern yourself with prudence and take all the precautions which shall be necessary in an affair of this nature. And if matters should come to an extremity, you will take care that it shall appear that any mischief which shall happen has been thro the management & order of the *civil authority*, and that the military are no way concerned, but in obeying the *civil magistrates*, and in supporting them in the execution of the laws."[64] Gage would ever desperately try to adhere to this principle in the next dozen years of worsening unrest which erupted into the American Revolution.

The mass murders committed against innocent Indians by the Paxton Boys the previous December had not satiated their hatreds. On February 5, 100 of them rode on Philadelphia. When they learned that all those troops were mustered against them the mob stopped at Germantown just outside the city. Gage later wrote that had the city been defenseless "much blood would have been spilled in the city; for as soon as the people heared that the Indians were in the barracks under the protection of the King's forces, they halted at a few miles from Philadelphia [and] . . . declared that if they had been only protected by the Legislature of the Province, that they would have put them all to death."[65]

Instead they demanded negotiations. Penn named head a seven man delegation, including Benjamin Franklin, that would negotiate with the terrorist leaders, Matthew Smith and James Gibson. The murderers and their supporters used the tense three day standoff as a chance to grandstand their views. It was finally agreed that the mob would disperse if Smith and Gibson could enter Philadelphia and pen a nine point "Remonstrance" to the government and public.

The remonstrance was completed by February 13 and submitted to Governor Penn, who in turn laid it before the Council the next day and the Assembly two days later. The most serious charge was a double standard whereby the government left the frontier unprotected while protecting Indians who aided the war parties: "the frontiers of this province have been repeatedly attacked and ravaged by skulking parties of Indians who have with the most savage cruelty murdered men, women, and children without distinction, and have reduced near a thousand families to the most extream distress. It grieves us to the very heart to see such of our frontier inhabitants as have escaped savage fury with the loss of their parents, their children, their wives or relatives, left destitute by the public, and exposed to the most cruel poverty and wretchedness while upwards of an hundred and twenty of these savages, who are with great reason suspected of being quilty of these horrid barbarities, under the mask of friendship, have procured themselves to be taken under the protection of the Government."[66] Furthermore the government heaped presents on Indians while refusing to compensate traders whose goods were looted. Even if these charges were true, did they justify murdering the innocent? Smith and Gibson claimed the Conestoga and Moravian Indians provided intelligence and shelter for war parties and thus were spies deserving of death.

More than Indian massacres riled the frontiersmen. Religion and region split Pennsylvania into near warring camps. Smith decried the underrepresentation of frontiersmen in the assembly. The three southeastern counties, Philadelphia, Bucks, and Chester, had 26 representatives and were predominantly Quaker, while the five frontier counties, Lancaster, Northhampton, York, Cumberland, and Berks, had only ten and were largely Presbyterian. In all, 22 of the 39 assemblymen were Quakers who voted as one. A related problem was the growing debt of frontier settlers to Philadelphia creditors. In short, frontier Pennsylvania was the exploited, neglected colony of Philadelphia and the surrounding counties.

The governor and assembly ignored all the demands but one. On July 7, 1764, Governor Penn would issue a proclamation which promised a bounty for every Indian scalp delivered. The glee of the frontiersmen at this news can be imagined.

Although the massacres of peaceful, Christian Indians cheered many frontier settlers, the butchery shocked and disgusted most Americans. Indian agent Thomas McKee reported that most people "condemned this as a most detestable murder, and not only contrary to the laws of government but Christianity and everything that ought to distinquish us from savages."[67]

To help sway public opinion against the murderers, Benjamin Franklin wrote his brilliant short work, "A Narrative of the Massacres." He systematically rooted his arguments in reason and psychology to discredit thoroughly the criminals and their excuses. He exposed the mob as cowardly hypocrites who claimed to be Christians and patriots but whose crimes vilely betrayed both their religion and country. He demolished their justification that they acted on "nothing less than the Word of God" by contrasting their pretended Christian piety with "heathens" of other faiths who acted on the belief to "turn the other cheek" and "thou shall not kill." He revealed them to be anarchists "who despise Government." Who could rationally dispute Franklin's logic that "If an Indian injures me, does it follow that I may revenge that injury on all Indians?" Finally he denounced the Paxton Boys as "unmanly men! who are not ashamed to come with weapons against the unarmed, to use the sword against women, and the bayonet against children" but tremble at the thought of marching against the hostile Indians. He ended his pamphlet with the words: "Mercy Still Sways the Brave."[68] Those sentiments were praiseworthy and impeccably argued. But they could not bring back the butchered.

All along William Johnson's diplomacy extended not just to the Indians but to British officials as well. He had to forge among all Indians and British a sense of common interests and policies to uphold those interests. No group was more important to convince than the ministers at Whitehall. After the uprising began, he sent one masterly report after another across the Atlantic analyzing the distribution of power among the Indians, the reasons for the revolt, and how a peace favorable to both sides could be forged.

The Indians had revolted because of a fatal mix of British arrogance, stingyness, exploitation, and weakness. British military and civilian leaders had deluded themselves into believing that the Indians "were an enemy of very little power or consequence & not worth our attention occassioned their being treated throughout the country with a neglect which never fails being resented by them."[69]

That was an extremely deadly mistake. The result was a war that had devastated the frontiers, thousands of lives, and vast wealth. Indians could not be defeated militarily because they "are no wise inferior to us in sagacity and strategem . . . their ideas of courage are different from ours . . . as they attack by surprise, and on failure of success . . . are able to repeat their attacks at the next advantageous place they meet with, killing many of our people in each encounter with a very small loss on their side."[70] Johnson believed the "northern Indians to be the most formidable of any . . . uncivilized people in the world. Hunting and war are their sole occupations, and the one qualifies them for the other, they have few wants, and those are easily supplied, their properties of little value, consequently expeditions against them however successful, cannot distress them."[71]

What then must be done? Although the Indians cannot be decisively defeated on the battlefield, powerful armies marching into their heartlands accompanied by envoys who promised a strict boundary, trade regulations, and respect in return for prisoners and peace could end the war. After that British wealth and security could only be served by genuinely stamping out abuses by greedy traders, expelling squatters, donating generous gifts, and treating the Indians with respect.

Whitehall's ministers carefully pondered Johnson's words. Then, within a week they sent him two replies that could not have pleased him more. On September 29, 1763, the four members of the Board of Trade signed a letter in which "we do entirely agree with you in opinion as to the cause of this unhappy defection of the Indians and are convinced that nothing but the speedy establishment of some . . . general for the regulation of our commercial and political concerns with them can effectually reconcile their esteem and affections. His Majesty's Ministers are entirely of the same opinion, and we have accordingly received His Majesty's commands to consider such a plan."[72]

The first step in that plan was sent a week later to Johnson and other colonial leaders a week later. On October 7, 1763, King George III officially proclaimed that henceforth the Appalachian Mountain watershed would divide British and Indians. Settlers were forbidden to clear land west of that divide; the provincial governments would remove any of their settlers already there. Only the provincial governments could purchase Indian lands in the king's name. Trade with the Indians was free to all; traders, however, could venture there only with a provincial government license after posting a bond which would be forfeited if the trader violated any regulations. The Indian Superintendents and their agents would work with the commander in chief and his troops in regulating the trade, enforcing all laws, and trying all offenders. The proclamation also converted Canada and East and West Florida to civilian rule. Each governor, Indian Superintendent, and colonel had the proclamation printed and posted.[73]

Johnson was ecstatic when he received a copy of the proclamation in December. The new policy was all that he had been requesting since 1760. The key to peace was separating Indians and settlers. The 1763 Proclamation gave him the authority to do that. In subsequent Indian councils he would make "the best use in my power of his Majesty's Proclamation for convincing the Indians here of his gracious & favorable disposition to do them justice & shall communicate the same to all the rest."[74] Implementation would depend on the commander in chief's approval.

Such decisions were no longer Sir Jeffrey Amherst's to make. While virtually all of His Majesty's troops in North America were deployed on the western frontier, their commander prepared to head the other way. On August 13, Lord Egremont wrote Amherst that King George III had granted his long-standing request for leave to England. Major General Thomas Gage would temporarily replace him. The king also expressed his appreciation for Amherst's long, meritorious service in America and confidence that the Indian uprising would be swiftly crushed. He ended, however, with the broad hint that, given Amherst's "well known zeal," the king would understand if the continued Indian uprising "make your presence in America essential . . . and your remaining there some little time longer necessary to keep the people quiet" His Majesty would certainly understand if Amherst did not immediately return home.[75]

Amherst ignored that last caveat when he joyfully received the news on October 7. Before he could pack he had to tie up a few loose ends, like the strategy for 1764. He wrote Johnson and Bradstreet to meet him at Albany. Setting out on October 17, Amherst arrived at Albany five days later. On October 22, he met with Bradstreet to brief him on the spring campaign. Johnson was delayed by a council and only arrived on October 24. After three days of conference, Amherst set sail down the Hudson River and reached New York on October 27. Now he had only to await his successor.[76]

On October 20, 1763, Brigadier General Thomas Gage received orders to immediately replace Amherst. Within days Gage had wrapped up his affairs at Montreal and embarked on the Lake Champlain route to New York. He arrived at Amherst's headquarters in New York City on November 16. The following morning Amherst briefed Gage on the next year's strategy. He embarked that evening on the HMS *Weasel*, a not inappropriate name for its most "illustrious" passenger. The *Weasel* set sail shortly after midnight on November 18.[77]

The general was eager to get away as soon as possible, a hope reciprocated by most of his officers and troops. When Captain Simeon Ecuyer heard that Amherst had been relieved, he wrote Colonel Bouquet that: "There are some revolutions sooner than one dared hope. I confess that the American army is very agreeably surprised; the Great Babylon has fallen. . . . What universal cries of joy and what bumpers of madeira are drunk to his prompt departure."[78] Just what official or private sins Amherst committed to deserve the sobriquette "the Great Babylon" is unclear. But he was surely despised by nearly all soldiers and civilians alike. Another officer, Lieutenant Thomas Basset, revealed that "we are told that Sir Jeffrey is ordered home, and a violent clamour is already begun against him as well among the civil as military part of the world."[79]

Genial, patient, and tactful Thomas Gage was a breath of fresh wind after Jeffrey Amherst's taciturn arrogance and blundering. Yet Gage faced an enormous challenge. A friend, William Smith of New York, warned Gage of what lay ahead: "Is not Mr. Amherst the happiest of men to get out of this trouble so seasonably? . . . Is not Gage to be pitied? The war will be a tedious one, nor it be glorious even though attended by success. Instead of decisive battles, woodland skirmishes, instead of colors and cannon, our trophies will be stinking scalps. Heaven preserve you my friend from a war conducted by a spirit of murder rather than a brave and generous offense."[80]

NOTES

1. Henry Gladwin to Wasson, August 16, 1763, Bouquet collection, Library of Congress, Washington, D.C., microfilm, A-1065.

2. Henry Gladwin to William Johnson, October 7, 1763, in James Sullivan and A. C. Flick, eds., *The Papers of William Johnson* (hereafter cited as *Johnson Papers*), 14 vols. (Albany: State University of New York, 1921–1965), 10:873.

3. Jean Baptiste De Couagne to William Johnson, September 8, 1763, *Johnson Papers*, 10:812; Collin Andrew to William Johnson, September 9, 1763, ibid., 10:812–13; Gavin Cochrance to William Johnson, November 5, 1763, ibid., 10:918–19; Court of Inquiry, September 1, 1763, in Sylvester K. Stevens, Donald H. Kent, Autumn L. Leonard, Louis M. Waddell, and John Totteham, eds., *The Papers of Henry Bouquet* (hereafter cited as *Bouquet Papers*), 6 vols. (Harrisburg: Pennsylvania Historical and Museum Commission, 1972–1994), 6:386; Jeffrey Amherst to Henry Bouquet, September 25, 1763, ibid., 6:397–99.

4. James Sterling to John Duncan & Co., September 8, 1763, Sterling letter-book, 112, William L. Clements Library, Ann Arbor, Mich. (hereafter cited as CL). For other accounts, see John Stoughton, September 16, 1763, *Johnson Papers*, 10:814; Alexander Duncan to William Johnson, October 1, 1763, ibid., 10:863–65; Henry Gladwin to William Johnson, October 7, 1763, ibid., 10:873; Franklin B. Hough, ed., *Lieutenant Jehu Hay, Diary of the Siege of Detroit in the War with Pontiac* (Albany, N.Y.: J. Munsell, 1860).

5. Jeffrey Amherst to McEllis, September 17, 1763, Bouquet collection, microfilm, A-1065. Jeffrey Amherst to Henry Gladwin, September 17, 1763, Bouquet collection, microfilm, A-1065. See also Charles Moore, ed., *Gladwin Manuscripts* (Lansing, Mich.: Robert Smith, 1897), 675.

6. John Clarence Webster, ed., *The Journal of Jeffrey Amherst: Recording the Military Career of General Amherst in America from 1758 to 1763* (Chicago: Ryerson Press, 1931), 322. For accounts of the massacre, see Jean Baptiste de Couagne to William Johnson, September 16, 1763, *Johnson Papers*, 10:815; William Browning to William Johnson, September 17, 1763, ibid., 10:816; George Etherington to William Johnson, September 17, 1763, ibid., 10:817–18; William Johnson to Jeffrey Amherst, October 6, 1763, ibid., 10:866–69; Journal of Indian Affairs, October 4–17, 1763, ibid., 10:892–94. For a discussion of different casualty accounts and good argument for the highest figures, see Alan Eckert, *The Conquerors: A Narrative* (1970) (reprint, New York: Bantam, 1981), 793.

7. Jean Baptiste de Couagne, November 11, 1763, *Johnson Papers*, 10:21–22.

8. Henry Bouquet to Jeffrey Amherst, September 7, 1763, *Bouquet Papers*, 6:85.

9. Simeon Ecuyer to Henry Bouquet, November 13, 1763, *Bouquet Papers*, 6:459–60.

10. William Browning to William Johnson, October 22, 1763, *Johnson Papers*, 10:906; John Blair to Cadwallader Colden, October 22, 1763, ibid., 10:908–9; William Johnson to Thomas Gage, December 5, 1763, ibid., 10:942–43.

11. Lord Halifax to Jeffrey Amherst, October 18, 1763, E. B. O'Callaghan and Berthold Fernow, eds., *Documents Relative to the Colonial History of the State of New*

York (hereafter cited as NYCD), 15 vols. (Albany, N.Y.: Weed, Parsons, and Co., 1856–1887); Jeffrey Amherst to James Hamilton, November 5, 1763, in *Minutes of the Provincial Council of Pennsylvania* (hereafter cited as MPCP) (1852) (reprint, New York: AMS Press, 1968), 9:74–75.

12. Cadwallader Colden to Lord Halifax, December 8, 1763, NYCD 7:586–87.

13. Jeffrey Amherst to James Hamilton, June 12, 25, 1763, MPCP 9:34, 34–35; James Hamilton to Council, June 20, 23, 1763, ibid., 9:30, 31; James Hamilton to Assembly, July 5, 1763, ibid, 9:31–33; Henry Bouquet to James Hamilton, July 6, 1763, ibid., 9:35; Assembly Resolution for 700 Men at Harvest, July 7, 1763, ibid., 9:36; Council, July 8, 1763, ibid., 9:6–37; Assembly Bill for Carriages for King's Service and Pay for Provincial Troops, July 8, 1763, ibid., 9:37.

14. James Hamilton to Assembly, September 12, 20, 29, 1763, MPCP 9:2–43, 52, 56–57.

15. Jeffrey Amherst to James Hamilton, October 16, 1763, MPCP 9:62.

16. Council, October 22, 1763, MPCP 9:63; Assembly to Hamilton, October 22, 1763, ibid., 9:64–66; John Penn Proclamation, November 1, 1763, ibid., 9:72–73.

17. Memorandum Concerning Indians, November 10, 1763, *Johnson Papers*, 4: 35–36.

18. Jeffrey Amherst to William Johnson, September 9, 1763, NYCD 7:547, 546–48.

19. Jeffrey Amherst to William Johnson, September 30, 1763, *Johnson Papers*, 10: 857, 856–59.

20. William Johnson to Jeffrey Amherst, October 13, 1763, *Johnson Papers*, 10: 880, 876–82.

21. Jeffrey Amherst to Henry Bouquet, August 7, 1763, *Bouquet Papers*, 6:346–49; List of New Officers, Instructions to Reduce the 42nd, New Establishment of the 42nd, August 1763, ibid., 6:352–57; List of Royal American Officers, August 1763, ibid., 6:57–59; Jeffrey Amherst to Henry Bouquet, September 7, 1763, *Bouquet Papers*, 6:387–89; State of 1st Battalion of 60th, September 30, 1763, ibid., 6: 415.

22. Jeffrey Amherst Order for Stoppages, September 22, 1763, *Bouquet Papers*, 6:399–400; Jeffrey Amherst Revised Stoppage Order, October 11, 1763, ibid., 6: 432.

23. Henry Bouquet to Jeffrey Amherst, October 24, 1763, *Bouquet Papers*, 6: 438, 436–39.

24. Simeon Ecuyer to Henry Bouquet, November 13, 1763, *Bouquet Papers*, 6: 460, 459–60.

25. Archibald Blane to Henry Bouquet, August 18, 1763, *Bouquet Papers*, 6:365, 365–66.

26. Simeon Ecuyer to Henry Bouquet, November 7, 1763, *Bouquet Papers*, 6: 460, 459–60.

27. Simeon Ecuyer to Henry Bouquet, November 20, 1763, *Bouquet Papers*, 6: 464, 462–66.

28. Henry Bouquet to Simeon Ecuyer, February 21, 1764, *Bouquet Papers*, 6: 497, 496–97.

29. Jeffrey Amherst to William Johnson, September 10, 1763, *Johnson Papers*, 4: 202, 201–2.

30. James Sterling to John Duncan & Co., August 7, 1763, Sterling letterbook, 111, CL.

31. George Croghan to Jeffrey Amherst, September 26, 1763, *Johnson Papers*, 10: 823–25.

32. George Croghan to William Johnson, September 28, 1763, *Johnson Papers*, 10:825–27.

33. Jeffrey Amherst to Henry Bouquet, September 25, 1763, *Bouquet Papers*, 6: 398. Either Croghan or Amherst got their dates wrong.

34. Jeffrey Amherst to William Johnson, September 30, 1763, *Johnson Papers*, 10: 858–59; George Croghan to Henry Bouquet, October 11, 1763, *Bouquet Papers*, 6: 430–31.

35. Henry Bouquet to Allan Campbell, August 12, 26, 1763, *Bouquet Papers*, 6: 363–64, 368–69; Henry Bouquet to Officer Commanding at Presqu'Isle, August 28, 1763, ibid., 6:375; see Jeffrey Amherst to Henry Bouquet, July 7, 1763, ibid., 6: 299–301.

36. Thomas Gage to Henry Bouquet, November 18, 1763, *Bouquet Papers*, 6: 460–62; Henry Bouquet to Jeffrey Amherst, December 1, 1763, ibid., 6:472–73; Henry Bouquet to Thomas Gage, February 4, 1764, ibid., 6:494–95.

37. Jeffrey Amherst to Henry Bouquet, August 7, 1763, *Bouquet Papers*, 6:350–52; Jeffrey Amherst to William Johnson, August 14, 1763, *Johnson Papers*, 4:186–89.

38. Lewis Ourry to Henry Bouquet, August 27, 1763, *Bouquet Papers*, 6:372, 371–74.

39. Henry Bouquet to Jeffrey Amherst, October 24, 1763, *Bouquet Papers*, 6: 437, 436–39.

40. Jeffrey Amherst to William Johnson, September 10, 1763, *Johnson Papers*, 4: 201–2; William Johnson to Cadwallader Colden, November 4, 1763, ibid., 4:229–32.

41. Adam Stephens to Henry Bouquet, November 5, 1763, *Bouquet Papers*, 6: 451, 451–52; Jeffrey Amherst to Adam Stephens, August 31, 1763, ibid., 6:380–81; Henry Bouquet to Adam Stephens, September 30, 1763, ibid., 6:421–22; Adam Stephens to Henry Bouquet, October 10, 1763, ibid., 6:427–29; Henry Bouquet to Adam Stephens, October 23, 1763, ibid., 6:434–36; Henry Bouquet to Jeffrey Amherst, October 23, 1763, ibid., 6:436–39.

42. John Stuart to William Johnson, December 10, 1763, *Johnson Papers*, 10:950–52.

43. John Richard Alden, *John Stuart and the Southern Colonial Frontier: A Study of Indian Relations, War, Trade, and Land Problems in the Southern Wilderness, 1754–1775* (1944) (reprint, New York: Gordian Press, 1966), 181–86; David H. Corkran, *The Creek Frontier, 1540–1783* (Norman: University of Oklahoma Press, 1967), 237–39.

44. Quoted in Howard Peckham, *Pontiac and the Indian Uprising* (Princeton, N.J.: Princeton University Press, 1947), 172.

45. Proceedings of Johnson with Indians, September 7–10, 1763, NYCD 7:558–59.

46. Journal of Indian Affairs, August 5–15, 1763, *Johnson Papers*, 10:794–802; Journal of Indians Congress, September 1, 1763, *Johnson Papers*, 10:828–55.

47. William Johnson to Thomas Gage, December 23, 1763, *Johnson Papers*, 10:

973–76. See also Journal of Indian Affairs, October 4–17, 1763, ibid., 10:891–900; Indian Congress, October 20, 1763, ibid., 10:900–906; Indian Conference, November 7–24, 1763, ibid., 10:930–33; Journal of Indian Congress, December 2–5, 1763, ibid., 10:945–49; Journal of Indian Congress, December 5–22, 1763, ibid., 10:957–72.

48. Villiers Instruction to Indian Nations, September 27, 1763, *Johnson Papers*, 10:819–21; Villiers to Inhabitants of Fort de Chartres, September 27, 1763, ibid., 10:821–22; Villiers to Inhabitants to Detroit, ibid., 10:822–23.

49. Robert Rogers to William Johnson, October 7, 1763, *Johnson Papers*, 10:870–72.

50. Hough, *Hay Diary*.

51. James Sterling to John Duncan, October 6, 1763, Sterling letterbook, 115, CL.

52. Henry Gladwin to Jeffrey Amherst, November 1, 1763, Michigan Pioneer and Historical Society 27:675–77; William Edgar to William Johnson, November 1, 1763, *Johnson Papers*, 10:914–15.

53. Instruction of Villiers to Indian Nations, September 27, 1763, *Johnson Papers*, 10:819–20.

54. Pontiac to Henry Gladwin and Reply, November 1, 1763, *Bouquet Papers*, 6: 449, 448–49.

55. Ibid.

56. Henry Gladwin to Jeffrey Amherst, November 1, 1763, *Bouquet Papers*, 6: 446–47; Thomas Gage to William Johnson, December 26, 1763, *Johnson Papers*, 4: 278–80.

57. The source uses leagues which I've converted to miles at that era's ratio of roughly three miles to one league. Indian Intelligence, Detroit, June 4, 1764, *Johnson Papers*, 11:218–29.

58. Thomas Gage to Lord Halifax, January 7, 1764, in Clarence Edwin Carter, ed., *The Correspondance of General Thomas Gage with the Secretaries of State, 1763–1775* (hereafter cited as *Gage Correspondance*), 2 vols. (1931–1933) (reprint, Hamden, Conn.: Archon Books, 1969), 1:9–11.

59. Henry Gladwin to Henry Bouquet, November 1, 1763, *Bouquet Papers*, 6: 445, 445–46.

60. William Browning to William Johnson, October 22, 1763, *Johnson Papers*, 10: 906–7; Gavin Cochrane to William Johnson, November 5, 1763, ibid., 10:918–19.

61. Thomas Gage to Lord Halifax, December 23, 1763, Gage papers, 1:4–7, CL; Jean Baptiste de Couagne to William Johnson, November 27, 1763, *Johnson Papers*, 10:936–37.

62. Thomas Gage to Henry Bouquet, December 22, 1763, *Bouquet Papers*, 6: 481–82.

63. Villiers de Neyon to Henry Gladwin, December 24, 1763, *Bouquet Papers*, 6: 483–86.

64. Thomas Gage to Captain Schlosser, February 6, 1764, Gage papers, CL. For a good overview and documents of the unfolding tragedy, see Wilbur R. Jacobs, *The Paxton Riots and the Frontier Theory* (Chicago: Rand McNally, 1967). For Gage's efforts, see Thomas Gage to John Penn, January 6, 1764, Gage papers, CL; John Penn to Thomas Gage, January 10, 1764, ibid.; Thomas Gage to Captain Robertson, January 10, 1764, ibid.; John Penn to Thomas Gage, January 12, 1764, ibid.; Cap-

tain Schlosser to Thomas Gage, February 9, 1764, ibid.; John Penn to Thomas Gage, February 9, 17, 1764, ibid.; Edward Shippen to John Penn, December 14, 27, 1763, MPCP 9:89–90, 100; Thomas Gage to John Penn, December 12, 31, 1763, January 6, 1764, ibid., 9:90, 104–5, 118; John Penn to Assembly, December 19, 1763, ibid., 9:92–93; Governor's Council, December 21, 1763, ibid., 9:93–94; John Penn to Assembly, December 21, 1763, January 16, February 4, 1764, ibid., 9:94–95, 122–23, 133–34; Governor's Council, December 29, 31, 1763, January 3, 23, 28, February 4, 1764, ibid., 9:100–101, 108–9, 123, 125–27, 132–33; John Hay to John Penn, December 27, 1763, ibid., 9:102–3; John Penn to William Johnson, January 5, 1764, ibid., 9:111–12; Thomas Gage to Captain William Murray of 42nd, January 6, 1764, ibid., 9:118–19; Assembly to John Penn, January 23, 1764, ibid., 9:123–25; William Johnson to John Penn, February 17, 1763, ibid., 9:137–38; Remonstrance by Matthew Smith and James Gibson to John Penn, February 13, 1764, ibid., 9:138–42; Assembly committee reponse to remonstrance, February 17, 1764, 9:142–45; Governors Council, February 18, 20, 1764, ibid., 9:146, 146–48.

65. Thomas Gage to Lord Halifax, January 7, 1764, Gage papers, 7–9, CL; Thomas Gage to Lord Halifax, May 12, 1764, ibid., 1:26.

66. To the Honorable John Penn . . . by Matthew Smith and James Gibson, February 13, 1764, MPCP, 138–42.

67. Thomas McKee to William Johnson, February 15, 1764, *Johnson Papers*, 11:56, 55–57.

68. Benjamin Franklin, "A Narrative of the Late Massacres in Lancaster County of a Number of Indians, Friends of this Province, by Persons Unknown, with Some Observations on the Same," in Leonard W. Labaree, ed., *The Papers of Benjamin Franklin* (New Haven, Conn.: Yale University Press, 1967), 11:47–69.

69. William Johnson to Lords of Trade, July 1, 1763, NYCD 7:526, 525–27.

70. William Johnson to Lords of Trade, September 25, 1763, NYCD 7:559–62.

71. William Johnson to Lords of Trade, November 13, 1763, NYCD 7:574, 572–81.

72. Lords of Trade to William Johnson, September 29, 1763, NYCD 7:567.

73. King's Proclamation, October 7, 1763, *Johnson Papers*, 10:977–85.

74. William Johnson to Thomas Gage, December 23, 1763, *Johnson Papers*, 10:973.

75. Lord Egremont to Jeffrey Amherst, August 13, 1763, NYCD 7:538–41.

76. Webster, *Amherst Journal*, 324–25.

77. Jeffrey Amherst to Thomas Gage, November 17, 1763, *Gage Correspondance*, 2:209–14; Thomas Gage to Lord Egremont, October 22, November 17, 1763, *Gage Correspondance*, 1:1, 1:1–2.

78. Simeon Ecuyer to Henry Bouquet, November 20, 1763, *Bouquet Papers*, 6:464, 462–66.

79. Thomas Basset to Henry Bouquet, December 10, 1763, *Bouquet Papers*, 6:478, 477–78.

80. William Smith to Thomas Gage, November 23, 1763. Quoted in John Richard Alden, *General Gage in America: Being Principally a History of His Role in the American Revolution* (Baton Rouge: Louisiana State University Press, 1948), 89–90.

6

Subjection

"To Be a Vassal to His Low Commanders"

What universal cries of joy and what bumpers of Madiera are drunk to his prompt departure.
—Captain Simeon Ecuyer on Sir Jeffrey Amherst's return to England

Is not Gage to be pitied? The war will be a tedious one, even though attended with success. Instead of decisive battles, woodland skirmishes; instead of colors and cannon, our trophies will be stinking scalps. Heaven preserve you, my friend, from a war conducted in a spirit of murder.
—William Smith to Thomas Gage

They would rather die with their tomahawks in their hands than live in slavery. . . . Be persuaded that we will not finish the war with the English whilst there remains one of us red men.
—Pontiac to Pierre Joseph Neyon de Villiers

Who was this new commander who so deserved to be "pitied"?[1] Although his exact birth date is unknown, Thomas Gage was about 44 when he replaced Amherst. He would remain His Majesty's Commander in Chief for North America from 1763 until 1775. The man who commanded British forces during that twelve years of worsening strife, which exploded with the Battle of Lexington and Concord, not only genuinely liked Americans and life in the New World but married Margaret Kemble, a beautiful young woman from New Jersey.

His recall for failure to crush the revolution in 1775 would be an unfortunate end to a proficient though hardly illustrious military career. His father may have bought him an ensign's commission as early as 1736 but definitely obtained for his son a lieutenancy in the First North Hampton regiment in January 1741. In May 1742, Gage transferred to Battereau's Foot and there rose to the rank of captain in January 1743. He saw no action until after Britain joined the War of Austrian Succession in 1744 and his regiment was sent to Flanders. Gage's efficiency and connections caused him to be named the second Duke of Abemarle's aide shortly before participating in the battle of Fontenoy. In 1745 he journied with Albemarle and much of the army to Scotland to help crush the revolt led by Bonnie Prince Charles, the Stuart claimant to the British throne, at the battle of Culloden. After a year's posting in Britain, Gage returned with Albemarle to Flanders for the campaigns of 1747 and 1748. During that last year of the war Gage became a major in the 55th which was soon renamed the 44th. On March 2, 1751, he was promoted to lieutenant colonel. From 1748 to 1755 the 44th was posted in Ireland.

When war with France broke out in America in 1754, the 44th was sent to Virginia along with the 48th in an expedition commanded by General Edward Braddock. Braddock would lead one of four campaigns against France's North American empire that year. The objective was Fort Duquesne at the forks of the Ohio River. Gage led the army's advance guard and was in the thick of the fighting when the Indians and French ambushed and nearly destroyed the column just nine miles from Fort Duquesne on July 9, 1755. Gage was slightly wounded when a bullet grazed his belly, and assumed command of the 44th when its colonel, Peter Halkett, was killed. The 44th would not not see action under his leadership. In 1757 he submitted to General John Campbell, the Earl of Loudoun, a proposal to found a light infantry regiment. Loudoun permitted Gage to form the 80th Light Infantry, the first such regiment in the British army. The 80th first saw action at the Battle of Fort Carillon on July 9, 1758, when Gage was slightly wounded and the British army lost nearly 2,000 killed and wounded in a suicidal assault. In 1759, Gage joined the staff of the new commander in chief, General Jeffrey Amherst, who dispatched him to lead British forces on Lake Ontario after Sir William Johnson took Fort Niagara. Gage's mission was to capture Fort La Galette on the upper St. Lawrence River and then descend to Montreal. After arriving at Oswego, Gage called off the campaign because of the late season, despite the arguments of Amherst, Johnson, and others who argued that plenty of time remained to at least capture La Galette. Gage's decision caused relations to cool briefly between him and Amherst. But Amherst recalled Gage to his staff for the next year's campaign which took Fort Presentation and finally Montreal on September 8, 1760. Amherst rewarded Gage's efforts by naming him governor of Montreal and its surrounding region in October 1760.

During his three years at Montreal, Gage was popular as an efficient, prudent, and honest administrator, and a genial and courteous man. He was promoted to major general in 1761. In 1762, he gained the colonelcy of the 22nd regiment as a fall back position should the army cut back its positions for generals. During 1763 he could only view the ever-worsening reports of Indian victories with increasing alarm. When he was named commander in chief, eight years of difficult experiences in North America had prepared him for that duty.

Yet Gage was certainly not above criticism. In his eagerness to please he was reluctant to make unpopular or unambiguous decisions. Captain Lewis Ourry described the frustration of prying a decision from the commander in chief: "he is so wavering that I can get no positive answer from him . . . on anything I ask him. And I find it is his way with everybody." Ourry did attribute Gage's indecisiveness in part to "his being unacquainted with the method of the services being carried on in our department, different from all others, owing to circumstances that none but those who have had the misfortune to serve in it, can have a just idea of."[2] This was an indirect jab at the ineptness of Gage's predecessor, Amherst.

Gage was supposed to serve as commander in chief for His Majesty's North American forces only until Amherst returned. But, safely back in England, Amherst confessed he had thoroughly wearied of North America and had no desire to see it ever again. The government accommodated Amherst's desire. On November 16, 1764, George III would officially commission Gage to replace Amherst as North American commander. Gage was allowed to retain his honorary and lucrative posts as the 60th Royal Americans' colonel and Virginia's governor.

Amherst left the bare bones of a strategy in Gage's hands. Over the next year, Gage, Johnson, Bouquet, and Bradstreet would give it flesh and blood. The strategy would be continually debated, decided, and then altered. But its essence remained unchanged.

Forts Pitt and Niagara would be the staging grounds for twin offensives against the Indians. The first objective was the cluster of Shawnee, Delaware, and Mingo villages in the Muskingum and Scioto valleys. That stronghold would be crushed by Colonel John Bradstreet's expedition from Fort Niagara and Colonel Henry Bouquet's from Fort Pitt. Gage envisioned "that the two attacks . . . could be made nearly at the same time; they would be of mutual assistance to each other & serve the more to terrify and throw the barbarians into greater confusion."[3] All along Gage encouraged Bradstreet and Bouquet to coordinate their campaigns. After assisting Bouquet in Ohio, Bradstreet then would head back to Lake Erie to subdue the rebellious villages on its shore, relieve Detroit, and then move against the Indians of the upper Great Lakes. That strategy would demand the mustering of 5,000 troops, to be evenly split between Bradstreet and Bouquet.[4]

The 1764 strategy did not take a military genius to devise. Given the disposition of Britain's forces and those of the enemy, it was really the only sensible way to try crushing the rebellion. And it was not even Amherst's idea. Bouquet had proposed it to the commander in chief shortly after the

Battle of Bushy Run. Amherst embraced the idea, then left it to Gage to realize.

Yet the strategy was deeply flawed in several important ways. For one, the campaign's command structure was curious, to say the least. Rather than directly command both field leaders, Gage subordinated Bradstreet to Bouquet. Given the distance between the expeditions, this would have been a highly questionable arrangement under any circumstances, especially since hundreds of miles of wilderness filled with hostile Indians separated them. Couriers would not only have to dodge war parties but somehow find and catch up to the other expedition. Adding to the awkwardness, Bradstreet's expedition would begin two months before Bouquet's.

Was it possible for those armies to reach let alone link up on the Scioto plains? Bouquet, for one, was highly skeptical. He warned Gage that Bradstreet "will find it very difficult if not impracticable to penetrate as far as the Indian towns upon the Scioto, the distance being not less than 90 miles" from Lake Erie.[5] Without horses all supplies would have to be carried. Given the distance and time those troops would probably not be able to carry enough to supply themselves. Bouquet argued instead that Bradstreet send a portion of his army via Presque Isle over the 20-mile portage to the Allegheny River and then down it to Fort Pitt; Bradstreet's main force would then row on to attack Sandusky and thus draw off Indians from the Scioto plains as Bouquet pushed forward.

In his reply, Gage not only rejected the idea of Bradstreet sending Bouquet reinforcements from Presque Isle, he also ignored the earlier plan of Bradstreet advancing from Lake Erie to attack the villages on the Scioto plains. Gage instead emphasized the importance of Bradstreet relieving Detroit and Michilimackinac. To satisfy Bouquet's call for reinforcements, Gage promised him that Johnson would send him Indians to serve as his eyes and ears in the wilderness. Johnson later repeated that pledge.[6]

Despite the exchange of letters among the four principal planners throughout the spring and summer of 1764, ambiguities lingered over just what each field commander's exact military and diplomatic mission was and how he would accomplish it. That ambiguity would lead to serious disappointments and accusations as the campaigns unfolded, especially toward Bradstreet.

While he could be ambiguous when forced to make a tough decision, Gage did illuminate some important issues. Unlike the former commander in chief, he bore no significant prejudice, if any, against Americans as soldiers. He knew well how undisciplined provincial troops could be. Yet during the late war they had fought just as bravely and, if truth be known, won more victories and suffered fewer defeats than the regulars. And for wilderness warfare only skilled, tough frontiersmen could match the Indians. Gage understood that it was "next to impossible to march in woods with regulars alone without being every moment subject to a surprise, from which a body of good woodsmen would affectually secure you."[7] Some provincials were already being raised. On November 15, 1763, Amherst had requested 1,400 of New York, New Jersey, Pennsylvania, Maryland, and Virginia to be split among those colonies in proportion to their respective populations. On December 9, Gage asked Massachusetts for 700 troops, 500 from Connecticut, 200 each from New Hampshire and Rhode Island.[8]

Nor did Gage harbor any reluctance to deploy Indians against Indians. To him the strategy made perfect sense: "I am sensible that a corps of Indians . . . will be eminent service in any expedition in this country. . . . They know the woods, dwellings, & hunting grounds of every nation; They can lead us to them & secure us from surprise which the troops know & will give them a confidence." Gage agreed with Johnson that treating the Indians with "equity, moderation, and kindness" and giving "them occasionally some small presents" was essential to gaining their loyalty.[9]

But the most important difference from Amherst was Gage's emphasis on diplomacy, which was completely missing from Amherst's strategy. To subjugate Indians demanded the deft, simultaneous wielding of carrot and stick. The new commander recognized that the military campaign could only succeed if it developed hand in hand with diplomacy. Indians could almost always evade expeditions sent to destroy them. However, they could be enticed with promises of gifts and respect for their land. And only diplomacy could achieve that.

Johnson more than anyone knew that diplomacy rather than arms would quell the uprising. Diplomacy should precede, accompany, and follow any military campaigns. But what was the best diplomatic strategy?

The better Johnson understood the exact reasons why the Indians revolted, the better he could devise policies that alleviated Indian grievances and kept the peace. In the fall of 1763, he dispatched Colonel William Eyre to the Great Lakes and Ohio valley regions to discover what had gone wrong and what should be done. In January 1764, with his mission completed, Eyre wrote Johnson a long report. He argued that only a drastic revision of Indian policy could prevent future wars. The core of his proposal involved withdrawing British troops, officials, and Canadian settlers from any forts west of Fort Niagara in New York and Fort Littleton in Pennsylvania. The western posts were liabilities rather than assets. They were expensive to maintain, irritants to the tribes, and vulnerable to destruction or isolation in war. Abandoning those posts would lose little trade and gain better relations with the Indians and enormous public savings in expenses. Traders would be allowed to rove freely through the Indian territory, at their own risk of course. Over time the frontier would gradually move west as the populations of the colonies expanded and their governments purchased more lands from the tribes. New forts could be erected to protect those populations.[10]

Trade rather than troops subjected the Indians. Diplomacy rather than troops would end the present war. The Indians had become so dependent on European products that after venting their rage and attempting to wipe the British from their land, they would be forced to grovel for goods. Eyre argued that the "most certain and effectual method to distress and punish the Indians now, or at any other time hereafter should they Attack us, will be, to cut off all supply of every kind, or have any intercourse with them; its now in our power by being wholly master of the country. . . . This [is] . . . the most safe and certain way, and that without putting the Crown to expense, for the Indians having been so long used to blankets, arms, ammunition, &c that the want of these articles would infaliably reduce them to great miseries . . . and moreover oblige them to sue for peace and our protection, in the most abject and supplicating terms: They cannot scarcely kill sufficient food without fire Arms being so much accustomed to them."[11]

These views were largely in accord with Johnson's. After mulling Eyre's report, he replied with a judicious analysis of the war's underlying causes: "First their jealousy of our growing power and occupancy of the out posts, where they neither met with the same treatment, nor reaped any of advantages which they enjoyed in time of the French. Secondly the reports . . . propogated by many of the French, tending to set our designs in the most odious light, and to represent the Indians on the brink of being enslaved. . . . The Indians began with remonstrances, represented many grievances, and demanded redress, these complaints I communicated from time to time with my sentiments and apprehensions . . . but the . . . opinion too universally entertained of their small power and abilities occasioned it to be treated with neglect. . . . I declared it as my opinion that the Indians should not be totally neglected, but that after redress of their grievances we should cultivate them to the utmost of our power a good understanding with them at least until our frontiers better established, and this I thought we could effect at an expense infinitely less than any other method, and on principles the best adapted for securing Peace, promoting trade, and increasing our frontiers."[12]

The consequences of Amherst's failure to follow Johnson's advice had been catastrophic: "The expence, difficulty, and dangers attending other expediants, the stagnation of our trade, destruction of our posts and frontiers, and the small advantages to be gained by a war with Indians, are now obvious to most people." It was not too late to adopt a proper policy: "I am pretty certain we can purchase all these advantages, and secure their inclinations by a proper treatment, which will gain us a sufficient credit with them, and a use of their country, as it will remove all their prejudices."[13] Johnson parted from Eyre over which frontier posts to retain.

For Johnson, the Seneca were the key to peace since they had been the catalyst for war. If he could forge peace with the Seneca the rest of the hostile tribes would soon follow. How could he convert the Seneca from enemies to allies?

To quell the Iroquois threat, Johnson now inflamed inter-tribal disputes. Johnson explained to Gage his strategy of "dividing them and preventing their unanimity. . . . The Six Nations on the one side and the Indians of [eastern] Canada on the other may be made an usefull barrier and Check upon the Western Indians, and the formenting a coolness between them and Jealousy of each others power will be the surest means of preventing a Rupture [with us], dividing them in their Councils, and rendering an union impracticable which cannot be too much guarded against."[14]

At a series of councils in January and February 1764, Johnson convinced the several hundred Iroquois, including Chenussio Seneca, who had gathered at Johnson Hall to join the British against the hostile Indians. Although the Iroquois refused to fight any defiant Seneca, they agreed to war against the Delaware and Shawnee. This was an essential step toward ending the war. It had taken seven months of nearly continuous diplomacy to shift the Iroquois League from ambiguous neutrals to lukewarm allies.[15]

How did Johnson do it? With the relief of Forts Detroit and Pitt the war had clearly shifted against the Indians. Until then Johnson's diplomacy had gingerly just tried to keep those who had not immediately joined the uprising neutral. But with those victories Johnson could be much tougher. At the councils he asserted that all who wished the benefits of trade with the British must join them in crushing the hostiles. This was especially true for once-belligerent villages which now sued for peace. They must prove their loyalty on the warpath and battlefield. Those who resisted would be destroyed.

The Iroquois had little choice but to accept Johnson's demands. The Six Nations were now surrounded by Union Jacks floating above frontier forts. Even their most remote villages were only a couple of weeks' march away from Albany, the staging area for invasion. Without the French to play off against the British, the Iroquois inevitably had to bow to the remaining power. With their own fur trade exhausted, the Iroquois were more dependent on British provisions and munitions than the western Indians. As the keeper of the western gate the Seneca were the least vulnerable to British military power, and thus freer to revolt. But the Seneca were just as dependent on British goods, especially ammunition. Once the British had recovered from their initial defeats and mustered armies for a counterattack it would only be a matter of time before they marched against the Seneca.

But Johnson's diplomacy involved more than threats and manipulation of the power imbalance. He also appealed to Iroquois prestige. The Iroquois claimed an empire that embraced the upper St. Lawrence and Ohio River valleys, the eastern Great Lakes and much of Pennsylvania, and suzerainty over all the tribes in that realm. That empire was largely in Iroquois minds. Although to varying extents those tribes grudgingly acknowledged a kind of elder status for the Iroquois, questions of war and peace were largely theirs alone to make. Nonetheless, Johnson argued that only a tough Iroquois response to the rebellion in their realm could revive their flagging prestige.

Although Iroquois power was but a shadow of its height a century before, it could still chill even the most fervent warriors of other tribes. Elders recalled to the young how just several generations earlier Iroquois war parties had ranged as far as Illinois and the Carolinas. Decades of war had exhausted the Iroquois and collapsed their power to a fraction of its former height. But their reputation for power had shriveled less than their means of living up to it. By joining the British the Iroquois hoped to rekindle a portion of the fear and respect with which they were once held.

Finally, war was as intregal a part of Iroquois culture as it was for any other tribe. The young men gained prestige and wealth by the bravery, skills, and leadership they displayed in battle, and the scalps and captives they paraded home. Most of those young men were itching for a chance to prove themselves. War was also a way to channel inner tribal tensions outward. Rivalries over prestige, wealth, and power strain any society. Those natural tensions had worsened with the Iroquois empire's decline. Joining the British in an easy victory against tribes already exhausted from the struggle could restore a sense of purpose and provide spoils to divide. Although the Seneca would have preferred to continue killing and scalping redcoats, now that the power balance had shifted they could simply redirect their attacks. Warring against their former allies the Shawnee and Delaware was better than no glory at all.

In early February, several war parties waded through the three-foot snowdrifts toward the enemy villages in the upper Susquehanna River valley. On February 9, Captain Henry Montour led 200 warriors and some rangers toward Captain Bull's small Delaware village on the Chemung River. On February 26 they surprised and burned the village, captured Captain Bull, the prophet Neolin's son, and 40 others. The raiders released some of the captives but dragged Captain Bull, eighteen men, eight women, and three children back to Johnson Hall. There Johnson sent Captain Bull and thirteen men down to New York City where they were incarcerated; he distributed the rest as prisoners to other tribes. In late February another raiding party of ten led by Indian Thomas King ambushed nine enemy warriors heading toward the settlements; they killed one, captured three, and scattered the rest. In mid-March, Captain John De Garmo and his men returned from a raid that netted 50 prisoners. An Oneida war party arrived at Johnson Hall on March 17 with fourteen male prisoners. Meanwhile, runners were sent to the distant hostile bands to warn them that the Iroquois would war against all who did not bury the hatchet with the British. Those who wanted peace were invited to a great council at Niagara in July.[16]

The raids frightened many of the remaining hostile Seneca into suing for peace. On March 5, Onondaga Chief Red Head with four of his men arrived at Johnson Hall to report that about 300 Seneca were approaching to seek peace. Fearing a trick, Johnson sent an Onondaga with a wampum belt to order the Seneca to halt at Canajohare while only their sachems proceeded. To further strengthen his hand, Johnson called out the militia on March 8; he retained some, sent a portion to Cherry Valley, and others to the Oneida villages to protect them while their warriors were raiding. Meanwhile, he conducted a series of talks with various chiefs who had assembled, including the Seneca. To contrast how the British treated friends and enemies, he handed out generous amounts of muskets, lead, gunpowder, clothing, and other gifts to his allies. He also issued an order that forbade merchants from trading with the Seneca. At council he pointedly ignored the Seneca while lavishing praise on the other chiefs.[17]

The raids continued. In early April, Captain Andrew Montour led 140 Indians, leavened by some rangers and Johnson's son John, toward some hostile Seneca villages to demand they bury their hatchets and send peace envoys to Johnson Hall. After they complied the war party then strode to Kanastio on the upper Susquehanna River whose two Delaware chiefs, Petacowacone (Long Coat) and Onuperaquedra (Squashcutter), had wreaked havoc on the frontier. The superintendent had offered 50 dollars each for their heads. Word of the approaching war party reached Kanastio and those people fled along with those of other villages in the region. Montour's raiders looted and burned Kanastio, Kankaghto, and several smaller villages before turning back with what livestock they had not slaughtered. The raiders returned to Johnson Hall on April 27. Montour and his men had little time to rest. On April 28, Johnson ordered them to reinforce Fort Niagara. Johnson stayed home.[18]

Throughout March and April the swelling number of Seneca chiefs at Johnson Hall had reached the psychological breaking point. The contrast between the dignity and generosity which Johnson bestowed on the other chiefs and the harsh contempt he showed the Seneca, combined with reports of raids or threats against defiant Seneca villages, converted their righteous anger into fatalistic meekness. When Johnson finally allowed them to speak, the Seneca begged for mercy. They took up their hatchets and declared they would mercilessly war against the hostile tribes. After sternly rebuking them for their treachery, Johnson issued his demands. The Seneca must release all prisoners, war against the hostiles, grant to Britain four miles of land on either side of the Niagara River, allow free passage through Seneca lands, promise forever to remain at peace with the British, and deliver hostages to ensure compliance with these concessions. The Seneca agreed and signed a preliminary treaty which would serve as the foundation for a more comprehensive treaty to be negotiated at Niagara in July. Johnson then invited the Seneca to join the Iroquois and other Indians for a war feast and dance. Although now most Seneca had promised to bury the hatchet, some hundreds remained defiant and the loyalty of many of the new allies was ambiguous at best.[19]

Of all those tribes who remained defiant, those of the upper Ohio River valley were the most belligerent throughout 1764. Shawnee, Delaware, and Mingo war parties haunted the forests of western Virginia, Maryland, and Pennsylvania. In early March a war party opened fire on Fort Pitt, killing one soldier and wounding another. Later that month Indians killed and scalped a man at Bedford. Those war parties evaded army pursuers. The raids began in earnest once the snows had melted in the mountains. War parties stalked deep into the frontier settlements, killing, looting, and burning. Over 100 Virginia settlers would die beneath Indian war clubs, muskets, and scalping knives that year. The carnage was less severe in the other two provinces where there were more troops and most frontier settlers had fled to eastern towns.[20]

Violence threatened to engulf the southern frontier as well. In December 1763, a Creek war party slaughtered fourteen settlers on South Carolina's frontier. A panic broke out and refugees streamed east. Governor Thomas Boone threatened to cut off all trade with the Creek until they surrendered the murderers. Knowing a harsh policy might well provoke a general war, Southern Indian Superintendent John Stuart tried to dissuade Boone from pursuing it.

Carnage continued to be committed by both sides. Pennsylvania Governor John Penn took a more controversial step in the war against the Indians. He first proposed a scalp bounty to his council on June 12, and informed them that he had written William Johnson for his advice three days earlier. The council deferred a decision until it received the Indian Superintendent's reply. On June 18, Johnson approved "gratifying the desire of the people of your province by a bounty on scalps, and I heartily wish success to the design."[21] A council approved the measure. Penn issued a proclamation on July 7, 1764, promising a bounty for Indian scalps and prisoners at a rate of 150 Spanish dollars for every male prisoner 10 years or older or 134 Spanish dollars for his scalp, and 130 Spanish dollars for every female 10 years or older or 50 Spanish dollars for her scalp. It was, of course, impossible to tell from a scalp whether it came from a hostile or friendly Indian. No doubt it was easier to rip scalps from the peaceful Indians living on the frontier than from the warriors and their families in the distant wilderness. Even more certain was how "gratifying" the bounty was to the frontier people.

Among the first to claim a bounty was one David Owen. In early June, Pennsylvania's wilderness disgorged him with a chilling tale to tell and evidence to prove it. He had deserted from the army four and a half years earlier, was captured, and then adopted into a Delaware band. There he married and fathered two children. In May 1764, he, his family, three men, two women, and a captured white boy went hunting on an eastern branch of the Susquehanna River. At some point something in Owens' mind snapped. He murdered seven of the Indians, including his wife and two children, and tore scalps from everyone but his offspring. Somehow two other women escaped. A couple of weeks later Owens arrived at Philadelphia with the boy and his scalps which he proudly displayed and then demanded the reward.

Having come only months after the massacres of the Christian Indians, Owens' murders provoked a fierce controversy. But did not Pennsylvania itself sanction murder by offering rewards for Indian scalps? Owens complained that he was retained rather than rewarded for his act. Perplexed at just how to treat Owens, Governor John Penn wrote Sir William Johnson for advice. In a stunning understatement Penn remarked that "this fellow has not the best of character; for which reason we are afraid to let him go."[22]

Among the Great Lakes and Ohio valley tribes, while Pontiac's ability to inspire a mass following had died, the British insults that had provoked the war continued to burn away in Indian hearts and minds. The long, frigid winter had made the Indians ever more hungry and enraged. With little ammunition their hunt had gone poorly. A succession of chiefs came to Detroit to demand ammunition from Gladwin. Huron Chiefs Teata and Takay, and Wyandot Chief Odinghquanooron (Big Jaw) visited Detroit expecting gifts; they returned to their villages angry. As a gesture of goodwill, all Gladwin could do was release Chief Winnemac back to the Potawatomi. Some of his warriors vented their rage by firing on the fort and wounding a private. Fearing an attack, Gladwin refused to allow other visitors like Potawatomi Chiefs Ninivois and Washee, Chippewa Chiefs Matchekewis and Minivavana, Mississauga Chief Wabbicomigot, and Ottawa Chiefs Manitou and Miniwaby to enter Detroit. Those chiefs turned away enraged by the insult.

A series of incidents occurred which sowed fear among Detroit's defenders that an attack was imminent. On the night of March 12 a torch was found leaning against the powder magazine door; it had extinguished before it could burn through. The British suspected that one of the Canadians in Detroit had placed it there. Had the powder magazine exploded it would have destroyed most of Detroit and left the survivors helpless before hundreds of surrounding vengeful Indians.

Then on March 23, Chief Osa of the Sauk reached Detroit to inform Gladwin that the Chippewa, Delaware, and Shawnee were circulating warbelts. Not only the distant Sauk but Winnebago Chief Taychee and Menominee Chief Oshkosh had also received belts. On March 30 a war party of thirteen warriors was spotted lurking near the fort. Gladwin ordered Lieutenant George McDougall to lead 20 troops against them. They brushed in the dark. Shots were exchanged. No British were killed or wounded. Casualties among the Indians were unknown. The Indians disappeared into the forest.

On April 4, the first supply convoys reached Detroit. A letter from General Gage to Major Gladwin informed him that his gallant, resourceful defense of Detroit had earned him the promotion to lieutenant colonel. Gladwin was to spread word through the region's tribes that they should send delegations and all their prisoners to the Grand Council to be convened by William Johnson at Niagara in July. Those Indians who remained hostile would be destroyed by two large British armies which would soon march against them. But Gage had sent no presents to be dispersed among the Indians and thus Gladwin's words would ring hollow.

On April 12, the schooner set sail with two Canadian prisoners, Mini Chene and Jacques Godefroy. The British had nabbed the renegades the previous fall. The Canadians had been locked up in the guardhouse ever since, as Gladwin and Gage debated what to do with them. Gladwin wrote asking for instructions. Gage replied that he had earlier sent Gladwin the authority to hold courts, bring the accused to trial, and issue judgments. It was time to wield that power so that "the delinquints in question will meet with their deserts, as it is most highly necessary for the King's service that examples should be made, and his new subjects taught to pay that obediance and allegiance which is due from them to their sovereign."[23] Despite virtually a direct order to try the prisoners, Gladwin finally decided to send the renegades east.

On the night of April 14, a prisoner who had escaped from the Saginaw Chippewa reached Detroit. He was prompted to escape when the Chippewa had eaten a girl captive and he feared he was next on their list. It took him eight days to reach Detroit and he ate not a bite the whole journey. Yet he said he was not very hungry. He must have had that butchered little girl on his mind.

Gladwin sent Mohawk subchief Aaron to take word to nearby villages of the Niagara council and approaching armies. The chiefs were in little mood to talk of peace. They had heard British promises and threats before. What they wanted was ammunition and other goods upon which they had become dependent. Yet most chiefs questioned the wisdom of carrying on the struggle. Huron Chiefs Teata and Takay met with Gladwin on April 29. Teata begged Gladwin to "take pity upon us, and be assured of our good intentions, as we have most faithfully repented of all the ill we may have done, and do sincerely promise never to be guilty of any bad thing for the future . . . let the earth turn as it will, we shall never be advised to do a bad thing again."[24]

Much further west, despite his promises, Pontiac refused to give up the warpath. In early 1764 he circulated a warbelt six feet long and four inches wide to most tribes between the Appalachian Mountains and the Mississippi River. Tribes as far south as the Gulf of Mexico received Pontiac's runners with his message to destroy their British overlords.

Why did Pontiac continue the struggle after nearly all his followers had abandoned him? Despite the breakup of his alliance, the truces the Detroit tribes had forged with Gladwin, France's loss of its North American empire, and the dearth of ammunition, Pontiac found a rationale for fighting on.

The Indians were not only undefeated but had destroyed nine forts and won nearly every battle with the redcoats. Only Detroit, Pittsburgh, and the Niagara forts remained west of the Appalachian divide. Those too might have fallen had not a lack of ammunition and the onset of winter forced the Indians from the field. Perhaps some new strategem could wipe out those strongholds as well. Also, Indian grievances had not been resolved. No treaty had been negotiated and signed. In exchange for a truce Gladwin had neither granted nor promised anything. Finally, pride may have fired Pontiac. Except for the Battle of Bloody Run, all of his strategies had met with humiliating failures. His once soaring popularity had plummeted. The motivation to prove to all that he was a great war chief may have been the strongest of all.

Still, Pontiac's prospects for reviving the alliance were bleak. Only 70 or so warriors of various tribes and their families had followed him to the Maumee village. He did talk Wyandot Chief Odinghquanooron (or Big Jaw) at his village near Lake Erie to agree to renew attacks in the spring. But only those two villages could be stirred by his magic along with a handful of Canadians like Pierre Barth, Baptiste Campeau, Alexis Cuillerier, John Maiet, and Jacques St. Vincent. Elsewhere his entreaties fell mostly on deaf ears. Those tribes which had already fought the British harbored hatred but little will to renew the struggle. It was a crushing descent from the intoxicating heights of the previous summer when his rhetoric had electrified nearly 1,000 warriors behind his schemes. But Pontiac's once powerful charisma had faded with his repeated failures to take Detroit. In 1764, Pontiac's "conspiracy" would be but a shadow of its former self.

As Pontiac's power waned his rage swelled. If he was impotent to destroy Detroit he could at least murder British captives under his thumb—or under the thumb of those who claimed allegiance to him. He decided to test Big Jaw's loyalty. In March he dispatched eight warriors to the Wyandot village to demand that Big Jaw execute two British, one a soldier and the other a trader. For whatever reasons, Big Jaw complied. Pontiac then tested his powers in his own village. He ordered the Canadian Alexis Cuillerier to murder a 7-year-old girl, Betty Fisher, who had been captured the previous summer. Probably fearing for his own life, Cuillerier drowned the child after Pontiac had hurled her into the freezing Maumee River. But this was the power of a murderous cult leader, not a great military commander.

How could Pontiac revive his power? Only unblooded tribes like the Illinois and Wabash tribes could muster some enthusiasm for war and they were far from the British forts. In March, Pontiac carried the warbelt to the Wea, Mascouten, Peoria, Kickapoo, Kaskaskia, Piankeshaw, and Kankankee who tepidly promised to fight the British.

He then headed to Fort de Chartres where, on April 15, 1764, he implored its commander, Captain Pierre Joseph Neyon de Villiers, to join the uprising. His oratory was as vivid as ever. Appealing to the Frenchman's pride, Pontiac revealed the British boast that "they keep the French in their pockets & that they knock them in the head as little flies that sting them, that for us they take us for a lump of earth which they break in their hands and give us to the winds to blow away like dust." Villiers protested that the war was over, and Pontiac should join hands with the British and French. Pontiac replied that "Thou knowest the Master of Life. It is he who has put arms in our hands, and it is he who has ordered us to fight against the bad meat that would come to infect our lands. . . . Be persuaded that we will not finish the war with the English whilst there remains one of us Red Men."[25]

But Villiers categorically refused to send any help and urged Pontiac to bury his hatchet. Pontiac refused and pressed more warbelts and demands on Villiers. His patience spent, Villiers kicked the warbelt. He demanded whether Pontiac was deaf to his words and castigated him for bringing misery to the Indians and Canadians at Detroit. Pontiac, angry and humiliated, stalked away. The next day Villiers gathered the local Illinois Indians and asked them to accept peace with the British.

Villiers sincerely tried to restrain the Indians. Garshum Hicks escaped from Indian captivity and reported that when a war party appeared before Villiers "he would not hear them and ordered the scalps thrown out of doors, telling them to go home again and take care of their wives."[26] British officials suspected Hicks of lying to spread disinformation. His reliability remains unclear. While Villiers may have sincerely advocated peace, merchants at Vincennes, Kaskaskia, and Cahokia sold munitions and other supplies to the Indians. In September alone it was reported that 800 pounds of gunpowder and lead in proportion had reached the hostile tribes. Some Canadians did all they could to inflame Indian passions for war. The most active Canadian during 1764 was Joncaire Chabert, who carried a warbelt from one village to the next from the Mississippi to the Scioto and Ohio to Lake Erie. It was probably Joncaire who circulated a phony letter from Louis XV saying that he had just awakened after a long sleep and was sending an army to reconquer Canada.[27]

Pontiac lingered at Fort de Chartres through midsummer. On June 15, Vincennes' commander, Captain Louis St. Ange de Bellerive, replaced Villiers who retired to France. Pontiac pressed St. Ange for aid just as persistently as he had Villiers. Although St. Ange was more sympathetic than Villiers, he refused to aid Pontiac. Throughout this time Pontiac's hopes were kept alive by Alexis Cuillerier's lies. Cuillerier displayed a letter which he claimed was from the French king promising that he had sent an army to help the Indians destroy the British. Despite all evidence to the contrary, Pontiac at first believed Cuillerier. But Pontiac's faith weakend. By July 1, when he finally left Fort de Chartres for the Maumee River villages, Pontiac was prepared to make peace.

Other Indians refused to give up. During the summer Shawnee Chief

Charlot Kaske replaced Pontiac as the most persistent leader for continuing and spreading the war. Kaske had a German father and British wife, both of whom were captives turned Indians. He hated the British and was obsessed with destroying their grip west of the Appalachians. In August 1764, Kaske led 60 Shawnee to the Illinois country to rally those tribes behind the revolt. He and his followers arrived at Fort de Chartres on August 27 and implored Captain St. Ange to supply them.

The commander dashed any hopes the Indians had that they would assist their rebellion. St. Ange patiently explained that the remaining French in the region were in an extremely vulnerable position and could not openly assist the rebels. To Louisiana governor d'Abbadie, St. Ange expressed "the embarrassment I labor under with those [Indians], who were every day making demands on me which tended only to vast expense and are contrary to the King's intentions and the orders you have given me on this hand. On the other hand, the fear of driving them against us, by rejecting all their demands; of their accusing the French of abandoning them entirely, and finally, that they should be driven to despair, has caused me to pass very uncomfortable moments. Their sojourn here has not failed to occassion heavy expenses for their subsistence alone. An Iroquois chief came here some twenty-five days ago. After having held such conversation as is usual among Indian nations, he asked me for assistance which I could not give him, having neither the right nor the ability to do so. . . . I cannot express to you, Sir, the uneasiness present circumstances give me; I should have to respond to all the Nations, and I am unable to do so. To speak to them of peace, that's all; nothing can afford them less satisfaction. There are at least fifty Red men here every day who must be fed, and who no longer recognize but this post where they have a father, most frequently leave very dissatisfied."[28]

Local merchants were not so reticent. They heaped munitions upon the Shawnee. Kaske convened a council of nine Illinois and Wabash tribes who agreed to go to war if the eastern tribes could sustain it. Kaske sent his men back east to fight the British. He then journied down the Mississippi to rally the southern tribes and gain Governor d'Abbadie's support. On December 20, 1764, he presented to the governor a warbelt with symbols of 47 villages supposedly united against the British and implored d'Abbadie to join them. The governor rejected Kaske's request and instead urged him to bury the hatchet with the British. Kaske persisted and was joined later in December by Illinois Chief Levacher. Yet their united pleas were no more successful in changing the governor's mind.

While first Pontiac and then Kaske rallied the Illinois tribes, British troops were trying to reach that region by the back door via the Mississippi River. Under the 1763 Treaty of Paris, the enlargement of the British Empire to the Floridas and the Mississippi River posed both a triumph and a challenge. Those lands had to be occupied and settled. Such a vast swath of territory could only be possessed in stages. British troops would first take over the Gulf of Mexico ports. By late 1763 the 3rd battalion of the 60th Royal Americans later the 22nd and 35th were sent to Pensacola, while the 34th occupied Mobile. The second stage was to ascend the Mississippi River and occupy the Illinois country. That effort would have to await the following spring and would prove to be far more challenging.

Imperialism involved more than simply planting the flag in forts. The governor and agents had to cement the loyalty of the region's whites and Indians. That would be no easy task. Like northern Indians the southerners preferred the light French or Spanish imperial presence to harsh British rule. The Indians knew that an influx of merchants and settlers would follow the Union Jack. Those whites would trample on Indian customs and sensitivities, cheat them of their furs and land, kill them off with alcohol and diseases, and eventually drive the remnants west across the Mississippi River.

How could British officials alleviate this animosity and fear? That antagonism could only be covered with presents, and the more the better. The governor, officers, and agents had to convene councils with the tribes in which they promised not to disturb Indian life while distributing gifts to show their sincerity.

The Indian reaction at the British occupation of Mobile was typical. The 34th's commander, Major Robert Farmar, "found the savages on his arrival much out of temper; and greatly displeased that the English should take possession without their previous consent; and angry with the French for abandoning the post. That in order to appease them, he had made them promises that we would give them the same good treatment the French had done; And had found himself under the necessity of making them considerable presents to reconcile those who appeared the most discontented."[29]

By spring 1764, the British were ready to embark on the second stage of subduing their new conquests. The man who would lead that expedition did not want to go and if he had to, wanted compensation. Major Edward Loftus made his case the previous December, asking Amherst to "consider how my present situation in being sent to the Illinois, a country almost unknown, which quite deprives me of all correspondence with my friends and acquaintances, the expense that attends an officer commanding at these posts . . . gives me hope that you will make some provision for me. . . . The French have a lieutenant governor there and they give him an allowance; if you would be pleased to give me this appointment I should be extremely happy, for really it requires both youth & health to march through this desolate country."[30]

By now Gage was in command. He offered his understanding of the challenges facing Loftus, then complimented the major and his regiment for their efforts so far. He did not, however, offer any extra "provision" to Loftus for simply doing his duty as a British officer.

Having wintered at Pensacola, Loftus and 400 troops of the 22nd regiment reached New Orleans on February 12. There, with the assistance of Governor d'Abbadie, Loftus gathered boats and supplies with which to ascend the Mississippi River. Despite warnings by d'Abbadie that the Indians might well resist, on February 27, 1764, Loftus left New Orleans with 320 troops, 30 women, and 17 children in ten bateaux and two pirogues on the tedious four-month row upstream to Fort de Chartres. They never made it. On March 19, at Roche a Davion or Tunica Bend, 240 miles above New Orleans, a war party of Choctaw, Tunica, Ofogoula, and Avoyelle lay in ambush on both sides of the river. Their fusilade killed four and wounded six of his troops. Loftus had a choice. He could try to land and scatter the Indians, he could turn tail and retreat to New Orleans, and then back to Pensacola, or he could push upstream against the current and firing.

That was an important decision. The arrival of Loftus and his troops at Fort de Chartres would have cut off an important source of supply, hope, and refuge for the warring Indians. The uprising's last embers might have been quickly extinguished. But Loftus chose to retreat. The back door to the Ohio country was left open and with it the dream of a French army rowing up the Mississippi to their rescue.

Gage received word of Loftus' decision on May 20 and immediately fired off an order for him to try again to ascend the Mississippi. Loftus replied that he hoped to reembark some time in August. This time he would lead the 34th; the 22nd's ranks were depleted by desertion, disease, and Indian sharpshooters. Meanwhile, Loftus accused Governor d'Abbadie of stirring the Indians against him, citing rumors and the friendly reception the Indian raiders received at New Orleans shortly thereafter. D'Abbadie heatedly denied the charge. Was d'Abbadie guilty as charged? Characteristically, Gage kept an open mind on the question. He wrote to the governor asking him to again help Loftus. The governor promised to do all that he could.

The second attempt to ascend the Mississippi would founder as well in lethargy, fear, desertion, and disease. Loftus delegated the mission to Lieutenant Campbell of the 34th. He deployed his troops on the Iberville River route clearing fallen trees and dredging the channel. Campbell and a small contingent would get no further up the Mississippi than Natchez by the year's end.[31]

Although disappointed by these reverses, Gage knew the Mississippi River route was a side show. Only the expeditions of Bouquet and Bradstreet could cow the Indians into accepting peace. On March 6, Gage ordered Bouquet to meet him in New York to plan that year's campaign. Bouquet's campaign goals were clear. He would move his army deep into enemy territory, destroy by any available means the enemy's capacity to wage war, free all the prisoners, and force the Indians to accept all the British peace demands. Just where the enemy lived was well-known. Most of the war parties which ravaged the Pennsylvania, Virginia, and Maryland frontiers emerged from clusters of Shawnee, Delaware, and Mingo villages in the

Muskingum and Scioto River valleys. Most of those who had lived in the Allegheny River valley had abandoned their villages, after the Battle of Bushy Run the previous year and more recent Iroquois raids.[32]

But how could Bouquet's army bring the Indians to their knees? A pitched battle like Bushy Run was unlikely. Bouquet's army would be too big to attack. At best, small war parties could hit and run from vulnerable British detachments. But that would only delay Bouquet's advance. If all went well his army would reach the Muskingum valley. Even then the Indians would most likely flee rather than defend their villages. What then could Bouquet do? There was only one choice. The Indians' livelihood depended on their corn, bean, and squash fields. The more of those fields the soldiers uprooted, the greater the number of Indians that would be stalked by starvation that winter, and thus the more likely they would be to sue for peace and emergency provisions. All that too was clear. But how long would such a "peace" last?

Ideally, the campaign would not have to resort to burning empty villages and uprooting fields. Only diplomacy backed by the threat of destruction could bring genuine peace. And only Johnson could negotiate a peace treaty. Bouquet's mission was to bring the Indians to Johnson. To do so he had to force them to accept a truce based on very specific tenets which were essentially a preliminary peace agreement. Curiously, the first demand on Bouquet's list was for the Indians to deliver the murderers of William Clapman and other traders; those murderers would be executed for their crimes. Next, all white prisoners, whether captives or adopted, would be released. Then a tribe which wanted peace had to renounce its alliance with belligerent tribes. The Indians also had to give up any right to all lands from the Appalachian watershed to the Atlantic Ocean. No Indian was allowed in ceded lands without permission. Trade would only be conducted at designated forts. Within seven years the Indians had to compensate with skin traders for all losses they had suffered. Hostages would be handed over to guarantee Indian compliance with these promises. If the Indians agreed to all this, what was left for them to concede to Johnson? The superintendent would essentially ratify this preliminary agreement into a formal treaty and reward the signatories with a small mountain of presents.[33]

How many troops would Bouquet's mission need? Johnson argued that 1,000 men would be the ideal amount. That number was enough to repel any attack and could move sooner and consume fewer supplies than the two or three thousand troops Bouquet and Gage envisioned. But, perhaps spooked by the near disaster at Bushy Run, Bouquet preferred marching with at least 2,000 or more troops even if it meant delaying the campaign until late summer. Desertion and disease had severely undermanned his regular regiments, the 42nd and 60th. Extracting troops and supplies from the assemblies of Pennsylvania, Virginia, and Maryland was as frustrating as ever. Johnson promised to send Bouquet Indians to act as scouts.[34]

The biggest question was how to get there. Thousands of draft animals and hundreds of wagons were vital to hauling the mountains of supplies from Philadelphia and other eastern towns first to Carlisle and then on to Fort Pitt. Beyond Fort Pitt only rivers and Indian paths etched the wilderness. If Bouquet chose to march overland, only pack animals could thread those narrow trails. The few grassy meadows en route would be quickly churned to mud by all the thousands of hoofs and teeth. Those animals would not only have to pack all the army's beans and bullets but also fodder to sustain themselves. Of course, it would be easier to row than walk to the enemy villages. The trouble was building over 100 bateaux necessary to convey all those troops and supplies down the Ohio and up the Muskingum or the Scioto if need be. But the winter and spring had been unusually dry; by May the water was believed too low on the Muskingum and Scioto to float heavily laden boats. By midsummer an attempt to row down the Ohio River was just as likely to founder.[35]

What then was Bouquet to do? By May 31 he had chosen the land route to the Muskingum valley. While he asked Johnson to confirm his objections to the river route, Bouquet concentrated on planning his overland expedition. The colonel harbored no illusions about the challenges that lay ahead. It would take at least two weeks and probably more to get the army from Fort Pitt to the heart of that cluster of seven villages which lined stretches of the Muskingum and its tributaries. From there it was another two weeks to the Scioto valley villages. The longer his supply line, the more vulnerable his army was to being cut off.[36]

Many forces would determine whether Bouquet's expedition succeeded or failed. His regular regiments alone were not numerous or skilled enough. He needed provincial troops, which only the assemblies could provide. Although on December 23, 1763, Pennsylvania's assembly had voted to raise 1,000 troops, it was not until a half year later, on May 30, 1764, that the legislators voted to raise 55,000 pounds to finance those reinforcements for Bouquet's expedition. It would take months to scrounge up that money and pay for all the uniforms, supplies, munitions, transport, draft animals, and salaries vital for those troops.[37]

Bouquet did what he could to prod Pennsylvania's government into fulfilling its pledge. On June 4 he wrote Governor John Penn and his council a detailed list of what the troops would need on the campaign. He also asked them to raise two troops of light horsemen or 50 of the 1,000 men to be enlisted. Finally, he asked them to import hunting dogs from England to help his troops rout out Indians on the campaign.[38]

To fill his depleted regular regiments, Bouquet asked Gage for permission to issue an amnesty for deserters. Gage agreed with the measure but avoided giving it official sanction. Bouquet pressed Gage to authorize him to do so. On June 11 the commander in chief reluctantly issued an amnesty proclamation directed to those who had "wantonly deserted" if they returned before July 31. But even that inducement enticed few men back to the colors.[39]

Bouquet was desperate for troops. Worried that Pennsylvania's assembly would fail its pledge, he called for any men "who are disposed to serve their country." The troops were to form into companies, could elect their own officers, and would receive all provisions. All that was standard. But the colonel also promised "whatever occasional assistance they might stand in need of in case of accidents during the campaign," and, more enticingly, "all those who shall take prisoners or scalps of enemy Indians . . . may depend upon proper certificates and recommendations to enable the reward offered by this government." All interested should join the army at Fort Loudoun by August 15 or at Pittsburgh by September 25. Those enthused by such offers might have been deflated by the notice's terse "P.S.: I hope the volunteers understand that it is not in my power to allow them pay."[40]

Gathering enough troops was trouble enough. Feeding them for weeks or months was a greater trial. Working closely with His Majesty's Commissary General for North America, Robert Leake, Bouquet shot off a flurry of letters to contractors. He asked Robert Callender in Philadelphia to supply his army 400 beeves the first week of July, another 400 by July 20, and 200 every month thereafter. In addition, by July 1, Callender should deliver 800 horses and as many wagons and teamsters as possible to Fort Loudoun. He asked the firm of Franks, Ingliss, and Barkly to supply other goods. In all, Bouquet expected that with "regulars, artillery people, Indians, volunteers, drivers, &c we shall have upwards of 2000 persons to victual, which will require about 3000 pack horses to carry six months flour at 160 pounds each, besides one year of provisions to be left at each fort, the ammunition, stores, & baggages, & 1600 beeves."[41] Bouquet planned to transport those supplies across Pennsylvania in convoys, each with an escort of four or five hundred troops. He would station 50 troops each at Forts Loudoun, Bedford, and Ligonier. Those troops would be responsible for escorting the smaller monthly convoys.

But before the convoys could move, the provincial troops had to be assembled. As the provincials slowly formed at Philadelphia, they were fully equipped but given only rudimentary training. Bouquet instructed Lieutenant Colonel John Reid that "the only exercise to be practiced is to march, run, & wheel in a rank entire with open files; from that order the line of march two deep. . . . The camp is to be formed by a single row of tents disposed in an oblong square and the fires made in the front."[42] He also reminded Reid to ensure his troops' muskets were cleaned and repaired.

Pennsylvania's government finally fulfilled its promise. At full strength the Pennsylvania regiment numbered 911 by late July. The 1st battalion mustered 521 troops at Lancaster on July 23, and the 2nd battalion 390 at Carlisle on July 30. Desertions would whittle away that regiment's manpower. Of those troops 750 were line infantry, 50 were light horsemen, and

200 were formed into four ranger companies. Only after those battalions achieved the fundamental tasks of organization, supply, and training, would they march on to Fort Loudoun and Bouquet's control.[43]

The constant frustrations involved in extracting troops and supplies from Pennsylvania and other provinces enraged Bouquet. With blistering contempt he demanded whether provincials "found it easier to kill Indians in a gaol than to fight them fairly in the woods?" The answer in his mind was clear. Bouquet was "so much disgusted at the backwardness of the frontier people . . . that I hope this will be the last time I shall venture my reputation and life for their sake."[44]

But Bouquet suffered a worse quandary. The notion of somehow coordinating his offensive with Bradstreet's, let alone linking up, seemed increasingly unrealistic. It would take all summer for Bouquet to concentrate enough troops and supplies at Fort Pitt. Bouquet recognized that Bradstreet's offensive would start well before his. Then, once on the march, Bouquet feared the danger of his expedition being cut off and ambushed. On June 21, he admitted to Gage that "we could not without great risk and difficulty penetrate in summer beyond the Ohio where there are no roads." Instead, Bouquet announced that he would delay his expedition until the beginning of October when "the leaves and weeds decay, and the woods are more open, and we shall still have two months for acting. . . . Bradstreet will, by that time, be near his return, and may indirectly be of service to us by appearing again about Sandusky; The first day of October may be fixed with him to make some diversion from Erie, if he can. If not we shall shift for ourselves."[45]

Much of that came to pass. But some controversial twists arose when Bradstreet tried to implement that strategy. The fault would lie mostly but not entirely with the colonel. Part of the problem was Gage's ambiguous instructions. He offered his most comprehensive orders to Bradstreet in two letters on April 2, 1764. Most were details about troops, supplies, and boats. He also spoke of the overall military and diplomatic situation with the Indians. Bradstreet and Bouquet were to campaign in harness against the Ohio Indians from different directions but at roughly the same time. That plan would change as Bouquet found it impossible to accumulate enough troops and supplies to start on time. Most crucial were Gage's instructions over treating with the Indians. While field commanders could make preliminary peace treaties, only Johnson could negotiate a final treaty. Bradstreet was to forward all Indian envoys to Johnson. Gage gave Bradstreet considerable leeway within which to accomplish his mission: "you will be at such a distance as not to make it possible to send for orders, and circumstances may change many things which can't be forseen at this distance. You must take upon yourself to manage them to the best advantage for his Majesty's service. You will be upon the spot and I must trust for the execution of everything to your discretion and judgment."[46]

Bradstreet's expedition would suffer its own share of delays, some because of foot-dragging by provincial assemblies and contractors, and just the tedious process of hauling enough supplies for the expedition. By early 1764, small mountains of provisions already lay along the Great Lakes route, including 5,000 barrels at Niagara and 1,000 at Oswego. Bradstreet called for another 10,400 barrels to sustain his troops for the year. That would take thousands of wagons, boats, draft animals, and men to move and store.[47] But the most important reason for the expedition's delay was Bradstreet's decision to wait until William Johnson had concluded his Fort Niagara council with the Indians.

Any council took a long time to organize. One as huge as Niagara demanded a series of preliminary councils along with a mountain of gifts and provisions as great as that for any army expedition. Throughout the spring and summer Johnson sent runners to distant tribes to invite them to the councils. A stream of chiefs and their followers arrived at Johnson Hall to negotiate preliminary understandings, polish the covenant chain, and receive food and gifts. Lieutenant Colonel William Browning, Fort Niagara's new commander, conducted his own councils with local Indians and organized the expedition until Johnson and Bradstreet could arrive.[48]

On June 15, William Johnson embarked on the Mohawk River near his home with 30 troops in three bateaux. The entourage was accompanied ashore by a swelling group of Indians which numbered 450 when they arrived at Fort Ontario on June 26. There they waited a few days while 100 Canadian Indians and 100 Oneida joined them.[49]

Colonel John Bradstreet reached Fort Ontario on June 27 and met with Johnson to discuss the pending campaign, share dinner, and council with the chiefs. Throughout the next few weeks Johnson carefully instructed Bradstreet on how to treat his Indian allies and conduct diplomacy. He was especially worried that the troops would alienate the Indians with insults. To avoid conflicts he asked Bradstreet to assign whites who spoke Indian languages to boats with those peoples. As for Bradstreet, he should always show friendliness and make frequent, short pep talks to groups of gathered Indians. He must grant any Indian requests for a council quickly and cheerfully. He should listen respectfully to the chiefs' advice and share his plans and their rationale with them. He should ensure that each warrior was properly dressed, armed, and fed. Bradstreet would violate all of this sound advice.[50]

Johnson also offered Bradstreet sound and explicit strategic advice. Acting in concert with Bouquet's campaign, expeditions of warriors and light troops could reach the Muskingum villages via the Cuyahoga River, or the Scioto villages via Sandusky. Of the two possibilities Johnson leaned toward the Sandusky route since that was the one preferred by their Indian allies. Bradstreet would reject this advice as well.[51]

Throughout June, Indian delegations began setting up shelters around

Fort Niagara. Not all the Indians converging at Fort Niagara had come in peace. In late June a war party of 17 Huron or Delaware killed a royal artilleryman on the Carrying Place. Learning of the killing, allied Indians quickly gathered and pursued but the raiders escaped.[52]

But danger lurked not just for stray soldiers stumbling about in the woods. As 20 friendly Indians approached a small stockade near Fort Schlosser they sang their war song and fired their muskets in salute. The sergeant commanding the post panicked and ordered a cannon loaded with grapeshot fired at the Indians, grievously wounding three of them. Fort Niagara's commander, Lieutenant Colonel William Browning, called a council to console the aggrieved and enraged Indians with presents and kind words. Then on June 24 the Onondaga war chief Red Head dropped dead during an alcoholic binge in the room of Major Alexander Duncan of the 55th regiment at Fort Ontario. Johnson performed the ceremony of covering the dead with gifts. For the Indians these tragedies were a terribly inauspicious beginning for what would prove to be a disheartening campaign.[53]

Johnson and Bradstreet finally arrived at Fort Niagara on July 7. The Indian Superintendent immediately got to work on last-minute preparations. The council officially began on July 11. Rather than convene one huge council, Johnson tried a new strategy. He negotiated separate agreements with each tribe. Although time-consuming, the separate negotiations had the desired effect of playing the tribes off against each other as they all feared the others were getting better deals.

Present were envoys of all Six Nations, two nonaffiliated tribes, and five other eastern tribes, along with eleven western tribes. The official head count for July alone was 1,725 Indians, of which only about 150 were women and children. Hundreds more would spend some time at the council. Notably absent, however, were Pontiac and his Ottawa, the Sandusky Huron, and the Ohio valley Shawnee and Delaware. Johnson negotiated and signed separate treaties with many of these tribes. Each treaty shared the promise made by the Indians to make peace; release prisoners, army deserters, and slaves; inform the British of any conspiracies; and join the British against rebel tribes. Some treaties included grants of land for existing or future forts. In return, Johnson made them all three promises. No British would be allowed to settle or buy Indian lands. All Indians who had taken part in the uprising would be pardoned. The tribes would be allowed to buy all they wanted from British traders. Polishing the covenant chain with so many Indians was very expensive. During the nearly four weeks of councils Johnson handed out 25,000 pounds worth of presents to the Indians. The Niagara council's total expenses included an additional 38,000 pounds for supplies, bateaux, and so forth.[54]

A danger lurked over the council. Four hundred Chenusio Seneca and 100 Delaware were encamped several days from Fort Niagara. Fears gripped both those Indians and the British. Johnson and Bradstreet worried that

they might attack troops and supplies traversing the Carrying Place. Imag-
ining a trap, the Seneca and Delaware stayed put, and they sent an insulting
message to Johnson. The superintendent replied on July 20 with an ulti-
matum that the Seneca and Delaware had only four days to reach Niagara
and beg for peace or he would march at the head of an army that would
wipe those tribes from the earth. The Seneca succumbed to Johnson's
threat. A mere three days later they arrived with fourteen prisoners and two
deserters. The Delaware, meanwhile, broke camp and fled west.[55]

Johnson was generous with British friends and tough toward foes. In his
council with them on July 24, he threatened to "reduce" the Chenusio
Seneca "to beggary without fighting, by only debarring you of trade. . . . If
you deceive us any more or continue obstinate, your ruin is inevitable. If
you faithfully perform your late engagement, the generous English will forgive you. Let me have your speedy answer, for I have no more time to lose,
nor have you any other alternative."[56]

The Seneca finally signed a peace treaty on August 6. In addition to
promising to bury the hatchet and surrender prisoners, the Seneca agreed
to cede to His Majesty all land four miles on either side of the Niagara River
from Lake Erie to Lake Ontario. They also had to deliver their former allies,
the Delaware Chiefs Ataweetsera and Onnusseraqueta within three weeks.
The treaty did release the Seneca from responsibilty for the two Kanastio
murderers, one of which had since died and the other who had fled.[57]

Johnson's diplomacy at Fort Niagara was backed by an impressive display
of military force. Nearly 1,500 British troops were camped around Fort
Niagara. The Indians knew that those troops would soon be heading west
to crush any hostile villages in their path. Among the regular troops were
the 17th regiment, whose ranks were filled from the 55th; the 46th's light
company; four companies of the 80th Light Infantry; and 50 royal artiller-
ymen and ten cannon. The provincial troops included 500 combined troops
from New Jersey and Connecticut, 500 from New York, and 300 Canadians.
Captain Henry Montour led 76 Indians and rangers. In addition to his
nearly 500 regulars and 1,000 provincials, about 500 Indians would start
out with the expedition to make a total force of 2,000 men. Second in
command to Bradstreet was Lieutenant Colonel John Campbell.[58]

Despite all these troops, Bradstreet refused to march them over the Carrying Place to Fort Schlosser until after the council broke up. He feared
suffering another massacre like that at Devil's Hole the previous year. But
had Bradstreet taken such reasonable precautions as deploying strong flanking, front, and rear guards, it is extremely unlikely that any Indians would
have considered, let alone dared an attack, especially during a peace council.
Bradstreet's timidity delayed his campaign by at least three weeks.

The Niagara council ended on August 6. Johnson returned to his home
while Bradstreet and his army headed west. Two days later, on August 8,
the troops embarked at Fort Schlosser in over 200 bateaux, each of which

was 44 feet long with pointed ends, flat bottoms, and two large sails. Eighty-eight men could pack into each bateau and man its 26 oars.[59] That day they began the long row westward on Lake Erie. Colonel Bradstreet had never commanded so many troops on such an important mission.

Just who was John Bradstreet? He was born in about 1714 in Nova Scotia of a British officer and Acadian mother. Although he received his ensign's commission in 1735, it would be another decade before his leadership was tested. At the siege of Louisbourg in 1745 he revealed his natural bravery and initiative as colonel of a Massachusetts regiment. Another eleven years would pass before his mettle was again tested. He bought a captaincy in the Royal American regiment on March 8, 1756 and was assigned to supply the isolated British post of Oswego on Lake Ontario. On June 8, 1756, nearly 700 French and Indians attacked his convoy eight miles from Oswego. Bradstreet rallied his panicked troops, then led a flanking movement which routed the enemy. That bold leadership earned him laurels but did not get him transferred from supply to combat troops. For the next two years he organized and managed the highly efficient bateaux corps which kept supplied the different fronts in New York. Then, during General James Abercromby's expedition against Fort Carillon in July 1758, Bradstreet was given command of the advanced guard after Lord George Howe was killed. After Abercromby's disastrous attack on the entrenchments before Fort Carillon, in which his army suffered nearly 2,000 casualties, Bradstreet was instrumental in restoring order among the demoralized troops. But his career's zenith would occur the next month when, after years of wrangling for the mission, he was allowed to lead a raid on Fort Frontenac on Lake Ontario. His force destroyed or captured a hugh cache of French supplies along with the fort. He served the war's remainder as one of Amherst's deputy quartermasters. On October 19, 1762, he received a colonel's commission. His rank, experiences, and reputation made him a logical choice to head the Lake Erie expedition.

So far, few could fault his military career. Many, however, deplored his character. He could be nasty with his subordinates, civilians, and even superiors. Most found him tactless, boastful, and rude. He seems to have abused his public duties for considerable private gain. But his audacity and victories had allowed Amherst to overlook his flawed character. Unfortunately, in 1764 his military skills were waning. He was no longer the tireless, impetuous warrior of the French and Indian War, whose physical and emotional strain had taken their toll on him. He was half a century old when he received the Lake Erie command; the fire of his youth was largely spent. Some chronic disease drained his energy and often confined him to bed.[60]

On August 12, Bradstreet and his army were encamped at L'Ance aux Feuilles on Lake Erie's south shore, 63 miles from the Niagara River head and just east of Presque Isle. A party of ten Indians was caught lurking nearby and brought into camp. The allied Indians wanted to torture their captives to death. The captives swore they were peace emissaries from the Sandusky Wyandot and Scioto Shawnee and Delaware; they were on their way to the Niagara council. Yet none were chiefs and they displayed only two wampum strings and a belt.

Those Indians were most likely scouts rather than diplomats. Yet, to the astonishment of his officers and Indians, Bradstreet not only believed the "envoys" but got them to sign a nine-article "treaty." All the chiefs whom the envoys represented must arrive at Sandusky with all their prisoners within 25 days to meet Bradstreet and his army. An eighteen-man peace delegation composed of six each of English, Canadians, and friendly Indians would be free to travel to tribes west of Sandusky. Any Indian who kills any whites after the treaty is signed must be delivered by his tribe for trial at Fort Pitt. Six envoys would remain as hostages; the others with an officer and friendly Indian would journey to the villages with the treaty. The peace treaty would last forever. Bradstreet then signed the treaty and granted peace "by the power invested in me by his Excellency Major General Gage Commander in Chief of all his Majesties Forces in North America."[61]

Bradstreet's action is puzzling. He was an experienced frontier officer, one of the few who had managed the art of wilderness warfare. Surely he must have realized that those Indians would have no authority to conclude treaties or order prisoners released. At best, they could serve as messengers from Bradstreet. Even more troubling was that Bradstreet was not authorized to conclude a treaty; only Sir William Johnson could do so.

What drove Bradstreet to such a rash action? Like many a commander throughout history, Bradstreet seems to have coveted all the campaign's "glory" for himself. He did not want to share any laurels with Colonel Bouquet and his troops, who would soon march toward the Muskingum and Scioto Rivers; nor with Sir William Johnson who negotiated peace treaties with the subdued tribes. He reveals his motivation in a letter to Bouquet written shortly after concluding his "treaty": "since I have reduced the Delawares and Shawnees without your aid . . . there is no longer any need of your advancing further."[62] General Gage later vividly explained that "had the interest of the public and a real sincere desire to use the most zealous efforts for her service outweighed jealousy, envy, and above all an immoderate vanity and self-opinion, and the pleasure to puff and bluster away a sort of reputation amongst the vulgar, these matters could have never happened."[63]

Bradstreet had no sooner committed one highly controversial decision when he committed another. With his treaty signed he reembarked his troops. They rowed the short distance to the Presque Isle peninsula's neck. There Bradstreet ordered the troops to drag their boats and supplies over the neck rather than row them around the peninsula. The labor was exhausting and actually took longer than if they had stayed afloat. Many boats were damaged from being dragged across and would leak badly in the weeks ahead.

On the neck's west side, the troops clamored back into the bateaux and bent their backs to the oars. At Sandusky a delegation of chiefs did greet Bradstreet with the promise that they desired peace. But they had no prisoners to deliver. Bradstreet accepted their promise to met him at Detroit to sign a formal treaty in two weeks. Then he and his army reembarked.

At the mouth of the Maumee River on August 26, Bradstreet dispatched Captain Thomas Morris of the 17th regiment with two interpreters, two servants, and nineteen Indians led by Thomas King up that valley and into the Illinois country to visit the tribes and get them to send peace delegations to Detroit. After doing so, Morris was to head to Fort de Chartres and take possession of that post for His Majesty. With that mission accomplished he would descend the Mississippi and warn all those adjacent tribes not to resist any British expedition which rowed upstream. As if all these missions were not challenging enough, a curious choice was made for one of Morris's guides. Earlier that year Gladwin had sent Jacques Godefroy and Mini Chene in chains back to Niagara to be tried for treason. General Gage had agreed to Bradstreet's request to pardon those men if they would act as interpreters.

The Morris mission was fraught with danger on every side and nearly ended in tragedy. He and his delegation reached Ottawa Chief Atawang's village eighteen miles upstream from Lake Erie on August 27; Pontiac's village was just a few miles beyond. Morris convinced Atawang, subchief Shamandawa, and visiting Miami Chief Naranea to join Bradstreet at a Detroit council. Morris courageously proceeded to Pontiac's village, whose inhabitants plundered the party's supplies and tried to separate the lieutenant from his Iroquois escort.

Who saved Morris from the torture fire? Pontiac was now ready to bury the hatchet, especially since an Iroquois war party accompanied Bradstreet. He handed Morris a huge peace wampum belt with 210 villages that would "make the road clear" on his mission. Pontiac, however, refused to journey to the Detroit council. For now he would sit down and see whether the French king would fulfill the promise he had made in a recent letter to send a huge army to his side; the letter was a Canadian forgery designed to encourage the Indian uprising.[64]

After three days with Pontiac, Morris and his escort proceeded to Fort Miami which they reached on September 7. The Miami seized, stripped, and beat Morris, then debated whether to torture him to death. Morris' escort pleaded for his life. Just before the Miami were about to begin their torture, Pontiac's nephew arrived and convinced them to release the captain. It was then that Morris learned that a delegation of fifteen Shawnee and Delaware had earlier passed upriver before him carrying a warbelt and boasting of having tricked Bradstreet into believing they favored peace. The Miami also displayed fifteen belts and five strings of wampum that they had recently received from the Seneca calling on them to continue the struggle against the British and reject any admonishments by the other Iroquois for peace. The Miami debated what to do. The Seneca and promised that the French army was far away while Bradstreet was nearby. It was better to send Morris away without killing him, the Miami decided. They would then wait to see whether their allies fulfilled their promises or Bradstreet marched against them. Morris and his escort hurried away and arrived at Detroit on September 17.

While Morris was struggling to fulfill his mission, Bradstreet and the expedition reached Detroit on August 28. There Bradstreet handed Major Gladwin orders which granted his request to be transferred. Lieutenant Colonel John Campbell replaced him as Fort Detroit's commander. Bradstreet dispatched Captain William Howard with 300 British troops and 100 Canadians in two companies to retake Fort Michilimackinac. He also sent Fort Sandusky's former commander, Ensign Christopher Pauli, with troops back to that site to reestablish the fort and receive the prisoners released by the Indians. He gathered all Canadians 14 years or older and had them reswear allegiance to the British Crown. He sent back a copy of his "peace treaty," an account of his actions until then, and a promise to conclude a general peace with the Detroit Indians by which they would hand over Pontiac "to be sent down the seacoast & maintained at his Majesty's expense the remainder of his days."[65]

Finally, Bradstreet sent runners to all the chiefs from the nearby villages for a council. The council met from September 5 to 7 and included Chippewa, Huron, Ottawa, and Potawatomi chiefs. Bradstreet demanded that the chiefs remain at peace, declare their loyalty to the British Crown, and surrender all their prisoners. This they promised willingly. But they demurred when he insisted they turn in Pontiac. Despite that disappointment, Bradstreet signed a treaty with the chiefs anyway.[66]

The illusion of Bradstreet's "peace" soon became apparent even to him. The ink was no sooner dry on the paper when, on September 13, Bradstreet received word that the Shawnee, Delaware, Miami, Wyandot, and other tribes remained as hostile as ever. Indeed the Wyandot had captured Ensign Pauli and his troops as soon as they stepped ashore at Sandusky. Upon learning what happened, Bradstreet embarked his troops and rowed to their rescue. The Wyandot fled with their prisoners.

Bradstreet encamped his men near the fort's ruins and pondered his next move. From Sandusky the upper Scioto plain villages were only a half dozen days' march away. Bradstreet rejected any notion of heading there, citing the lack of draft animals to convey their supplies. It was true that his entire army, minus a contingent to guard the bateaux, would have had difficulty marching there and back with just the provisons they could carry. Yet a picked force of Indians and rangers could have marched to those villages and destroyed them in retaliation for the Indian refusal to comply with the August 12 "treaty." The Indians and most of his officers urged him to do so. But Bradstreet shrugged off their advice and continued to sit tight.[67]

Meanwhile, on August 23, Bouquet received Bradstreet's missive calling on him to cancel his campaign. What should Bouquet do? Bradstreet had clearly violated orders. But what if he had done as he claimed? What if the Indians really had laid down their weapons and sincerely accepted peace? What would be the effect on them of another army marching through their lands? Would they then return to the warpath to defend their homes?

The only sensible thing to do was reject Bradstreet's "treaty." The campaign must proceed. The Indians must be crushed. The remnants must make a treaty with the only man with the powers to do so, Sir William Johnson, His Majesty's Indian Superintendent. All this Bouquet quickly decided. He angrily scribbled a letter to General Gage and sent it off by express. Bradstreet's treaty "compromised the honor of the nation by such disgraceful conditions; and that at a time when two armies, after long struggles, are in full motion to penetrate into the heart of the enemy's country." Bouquet vowed he would "take no notice of his peace, but shall proceed to the Ohio, where I shall await till I receive your orders."[68]

Gage was furious when he learned from Bouquet of Bradstreet's actions. He fully agreed with Bouquet that Bradstreet's "peace" "obtains not the least satisfaction for all the cruelties those barbarians have been guilty of . . . [and] add dishonor to our arms amongst the Indians, and can serve no purpose but be the basis of future massacres." He urged Bouquet "to proceed in your operations. I annull and disavow the peace. Attack and use every means to extirpate . . . and listen to no terms of peace till they deliver the promoters of the war unto your hands to be put to death, and send the deputys to Sir William Johnson to sue for peace."[69]

Bradstreet's folly was only the latest frustration in an ever lengthening list for Bouquet. He had reached the army's staging post at Carlisle on August 5. The army was short of supplies, wagons, draft animals, and troops. The steady rains had not only converted the roads to quagmires but had soaked much of the gunpowder. Indians skulked in the surrounding forest; on August 22 they killed six soldiers. Within days over 200 Pennsylvanian troops had deserted.

What could cement troops to the campaign? Bouquet reasoned that only ample coin could fill the want of patriotism. He shot off a letter to Governor Penn requesting that Pennsylvania's government make up the shortfall by offering "twenty shillings p[er] man to the officers for recruiting & three pounds advance money to such as should be recruited for that purpose."[70] The government complied even though Bouquet's request was "thought somewhat unreasonable, as no demand of the like nature had been made in any former campaign."[71]

Although relieved at their prompt compliance, Bouquet knew it might take months before more men could be recruited, equipped, and dispatched to the campaign. He looked in other directions for troops to fill the shortage. He wrote to Colonel Andrew Lewis asking him to send 200 Virginian troops. As an afterthought he sent Lieutenant William Brown of the 60th with 300 pounds to offer bounties to Lewis and his volunteers. Lewis could be relied on to provide troops. But another Virginia colonel could not be trusted. Colonel Adam Stephens had earlier not only denied Bouquet's request for reinforcements but had diverted supplies intended for the Ohio campaign to his own needs. Bouquet wrote Governor Francis Fauquier asking him to reprimand Stephens.[72]

What about the Indians that Gage and Johnson had promised? Bouquet would be disappointed there as well. Johnson finally wrote him on September 1 to apologize that the Indians he had raised preferred to journey with Bradstreet rather than Bouquet. An irritated Bouquet complained that if Johnson "could not send me any Indians I wish he had not promised them."[73]

Hostile war parties stalked the surrounding forests. On September 15, Indians ambushed two soldiers carrying letters on horseback. They dragged one away into captivity. The other was decapitated and his head stuck on a pole in the road.[74]

Bouquet and most of his army reached Fort Pitt on September 18. Ironically, Bradstreet's "peace" had provided him a diplomatic opening. The previous day ten Delaware appeared on the shore opposite Fort Pitt. Chiefs Captain Pipe, Captain Jacob, and Captain John had paddled over with a white prisoner to Fort Pitt and asked if the peace were true. They received a rude answer when Captain William Grant promptly accused the Indians of being spies and had them arrested. Learning the fate of their brothers, the other Indians swiftly disappeared into the forest.

Bouquet met with the prisoners and on September 20 sent Captain Jacob to his village with a bundle of letters from himself and Gage to Bradstreet and the message to the tribes that Bradstreet's "peace" was annulled, since the Indians had continued their murderous attacks. He warned that his army would sweep through their land burning and killing all if the Indians did not immediately lay down their arms and safely escort two messengers to Bradstreet and back within 20 days. If any harm befell the messengers, the two remaining hostages would be executed.[75]

Meanwhile, Bouquet made final preparations for his campaign. On September 28, Lieutenant Colonel John McNeil arrived at the head of 110 Virginia volunteers. Those troops were assembled and informed of the strict orders that regulated the army. Bouquet was a stickler for cleanliness and sobriety, reasoning that it saved lives and boosted morale by limiting disease. Linen should be washed daily. Rolls were called four times daily where soldiers would appear with faces and hands washed and hair combed. Firing or shouting in camp was forbidden. Troops were supplied with one-quarter pound of powder and three flints. To save ammunition, loads were drawn each day rather than fired.

Discpline was harsh. Concerned with minimizing any looting his troops might commit, he decreed that the perpetrators and their officers would be severely punished. During the campaign at least a dozen men received from 50 to 1,000 lashes for crimes including drunkenness, theft, disobedience, selling equipment. Despite the risk, deserters gnawed away the army. Most got away. Some unfortunates were caught. On September 26, Bouquet had the army assembled in a three-sided square. Two deserters, one from the 42nd and another from the 60th, stood on the open side before a file of soldiers. They were shot to encourage the others.[76]

On October 2, two Iroquois, an Oneida, and an Onondaga arrived at Fort Pitt. Bradstreet had dispatched them through the Scioto and Muskingum villages. They assured Bouquet that they were gathering their prisoners, and apologized for their past conduct. Bouquet sent the envoys back to the Ohio tribes with the message to lay down their arms and surrender their prisoners. The envoys were then to carry letters to Bradstreet.[77]

That same day, on October 2, the army crossed over to the Ohio River's north bank and camped for the night. Early on the morning of October 3 the army began a slow, careful march through the thick forests toward the Muskingum.[78] Determined to prevent any ambush, Bouquet ordered his troops to maintain strict formations on the march and camp. The Virginia volunteers formed the advanced guard with scouting parties well to the front and on either flank. Following them were the axe men who cut away fallen logs and widened the trail. Two light infantry companies guarded them, followed by eight light horsemen. The main body advanced in a hollow square with several companies of the 42nd at the front, companies of the 42nd and 60th regiments on the right flank, and the 1st battalion of Pennsylvanian volunteers on the left. The reserve corps consisted of two grenadier platoons flanking the 2nd battalion of Pennsylvanians. Eight light horsemen followed. The 2nd battalion of Virginia volunteers formed the rear guard. Scouting parties paralleled its flanks and rear. The supply convoy was in the very center of the hollow square on the trail. First came those animals bearing ammunition and tools, followed by those with the officers' tents and baggage, and hospital stores, and finally the four separate droves of oxen and sheep. Each of the 80 light horsemen led his horse with a 125-pound flour sack on its back. That flour would be eaten first whereupon the trooper could mount his horse. In all, there may have been as many as 1,530 horses to carry supplies, the light cavalry, and officers.

The troops camped in the same formation that they marched. The drums beat reveille at daybreak. At assembly officers would ensure that the men's canteens were full and their cartridges dry and intact. The troops were to march in complete silence. The amount of food they carried varied. The first three days of each week, each soldier drew rations of four pounds of beef and three pounds of flour, and the next four days drew five pounds of beef and four pounds of flour. Whenever a halt was called or an attack commenced, each soldier should immediately face outward two paces from his comrades while the light horsemen entered the square. At night sentries took cover behind trees, and would neither move nor talk. Officers would make the hourly rounds. During a night attack all troops would face outward and lie down with their arms thrust forward.

The orders were just as clear over how to act before peaceful Indians. The troops were neither to fire on any Indians unless ordered to do so, nor were they to show any signs of friendship with any Indians who arrived to discuss peace. Soldiers were forbidden to "hold any kind of friendly intercourse with them by speaking, shaking of hand or otherwise, but on the contrary to look upon them with utmost disdain and with that stern and manly indignation justly felt for their many barbaritys to our friends and fellow subjects. They will continue to be regarded as enemys till they submit to the terms that will be offered them and till they have in some measure expiated the horrid crimes they have been guilty of."[79]

The troops marched about a dozen miles daily in a low arc first along the Ohio River and then inland. On October 13 they reached Sandy Creek, a tributary of the Tuscarora River and 92 miles from Fort Pitt. The next morning, on October 14, the Iroquois Bouquet had dispatched reached his camp to reveal that the Delaware had forbidden them to continue to Detroit. They did have some good news. A delegation of Shawnee, Delaware, and Seneca chiefs were on their way to negotiate with Bouquet. But they wanted assurance that the hostages Captain Pipe and Captain John were safe. Bouquet replied that the hostages were safe and that their delegation could "come to me without fear, for I will not hurt or detain anyone of you."[80]

The colonel ordered his army to march on to the juncture of Sandy Creek and the Tuscarora River where they camped that night. Bouquet issued orders designed to give his army the most formidable appearance possible. The troops were ordered to clean their muskets and linen, and ensure their ammunition was in good order. It was forbidden to insult any Indians. The troops should maintain constant vigilance. Sentries should halt the delegation when it arrived and send word to the field officer of their arrival. The officer would then give them permission to enter. Guards would escort the envoys to Bouquet's tent.

On October 16, Bouquet met with two Delaware and four Seneca who declared their desire for peace and explained that they had not arrived earlier because Bradstreet "had invited us to go & see him upon the lake, at the same time you expected us at Fort Pitt, we were at a loss which way to go."[81] As for the Shawnee, they would come tomorrow.

On October 17, the council convened. Present were Seneca Chief Kayashuta with fifteen men, Shawnee Chief Keisinautchta with six men, Delaware Chiefs Beaver, Kitchi or Turtle's Heart, and Custaloga (or White Eyes) with 20 men, and eighteen prisoners. Each chief rose to blame the western Indians for the war and announce that his people were ready for peace. They would release their remaining prisoners but, referring to their August 12 treaty with Bradstreet, they wondered which commander should receive them. As etiquette demanded, Bouquet was not to respond until the next day, but a fierce storm forced a delay.[82]

The council did not reconvene until October 20. With Indian agent Alexander McKee at his side, Bouquet castigated the Indians for the treachery, mass murder, and destruction they had wrought. He swore that he would destroy any tribes that remained on the warpath. He then gave them twelve days to return all the prisoners, deserters, French, and escaped slaves, even those who had been adopted. A formal treaty could only be negotiated by the Indian Superintendent Sir William Johnson and would only be concluded after the tribes had surrendered any whites in their midst and left the warpath forever. And to guarantee their word, some of chiefs would remain with Bouquet as hostages. He concluded by asserting that "you deserve the severest chastisement—but the English are a merciful and generous people averse to shed the blood, even of their most cruel enemies—and if it was possible that you could convince us that you sincerely repent of your past conduct and that we could depend on your good behavior for the future, you might yet hope for mercy and peace."[83]

The next day the chiefs agreed to Bouquet's demands and gave up their hostages—the Seneca Kayashuta, Shawnee James Smith, and Delaware Turtle's Heart and Custaloga's son. The council broke up. The delegations scattered to their villages; most would fulfill their promises. But Bouquet was determined to maintain pressure on them. On October 23, the army marched another fifteeen miles downstream to where the Tuscarora River and Walhondling River form the Muskingum River. His army was now 120 miles from Fort Pitt. The Shawnee village of Wapatomica stood on the west bank and the Delaware village of Goschachgunk on the east bank. A constellation of other villages were scattered across the region. The Shawnee and Delaware often held councils at the river forks. Bouquet had his troops fortify their camp and then waited for the prisoners. Three days later, on October 25, Bouquet moved camp again, this time another ten miles. They were now 130 miles from Fort Pitt. This would be their furthest advance.

The Indians did as they had promised. They had little choice. Many of their prominent chiefs were literally under the gun. Their villages were not far away from Bouquet's army. Over the next few weeks the Indians brought most of their prisoners and adopted alike to Bouquet's camp. Prisoners released were separated according to sex and age and then interviewed so that their names and homes, and physical descriptions were recorded. Soldiers were warned that "there will be many among them who are very much attached to the savages by having lived with them from their infancy. These if not narrowly watched may be apt to make their escape after they are delivered up. The guards and sentinels therefore on this duty must be particularly attentive to prevent such acccidents happening."[84]

Reinforcements arrived during this time. Colonel Andrew Lewis and 200 Virginia troops caught up to Bouquet on the march. Forty-three Maryland volunteers reached Bouquet's camp on October 20. On November 9, Bouquet dispatched Captain Abraham Buford and a detachment to escort 110 released whites to Fort Pitt. Although Indian parties warily shadowed Bouquet and those detachments, no violence exploded.

Then, on November 7, the peaceful proceedings nearly died when a soldier was found dead in the woods. Bouquet demanded that the murderer be surrendered and used the crime to heighten pressure on the surrounding villages to hurry the delivery of the whites among them; the murderer would not be found. Councils between Bouquet and various delegations alleviated the animosities on October 30, November 1, 9, 10, 11, 12, and 14. On November 11 the Indians agreed on six hostages each from Mingo and Delaware to stay with Bouquet and five envoys each to be sent to Johnson. The Shawnee remained reluctant and finally conceded, under threats, on November 13. Bouquet then closed the council by declaring: "I came here determined to strike you with a tomahawk in my hand, but since you have submitted, it shall not fall upon your heads.·I will let it drop and it shall no more be seen. I bury the bones of all the people who have fallen this war and cover the place with leaves."[85]

Bouquet had accomplished most if not all of his mission. The chiefs had agreed to bury the hatchet, release the prisoners, and submit hostages. Those who started the war, however, remained free. Bouquet explained to Gage that had he tried to catch "the authors of the war, to be put to death . . . the savages . . . would have dispersed . . . and necessity would have forced them to fall on our frontiers, which must have remained exposed to their depradations at least for another year as I had neither troops nor provisions to take post in their country."[86]

The army began the long march back on November 15 and arrived triumphantly at Fort Pitt on November 28. Accompanying the army were the Indian envoys, fourteen hostages, and 207 released whites including 32 males and 59 females from Virginia and 49 males and 67 females from Pennsylvania. In all, over 300 whites were released when those who marched back in early November were included. Not all of the hostages reached Fort Pitt. Two Shawnee were too sick to travel and were left behind. En route, the Mingo stole some horses and rode off. A Maryland soldier murdered and scalped an Indian near Fort Pitt which prompted the two remaining Shawnee hostages to flee. Still, Bouquet was confident that the envoys sent to Johnson would agree to a lasting peace.[87]

In all, Bouquet's 1764 campaign was a model of wilderness warfare. His tight formation on the march and in camp deterred any attack. His steady but peaceful advance to the heart of the Muskingum intimidated the Indians into coming to council rather than fighting or fleeing. His unyielding but fair diplomacy forced them to bury the hatchet. In all, he freed 363 former captives. He accomplished his mission without his men firing a shot at the enemy.

The troops were dispersed to winter quarters. The 60th Royal Americans began the long march east on November 29, followed the next day by the provincial regiments. The 42nd Highlanders would garrison the string of forts with five companies under Captain William Murray at Fort Pitt, a company under Captain John Stewart at Fort Ligonier, a company at Fort Bedford under Captain William Grant, a half company at Fort Cumberland under Lieutenant McIntosh, and a half company at Fort Loudoun under Lieutenant James Eddington.[88]

During this time a Canadian named Louis Hertel arrived with a message for Bouquet from Bradstreet. The message solved a lingering mystery for Bouquet: Just where was Bradstreet?

Bradstreet and his army remained encamped at Sandusky as Bouquet's expedition marched toward the Muskingum. Indian problems preoccupied Bradstreet. The hostiles refused to come in for peace and the friendlies refused to go out for war. Without the hostiles' presence he could not ask them why they failed to fulfill the "treaty" signed by their "envoys." That treaty required all the chiefs to bring all their prisoners to Sandusky no later than September 8. Nearly a month had passed since the deadline and those Indians remained hidden.

But his allies gave him an earful of explanations for their inaction. On October 4 the Indians announced that they wished to go home—Bradstreet's fumbling diplomacy since the August 12 treaty had chilled the passions aroused among them at the Niagara council. Bradstreet responded by giving them a warbelt and request to war immediately against the Shawnee and Delaware on the Scioto. The Iroquois counciled among themselves, then met with Bradstreet on October 5. Speaking for the Five Nations, Oneida Chief Thomas King announced that they would send out a small war party as a test. If it brought in prisoners and scalps all the Indians would march en masse against the Scioto villages; if it failed they would all go home. Bradstreet was dismayed but could do nothing to change their mind.[89]

Bradstreet was still awaiting the war party's return when a packet of letters from Gage and Bouquet arrived on October 13. Both men were more restrained in their remarks to Bradstreet than in their comments to each other about his conduct. Bouquet politely begged Bradstreet "to postpone the final conclusion of your treaty." Gage's letter was more cutting. He annulled and disavowed the "treaty" and ordered Bradstreet "to let nothing prevent your attacking them . . . and use every means in your power to destroy them."[90] Both called on Bradstreet to march immediately against the Scioto villages.

Nonetheless, the rebukes stung and the orders rankled. Bradstreet was to tear up his "treaties" and attack the Scioto River villages. But how could he do that with no pack animals? While he was mulling that conundrum and probably cursing his commanders, he received word from Detroit that Morris' mission had failed. Then there were the ever more troubled relations with the Indian allies. The expedition's failures were piling up.

Bradstreet sunk deeper into a lethargic depression. For days he issued no orders to fulfill those of Gage. The war party returned with neither scalps nor losses. But the Indian allies wanted to go home anyway. Bradstreet decided to do the same. On October 14 he dispatched the Canadian Louis Hertel with some Indians to carry a message to Bouquet. The season was too advanced to march on the Scioto, he informed Bouquet; he would lead his army back to Niagara for the winter.[91]

Still hoping that the Indian peace emissaries might actually appear, Bradstreet tarried at his Sandusky camp. He finally gave up that illusion on October 16. He ordered his troops to pack up and embark so hastily that he left behind two New Jersey privates who had gone fishing for the colonel's dinner, and five Iroquois out hunting.

Nature turned their retreat into a rout. The expedition got no further than the Cuyahoga River mouth on October 21 when a storm slashed them for three miserable days. The waves and winds battered the boats against the rocky shore, destroying 25 and leaving most of the rest leaking wrecks. The incessant downpour soaked most of their provisions and gunpowder. Six cannon sank with the boats. Bradstreet buried his remaining cannon and extra ammunition. He then packed his regulars in the undamaged bateaux and ordered 150 of his provincials and all the Indians to make their own way along the wooded shore back to Niagara. Like whipped bedraggled dogs, Bradstreet's regulars filed into Fort Niagara on November 4. Hundreds more provincials and Indians were still straggling along the Lake Erie shoreline; several would die from starvation and exposure to the freezing temperatures. The trials of Bradstreet's expedition seemed unending. After resting briefly at Fort Niagara he embarked most of his troops on Lake Ontario. Storms drove ashore the sloops *Mohock* and *Johnson Snow*, ruining yet more provisions.[92]

While Bouquet returned to a stream of accolades, Bradstreet met a fire of criticism. The Indians who accompanied Bradstreet bitterly denounced him before Johnson: "this is the first time we ever joined our brethern the English, and we are sorry to say we never experienced such hardships and ill treatment from the French, nor so unsuccessful a campaign."[93] To the Board of Trade, Johnson wrote a scathing indictment of Bradstreet's inept diplomacy, arguing that it did more harm than good because it alienated friendly and emboldened hostile Indians.[94]

Bradstreet had indeed exceeded his rather ambiguous orders. Yet how badly did he foul the strategy? Quixotic, vainglorious, and much criticized as his actions were, they did not actually undermine Britain's war effort. Nearly all of the Indian tribes had already given up. All that remained was to secure a peace with them.

On December 13, 1764, Gage wrote Lord Halifax, Secretary of State for the Southern Department, that "the country is restored to its former tranquility and that a general and, it's to be hoped, lasting peace is concluded with all the Indian Nations who have lately taken up arms against his Majesty."[95]

That assessment proved to be somewhat premature. The Indians had not been crushed or even defeated. They had simply signed peace treaties and returned prisoners. Pontiac remained at large.

Bouquet and Bradstreet had primarily led diplomatic rather than military missions. The presence of large armies in their homelands probably could not defeat the Indians in battle but could certainly awe them into laying aside their hatchets. The military commanders made preliminary agreements which William Johnson would elaborate, codify, and then seal with gifts.

Even then, Johnson could only do so much. Like everyone else, he was largely the prisoner of events beyond his influence let alone control. The Indian Superintendent's powers rested mostly on his ability to persuade hostile tribes to lay down their hatchets and friendly tribes to take up theirs in defense of British interests. When the uprising first exploded, his efforts centered on trying to contain it, to keep it from worsening. As Indian power quickly peaked and receded he tried to tip the power imbalance toward Britain and dilute the rebellions' passions. He accomplished these goals with measly powers to grant gifts or threaten retaliation. All along his most powerful diplomatic weapon was his own dazzling moral character, his reputation for fairness, sincerity, and understanding. At best, however, he could only deal with the uprising's symptoms rather than underlying reasons.

That changed by late 1764. The war had sputtered out, replaced by a haphazard patchwork truce rigged with promises and a few formal treaties. With this breathing space Johnson could now look far beyond the immediate task of ending the uprising. He would build upon that fragile truce by beginning to treat the causes. Over the next three years he and his agents would negotiate and implement a series of Indian treaties, trading regulations, restrictions on new white settlements, and the often resentful cooperation of provincial governments that would culminate with the Fort Stanwix Treaty of October 24, 1768. With that treaty, eight years after the British formally conquered Canada, they formally subjugated the Indians by informally granting them a strict territorial, economic, and political autonomy.

How did Johnson do it? Here again his powers were limited. Although Whitehall had issued the 1763 Proclamation splitting white and red worlds at the Appalachian watershed, it had provided no laws and money to implement it. Then, on October 11, 1764, Johnson received the first sign of hope. A letter from Lords of Trade requested that the Indian Superintendent give "my sentiments & remarks on a plan for the better regulation of Indian affairs & for making several necessary establishments in my Department as well as for preventing abuses in trade."[96]

In July 1764, Whitehall enhanced the 1763 Proclamation by submitting to its Indian Superintendents the 43-point "Plan for the Future Management of Indian Affairs." All tribes in the British Empire would be in the jurisdiction of either the northern or southern superintendencies, with 42 tribes in the former and thirteen in the latter. Chiefs were appointed for each village and each tribe with powers to negotiate binding treaties. The superintendents had to approve and could veto all agreements made by their assistants, governors, and military officers. The northern superintendent received three deputies and the southern superintendent two deputies. Four missionaries from the Society for the Propogation of the Gospel in Foreign Lands would be allowed to proselytize in each district. Whitehall repealed all existing provincial trade laws for the Indians and imposed uniform laws in their place. Trade would be free to all those who applied and paid for a one-year renewable license, posted a bond, and promised to uphold all regulations. Trade could only be conducted at forts under the watchful eye of commissaries, assisted by interpreters and blacksmiths. Prices were fixed. Extending credit to Indians was forbidden. Traders could sell muskets but not rifles to the Indians. Liquor was also forbidden, although some could be brought into Indian territory only for personal consumption. Indian superintendents, deputies, and commissaries or agents were empowered to enforce all trade laws. Anyone who violated the regulations could forfeit his license, bond, any trade goods, the possibility of trading again in Indian lands, and even his liberty, depending on the crime's severity. Only the superintendents could purchase Indian lands and only then with the agreement of all a tribe's principal chiefs. The annual budget for the superintendents would be about 20,000 pounds, to be defrayed by duties on the Indian trade.[97]

The plan was a dream come true for Johnson. When asked for his comments he replied with an in-depth, point-by-point commentary. He disagreed only with the total prohibition of rum since "the Indians will be universally discontented without it." He called instead for commissaries to supervise the sale and consumption of watered-down liquor to the Indians.[98]

Whitehall shelved all the commentaries it received from the superintendents, governors, and the commander in chief. The plan remained only a proposal without the force of law. Nonetheless, Johnson used its tenets as the basis for his own diplomacy toward the Indians and regulations for the merchants. But to make that work he had to forge a consensus with other colonial leaders on just what would lead to a lasting peace. They would squabble for years over that question.

At least he had the commander in chief's support. What a relief for Johnson after the years he had vainly argued with Jeffrey Amherst that peace could only be maintained with generosity rather than severity. Amherst had rejected his advice; war had followed. In stark contrast, Amherst's successor Thomas Gage firmly grasped that simple truth. Intelligent, tolerant, and experienced in dealing with Indians, Gage was of one mind with Johnson on how to govern the new empire and its subjects. They developed and coordinated their policy through a series of letters and meetings over the years. Together they worked to implement their policy at all levels, through British officers and Indian agents, traders, provincial governments, and settlers. It was an unending, frustrating labor, but they largely succeeded.[99]

The key to peace was to respect and legally uphold the Indian assertion of sovereignty. To do otherwise would bring war. Although the European powers might trade territorial claims in the poker game of international relations, the Indians living on those lands would never subject themselves to any foreign ruler "or will ever ever consider themselves in that light whilst they have any men, or an open country to retire to, the very idea of subjection woud fill them with horror."[100] Johnson asks Gage to "Imagine to yourself, Sir, how impossible it is to reduce a People to subjection who consider themselves independent thereof both by nature and situation, who can be governed by no laws, and have no other ties among themselves but inclination." Indeed, according to Johnson no Indian language had a word that conveyed the British concept of subjection. Thus he called for prohibiting its use in any treaty to avoid future problems: "it may prove of dangerous consequences to persuade them that the Indians have agreed to things which (had they ever even assented to) is so repugnant to their principles that the attempting to enforce it must lay the foundation of greater calamities than has yet been experience in this country."

The details of any peace treaty rested upon that concept of native sovereignty. While conceding that basic point, Johnson and Gage were hardnosed diplomats: "we must show firmness where it's proper and & yeild in trifles when it becomes necessary to gain their affections."[101] In all, Johnson faced a Sisyphean challenge.

NOTES

1. John Richard Alden, *General Gage in America: Being Principally a History of His Role in the American Revolution* (Baton Rouge: Louisiana State University Press, 1948).

2. Lewis Ourry to Henry Bouquet, June 8, 1764, in Sylvester K. Stevens, Donald H. Kent, Autumn L. Leonard, Louis M. Waddell, and John Totteham, eds., *The Papers of Henry Bouquet* (hereafter cited as *Bouquet Papers*), 6 vols. (Harrisburg: Pennsylvania Historical and Museum Commission, 1972–1994), 6:566–67.

3. Thomas Gage to Henry Bouquet, April 4, 1764, *Bouquet Papers*, 6:508, 507–8. For Amherst's dispositions and plan, see Jeffrey Amherst to Thomas Gage, November 17, 1763, in Clarence Edwin Carter, ed., *The Correspondance of General Thomas Gage with the Secretaries of State, 1763–1775* (hereafter cited as *Gage Correspondance*), 2 vols. (1931–1933) (reprint, Hamden, Conn.: Archon Books, 1969), 2:209–14; For Gage's innovations see Thomas Gage to Welbourne Ellis, January 20, June 8, 1764, ibid., 2:217–19, 229–31; Thomas Gage to Charles Jenkinson, February 10, 1764, ibid., 2:221–22.

4. Thomas Gage to Henry Bouquet, April 4, 1764, *Bouquet Papers*, 6:507–8, 517–19.

5. Henry Bouquet to Thomas Gage, May 2, 1764, *Bouquet Papers*, 6:533, 532–35.

6. Thomas Gage to Henry Bouquet, May 14, 1764, *Bouquet Papers*, 6:538–40.

7. Thomas Gage to Henry Bouquet, November 18, 1763, *Bouquet Papers*, 6: 461, 460–62.

8. Thomas Gage to Lord Halifax, December 9, 1763, *Gage Correspondance*, 1: 2–4.

9. Thomas Gage to William Johnson, December 12, 1763, in James Sullivan and A. C. Flick, eds., *The Papers of William Johnson* (hereafter cited as *Johnson Papers*), 14 vols. (Albany: State University of New York, 1921–1965), 10:953.

10. William Eyre to William Johnson, January 7, 1764, *Johnson Papers*, 11:5–10.

11. William Eyre to Robert Napier, April 12, 1764, in Stanley Pargellis, ed., *Military Affairs in North America, 1748–1765: Selected Documents from the Cumberland Papers in Windsor Castle* (1936) (reprint, Hamden, Conn.: Archon Books, 1969), 462.

12. William Johnson to William Eyre, January 29, 1764, *Johnson Papers*, 11:21–22, 20–24.

13. William Johnson to William Eyre, January 29, 1764, *Johnson Papers*, 11:22.

14. William Johnson to Thomas Gage, January 27, 1764, *Johnson Papers*, 4:308–68.

15. Journal of Indian Affairs, January 2–31, 1764, *Johnson Papers*, 11:24–35; Indian Conference, February 1–4, 1764, ibid., 11:37–43; Journal of Indian Affairs, February 6–7, 1764, ibid., 11:45–50; Indian Congress, February 16–17, 1764, ibid., 11:59–677; Indian Conference, February 23–28, 1764, ibid., 11:80–85.

16. William Johnson to Thomas Gage, February 3, 1764, *Johnson Papers*, 11:36; Instructions to Henry Montour, February 9, 1764, ibid., 11:51–52; William Johnson to Ralph Burton, February 11, 1764, ibid., 11:54–55; Henry Montour, William Hare, and John Johnston to William Johnson, February 28, March 2, 1764, ibid., 11:86, 87–88; William Johnson to Cadwallader Colden, March 16, 1764, ibid., 4: 364–66; William Johnson to John Stuart, March 18, 1764, ibid., 11:103–4; Journal of Indian Affairs, March 11, 1764, ibid., 11:108–15; William Johnson to Lords of Trade, May 11, 1764, in E. B. O'Callaghan and Berthold Fernow, eds., *Documents Relative to the Colonial History of the State of New York* (hereafter cited as NYCD), 15 vols. (Albany, N.Y.: Weed, Parsons, and Co., 1856–1887), 7:624–26.

17. Indian Congress, March 4–5, 1764, *Johnson Papers*, 11:88–96; Journal of Indian Affairs, March 5–23, 1764, ibid., 11:105–6.

18. William Johnson to Thomas Gage, April 16, 1764, *Johnson Papers*, 11:131–32; William Johnson to Cadwallader Colden, April 28, 1764, NYCD 7:628–29; William Johnson to Henry Montour, April 28, 1763, *Johnson Papers*, 4:411–13.

19. Indian Conference, March 24–April 23, 1764, *Johnson Papers*, 11:134–61; William Johnson to Thomas Gage, April 27, 1764, ibid., 11:162–65; Articles of Peace with Seneca, April 3, 1764, NYCD 7:621–23.

20. Henry Bouquet to Thomas Gage, March 8, 1764, *Bouquet Papers*, 6:500; Lewis Ourry to Henry Bouquet, March 24, 1764, ibid., 6:503–4; William Murray to Henry Bouquet, June 5, 1764, ibid., 6:559–60.

21. William Johnson to John Penn, June 18, 1764, *Minutes of the Provincial Council of Pennsylvania* (hereafter cited as MPCP) (1852) (reprint, New York: AMS Press, 1968), 9:189–90; Governor's Council, July 6, 1764, ibid., 9:188–89; John Penn Proclamation, July 7, 1764, ibid., 9:190–92.

22. John Penn to William Johnson, June 9, 1764, *Johnson Papers*, 11:224–25; William Johnson to John Penn, June 18, 1764, ibid., 11:241–42.

23. Thomas Gage to Henry Gladwin, January 9, 1764, Gage papers, William L. Clements Library, Ann Arbon, Mich. (hereafter cited as CL); Thomas Gage to Henry Gladwin, December 22, 1763, ibid.; Henry Gladwin to Thomas Gage, December 30, 1763, January 9, 1764, ibid.; Villiers Council with Pontiac, April 15, 1763, included in Farmar to Thomas Gage, December 21, 1764, ibid.

24. Franklin B. Hough, ed., *Lieutenant Jehu Hay, Diary of the Siege of Detroit in the War with Pontiac* (Albany, N.Y.: J. Munsell, 1860); Henry Gladwin to William Johnson, May 11, 1764, *Johnson Papers*, 11:191–92.

25. Minutes of De Villiers Meeting with Pontiac, April 15, 1764, Gage papers, CL; Indian Intelligence, Detroit, June 9–11, 1764, *Johnson Papers*, 11:226–30.

26. William Grant Examination of Garshum Hicks, April 19, 1764, *Bouquet Papers*, 6:522–26.

27. Thomas Smallman to Alexander McKee, November 8, 1764, *Johnson Papers*, 11:403–4.

28. St. Ange to M. d'Abbadie, November 9, 1764, NYCD 10:1157–58.

29. Thomas Gage to Lord Halifax, March 10, 1764, *Gage Correspondance*, 1:19.

30. Arthur Loftus to Jeffrey Amherst, December 15, 1763, Gage papers, CL; Arthur Loftus to Jeffrey Amherst, December 20, 1763, ibid.; Thomas Gage to Loftus, March 29, 1764, ibid. For details of the expedition, see Thomas Gage to Lord Halifax, April 14, 1764, NYCD 7:619–20; Thomas Gage to William Johnson, May 28, 1764, *Johnson Papers*, 4:432–34. See also John Shy, *Toward Lexington: The Role of the British Army in the Coming of the American Revolution* (Princeton, N.J.: Princeton University Press, 1965), 152–53.

31. Thomas Gage to Lord Halifax, April 14, May 21, July 13, September 21, November 9, 1764, *Gage Correspondance*, 1:25, 29–30, 31–33, 36–38, 41–44.

32. Thomas Gage to Henry Bouquet, March 6, April 4, 1764, *Bouquet Papers*, 6:498–99, 506–8.

33. Henry Bouquet to Thomas Gage, May 2, 1764, *Bouquet Papers*, 6:532–35.

34. Henry Bouquet to Thomas Gage, May 20, 1764, *Bouquet Papers*, 6:542–45; Henry Bouquet to William Johnson, May 31, 1764, ibid., 6:551–54; William Johnson to Henry Bouquet, June 17, 1764, *Johnson Papers*, 11:239–40.

35. Henry Bouquet to Thomas Gage, May 27, 1764, *Bouquet Papers*, 6:547–49.

36. Henry Bouquet to Thomas Gage, May 31, 1764, *Bouquet Papers*, 6:549–51; Henry Bouquet to William Johnson, May 31, 1764, *Johnson Papers*, 11:210–13.

37. Henry Bouquet to Thomas Gage, May 31, 1764, *Bouquet Papers*, 6:549–51.

38. Bouquet to Penn and Commissioners, June 4, 1764, *Bouquet Papers*, 6:554–55.

39. Henry Bouquet to Thomas Gage, May 27, 1764, *Bouquet Papers*, 6:547–49, 562–64; Thomas Gage to Henry Bouquet, June 5, 1764, ibid., 6:556–58; Gage Amnesty Proclamation, June 11, 1764, ibid., 6:570.

40. Bouquet Advertisement, August 11, 1764, *Bouquet Papers*, 6:602–3.

41. Henry Bouquet to Thomas Gage, June 21, 1764, *Bouquet Papers*, 6:576, 575–78; Henry Bouquet to Robert Callender, June 6, 1764, ibid., 6:561–62; Henry Bouquet to Thomas Gage, June 7, 1764, ibid., 6:562–64; Henry Bouquet to Plumstead and Franks, June 16, 1764, ibid., 6:579–80; Plumstead and Franks Account with the Crown, June 20, 1764, ibid., 6:580–81; Bouquet Remark on Enclosed Account, ibid., 6:581; Gage Remark on Account, ibid., 6:582; Henry Bouquet to Contractor's Agents, June 16, 1764, *Gage Correspondance*, 2:249–50; Articles of Agreement, Robert Callender and Robert Leake, July 6, 1764, ibid., 2:250–52.

42. Henry Bouquet to John Reid, June 15, 1764, *Bouquet Papers*, 6:570–71.

43. Edward G. Williams, ed., *Bouquet's March to the Ohio: The Forbes Road* (Pittsburgh: Historical Society of Western Pennsylvania, 1975), 43–51. For another primary source, see William Smith, *An Historical Account of the Expedition against the Ohio Indians in the Year 1764 under the Command of Henry Bouquet* (1765) (reprint, Cincinnati, 1907).

44. Henry Bouquet to John Harris, July 19, 1764, *Bouquet Papers*, 6:594–95.

45. Henry Bouquet to Thomas Gage, June 21, 1764, *Bouquet Papers*, 6:575, 575–78.

46. Thomas Gage to John Bradstreet, April 2, 1764 [2nd of 2 letters], Gage papers, CL. See also Thomas Gage to John Bradstreet, December 12, 1763, ibid.; John Bradstreet to Thomas Gage, December 22, 1763, ibid.; Thomas Gage to John Bradstreet, December 25, 1763, ibid.; Thomas Gage to William Browning, December 26, 1763, ibid.; Thomas Gage to John Bradstreet, January 2, February 6, 19, 1764, ibid.; John Bradstreet to Thomas Gage, January 10, February 20, 1764, ibid.; James Furniss to Thomas Gage, March 28, 1764, ibid.; Thomas Gage to Joshua Loring, April 1, 1764, ibid.; Thomas Gage to John Bradstreet, April 15, 22, 1764, ibid.; John Bradstreet to Thomas Gage, May 11, 16, 1764, ibid.

47. Thomas Gage to John Bradstreet, December 28, 1764, Gage papers, CL.

48. Thomas Gage to Henry Bouquet, July 18, 1764, *Bouquet Papers*, 6:592–94; Thomas Gage to William Johnson, April 30, 1765, *Johnson Papers*, 11:167–68; William Johnson to Thomas Gage, May 3, 1764, ibid., 11:171–75; Thomas Gage to William Johnson, May 4, 1764, ibid., 11:175–76; Indian Conference, May 7–10, 1764, ibid., 11:176–80; Journal of Indian Affairs, April 24 to May 11, 1764, ibid., 11:180–89; William Johnson to Thomas Gage, May 11, 1764, ibid., 11:189–90; William Johnson to Thomas Gage, May 17, 1764, ibid., 11:194–95; William Browning to William Johnson, May 23, 1764, ibid., 11:196; Henry Montour to William Johnson, May 23, 1764, ibid., 11:197–98; William Johnson to Thomas Gage, May

26, 1764, ibid., 11:200–202; William Browning Niagara Indian Congress, May 26, 1764, ibid., 11:202–3; Journal of Indian Affairs, May 21–23, 1764, ibid., 11:204–9; Journal of Indian Affairs, June 2–14, 1764, ibid., 11:233–37.

49. William Johnson to John Bradstreet, May 31, 1764, *Johnson Papers*, 11:209–11; William Johnson to Thomas Gage, June 29, 1764, ibid., 11:245–47; Journal of Indian Affairs, June 15–July 3, 1764, ibid., 11:250–54.

50. William Johnson to John Bradstreet, May 11, 1764, *Johnson Papers*, 11:192–93; Heads for Colonel Bradstreet's Inspection, June 12, 1764, ibid., 11:231–33.

51. Heads for Colonel Bradstreet's Inspection, June 12, 1764, *Johnson Papers*, 11:231–33.

52. William Johnson to Thomas Gage, June 29, 1764, *Johnson Papers*, 11:245–47.

53. Ibid.

54. Peace between William Johnson and Hurons, July 18, 1764, NYCD 7:650–60; Conference with Foreign Nations, July 9–14, 1764, *Johnson Papers*, 4:466–81; Conference with Indians, July 9–14, 1764, ibid., 11:262–73; Indian Congress, July 15, 1764, ibid., 11:273–76; Indian Congress, July 17–August 4, 1764, ibid., 11:278–324.

55. William Johnson to Thomas Gage, August 5, 1764, *Johnson Papers*, 11:324–27; William Johnson to Cadwallader Colden, August 23, 1764, ibid., 4:511–14.

56. Indian Congress, July 24, 1764, *Johnson Papers*, 11:293.

57. Treaty of Peace with Senecas, August 6, 1764, *Johnson Papers*, 11:327–28.

58. Thomas Gage to Welbourne Ellis, June 8, 1764, *Gage Correspondance*, 2:229–31; Thomas Gage to Halifax, May 12, September 21, 1764, ibid., 1:26–29; 36–38; William Johnson to Thomas Gage, September 1, 1764, *Johnson Papers*, 4:518–20.

59. James Dow to Henry Bouquet, July 22, 1764, *Bouquet Papers*, 6:596–57.

60. William G. Godfrey, *Pursuit of Profit and Preferment in Colonial North America: John Bradstreet's Quest* (Waterloo, Ont.: Wilfred Laurier University Press, 1982).

61. Treaty of Peace, August 12, 1764, *Johnson Papers*, 11:328–33; Indian Proceedings, December 2–16, ibid., 500–508.

62. John Bradstreet to Henry Bouquet, August 14, 1764, in Franklin B. Hough, ed., *Diary of the Siege of Detroit in the War with Pontiac. Also a Narrative of the Principal Events of the Siege by Major Robert Rogers; A Plan for Conducting Indian Affairs by Colonel Bradstreet; and other Authentick Documents, never before printed* (Albany, N.Y.: J. Munsell, 1860)

63. Thomas Gage to William Johnson, November 29, 1764, *Johnson Papers*, 4:605, 605–6.

64. Testimony of Thomas King, October 3, 1764, *Johnson Papers*, 11:369–72; Thomas Gage to William Johnson, October 26, 1764, ibid., 11:391–92; Courts of Inquiry, March 11, 16, 28, April 6, 1765, ibid., 4:670–79.

65. John Bradstreet to Thomas Gage, August 28, 1764, *Johnson Papers*, 11:340, 340–41.

66. Congress with Western Indians, Detroit, September 7, 1764, *Johnson Papers*, 11:349–51.

67. Indian Proceedings, December 2–16, 1764, *Johnson Papers*, 11:500–508.

68. Henry Bouquet to Thomas Gage, August 27, 1764, *Bouquet Papers*, 6:621–22.

69. Thomas Gage to Henry Bouquet, September 2, 1764, *Bouquet Papers*, 6:626.

70. Minutes of Commissioners for Paying the Pennsylvania Forces, August 16, 1764, *Bouquet Papers*, 6:613.

71. John Penn to Henry Bouquet, August 16, 1764, *Bouquet Papers*, 6:611, 611–12.

72. Henry Bouquet to Benjamin Franklin, August 10, 1764, *Bouquet Papers*, 6:600–601; Henry Bouquet to Thomas Gage, August 10, 1764, ibid., 6:601–2; Andrew Lewis to Henry Bouquet, September 10, 1764, ibid, 6:634–35; Report and Resolves of Virginia Investigation of Stephens, December 15–25, 1764, ibid., 6:727–30.

73. Henry Bouquet to Thomas Gage, September 5, 1764, *Bouquet Papers*, 6:632, 631–32; William Johnson to Henry Bouquet, September 1, 1764, ibid., 6:625–26.

74. John Reid to Henry Bouquet, September 16, 1764, *Bouquet Papers*, 6:640–41.

75. Henry Bouquet Speech to Delaware, September 20, 1764, *Bouquet Papers*, 6:649–51; Henry Bouquet to Thomas Gage, September 26, 1764, ibid., 6:646–49.

76. Henry Bouquet to Thomas Gage, September 26, 1764, *Bouquet Papers*, 6:646–49.

77. Onondaga and Oneida Speech to Bouquet, October 2, 1764, *Bouquet Papers*, 6:653–55; Bouquet Reply, October 2, 1764, ibid., 6:655–57.

78. For the best primary source on Bouquet's 1764 campaign, see Edward G. Williams, ed., *The Orderly Book of Colonel Henry Bouquet's Expedition against the Ohio Indians, 1764* (Pittsburgh: Mayer Press, 1960). See also Alexander McKee to William Johnson, October 21, 1764, *Johnson Papers*, 11:385–86.

79. Williams, *Orderly Book*, 28.

80. Henry Bouquet to Delaware, October 15, 1764, *Bouquet Papers*, 6:661–62; Delaware Reply to Bouquet, October 14, 1764, ibid., 6:660–61.

81. Ohio Senecas and Delawares to Henry Bouquet, October 16, 1764, *Bouquet Papers*, 6:666, 665–67.

82. Speeches of Seneca and Delaware Chiefs, October 17, 1764, *Bouquet Papers*, 6:669–71.

83. Indian Proceedings, October 13–November 16, 1764, *Johnson Papers*, 11:443–44, 435–68; Bouquet Speech to Chiefs, October 20, 1764, *Bouquet Papers*, 6:671–75; Henry Bouquet to Thomas Gage, October 21, 1764, ibid., 6:675–77; Henry Bouquet to William Johnson, October 21, 1764, ibid., 6:679–80.

84. Williams, *Orderly Book*, 40.

85. Bouquet to Shawnee Chiefs, November 13, 1764, *Bouquet Papers*, 6:701, 698–703; Minutes Council with Chiefs, November 11, 1764, ibid., 6:692–97; Henry Bouquet to John Penn, November 15, 1764, MPCP 9:206–8.

86. Henry Bouquet to Thomas Gage, November 15, 1764, *Bouquet Papers*, 6:703–6.

87. Henry Bouquet to William Johnson, November 30, 1764, *Bouquet Papers*, 6:716; Henry Bouquet to Delaware, December 3, 1765, ibid., 6:717; Henry Bouquet to Iroquois, December 11, 1764, ibid., 6:720–21; Henry Bouquet to Horatio

Sharpe, December 20, 1764, ibid., 6:738–40; Alexander McKee to William Johnson, December 3, 1764, *Johnson Papers*, 11:482; Captives Delivered to Bouquet, December 3, 1764, ibid., 11:484–91; George Croghan to William Johnson, January 1, 1765, ibid., 11:519.

88. Henry Bouquet to Thomas Gage, November 30, 1764, Gage papers, CL.

89. Indian Conference, October 5, 1764, *Johnson Papers*, 11:373–74.

90. Henry Bouquet to John Bradstreet, September 5, 1764, *Bouquet Papers*, 6:629; Thomas Gage to John Bradstreet, September 2, 1764, ibid., 6:637–38. See also Henry Bouquet to John Bradstreet, September 12, 1764, ibid., 6:635–36.

91. John Bradstreet to Henry Bouquet, October 17, 1764, *Bouquet Papers*, 6:667–68.

92. William Johnson to Thomas Gage, November 8, 20, December 6, 1764, *Johnson Papers*, 11:399–402, 471–74, 491–96; Johnson's Remarks on Bradstreet's Conduct, November 24, 1764, ibid., 4:599–604.

93. Indian Proceedings, December 2–16, *Johnson Papers*, 11:505, 500–508.

94. William Johnson to Lords of Trade, December 26, 1764, NYCD 7:685–89.

95. Thomas Gage to Lord Halifax, December 13, 1764, *Gage Correspondance*, 1:46.

96. William Johnson to Thomas Gage, October 17, 1764, *Johnson Papers*, 11:382–84; William Johnson to Thomas Gage, July 6, 1765, ibid., 11:830–32.

97. Lords of Trade to William Johnson, Plan for the Future Management of Indian Affairs, July 10, 1764, NYCD 7:634–41.

98. William Johnson to Lords of Trade, NYCD 7:661–66.

99. William Johnson to Thomas Gage, September 30, 1764, *Johnson Papers*, 11:364–66; Thomas Gage to William Johnson, October 14, 1764, ibid., 11:375–78.

100. William Johnson to Thomas Gage, October 31, 1764, *Johnson Papers*, 11:394, 393–96.

101. Thomas Gage to William Johnson, December 6, 1764, *Johnson Papers*, 11:497, 496–98.

7

Settlements

"Nay Think Us Conquered, and Our Country Theirs"

Why, children, do you continue the war? And what will it avail you thus to redden the earth with your own blood?
                    —Governor d'Abbadie to Kaske and Levacher

I got the Stroke of a hatchett on the Head but my Scull being prety thick the hatchett wou'd not enter, so you may see a thick Scull is of Service on some Occasions.
                                    —George Croghan

Father, we have all smoked out of the pipe of peace. It's your children's pipe, and as the war is over and the Great Spirit and giver of light, who has made the earth and everything therein, has brought us together this day for our mutual good to promote the good works of peace.
                                              —Pontiac

After "Amherst's War" sputtered out in 1764, Johnson, Gage, and their men struggled desperately to sustain the tense truce. Not battle but logistics had forced the Indians to lay aside rather than bury their war hatchets. The truce would persist for two reasons. First was the resumption of trade which allowed the Indians to replenish their ammunition, food, and other essentials. As important were repeated British promises to negotiate a boundary as mandated by the Crown's October 7, 1763 Proclamation.

But it took four years to fulfill that promise. Whitehall, consumed with more pressing problems with the colonies and elsewhere, failed to agree on just where and how to draw the line. Without specific instructions and funds Indian Superintendents William Johnson and John Stuart were hamstrung in their Indian councils. Meanwhile, British squatting, murders, and cheating against Indians on their land raised tensions to a fever pitch. The Indians remained unconquered, defiant, and ever more eager to avenge years of British crimes and insults with their scalping knives. The frontier teetered on the brink of yet another devastating war. Gage, Johnson, Stuart, and various colonial governors and assemblies repeatedly wrote London imploring the government to grant them the necessary instructions, powers, and funds to settle the boundary. Each offered variations on the same argument—"should this boundary be established, these frequent causes of Indian disatisfaction would be removed, at least for many years."[1] But such pleas elicited only silence.

That silence had a reason. Britain's leaders were deadlocked over imperial policy. Some argued the price of empire was too high; maintaining troops and Indian agents was an enormous drain on the government budget. The forts were a liability, expensive to keep up during peace and easily isolated and taken during war. Why not withdraw the administration behind a firm boundary and allow traders beyond to operate at their own risk? Some went even further. Why not abolish the Indian superintendencies and allow the colonies to shoulder the expense, time, and efforts of Indian relations? Thus could the maximum amount of wealth be extracted from the Indian lands for the empire at minimum cost. Others countered that an ounce of prevention was worth a pound of cure. British agents and troops kept the peace. Withdrawing them would precipitate a war which would cost the empire enormous treasury and blood to win, and require sending back the troops and agents after all. And so the debate persisted along with the fear of another Indian war.

Just what were the prevailing sentiments among the tribes for renewed war or grudging peace? Each village's politics teetered between war and peace factions. To varying degrees most Indians in most villages burned with hatred toward the British. Yet practical realities checked those passions. To varying degrees virtually all Indians had suffered from the collapse of trade. The French on the Mississippi and Wabash could buy only a portion of their furs and supply only a portion of their powder, lead, and other necessities. Some villages mourned the loss in battle of their finest warriors. Even more murderous were smallpox and other diseases that had eaten their way across the region during the war. Smallpox reportedly killed 149 men and as many women and children among the Shawnee alone during 1765; similar losses undoubtedly afflicted the other tribes.[2]

Even the allied Iroquois tribes burned with resentment. At a council at Johnson Hall on May 4, 1765, the Onondaga spokesman bitterly recounted British insults, betrayals, and thefts. He then ended his harangue by asserting that "we have told you our minds. If it does not please you, it is none of our faults. We were always ready to give, but the English don't deal fairly with us. They are more cunning than we are. They get our names upon paper very fast, and we often don't know what it is for—We would do more for the King, but it is hardly in our power, and some of us don't like it because we are so often imposed upon."[3]

Despite this anger, the Iroquois remained a powerful force for peace. By first remaining neutral and then contributing war parties to the British they had pressured the hostile tribes to lay aside their arms and surrender their captives. The Delaware and Seneca joined the other Iroquois at Johnson Hall in council from April 29 to May 22, 1765. The two defiant tribes disgorged 25 prisoners and signed a treaty promising that they would remain at peace with the British.[4]

Although the Iroquois League had upheld its alliance with Britain, some sought to trim its power. New York Lieutenant Governor Cadwallader Colden argued that "the Six Nations assumed too much to themselves in directing affairs with all the other Nations & some method ought to be taken to check their ambition of having the lead everywhere. . . . Now that all our apprehensions of the French are removed, our principles of negotiating with the Indians are quite changed."[5] Colden suggested that Johnson treat separately with the tribes, encourage their independence from the Iroquois, not invite representatives of the Six Nations to those councils, and not recognize Iroquois claims over the other tribes. Thus did Colden hope that Iroquois power would eventually wither. But Johnson needed that power for now and maintained the old system of acknowledging Iroquois hegemony.

While Johnson depended on the Iroquois League to bring the eastern Indians to council, he believed that only one man determined whether the war in the west continued or ended. No chief was seen as more important than Pontiac. Peace among the tribes from the Maumee valley to Fort de Chartres depended on wooing him. Gage reckoned that "if Pontiac's fears do not prevent him I think he will come in to us; and he certainly may do us great service. Nothing but French influence I think can oppose us with all the Western Tribes."[6] Johnson agreed, describing Pontiac as "certainly very busy amongst the Indians backed & supported by the French, yet I don't despair of convincing him of his folly & rashness provided an interview can be effected either by me or my deputy."[7] He advised George Croghan that "Pondiac will be a very proper person to make a friend & shew favours to in proportion to his alacrity. If his doubts and fears are once removed he may prove of great service."[8] Johnson himself looked forward personally to polishing the friendship chain with him.[9]

What were the odds of scoring that? Gage and Johnson were right. Pontiac had wearied of the struggle and was ready for peace if the terms were just. And once Pontiac buried his hatchet the war in the West would effectively end. The problem was how to find him and then convince him to sign.

Yet while Pontiac may have been ready for peace, other chiefs remained defiant. Shawnee Chief Kaske and Illinois Chief Levacher persisted in lobbying the Louisiana governor throughout the winter and spring of 1765. A fever killed Governor d'Abbadie on February 4, 1765. Kaske and Levacher soon gained an audience with d'Abbadie's successor, Captain Charles Philip Aubry, Louisiana's commander. The new governor could only repeat his predecessor's arguments. France had surrendered its North American empire. Those tribes between the Mississippi River and the Appalachian Mountains were now subjects of the British king. It was time that they made peace with him. Those two chiefs would be joined by a third, Kaskaskia Chief Chacoretony, later that spring. The three chiefs met with Aubry and endured the same bitter message.[10]

The Indians were just as trapped among destructive forces beyond their control. Kaske lamented that "the English are coming here and saying that the land is theirs and that it is the French who have sold it to them. You know very well that our Fathers have always told us that the land is ours, that we were free on it, that the French did come to settle there only for our protection and defense, as a good father protects and defends his children. You placed the tomahawk in our hand to strike the English, which we did. . . . I am deputed by all the chiefs to demand aid from you to continue the war, and to know from you what you wish us to do. We have adopted you as our Father and will never hearken save to your word. Send us traders; we shall pay them well; we are rich in furs; our women and children are all naked since the French have ceased coming to trade with our Nation. If the French do not abandon us, the English will never take our lands." To this, the governor could only ask had they not heard that the "Great Emperors of France and of English had made peace? . . . Why, children, do you continue the war? And what will it avail you thus to redden the earth with your blood?"[11]

Those envoys from the Ohio tribes would receive no support to carry on their struggle. As the northern Indian war sputtered to an end, another threatened to explode on the southern frontier. Tensions had been at a fever pitch since the British conquest. In October 1764, rumors had spread that eighteen southern tribes had formed an alliance to overthrow British rule. Upper Creek Chief Mortar and Choctaw Chief Alabama Mingo were accused of being the ringleaders. John Stuart, Indian Superintendent for those colonies south of Maryland, tried to stifle any possible explosion with a series of councils among the tribes. In May 1765, at Mobile, Stuart counciled with the Chickasaw and Choctaw. Chiefs of those tribes surrendered their French medals, flags, and commissions in return for British ones. But the upper Creek remained defiant.

To keep the region subdued, the British played the classic "enemy of my enemy is my friend." Ancient rivalries split those tribes. The British tried to worsen those animosities. William Johnson suggested that the "quarrel between the Creeks & Chactaws might be of advantage to us as differences amongst themselves will always keep those at variance from giving us any trouble."[12] Stuart took his advice.[13]

Heightened suspicions among the tribes enhanced British security. War, however, literally killed British interests as Indian hunters and sometimes merchants died while fur production and trade collapsed. It was a tough diplomatic balancing act.

The British only promoted war among the tribes when they themselves were attacked. During the 1763 and 1764 uprisings the British had encouraged Cherokee war parties to stalk north up the Warrior Path to attack the Ohio valley tribes. That would divert at least some northern warriors from attacking settlements there. The trouble was that many battles between the Cherokee and northern Indians took place on Virginia soil. War parties from either side might ambush settlers and then claim the other side did it. Now that the war was over, Virginia Governor Francis Fauquier urged Johnson to foster peace between the Cherokee and northern tribes. Johnson agreed to try, although he reckoned it would be quite a challenge. Once the war genie had escaped the bottle it was difficult to stuff him back in.[14]

Peace with the Cherokee had to await attention to more pressing needs. In the northern district, Johnson and his agents faced the Sisyphean dilemma of reknitting an endlessly fraying peace. While some chiefs and their followers remained defiant, the worst obstacles to peace were British rather than Indians. Frontier bullies, murderers, squatters, and unscrupulous traders enraged the Indians. General Thomas Gage would have been optimistic over a "general pacification unless it is interrupted by the lawless and licentious proceedings of the frontier inhabitants. If those people can't be kept within their boundaries and forced into a subjection to the laws, we must expect that quarrels will be renewed with the Indians."[15]

After the hostilities petered out, a wave of settlers poured back into the territory to claim vast reaches of land owned by the Indians. The Ohio valley Indians demanded that British officials expel those along Red Stone Creek on the Monongahela River and the Cheat River which flows into the Ohio. Conflicting jurisdictions and cowardice prevented British officials from fulfilling their repeated promises to remove the squatters. Although General Gage and most governors agreed that the squatters must go, none wanted to roust settlers at bayonet point from their homes. They feared provoking a civil war on the frontier.[16]

Bands of frontier bullies terrorized Indians and officials alike, and were especially virulent in squatter and legal frontier settlements in western Pennsylvania and Virginia. Indian Agent Thomas McKee's experience at Fort Augusta was typical. McKee's mission was to forge peace with the Delaware, Shawnee, Nanticook, and Munsee who lived in the upper Susquehanna region. But ruffians harassed not only those Indians but McKee and his family: "I dare not move a step from my house, otherwise I should most certainly fall a victim to their rage and infatuation. I dread that any Indians should come on the frontiers, as the inhabitants declare they will murder all who do; and it is not to be wondered at as there is no kind of government among them."[17]

The Virginia frontier was just as violent. In early 1765, frontiersmen murdered perhaps as many as ten Shawnee in those borderlands alone. General Gage called on Virginia governor Francis Fauquier to lead efforts to bring the murderers to justice. But Fauquier's authority died at the frontier. Gage feared that "unless satisfaction is given the Indians, and the people restrained and punished for their lawless proceedings, we shall lose all the fruits of our expeditions and treaties, and our affairs thrown into worse confusion than ever."[18]

When it came to frontier criminals, Gage thoroughly sympathized with the Indians: "I am really vexed at the behavior of the lawless bandits upon the frontiers, and what aggravates the more is the difficulty to bring them to punishment. The true cause of which is . . . their flying from province to province, rescued by their comrades. . . . The disorder lies in the weakness of the governments to enforce obediance to the laws, and in some, their provincial factions run so high that every villain finds some powerful protector."[19] Another Indian war would likely result if a proper system of governing the frontier were not established. Yet Gage was unwilling to back frontier justice with regular troops.

The commander in chief was more decisive in acting against rapacious merchants. On January 16, 1765, he issued regulations governing the Indian trade. All traders had to apply for a license from their colonial governors. Traders must never cheat the Indians. "Spiritous liquors" could only be sold at forts. Post commanders would enforce the trade laws.[20] Yet these rules fell far short of what Johnson advocated. They were, however, the most politically feasible at the time and laid a legal foundation that could and would be expanded.

The merchants protested and pointed to the 1763 Proclamation which, among other things, guaranteed "free trade." Groups of merchants submitted petitions to Johnson demanding that their rights be observed.[21] Johnson deftly handled these complaints. He played good cop to the Crown's bad cop, insisting that he was required to uphold the law. But he also argued that the strict laws had been imposed because of the predatory actions of some traders. Nonetheless, he saw merit in some of their arguments, especially that of being allowed to winter with the distant tribes instead of remaining confined at the posts. He deferred that decision to Gage. The general agreed it was a tough call. The fear was that if they granted freedom to some traders all would demand the same. Control would disappear. Abuses would proliferate. Indian anger would again explode into war. So, in the end, Johnson and Gage put the interest of keeping a troubled peace before short-term profits.[22]

Then there was the debate over whether the military posts on Indian lands kept the peace or provoked conflict? If they kept the peace were they all equally cost-effective? Could the smaller posts be abandoned or were they all essential?

Johnson and Gage had no doubts that troops, Indian agents, and forts were essential to preventing another war. But they also agreed that for reasons of economy rather than security some of the smaller posts could go. Those posts which held too few troops to intimidate the local tribes or prevent traders from exploiting the Indians were liabilities rather than assets. Yet it was difficult to pinpoint just which forts cost the British Empire more than they saved. After all, any post could be a listening post for Indian rancor or French intrigues—that is, if the commander and his troops nurtured ties with the local Indians and civilians. What price could be levied on information that might prevent a war? In contrast, the budget for the system of troops, agents, and forts was easily calculated and exhorbitant.

While cognizant of the system's costs, Johnson feared more the alternative. Peace promoted trade and war destroyed it. Troops and agents helped keep the peace, though imperfectly. Withdraw them, allow greedy merchants the freedom to cheat and steal, and another war was inevitable. The expense of subduing hostile Indians with armies and presents far exceeded the present system's budget. Johnson reckoned the result would be "bloodshed & infinite expense, & perhaps cost us half a century to put matters on their former footing."[23]

Being further removed from Indian affairs, Gage could see the concrete expenses and not the subtle benefits of the military posts. He was willing to abandon the lesser posts and concentrate British power in a few strategic garrisons like Forts Detroit, Pitt, Niagara, Michilimackinac, Oswego, and Presque Isle. But that decision was deferred. It seemed more prudent to maintain the existing expensive system than eliminate links of it that might prove to have been essential.[24]

Ironically, while that debate droned on, British forces were attempting to add yet another fort to the empire. In 1765, Thomas Gage, William Johnson, and John Stuart each launched his own diplomatic mission which would infiltrate the Illinois country to negotiate peace from those tribes and occupy Fort de Chartres. Each attempt would face harsh challenges. Most would fail.[25]

Once again an expedition was ordered to ascend the Mississippi River. Once again it was delayed, this time by squabbles among the British rather than Indian sharpshooters. At his Mobile headquarters Governor George Johnston accused both Major Arthur Loftus and Major Robert Farmar of impeding the performance of his office, including preempting Indian diplomacy. Those officers in turn accused Johnston of "cruel treatment" and "violent and tyrannical behavior."[26] In March, Farmar finally left Mobile with the 34th regiment for New Orleans. He had planned to ascend the Mississippi with his troops from New Orleans on April 13. He was delayed by a lack of funds to pay for bateaux he had ordered. The 34th would remain camped outside of New Orleans through the summer, its ranks steadily diminishing from disease or desertion into the city.

Meanwhile, two other envoys trekked overland from Mobile to Fort de Chartres. On February 18, 1765, Captain Villiers received Lieutenant John Ross and trader Hugh Crawford who had been dispatched by Farmar several months earlier. The Illinois tribes were still out hunting so Ross had to wait impatiently until early April before they returned. On April 4, 1765, Ross opened a council with chiefs of the Kaskaskia, Cahokia, Michigamea, and Peoria among the Illinois, along with Osage and Missouri. The Illinois Chief Tamarois rejected Ross's message and ordered him to leave their country. Ross departed down the Mississippi River on April 7.

Although Ross and Crawford were undoubtedly disappointed, their expulsion was a blessing in disguise, saving them from prolonged terror and perhaps even death. The next day Pontiac, accompanied by Ottawa warriors and some Chippewa and Potawatomi subchiefs, arrived at Fort de Chartres. He and his delegation joined a council with the Illinois tribes, Osage, and Missouri. But those tribes were no more eager to join Pontiac in war against the British than they were to subject themselves to the British. Disappointed, Pontiac and his followers lingered indecisively at Fort de Chartres.

Meanwhile, another British envoy was approaching. In mid-January Gage ordered French-speaking Lieutenant Alexander Fraser of the 77th regiment and Deputy Indian Superintendent George Croghan to journey to Fort de Chartres and there secure peace from the Illinois tribes. Croghan was delayed at Fort Pitt by the failure of Indian gifts to arrive. On March 22, 1765, Fraser boldly embarked by canoe down the Ohio River, accompanied by its crew and a few Indian guides. They reached Fort de Chartres on April 17. There he would spend several hellish months during which he was never far from being burned at the stake.

The first of his gut-wrenching moments began almost immediately. Fraser was meeting with St. Ange when Pontiac and eight warriors crowded angrily into the room and insisted that the French commander surrender the British envoy to them. St. Ange promised to hand over Fraser the next morning. Pontiac and his men stormed off. Meanwhile, the Illinois captured two of Fraser's rowers and spirited them away to Kaskaskia, eighteen miles downstream. Once again Pontiac seems to have changed his mind over what to do. He did not appear the next morning to take Fraser. This allowed Fraser to convene a council with the Illinois chiefs and demand that they subject themselves to the British Crown or suffer the consequences. He explained that now that the eastern tribes had buried the hatchet, the British army would soon arrive to occupy the Illinois country. If those tribes were hostile they would be slaughtered. The chiefs were noncommittal. Fraser then called Pontiac to a private meeting and delivered the same message. Pontiac refused to believe that the Shawnee, Delaware, and Mingo had bowed to British power or that France had surrendered Illinois along with Canada.

That afternoon Fraser and St. Ange sent runners to all the chiefs to assemble with all their people. Nearly 500 Indians gathered before Fort de Chartres. The British and French officers called on the crowd to accept peace and British rule. Chief Tamarois replied that such a decision could only be made by their "elder brothers" the Ottawa.

Thus did a decision for war or peace rest once again in Pontiac's hands. And once again he flip-flopped. To the astonishment of all, Pontiac declared that "I submit to the wish of the king, my father. I do not desire to oppose him longer and consider from this moment that you have restored peace to all these children. For the future we will regard the English as brothers, since you wish to make us all one."[27]

An enormously relieved Fraser secured the release of his two boatmen and readied a delegation of chiefs to meet Croghan, who, he hoped, was on his way. The chiefs departed on April 24. Fraser remained as St. Ange's guest. Yet the Illinois remained ambivalent about British rule and even Fraser's presence. Death threats were muttered.

Then on April 28 a delegation of Chippewa, Potawatomi, Kickapoo, and Mascouten chiefs and warriors arrived at Fort de Chartres. When St. Ange refused their demand for brandy they ordered him to hand over Fraser instead. St. Ange hid Fraser. Traders sold alcohol to the Indians, who got drunk. They captured the British rowers and threatened to torture them to death. Hoping to save his men, Fraser surrendered himself. Fortunately, the Indians delayed killing the British until the next day. Now sober they sheepishly apologized for their behavior, released the British, and opened a council with Fraser. Fraser had no sooner talked the chiefs into going to meet Croghan when a runner appeared with a rumor that a British and Cherokee war party had killed fourteen Illinois. Now the Illinois clamored for Fraser's scalp. Pontiac then intervened with his warriors and asserted that the Illinois could only kill Fraser if they first killed him and his men. The fear of war with the Ottawa and other Great Lakes tribes overcame the Illinois lust for vengeance; they backed off. Although Fraser had again avoided a gruesome death, tensions lingered. Then a few days later the Illinois Indians thought to have been killed reached Fort de Chartres. The Illinois moved to Kaskaskia to greet Croghan. Fraser could breathe easy—but not for long.

Within days Kaske arrived at Kaskaskia to lie that the French king had renewed war with Britain and Governor Aubry was sending supplies and troops. The Illinois seized Fraser and his men and beat them. Once again Fraser's life hung in the balance and Pontiac saved him. The Ottawa chief strongly voiced his skepticism over Kaske's words and demanded that the Illinois desist from killing him and his men. The Illinois agreed and released them. Then the Illinois delegation that had journied to the Wabash River mouth to await Croghan returned on May 18 to announce that he had never showed up. As the Illinois debated whether to recapture the British, the intrepid lieutenant secretly sent his men downriver the night of May 19. He then confidently placed himself under Pontiac's protection. He found Pontiac "the most sensible man among all the nations and the most humane Indian I ever saw. He was as careful of me and my men as if we were his own children, and has twice saved my life since I came here."[28]

That favorable image would soon be challenged. Murderous passions seethed beneath Pontiac's genuine affections and desire for justice. One night he got drunk and threatened to murder Fraser. He resisted the impulse and asked Fraser for forgiveness once he had sobered up. Fraser again tried to convince Pontiac that the eastern tribes had submitted and it was only a matter of time before the British army would arrive to impose their rule over the Illinois country. Pontiac admitted that Fraser was persuasive and "I will believe none who will tell me the contrary hereafter. I believe that the nations on the Ohio have made a peace and that they come with Croghan. As soon as I see them or I am informed by them that they made peace, I will do the same, and you may be assured that as soon as my hatchet is buried all others in this quarter will."[29]

In June, Fraser received diplomatic reinforcements when Pierce Acton Sinnot, the Deputy Indian Superintendent for the Southern Colonies, reached Fort de Chartres, accompanied by French Captain Harpain de La Gauterais. Sinnot assembled the Illinois chiefs, called on them to remain at peace, and then distributed gifts. The Illinois were mollified. Two runners arrived with a letter from Croghan promising he would soon arrive. But the Deputy Indian Superintendent for the Northern Colonies failed to show up and the Illinois grew disgruntled again.[30]

Just where was George Croghan? He spent early February on a shopping trip. Gage had given Croghan 2,000 pounds of credit in Philadelphia to purchase the necessary gifts. There Croghan found what he needed, but he went more than double over budget. The extra was charged to the Crown. He arranged to have the goods transported to Fort Pitt where they would be stored until they could be packed on bateaux for the trip downriver. Upon finishing these arrangements he hurried on to Fort Pitt to organize councils and await the gifts.[31]

By late February an enormous packtrain with drovers had been assembled in Philadelphia. As much as 20,000 pounds worth of goods were packed on 80 horses, including 4,043 pounds worth of gifts bought by Croghan for diplomacy. The caravan departed for the several weeks' trek across Pennsylvania to Fort Pitt. On March 6 it was at Sideling Hill twelve miles west of Fort Loudoun when perhaps 100 members of a gang of frontier outlaws known as the "Black Boys" ordered it to halt. With blackened faces and other disguises they strode confidently among the animals and drovers, slit open the packs, stole or destroyed 63 of the 81 loads, and killed three horses. The outlaws justified their crime by asserting that they were preventing ammunition and other necessities from getting through to the Indians, who could have used those goods to attack the settlements. The drovers hurried back to Fort Loudoun with the news. Fort Loudoun's commander, Lieutenant Charles Grant, dispatched Sergeant McGlashan and twelve 42nd Highlanders to the site. Shots were exchanged. The outlaws fled. The detachment captured two stragglers. En route back to Fort Loudoun McGlashan and his men were confronted by 50 other outlaws. McGlashan managed to push his troops safely through the mob and reach Fort Loudoun. There the prisoners were released after posting their rifles as bail.[32]

A scandal soon arose on the heels of crime. Many of those merchants whose goods were lost were unlicensed. The packtrain was traveling on a side trail that paralleled the public road. All signs indicated that the merchants were deliberately trying to dodge the law.

That was bad enough. What worsened the scandal was that George Croghan was accused not only of allowing the traders to proceed without a license but also of mixing his own and official goods. As Gage put it, the disaster occurred because of "Croghan troubling his head more about trade than the business he was employed in. Had he thought proper to have followed his instructions, and made use of Colonel Bouquet's permit to get up his presents, which would if necessary have procured him an escort at every post, no accident could have happened. He takes upon himself to enter into leagues with traders to carry up goods in a clandestine manner under cover of the business he was employed in . . . and under pretense of having goods ready when the trade should be opened."[33]

Those were very serious charges. Were they true? Upon learning of the crime and scandal, William Johnson fired off a letter to his deputy asking his version. Croghan angrily denied the charges. Johnson also interviewed the prominent Philadelphia merchant Samuel Wharton who asserted that Croghan "had not the least interest in or concern with the goods."[34] After carefully reviewing these accounts, Johnson stood by his man. To the Board of Trade, he asserted that "Mr. Croghan had nothing to do in the affair, only told them that the Indians at Illinois would expect a trade to be opened with them as soon as possession was taken."[35]

Was Johnson right? An impartial review of the evidence reveals that Croghan was most likely guilty as charged, although he and his confederates would never be indicted. Nearly all of the goods in that packtrain were owned by the powerful Philadelphia firm of John Baynton, Samuel Wharton, and John Morgan. Croghan had conspired with those partners along with Robert Callender and Robert Field to use his own 4,043 pounds worth of official Indian gifts as cover for the private venture which would circumvent the law to be the first to reach the Ohio valley Indians.[36]

The charges against Croghan of corruption and conflict of interest were nothing new. They had been whispered or angrily shouted for years. Many frontier settlers had despised George Croghan along with other Indian agents not just for treating Indians diplomatically but for making small fortunes off the privilege. Henry Bouquet wrote that the "country people appear greatly incensed at the attempt they imagine has been made of opening a clandestine trade with the savages under cover of presents."[37]

Making those charges was easy and believable enough. Proving them, however, would be far more difficult. While his accusers may have had a weak legal case, the practical reasons for leaving Croghan alone were even stronger. He was indispensable to Johnson's diplomacy. The superintendent could not be everywhere at once. Croghan ventured deep into the wilderness to places denied Johnson because of his wretched health and endless duties. On April 20, Johnson ordered Croghan to continue on his diplomatic mission to the Ohio valley and Illinois tribes.[38]

Croghan was off the hook. But what about the other accused merchants? They all vigorously denied any wrongdoing, insisting that they did indeed intend to use those goods for the Indian trade but only after obtaining a proper license; until then they had intended to store those goods at Fort Pitt. They announced their intention to send west another load and applied for permission to store it at Fort Pitt.

Necessity may have forced Johnson to turn a blind eye toward his deputy. But for the merchants, he judged it as an open-and-shut case. All traders needed a license not only to trade with the Indians but also to move goods westward. Those merchants had broken the law. But while Johnson could judge he could not sentence. The alleged crimes were not strictly in his jurisdiction. Justice depended on Pennsylvania Governor John Penn, who journied to Carlisle to investigate the crime and various accusations. Most folks sympathized with the Black Boys. Few among the few who did not were brave enough to bear witness against them. Penn did not find enough compelling witnesses or evidence to call a grand jury. The merchants escaped justice as well. No one would step forward to testify against Wharton and his associates in Philadelphia. Pennsylvania teetered on the verge of anarchy. In the end no one served any time for the crimes.[39]

Croghan meanwhile tied up the preparations for his diplomatic mission. Before he could embark he had to await more gifts and polish the friendship chain with upper Ohio valley tribes. Only after securing a preliminary peace agreement with them and sending their chiefs on to meet with Sir William Johnson could he head for the Illinois country.

It was not until May 9 that 105 Shawnee, 215 Delaware, 125 Seneca, and 38 Wyandot warriors, along with their women and children arrived at Fort Pitt. With them were 44 whites, 21 males and 23 females, whom the chiefs released with the greatest reluctance. Few of those whites were recent and defiant captives. Most had become Indians and resisted being torn from their families. One can almost hear the sobs in his voice as Shawnee Chief Lawoughqua addressed the council the next day: "Father, here is your flesh and blood . . . they have all been tied to us by adoption, although we now deliver them up to you. We will always look upon them as relations, whenever the Great Spirit is pleased that we may visit them. We have taken much care of these prisoners, as if they were our own flesh and blood; they are become unacquainted with your customs and manners, and therefore, Father, we request you will use them tender and kindly, which will be a means of inducing them to live contentedly with you."[40] The fate of those bewildered adoptees sent back into a white world that scorned and pitied them remains unknown.

The council lasted three days. Although the Indians promised peace and turned over their prisoners, Croghan had no gifts to give them. He promised that presents would soon arrive and pleaded with the Indians to remain patient. He wrote Johnson to tell of the council's success and also to warn that if trade is not soon resumed with the Indians peace "will have but a short duration."[41] He sent a delegation of Shawnee, Mingo, and Delaware chiefs to Johnson Hall where they met from July 4 to July 14 and signed a peace treaty.[42]

Meanwhile, Croghan asked for and received a delegation of Seneca, Shawnee, and Delaware chiefs to accompany him to the Illinois country. They embarked on May 15 and reached the Wabash River mouth on June 6. There Croghan sent two runners overland to Fort de Chartres with word of his approach and set up camp to await a response. On June 8, 80 Kickapoo and Mascouten attacked, killing two British and three Shawnee and wounding everyone else including Croghan. The deputy laconically recalled that "I got the Stroke of a hatchett on the Head but my Scull being prety thick the hatchett wou'd not enter, so you may see a thick Scull is of Service on some Occasions."[43]

Why had the Kickapoo and Mascouten attacked the peace delegation? Apparently, they had believed the rumor that Croghan and his followers were actually a prowling British and Cherokee war party. Although at first depressed, Croghan soon realized that the attack had been a blessing in disguise: "It will turn out for the good of his Majesty's Indian interest, as it has broke & divided that great confederation of eighteen western nations which the French has been this three years endeavoring to bring about with great pains & expense to oppose our getting possession of this country."[44]

And indeed, that is what happened. The murder or wounding of the Shawnee, Delaware, and Seneca chiefs terrified the Kickapoo and Mascouten that those nations would soon war against their peoples. They released their Indian captives and pleaded with them for forgiveness. A Kickapoo and Mascouten delegation joined the Shawnee, Delaware, and Seneca party to journey to Fort de Chartres and negotiate with Sinnot and Fraser. The others retained Croghan and his men as hostages, hoping to exchange them in return for a British and Indian promise not to retaliate.

What had happened to Fraser and Sinnot? The arrival of Croghan's delegation at Fort de Chartres shifted popular opinion once again over whether to protect or murder the British envoys. They were released. Sinnot stayed. Fraser was fed up. He and his men embarked downriver for New Orleans.[45]

Meanwhile, Croghan and the other hostages were taken by canoe up the Wabash to Vincennes. The Piankeshaw living at Vincennes were horrified when they learned that the Kickapoo and Mascouten had attacked a British and eastern Indian peace delegation, and urged them to release their hostages. Instead, the war party soon departed for Fort Ouiatenon where fourteen French families and a Wea village lived beside Kickapoo and Mascouten villages. On June 30 the Kickapoo and Mascouten chiefs returned to Ouiatenon from Fort de Chartres where they had made peace with Fraser and Sinnot. Croghan and his men were released. The deputy began talks with the chiefs and sent runners to more distant tribes calling for a council. On July 13, Croghan convened a council of Kickapoo, Wea, Mascouten, Ottawa, Piankeshaw, and Miami chiefs who agreed to his request, which was really a demand packaged in diplomatic guise, that they allow the British to reestablish forts throughout the region.[46]

But Croghan was not out of the woods yet. One man remained the key to any lasting peace: "Pontiac has great sway amongst those nations and is on his way here. He sent me a message by a Frenchman that came here yesterday that he would be glad to see me and that if he liked what I had to say he would do everything in his power to reconcile all nations to the English as he is an old acquaintance of mine I hope I shall be able to settle matters with him on a good footing."[47]

Where was Pontiac? He had left Fort de Chartres with a delegation of Illinois chiefs along with the Seneca, Shawnee, and Delaware chiefs that Croghan had dispatched there. Croghan and his delegation departed Ouiatenon on July 18. The next day the two delegations met on the trail linking the two forts and returned to Ouiatenon.

There at a council on July 20, Pontiac submitted to Croghan who informed him he must journey on to formally surrender to Sir William Johnson. Pontiac agreed as long as the British promised that only troops and traders would rent the forts in Indian lands and would allow no settlers to arrive. Croghan was not authorized to make such a promise but did encourage Pontiac to believe that Johnson would agree to keep settlers from Indian country if the Indians remained at peace. Croghan sent to Gage a letter saying that British troops could be returned to the forts. Then on July 25, Croghan, Pontiac, the other chiefs, and their men hurried on to Detroit.

Lieutenant Colonel John Campbell greeted the delegation at Detroit on August 17, 1765. Croghan held councils first with the Miami, Mascouten, Kickapoo, Wea, and Piankeshaw on August 23, and then on August 27 with the Ottawa, Chippewa, Huron, and Potawatomi. Speaking for the Detroit tribes, Pontiac promised peace: "Father, we have all smoked out of the pipe of peace. It's your children's pipe, and as the war is over and the Great Spirit and giver of light, who has made the earth and everything therein, has brought us all together this day for our mutual good to promote the good works of peace."[48]

Although conciliatory, Pontiac firmly held out for a promise that the British would pay dearly for the privilege of having forts and trading posts on Indian land, and that settlers would not arrive on the heels of the British soldiers and merchants. Croghan delicately tiptoed around the reality that the British government did not regard the Indian peoples as civilized members of the "family of nations" and thus rejected their land claims.

The council realized British hopes. Colonel Campbell for one was convinced that peace was at hand: "Pondiac . . . will do all the good actions in his power to ingratiate himself with the English. He certainly has vast influence over the Indians and I firmly believe he will exert himself for the future in behalf of the English interest, as much as he formerly did against us."[49]

On September 26, Croghan left Detroit for Niagara. Pleading illness, Pontiac did not accompany Croghan. He did promise to meet Johnson in the following spring of 1766 for a Grand Council at Niagara.

As one report after another trickled into his New York headquarters, Gage grew more satisfied at the progress. At best making peace with the Indians was a process of two steps forward and one backward. There were still plenty of loose ends to tie up. One of the more glaring was that the fleur de lis still flew over Fort de Chartres. In late summer Gage ordered yet another detachment to attempt that elusive goal. Captain Thomas Stirling and 100 Highlanders of the 42nd left Fort Pitt on August 24 and reached Fort de Chartres on October 9. Captain St. Ange formally surrendered Fort de Chartres to Stirling on October 10, 1765, then retired with his troops across the Mississippi River to St. Louis, which had been founded the previous year.[50]

Around that same time news of a tragedy reached New York. Earlier that year, on March 16, 1765, Gage had recalled Colonel Henry Bouquet. The following month, on April 15, he gave Bouquet his next assignment, command of British forces in the Floridas, and promoted him to brigadier general. It would be a difficult mission. That region's tribes were resentful of British rule. Animosities poisoned relations between Governor George Johnston and the senior officers. Serious accusations of corruption and cowardice were lodged against Major Robert Farmar. Fever ravaged the troops. Bouquet never got a chance to confront these challenges. He sailed from Philadelphia for Pensacola on June 20. He had no sooner settled into his new post when yellow fever killed him on September 3, 1765.[51]

Henry Bouquet may have forseen his premature death. He wrote a detailed last will and testament not long before he embarked.[52] To Elizabeth, the sister of Margaret Oswald, the woman he hoped to marry, he asked that she "forgive & forget all my sins and iniquities."[53] Whatever those may have been, they are lost to history. But Bouquet's real or imagined "sins & iniquities" clearly preyed on his mind. Most poignantly, Bouquet wrote to Margaret that she had "become my habitual thought . . . While I breath I shall remain irrevocably yours."[54] Sadly, a "habitual thought" was all she would ever be to that lonely, passionate man destined to suffer a life of unrequited loves.

While Bouquet's friends mourned his death, they could cheer at that year's diplomatic successes. Peace treaties had been negotiated with most tribes. Most prisoners had been released. Even Pontiac had abandoned the fight. The Union Jack flew over Fort de Chartres. On December 4, Major Farmar's expedition finally reached that fort and relieved Captain Stirling.

But a key problem remained. How were the British to fulfill all their promises to the chiefs? The hands of Johnson and Gage remained tied with regard to policy. Whitehall's silence on their repeated requests for greater authority, personnel, and funds to negotiate a definitive treaty deeply frustrated the superintendent and general. Gage bitterly complained that "I am at a loss how to act, since I am neither empowered to incur any expense but at my own hazard nor have I officers near sufficient to discharge the duty within my department which has become very expensive since the reduction of Canada."[55]

As the wilderness war wound down, the worries of British officials would shift elsewhere. The simmering Indian troubles on the distant frontier would be eclipsed by more immediate ones that engulfed nearly all Americans. The attempts by Johnson and Gage to forge a lasting peace with the Indians were continually thwarted and diverted by the worsening political crisis between Parliament and the colonies. On August 11, 1765, Lord Halifax issued a letter to the governors informing them that Parliament had passed the Stamp Act which imposed a tax on all legal transactions that required an official seal. The logic behind the tax was that Americans should pay for at least part of the cost of defending them.[56]

Most Americans disagreed. Riots broke out. Stamps were seized. Officials were driven to the safety of British forts and warships. Many feared that the colonies were on the verge of revolution. Although Whitehall tried to quell the disturbances by repealing the Stamp Act on March 31, 1766, they issued other taxes and repressive measures that would provoke the American Revolution within a decade.[57]

Like most British officials and wealthy landowners, Sir William Johnson sided with the Crown against the colonists. He associated the protesters with mob rule, the kind that violated Indian trade laws or most evilly slaughtered peaceful Indians. He denounced "the clamorous conduct of a few pretended Patriots, who have been always remarkable for opposing government in every article, & its officers in every character, & have propogated their Republican principles amongst an ignorant people whose religious and civil tenets incline them to embrace that Doctrine."[58] Johnson prudently confided his views only to his close friends. Although he was "a lover of the British Constitution," he gingerly sidestepped debates.

Yet Johnson recognized the dilemma in imposing troops on the colonists to enforce the collection of taxes that helped pay for those troops. The solution, for Johnson, was simple: "If they can get away the troops, there will be little occasion for the late duties & they will besides get rid of . . . the . . . braggadocios the more sensible Americans must consider." Yet he rejected any notion of "abandoning the frontiers & leaving us to our own discretion . . . or the withdrawing of troops at any time from a region so distant from the Mother Country."[59] Like so much of Johnson's other advice over the years, Whitehall ignored that possible remedy to a worsening crisis.

There was also the continued fear that the French would stir up trouble and divert trade. Although British leaders were pleased that Spain had taken over France's Louisiana territory, they feared that the French would continue to rule while the Spanish reigned. Johnson's assessment was typical: "Altho the Spaniards should possess New Orleans &c and are a less active people . . . the French will still remain and act the same part under the Spanish government which they practise under their own, whilst those at the Illinois (now British subjects) having a property & interest in that country and being all traders, will doubtless act in conjunction with them and thereby divert the trade from the proper channel to the great prejudice of the Crown and the mercantile people."[60]

It was one thing to accept the persistence of French intrigues and another to believe they were the source of all troubles in Britain's western empire. A skeptical Croghan reported the Indian claim that the French had provoked the war: The "principal men of those nations seem at present to be convinced that the French had a view of interest in stirring up the late difference between his Majesties Subjects & them & call it a beaver war, for neither Pontiac nor any of the Indians which I met with ever pretended to deny but the French were at the bottom of the whole & constantly supplied them with every necessary they wanted."[61] Croghan, Johnson, Gage, and most other British leaders agreed that Amherst's punitive policies were the war's underlying cause. Those in turn provoked Indian conspiracies which were exacerbated by French supplies and encouragement.

Yet there was no question that the Indians remained nostalgic for French rule. The imposition of British power "has not changed the Indians affections to them. They have been bred up together like children in that country & the French have always adopted the Indians customs & manners, treated them civily & supplied their wants generously, by which means they gained the hearts of the Indians & commanded their services & enjoyed the benefit of a very large fur trade. . . . The French have in a manner taught the Indians . . . to hate the English."[62]

British fears of French intrigues lifted somewhat when they learned that on March 5, 1766, Don Antonio de Ulloa arrived at New Orleans with 100 troops to take possession of Louisiana and serve as its first Spanish governor. The transfer of power pleased the British. In all, Spanish rather than French imperial neighbors were preferred. Southern Superintendent John Stuart summed up the British view that since "Spaniards are now in possession of French Louisiana it is to be hoped that we shall not in future be plagued with such a competition in Indian concerns as it is not in the genius of the Spaniards to be so enterprising as the French."[63] But the French did not accept their new overlord. When the French protested, Ulloa retreated to Fort Balize below New Orleans where he awaited reinforcements from Havana. French governor Aubry remained in power. The standoff would not be resolved until July 1769, when Governor Alexander O'Reilly arrived with 2,000 Spanish troops, crushed the rebels, and took the province's helm.

The French may have lost their empire but they continued to intrigue against the British. If the struggle for formal ownership of territory had ended, that for national pride and personal profits continued. Captain St. Ange at St. Louis would not give up. He sent warbelts among the Illinois urging them to resist the imposition of British rule and carry the belts on to the Detroit tribes. When he heard of the conspiracy, Pontiac promptly informed the British.[64]

In all, although they had lost their own empire the French remained a thorn in the British Empire's side. With peace French ships docked again at New Orleans and disgorged trade goods. Those goods were packed on barges for the four-month trip up the Mississippi River, bound now for St. Louis rather than Fort de Chartres. That region's furs still largely ended up in French hands. The French enticed more than furs to St. Louis. They convinced entire villages of Indians to migrate west across the Misssissipi River. That migration not only deprived the British of furs but food as well. The British garrison and traders at Fort de Chartres and elsewhere in the western empire depended on buying crops from the local tribes to sustain themselves. Surplus food dwindled with Indian populations.

How could the loss of furs and food be stemmed? Why not create a British colony in Illinois, many a land speculator suggested. Gage and Johnson debated whether to allow a limited white settlement on vacated Indian lands. The paradox was that their garrisons needed food but any settlement would inevitably lead to others which could provoke an Indian war.[65]

Policies toward the Indians and western empire could conflict in principle and practice. Gage and Johnson repeatedly called for a strict boundary separating British and Indian settlements and strict trade regulations. Yet they finally agreed to back a Whitehall scheme for creating a new colony in Illinois that would be settled by free land grants to war veterans, based on their respective ranks. Johnson described it as "so reasonable and so well calculated for the mutual interests of Great Britain & its Colonies. . . . It will . . . prove a means of checking the attempts of the French or Spanish towards establishing a colony on the other side of the Mississippi which might draw off our new acquired allies, and deprive us of the great benefits we may expect from a commerce with so many nations, whilst at the same time it will tend to the security of our southern frontiers & enhance the public revenue."[66]

Were those sentiments sincere or merely calculated to appease Whitehall? It is difficult to say. The proposal did advance its avowed strategic goals while simultaneously making an Indian war much more likely. But any settlement let alone colony would take years of toil and treasure to plant.

For now, Johnson and Gage remained preoccupied with nurturing the precarious truce into a genuine peace with the Indians. They moaned frequently of the lack of detailed instructions and disbursements from Whitehall that would allow them to forge a lasting peace. They claimed that their limited power threatened to undo all that had been done. Peace remained fragile and could easily be shattered by some incident. Gage, Johnson, and most other leaders feared another devastating Indian war was imminent.

Yet, in retrospect, their complaints are puzzling. Whitehall did grant them the authority if not the funds to accomplish their mission. All along Whitehall thoroughly backed Johnson's peace efforts, including such specific policies as enforcing the 1763 Proclamation and eliminating the Redstone Creek settlement. The Indian agency was becoming increasingly professionalized. Indian agents received assignments with standard and detailed requirements. They were empowered to inspect all trade, investigate all Indian or trader complaints, enforce price controls, employ a blacksmith and interpreter, and maintain strict accounts of expenditures. Still, Johnson and his agents could not fulfill all Indian demands. It was easy to scapegoat Whitehall for any problems.[67]

And there were plenty of those. Despite all the British promises, the change in official policy, and the troubled peace on the frontier, rage among the Indians remained ubiquitous and with it the chance for another war. Johnson informed the Board of Trade, in June 1766, that "there has lately arisen a fresh discontent amongst most of the Indian Nations . . . occasioned by many late acts of oppression, by murders, robberies, & encroachments on their native rights and possessions, and as these acts of cruelty and injustice continue or rather gain ground, the discontent and clamours of the Indians is daily increasing, and will in all probability end in a general war."[68]

The subjection of the tribes prompted some frontiersmen gleefully to murder stray Indians. In early May 1766, criminals butchered five Shawnee on the Ohio River, stole their canoes, blankets, and fled downriver. The chiefs issued their bitter complaints to the commander and Indian agent at Fort Pitt. Gage worried that "these villians will sooner or later bring us into a war. . . . I most sincerely wish that the Indians had killed them that we might shew them our approbation in the punishment of such execrable villians."[69]

Murders in New Jersey prompted Johnson to write Governor William Franklin of his hope that "you will use all your endeavours for bringing the murderers of the Indians to justice, the conduct of the frontier inhabitants in many colonies being such as give us all great reason to dread a renewal of that cruel war from which we are but just freed."[70]

No matter what the evidence for the crime, juries would not convict peers or even slaves who murdered Indians. Gage complained that the "difficulty in bringing those lawless ruffians to punishment encourages them to every excess. They escape out of one province into another. If by chance apprehended, they are rescued and it is said the bringing them to trial signifies little, as no jury would condemn them for murdering or ill treating an Indian."[71]

The worsening frontier anarchy did not just plague Indians. Many of the same ruffians who had plundered Croghan's supply train the previous year continued to harass Fort Loudoun. They robbed messengers and Indian traders, and in April 1766 "surrounded Fort Loudoun for the space of a day and a night firing some thousands of shots at it. The soldiers were covered by the stockades so that fortunately none were killed or wounded. The garrison did not return a single shot, a remarkable instance indeed of their temper and coolness. The ringleader as well as most of the rest are known, but I have not been able to get an satisfaction."[72]

Ever more squatters elbowed their way on Indian land, sometimes following and sometimes preceding the soldiers and traders. Land companies petitioned Gage and Johnson for permission to settle tracts in Indian territory. Permission was denied. Settlers flocked to those regions anyway. Tensions rose with the Indians.

The Indians complained most about the swelling squatter settlements at Redstone Creek and the Cheat River. Gage and Johnson favored deploying troops to expel the squatters but the worsening crisis between Parliament and the colonies stayed their hand. Although Johnson hardly needed reminding, Gage warned that if in expelling the squatters "a skirmish happens and blood is shed, you know what a clamor there will be against the military acting without civil magistrates."[73] So Gage and Johnson appealed to the colonial governors to muster their militia and roust the settlers. Most colonial governors sympathized with the king and Parliament rather than their colonial assembly and inhabitants. Yet they dared not use force. They feared exacerbating the worsening relations between themselves and ever angrier and more assertive populations provoked by the Stamp, Townsend, and other repressive parliamentary laws. And besides, it was not at all clear which provincial jurisdiction was being violated. No boundary had then been demarcated that far west between Virginia and Pennsylvania.

Within Johnson's shadow in the lower Mohawk valley, Ury Klock and his son George continued to eat away at Iroquois lands by debauching and bullying local Indians. Mohawk and other Iroquois sachems had been protesting Klock's land thefts for years. But Johnson could do nothing. Klock had powerful political allies and could point to legal documents signed by drunk chiefs.[74]

The British had their own complaints. The loudest protests came from established merchants and traders who wanted to enrich themselves further from business with the Indians. They despised the new policy of regulated trade. They protested that the requirement that they trade only at military posts lost them an enormous amount of business and raised costs. Not only the British but tribes distant from the posts suffered when traders were forbidden to winter with them. French traders filled the void; profits shifted to them and flowed down the Mississippi to France. This was an ironic turnabout from the decades leading to the French and Indian War. Then it was the French traders who complained that their British rivals enjoyed an advantage.[75]

The Indians joined the merchants in protesting the restrictions. They "complained that they could not subsist during the winter without them & that the traders were extremely sollicitous for such permission." Johnson was thoroughly unsympathetic to such claims: "I see plainly how it is now throughout the continent. People expect to do now as they please." He went on to argue that free trade will allow abuses that provoke another disastrous Indian war. Thus were some trading losses offset by the enormous savings accrued by continued peace.[76]

Always the skilled diplomat, Johnson made it appear that he sided with the merchants while at the same time arguing that the new regulations would increase trade and profits rather than the reverse. He asserted his opposition to the rise of any monopoly over the trade. He also claimed that London tied his hands and "it is not in my power to do any thing contrary to the intentions of His Majesty."[77] Johnson provided powerful documentation and arguments packaged in diplomatic niceties to those British in Canada who claimed lands granted by the French regime.

Merchants also struggled to receive government compensation for losses suffered during the war. Major Thomas Smallman's plight in western Pennsylvania was typical. He reported losses of 15 beaver packs worth 450 pounds, 44 packs of tanned deerskins worth 440 pounds, 22 packs of deer furs worth 165 pounds, 2,800 racoon skins worth 280 pounds, 100 wildcat and fox skins worth 280 pounds, 128 otter skins worth 64 pounds, 11 horses with saddles and bits worth 99 pounds, three canoes worth 45 pounds, and a bateau worth 30 pounds. With some miscellaneous losses the total damage was 3,085 pounds, a fortune in those days.[78] How much, if any, compensation he received is unknown.

Indians robbed and sometimes murdered stray traders or hunters who ventured into their territory. Of course, most of those were trespassers who entered Indian lands at their own risk. And sometimes their crimes were even more serious.

On February 4, 1766, St. Joseph Potawatomi murdered two redcoats. Learning of the crime, Lieutenant Colonel Campbell sent a message to the chiefs annoucing that trade would be cut off with that tribe until the murderers were delivered to Detroit. It would be difficult enough to get an extradition under any circumstances; with two sons of chiefs implicated it would be nearly impossible. Campbell then aggravated the situation by committing a serious and potentially explosive gaff. A runner informed him that a Potawatomi delegation was approaching to offer condolences and a slave in compensation rather than the accused. Campbell set up an ambush "in order to waylay them and take them prisoners if possible." He seems to have envisioned holding the envoys as hostages to be exchanged for the murderers. But Campbell's scheme could not have been more stupid. By violating both Indian and European notions of diplomacy it could have been a casus belli. It was also impractical. Why Campbell chose to try capturing the delegation in the wilderness rather than simply interning them when they arrived at Detroit is a mystery. The trap sprang poorly. The troops did capture two men and a woman but the others fled. The Potawatomi would not trade the accused for the hostages. Thus did Campbell savage his own reputation. Friendly and hostile Indians alike now saw Campbell as untrustworthy, even treacherous. Campbell compounded the crisis by threatening to march against the Potawatomi village if he did not receive the accused. That was mere bluster and the Indians knew it, which further damaged Campbell's esteem. It is from such arrogant, insensitive, and aggressive blunders that Indian wars often explode. Fortunately, the mutual animosities simmered but did not boil over.[79]

As alarming was Campbell's failure to address the murderers' motive. Those two soldiers had raped one of their women. The husband and others killed the rapists in an act of vengeance and justice. That oversight was especially ironic, since a similar crime occurred near Detroit, this time involving a black slave who raped and murdered an Indian woman. When he learned of the crime, Lieutenant Colonel Campbell launched an investigation and had the slave arrested and charged with murder. Campbell wished "with all my heart he could be tried here & if condemned to suffer death, his being made an example of in the presence of the Indians." But that was not to be. Accused civilians had to be sent back to the eastern settlements for trial. If the slave was extradited "the Indians will be very apt to believe he is sent on purpose out of the way."[80] Gage heartily agreed. He blasted the civil law which aggravated relations with the Indians and hoped that "the Negro is past all doubt guilty . . . [and] the Indians had put him to death & saved us [the] trouble."[81] In the end none of the murderers met justice.

Sir William Johnson hoped to resolve the worsening tensions at a Grand Council at Fort Ontario during the summer of 1766. During late spring envoys carried wampum invitations to the distant tribes. Unable to go himself, George Croghan dispatched Hugh Crawford to Detroit to gather and escort the tribes of that region to the council. Crawford reached Detroit on May 6 and began visiting each tribe to council with the chiefs. He had his hands full.

The British policy of dividing and subjecting the tribes by playing off the chiefs against each other was working too well. Animosities within and among the tribes had become explosive. The Indians could only sublimate their rivalries by opposing a common enemy, ironically, not the British this time but one of their own.

Bitter resentment rather than adulation greeted Pontiac when he reached Detroit in June. The antagonism came not so much from Pontiac's failure to destroy Fort Detroit but from rumors that the British rewarded his loyalty with ten shillings a day. Then, on the way to Detroit, Pontiac got into a drunken fight with three Illinois chiefs and stabbed one. The wounded chief could not attend the council. Many Indians may have seen the stabbing as a metaphor—Pontiac had first walked with then turned against his Indian brothers. Indian agent Norman MacLeod shared a belief that the rumors about Pontiac were "used by his enemys to create a jealousy amongst the Indians that will end in his ruin. The Frenchmen offered to lay me a beat that Pontiac would be killed in less than a year, if the English took so much notice of him."[82] It would actually be another three years before an Indian murdered Pontiac, but jealousy would be the most likely motive.

Tensions mounted on June 20, as 40 chiefs from a dozen tribes crammed into bateaux at Detroit. They were escorted by Crawford, Indian affairs commissary Lieutenant Jehu Hay, and interpreter Mini Chene. Upon arriving at Fort Erie on June 27, Pontiac's composure broke when he heard musket shots. His terror was unfounded; the shots came from soldiers bird hunting on the lake. But the incident must have further diminished his stature. Then the grudge against Pontiac worsened when he signed, with Fort Erie's commander Lieutenant John Carden, an agreement which surrendered land around Detroit. Pontiac had no authority to do so; nor did Carden, for that matter.

The chiefs finally reached Fort Ontario on July 3. A sickly Johnson sent word for the chiefs to join him at his home, Johnson Hall, in the lower Mohawk valley. But the chiefs refused to venture any deeper into British territory. Johnson finally agreed to journey to Fort Ontario. During these negotiations it fell upon the fort's commander, Captain Jonathan Rogers, and commissary Norman McLeod to entertain the chiefs.

On July 22, Johnson arrived, accompanied by his sons-in-law and officials Daniel Claus and Guy Johnson, along with Captain John Butler. Johnson convened the council on July 23. As usual, when he counciled with many tribes, Johnson used their main gathering as a pageant to impress the Indians while he cut deals with individual chiefs behind the scenes. When it was his turn on July 25, Pontiac declared to Johnson that "I speak in the name of all the Nations to the westward whom I command, it is the will of the Great Spirit that we should meet here today and before him and all present I take you by the hand and never will part with it." As Pontiac spoke, he punctuated each point of his speech by handing small wampum belts to Johnson. He concluded his peace speech by promising, "Father, it will take some time before I can make known to all the nations what has passed here, but I will do it even from the rising of the sun to the setting and from north to south."[83] Pontiac would largely be good to his word. Yet it is unlikely that many Indians believed that he spoke for them.

Pontiac and the other chiefs signed the standard treaty by which they agreed to accept peace and return any whites or blacks among them, in return for a resumption of trade and forgiveness for the war. Handing over those non-Indians among them was the most controversial issue. Scores of whites and escaped slaves remained among the Indians, most voluntarily after having grown to love the culture they were forced to adopt. But under the treaty the chiefs promised to return all whites whether or not they were willing to leave their Indian families. In all, Johnson deemed the council a grand success, having settled "matters with Pondiac and the Western Chiefs much to my satisfaction and beyond my expectations as they were greatly discontented."[84] Pontiac and most other western chiefs left Oswego on July 31 and reached Detroit exactly a month later on August 31, after prolonged halts at Forts Niagara and Erie. By early September, Pontiac had returned to his Maumee village.

While Johnson tried to mollify the New York and Great Lakes Indians, Croghan worked just as assiduously to forge relations with the Illinois tribes. He held a council with chiefs from 22 villages of eight tribes at Fort de Chartres on August 25, 1766. His diplomacy appeared to work. At the council's end the chiefs collectively declared their friendship with the British. How many of the chiefs secretly gritted their teeth when they uttered the platitude was not clear. Croghan recognized that possibility. Yet he was guardedly optimistic that he had defused a potential regional explosion against British rule, at least for the present.[85]

All along, Southern Indian Superintendent John Stuart continued to play a vital supporting role in quelling war. Like Johnson, Stuart tried to subdue and exploit the tribes by subtly wielding carrot and stick policies. He defused Indian rage by resuming supplies of ammunition and other essential goods while promising to restrain British settlers east of the Appalachian watershed. But after those "carrot" policies, divide and conquer was the most avidly practiced British imperial policy. The Indian warrior cultures demanded that they almost always raid someone. British diplomacy encouraged them to raid tribes actually or potentially hostile to the colonies. Stuart was just as adept in employing that strategy as more conciliatory ones.

In early 1766 the debate continued among Gage, Johnson, and Stuart over whether to mediate a peace between the Cherokee and Iroquois or continue to exacerbate the war between them. Cherokee war parties were useful in diverting what the British feared was another conspiracy budding among the northern Indians. It also inhibited the resumption of the Cherokee war against the British. In late spring, the murder of some Cherokee in Augusta County, Virginia threatened to ignite an Indian war on that frontier. When he learned of the murders, upper Creek Chief Mortar offered to join the Cherokee with 700 of his warriors. Stuart feared an Indian war would engulf the entire southern frontier. He found the Creek "very insolent and ungovernable, and have of late been endeavoring to form a confederacy among the great nations in this department."[86] The Creek killed two traders and threatened to murder any others caught on their lands. But somehow the fragile peace was maintained.[87]

Amid these delicate negotiations in the northern and southern districts, Gage sent orders to the superintendents to cut expenses. Keeping the peace was indeed expensive. The personnel expenses of the northern Indian superintendency alone cost 3,299 pounds in 1766. Johnson drew a rather modest 600-pound salary, while his three deputies, George Croghan, Daniel Claus, and Guy Johnson got 200 pounds each. Five commissaries along with interpreters and blacksmiths were employed at key posts. The commissaries included Edward Coles at Fort de Chartres, Jehu Hay at Detroit, Benjamin Roberts at Niagara, Alexander McKee at Fort Pitt, and Norman McLeod at Fort Ontario, the first two of whom made 200 pounds, and the latter three 150 pounds a year. The salaries for the interpreters and blacksmiths varied considerably. Johnson estimated that his proposal for additional personnel at Fort Edward Augustus, Chicoutami on the Sagninaw River, Fort Halifax on the Kennebec River, and ones at Montreal or Carillon would annually cost an additional 1,550 pounds. Whitehall not only would not grant Johnson his wish list but implored him to trim his current personnel.[88]

Nor would Whitehall accept either superintendent's recommendations on the relationship between them and other colonial leaders. Johnson had lobbied Whitehall for autonomy between the military and the Indian superintendencies. John Stuart favored the subordination of the superintendents to the provincial governors. Whitehall rejected both notions, stating unequivocally that they would continue to be subject to the commander in chief's orders so that they might act in concert.[89]

As if salaries were not expensive enough, diplomacy cost thousands of pounds more. Croghan's expenses alone were 8,408 pounds for 1766. He, like other agents, often paid out of his own pocket and then awaited government compensation. The uncertainty of repayment only worsened a highly stressful job.[90] Yet General Gage for one not only believed Croghan spent too much, but suggested that he may have diverted some funds to his own pocket. For years Gage tiptoed around accusations of Croghan's corruption. He respected Croghan's indispensable diplomatic skills and Johnson's faith in him. Yet the circumstantial evidence surrounding the accusations seemed formidable. He tactfully pointed that out to Johnson, arguing that "no man however good his character is to be trusted with the money of the public without checks and very satisfactory proofs of his disbursements."[91] Gage asked Johnson to pressure Croghan to curb his expenses. While claiming he reserved judgment, Gage asserted that "everybody . . . has complained of his unnecessary and lavish expense in all his Indian transactions."[92] But nothing came of the accusations.

As if all this were not trouble enough, there was Robert Rogers. By all accounts Rogers was a brilliant, daring, and tireless ranger leader, arguably the best wilderness fighter on either side during the French and Indian War. Yet those who knew him, friends as well as enemies, questioned his character. Money slipped through his fingers like quicksilver. His debts piled up no matter how much money he raked in from his business deals, legitimate and otherwise. He scammed constantly for a quick buck.

None of this would have mattered if Rogers had slipped into an obscure retirement. But he was eager for a command and the perks and business deals it provided. In March 1764, Rogers had somewhat desperately petitioned Gage for a post, any post, along with 1,000 pounds in compensation for a ranger company he claimed to have raised and paid for to relieve Detroit in July 1763. He would be disappointed. Gage expressed sympathy over Rogers' financial trials which seemed to be leading him toward debtors' prison: But while "I am very well convinced of your abilities, and knowledge of that particular service, but do not know of any rangers to be raised at present, nor of any command to be given at any of the frontier posts. . . . Should any opportunity offer itself of employing you to your advantage, I should gladly embrace it. In respect of your transactions in this place, I have nothing to offer. I could wish to hear less of them."[93] That last line was classic Gage, the iron fist packed in a velvet glove. The general was politely ordering Rogers either to clean up his act or get out of town.

And that is what Rogers did. As Gage opened an investigation in his wake, Rogers set sail for London to petition the Crown for a frontier post. What Gage discovered confirmed all the nasty rumors swirling about Rogers. He corresponded with various post commanders well acquainted with him. To Henry Gladwin, Gage wrote that "Rogers talks of a company he commanded of rangers [and] has given a demand of a thousand sterling for their subsistence. I can find none he had but provincials who had their provincial pay, and some are now demanding a bounty for their extraordinary service with the Major, having not got a penny from him, on that account. If you can give any intelligence of this company, pray inform me. I can find neither muster nor return of such a company during his whole stay at Detroit. And I can't pay such a sum without more authority than he has yet produced. Sir Jeffrey Amherst certainly knows nothing of it."[94]

Rogers spent a year and a half lobbying various influential men in London before he scored his prize—he would become commandant of Fort Michilimackinac. He was keen on taking that post not just because it was the magnet for the upper Great Lakes' fur trade, but a springboard to fulfill a dream. Rogers hoped to discover the fabled Northwest Passage across the American West to the Pacific and beyond!

He returned to New York on January 9, 1766 and the following day received an audience with Gage. The general had no choice but to accept the Royal Commission Rogers presented him.[95] Johnson was astonished when he heard the news. He fired off a letter to Gage in which he accused Rogers of being "puffed up with pride and folly from the encomiums & notice of some of the provinces" of his wartime exploits which "spoiled a good ranger for he was fit for nothing else, neither has nature calculated him for a large command . . . he has neither understanding, education, or principles."[96]

To forestall any wrongdoing, Johnson recommended keeping Rogers under constant surveillance and obliging him to submit detailed reports on all his transactions. Gage accordingly sent orders to his officers, interpreters, and commissaries at Fort Michilimackinac to watch Rogers constantly and even open his letters for any sign of malfeasance. He assured Johnson that "if you find he will not do, that complaints are made, and that the King's affairs are going into confusion thro Major Rogers' bad management . . . I shall certainly then remove him from Michilimackinac to some other post where he can do less mischief."[97] Johnson's instructions to Rogers were explicit. He was to enforce strictly the trade laws, sooth relations with the tribes, keep strict financial accounts, and send back detailed reports of all his activities every six months.[98] The suspicions about Rogers would prove partly true and provoke fears of another Indian conspiracy.

As 1767 began, Johnson issued a set of very explicit trade regulations that he hoped would eliminate the abuses that fostered animosities and sometimes war. Those who wished to trade with the Indians were required first to get a license from the governor and post a bond. Traders had to show that license and their goods at every post they reached. Trading was only permitted at those posts under the watchful eyes of the local official. Prices, weights, and measures were fixed. Traders issued credit at their own risk and were forbidden to beat Indians or coerce payments. Anyone who violated the regulations would be prosecuted.

Yet those regulations did not go far enough to suit General Gage. He insisted that "the price of goods should be fixed, for every part of the country, that no trader should trade without a license, in which the prices of his goods should be inserted, and a very small fee taken for such license; that the traders should give security for their good behavior and observation of all rules and restrictions. That tho' licensed in one province they may be brought to punishment in all, for any frauds or misdemeanors, or in any shape breaking the condition of their bonds by which they obtain their licenses. That every trader should be obliged to return with his peltry to that province from whence he received his license, and make returns of the quantity and nature of the peltry he brings with him. That the Indian commissarys should be so stationed that every nation may be able to lay their complaints before some of these commissarys who should be impowered to do them justice in case of misusage or fraudulent dealings on the part of the traders."[99] Johnson, of course, heartily agreed with these ideas. But he felt constrained to impose such regulations.

The array of problems continued to fester. Merchants protested that these newest regulations would destroy the fur trade.[100] Any goodwill generated by Johnson at the 1766 Council soon dissipated. The British failed to fulfill their promises to send enough munitions and other goods to the Indians. Traders cheated and browbeat their customers. The promised boundary line remained unrealized.

In all, animosities worsened between the British and the Indians, with French intrigues, the unpunished crimes of British murderers, the greed of merchants and squatters, and the inability of the Indian agents and troops to quell those problems all contributing. British officials at Whitehall and in the colonies understood the conflict's roots: "Abuses committed in the Indian trade and the disorders in the back settlements have had their source principally in the fraudulent purchases and grants from the natives, which have so long been suffered and even countenanced in by His Majesty's Governors, from shameful motives of self-interest very unbecoming their station."[101] If the cause was clear the solution was not.

Meanwhile, the debate continued among British military and diplomatic leaders over whether to close all but a handful of western posts, a policy that would at once reduce government expenses, vulnerabilities to Indian uprisings, and fur trade profits. If they closed the western posts, much of that region's trade would be diverted to French living in settlements west of the Mississippi River in Spanish territory. Gage and Johnson finally agreed to abandon, in 1767, several unnecessary posts including Fort Stanwix. As for the squatters, in June, Gage actually dispatched Captain Murray with troops and some chiefs to expel the settlers from Redstone Creek and the Cheat River. Those squatters moved off, then returned after the troops had left.[102]

Unrest among the tribes worsened. Two Chippewa murdered a trader at Detroit. A war party of Ottawa and Chippewa murdered eleven traders on the Ohio River. The Shawnee and Delaware resisted the influx of settlers into the upper Ohio River valley. These tribes sent envoys to St. Louis to ask St. Ange for ammunition and other supplies. Many chiefs refused to attend that year's council, including Pontiac, although he did turn in three prisoners at Detroit. The Cherokee pressed Gage and Johnson to broker a peace between them and the northern tribes. But those leaders demurred, hoping that the war between those tribes deterred a general war against the British.

Learning of the disturbances, William Johnson dispatched the indefati-
gable George Croghan to the region to defuse the explosive situation.
Croghan met with Shawnee, Delaware, and Iroquois chiefs at Fort Pitt on
June 3. Not suprisingly, they complained of white settlers on their lands
and insisted that "the country west of the Allegheny Mountains was their
property—that they had never ceded it, either to their Father the King of
Great Britain or to his Subjects."[103] To this Croghan could merely promise
that a boundary treaty would eventually be negotiated and signed that satisfied Indian rights. Until then he asked for their patience and understanding.

Johnson sought to alleviate the worsening tensions by calling yet another
council in 1767 where each side could repolish the chain of friendship between them. The British would give presents and the Indians would hand
over their remaining prisoners. The council followed the familiar pattern.
The chiefs complained bitterly about the ever-more squatters, murders, and
cheating, all of which were related to the British unwillingness to set a
boundary and keep their people on the other side. Johnson could only cover
these complaints with presents and promises of eventual justice.[104]

Pontiac never showed up at Johnson's council. He did send his regrets
to the superintendent for not meeting with him that summer. He was going
hunting instead but promised to visit Johnson in 1768. He tried to reassure
the British of his peaceful intention, claiming that he "was not a one of
those who like dogs did nothing but try to bite whatever they could."[105]

That year Pontiac was dragged into a murder trial. At Detroit, Antoine
Cuillerier was apprehended and charged with drowning 7-year-old Betty
Fisher who was captured in 1763 after her parents were slain. Detroit's
Indian commissary Jehu Hay called on Pontiac to appear as a witness at the
trial. Although Cuillerier escaped on August 17, Pontiac still gave testimony
when he arrived on August 29. He confessed to tossing the child into the
Maumee River when the stench of her dysentery disgusted him, then ordered Cuillerier to finish her off. Cuillerier complied and then buried the
child. After several days Pontiac changed his story to confess that he rather
than Cuillerier had drowned the child. It is assumed that Cuillerier's family
and friends bribed Pontiac into assuming complete blame for the crime. The
treaties had absolved the Indians of any atrocities they may have committed
during the war, so Pontiac and others could freely confess even the most
abominable acts without fear of persecution.[106]

George Croghan was not present at that gruesome confession. After concluding his summer diplomacy he journied to Johnson Hall to report and
receive instructions. By October 16 he had returned to Fort Pitt for yet
another meeting with local chiefs. On October 24 he was off to Detroit. At
each village along the way he counciled with the chiefs. On November 6
he reached Sandusky where he met with the Wyandot, along with Shawnee,
Mohican, and Caughnawaga Iroquois. He arrived at Detroit on November

15 and held a series of talks with the Huron, Chippewa, Ottawa, and Pot-awatomi. He had hoped to meet Pontiac but that chief was said to be hunt-ing far away. Croghan left Detroit on November 24 and was back at Fort Pitt on December 9, 1767. There he promptly counciled with delegations of Shawnee, Delaware, and Mingo. Croghan appeared before General Gage at New York on January 12, 1768. It had been a typically hectic year of endless rounds of polishing covenant chains, speaking, listening, cajoling, and distributing presents.[107]

From an official point of view, the trade regulations worked. Gage reck-oned that, since they were imposed, he had "never heard the least complaint about their trade. . . . Every precaution and care has been to prevent any impositions or frauds being practiced by the traders, and most people have agreed in general that they have bought their goods much cheaper than they had done for many year's past."[108]

Merchants bitterly disagreed. They complained that the regulations caused the trade's "deplorable and ruinous condition . . . that . . . only threatens ruin and bankruptcy."[109] Was this true? While some undoubtedly suffered, most made piles of money despite the hated rules.

Ever greater mountains of furs passed through the trading posts en route to eastern markets. The pounds of skins trans-shipped through Fort Pitt alone in 1767 included 10,587 pounds of beaver, 755 pounds of otter, 3,539 of wildcat and fox, 15,253 of racoon, 785 of bear, 82 of elk, and 282,629 of deer, while Fort Detroit counted the skins of 1,260 pounds of muskrat, 150 of fawn, 297 of fisher, 2,656 of otter, 6,131 of bear, 14,092 of redskin, 44,416 of deer, 311 of mink, 564 of martin, 431 of fox, 3,696 of wildcat, 101 beaver robes, 32 buffalo, 114 wolf, 511 elk, 62,929 racoon, 27,844 beaver, 458 parchment, 7 arincalle, and 4 tiger. As for merchandize including rum, 26,157 pounds worth officially passed through Fort Pitt and 25,951 pounds through Fort Detroit, though the Indian agents believed that at least twice that amount actually reached Indian country through those posts. At Niagara from May 14, 1767 to November 24, 1768, 313 bateaux with 886 men arrived from Detroit and other upper Great Lakes posts.[110]

But that silver cloud had a dark lining. Danger grew with the profits. Problems and hatreds festered. Rumors persisted of circulating warbelts and French intrigues. During 1767 alone the Chippewa, Seneca, Shawnee, and Illinois were all reputed to have exchanged warbelts. The Seneca belt to the Shawnee and Delaware issued a powerful challenge: "Brethern, those lands are yours as well as ours. God gave them to us [to] live upon & before the white people shall settle them for nothing we will sprinkle the leaves with their blood, or die every man of us in the attempt."[111]

The council diplomacy of presents and promises combined with strict enforcement of trade regulations had so far averted war, but for how long no one could say. British officials despaired of stemming the tide. General

Gage could only watch in impotent fury as a vicious cycle exacerbated hatreds and problems. The colonial assemblies and settlers had an interest in pushing forever westward and exploiting wealth from Indian lands. The governors "are afraid to desire assistance from me . . . and set forth their inability to enforce obediance, which they own nothing but a military force can effect."[112] The weakness of governors in turn emboldened the assemblies, land companies, traders, and settlers, while worsening relations with the Indians. Gage's inability to halt the influx of squatters, which would inevitably spark another bloody Indian war, so infuriated him that he expressed the stunning hope that "if the Indians do break out . . . [they] should confine their hostilities to those spots only, tho' the killing of people must be shocking humanity."[113] If the governors would not back his expulsion of the squatters with redcoats, he would shed no tears if they were exterminated by redskins.

An Indian war could have potentially exploded from any number of villages in 1767. But that year British officials especially feared for the fate of one particular post and from an unexpected source—Michilimackinac and its commander, Robert Rogers. The harsh suspicions Johnson and Gage harbored over Rogers may not have been harsh enough, if the informants' reports were true. Since arriving at the post on August 10, 1766, he was accused of a range of high crimes and misdemeanors. He stole rum and sold it to the Indians. He lined his pockets with bribes. He bought a small fortune of goods on credit and gave them away to the Indians to gain their personal allegiance. But those paled before the most serious whispered charge—Rogers conspired with the Indians and French to destroy Michilimackinac, after which he would lead an army to sweep the British from the Great Lakes!

Treason was a capital offense. The evidence seemed damning. No man during Detroit's siege was more fearless than Captain Joseph Hopkins, who led a score of sorties against the enemies. But like his fellow ranger Robert Rogers, Hopkins was abrasive and dabbled in shady ways to make money. After the rebellion sputtered out, his ranger company was abruptly disbanded. In disgust, the soldier of fortune joined the French army. Learning that Rogers was Michilimackinac's commandant, Hopkins wrote him letters encouraging him to carve out an independent colony in the upper Great Lakes or, if that failed, to escape down the Mississippi to New Orleans.

Who reported these schemes? Rogers' secretary, Nathaniel Potter, informed second in command Captain Frederick Spiesmacher. Acting on secret authority from Gage, Spiesmacher superseded Rogers' authority and had him arrested on December 6, 1767. Rogers' legs were clamped in irons and he was thrown in the guardhouse. There he languished in misery until spring, when he was carried down to a Montreal jail.

The trial did not open until October 20, 1768. Rogers was charged with three crimes—conspiracy to commit treason, correspondence with His Majesty's enemies, and disobeying orders about economy with the Indians. Ironically, the fate of America's most famous American war leader would be decided while the Indian superintendents were concluding treaties with Indians at Fort Stanwix and Hard Labour that would dramatically redraw the frontier.

Was Rogers like Benedict Arnold a dozen years later, a war hero and patriot turned scoundrel and traitor? Unlike Arnold, there was no smoking gun that proved Rogers had actually contemplated, let alone conspired, to commit Hopkins' plan of treason or conspired with the Indians. In a brilliant and eloquent defense, Rogers countered every charge and smeared the credibility of his accusers. He admitted receiving a letter from Hopkins, but claimed that he not only dismissed the scheme but forwarded the letter to Gage; it was lost en route. The debts he had incurred with the local traders kept the garrison fed and the Indians peaceful. His presents and speeches to the Indians helped bind them to the British Crown, not to Rogers personally. Witnesses confirmed all of his arguments. On October 31, the jury rendered its verdict—Rogers was not guilty of all three charges against him.[114]

Nonetheless, Gage kept him in prison until February 1769, when a personal order from King George III set Rogers free. Though acquitted and free, his military career ground to a humiliating halt and his personal life crumbled. A slander suit against Gage was dismissed. He sank ever deeper into drink and debt. His wife, Betsey, won a divorce on grounds of adultery. He was twice thrown into debtor's prison. But his career had not yet ended. He would surface briefly during the American Revolution. Congress denied him a ranger's commission, but the King granted him one. He headed the Queen's Rangers for a year, but he displayed a mere shadow of his former prowess and was dismissed. He sailed to London, where the frontiersman lived in drunken squalor in that city's dark labyrinth until his death in 1795.

Perhaps until his dying breath Rogers brightened his abyss with dreams of the Northwest Passage. What had happened to his expedition? He recruited former ranger Captain James Tute, map-maker Jonathan Carver, and several others, and sent them west on September 12, 1766. Inspired by Indian tales of the lands far beyond the horizon, Rogers instructed his men to head first to the upper Mississippi valley and winter among the Dakota. The following spring they were to trek to the forks of the Saskatchewan River and winter at Fort La Prairie. With the snow melting they would trace the Saskatchewan to its source, cross the divide to the Ourigan (Columbia) River, and float down to the Pacific Ocean. Upon their return the expedition could split 2,000 pounds of a 20,000 pound prize offered by the Crown; Rogers presumably would enjoy the remainder.

But Rogers' dream was too grandiose to achieve with the paltry trade goods and will among his adventurers. The men split up. Carver got the farthest west. In a year's travel he journied as far as a Dakota (Naudowessie)

village on the St. Peter's River amid Minnesota's tallgrass prairies. What lay
further West? Where was the Northwest Passage? The Dakota told Carver
of months of travel across treeless plains until they reached stony mountains
that rose miles into the sky. And beyond? The old men could only shrug.[115]

Critical events overshadowed Rogers' arrest, imprisonment, and trial. In
January 1768 word of yet another vicious mass murder spread among Indians and Americans alike and threatened once again to drench the frontier
in war.[116] On January 10, four Delaware men and two women appeared at
the home of Frederick Stump and his servant, John Ironcutter, on Middle
Creek in Cumberland county. Stump invited them in and plied them with
liquor. When the Indians were nearly senseless he took an axe and caved in
the heads of five while his servant murdered the sixth. They dragged the
bodies, one by one, through the snow down to the Susquehanna, broke a
hole in the ice, and shoved them under. Stump's work was not yet done.
He strode the fourteen miles to the home of one of those Indians. A wife
and three children huddled inside. Stump butchered and incinerated them
within their cabin. Was there any motive besides hatred? Perhaps Stump
hoped to hide away the scalps for a future war in which he could enjoy a
sizable bounty. One scalp was especially grisly—it included the man's ears.

Two days later he boasted of his deed to neighbor William Blyth who,
fearing another Indian uprising, nervously told Will Allen, a Philadelphia
magistrate. On January 19, when Governor Penn learned of the crime, he
got the council's approval to post a 200 pound reward for the capture of
the murderers. Penn wrote to the Cumberland county sheriff, asking him
to track them. He informed Gage and Johnson of the crime and what he
had done to solve it. To the chiefs living in that area he sent a promise to
bring the murderers to justice and cover the dead with generous amounts
of gifts.

On January 28, Sheriff John Armstrong and a posse nabbed Stump and
Ironcutter, who were sheltered in the home of sympathizers. He incarcerated them in the Carlisle jail. But the sheriff refused repeated orders by the
governor himself to bring the confessed murderers down to Philadelphia to
stand trial. Armstrong explained that the murderers were heroes in the
minds of most frontier people. They demanded that the accused be tried by
a jury of their peers according to law, but of course such a jury would surely
acquit Stump and Ironcutter.

On January 29, 80 men galloped into Carlisle, surrounded the jail, and
demanded their heros' release. With muskets in their hands, Armstrong and
four deputies faced the crowd. The sheriff "stood on the steps under the
door. He addressed himself frequently to the armed company who were
about him, and used many arguments to persuade them to desist from their
lawless undertaking, and told them, among other things, that they were
about to do an act which would subject themselves and their country to
misery. That while . . . Armstrong was speaking . . . one of the armed men

[took] hold of him and draw him down the . . . steps, upon which . . .
Armstrong by violence pushed back the person . . . saying that they would
take his life before they should rescue the prisoner."[117] But some outlaws
got inside the jail and freed the prisoners. Suddenly Stump and Ironcutter
were racing on horseback out of town with the other outlaws. Once they
were safely away, the murderers were released. They were last seen riding
hard toward Virginia. Their fate is unknown.

On February 16, Governor Penn asked the Pennsylvania assembly for
3,000 pounds in gifts to the Indians to cover their dead. The assembly
complied. Johnson received 1,300 pounds of that money to disperse at his
councils, while the rest was distributed to Pennsylvania Indians. Whether
that prompt generosity prevented another Indian war is impossible to determine, but tensions still sizzled along the frontier.

The commander in chief for North America faced an agonizing dilemma.
His job was to keep the peace, to deter and if necessary crush rebellion not
only from Indians but from Americans as well. But the policies that might
dampen animosities with potential Indian rebells might enflame them with
potential American rebells, and vice versa. British peace envoys to the Indians faced death threats by enraged settlers. For example, in April General
Gage was forced to detach 30 troops "from Philadelphia to escort Mr.
Croghan . . . to Pittsburgh in order to protect him from the frontier people
who have threatened his life, and to plunder the Indian presents he was
carrying with him."[118]

Gage despaired the "fact that all the people of the frontiers from Pennsylvania to Virginia inclusive openly vow that they will never find a man
guilty of murder for killing an Indian." The solution, as Gage proposed to
Secretary of State for the Southern Department William Petty Shelburne,
was "removing the trials to the capitals of the provinces where the jurys
would be composed of men more civilized than those of the frontiers."
Finally he deplored the shortsightedness and hypocrisy of those distant settlers: "It may be thought extraordinary that those who always are . . . the
first victims to an Indian war should be the first to provoke them to hostilities. And when they have brought such a misery upon the country, they
are the first to call out for help and bewail their misfortune."[119]

The trouble with Gage's proposal was, of course, that violating such a
fundamental British right as trial by a jury of one's peers could spark a
frontier rebellion. Gage already faced growing opposition, protests, and even
violence to Whitehall's taxes in the eastern cities and towns. He warned the
Crown that the Americans "will struggle for independence . . . From the
denying the right of internal taxations, they next deny the right of duties
on imports, and thus they mean to go on step by step till they throw off all
subjection to your laws." To prevent that Gage advised that Whitehall "keep
them weak as long as possible . . . and avoid anything that can contribute

to make them powerful," such as preventing new immigrants from swelling the population and the development of domestic industries from enhancing American economic strength.[120]

Given Gage's belief that an American assertion of independence was not far off, why would he alienate the pioneers as well? Then nearly all Americans might unite against the Crown. Gage was willing to take that chance if he could forestall the more immediate threat of another Indian war. But Shelburne would not authorize him to move the trials.

Despite the vicious crime that opened the year, in 1768 the boundary line's last gaps would finally be filled. On December 23, 1767, the Board of Trade recommended to Shelburne that Johnson be granted the necessary authority to settle the boundary. Word of that decision did not reach General Thomas Gage at New York City until April 18, 1768. Unfortunately, the message from Shelburne remained maddeningly vague. Shelburne merely called on Gage and Johnson to forge a consensus with the governors over a just line, and then negotiate that line and other outstanding issues with the Indians. Essential questions remained unanswered. How would costs would be split among the Crown, provinces, and superintendents? Where, specifically, should the boundaries of New York and Pennsylvania be drawn? Would Whitehall insist that the colonies pass uniform laws regulating the Indian trade? These and other important questions remained a mystery. It was up to Gage and Johnson to fill in the blanks.[121]

Where to draw the line was not hard to resolve. Gage and Johnson agreed to allow the Indians to "fix the point to which they allowed the jurisdiction of each province to extend, beyond which they would not suffer any purchase to be made, but reserve all beyond it to themselves and posterity."[122] The tough part was scraping up enough goods for the council. That vital need was filled by resolving another question that had lingered for years— which forts should be retained and which abandoned. In early August, Gage finally decided to keep Forts Pitt, Niagara, Detroit, Michilimackinac, and de Chartres. The rest would be abandoned.

And then there was the question of what to do about squatters on lands reserved to the Indians. Gage was firmly resolved that they would be removed. But he gave "the strictest orders . . . to treat the inhabitants on all occassions with lenity, moderation, and justice; that they shall not suffer any insults either from officers or soldiers, but be permitted to enjoy unmolested the common rights of mankind, and be protected against all violence towards their persons and properties."[123]

Whitehall resolved yet another problem that year. The Mohawk had granted Johnson a huge tract of land north of the Mohawk River in 1760. It would take nearly eight years before the Crown approved that grant. With the 1763 Proclamation His Majesty had decreed that lands from the Indians could only be made in the king's name for the king. Johnson got New York lieutenant governor Cadwallader Colden to appeal to Whitehall to approve the land grant. When that did not work, Johnson submitted his own petition. It was not until February 10, 1767 that the Lords of Trade recommended that the grant be approved in gratitude for Johnson's long, arduous, and expensive service.[124]

So it was with renewed enthusiasm that Johnson organized that year's council. It would be preceded by a series of preliminary councils. During these early negotiation rounds, agents had to redress as many specific grievances as possible while hammering out a consensus on the exact boundary to be accepted by all the tribes. William Johnson sent out instructions to his agents and runners to the tribes. The tribes would cluster for negotiations with either George Croghan at Fort Pitt or William Johnson at his home in the lower Mohawk valley. That preliminary diplomacy would be very expensive. The northern superintendency's personal expenses for the six months from March 24 to September 25, 1768 were 7,200 pounds. That included Johnson's 857-pound salary plus salaries for ten field agents and various interpreters, blacksmiths, surgeons, storekeepers, and clerks. During that same period Johnson and his men gave 905 pounds worth of presents to the Indians outside of the Fort Stanwix Treaty.[125]

In early March, Johnson hosted over 850 Indians, with whom he not only had to forge agreement but whom he had to feed and then disperse laden with gifts. Always tedious, the negotiations with the Indians worsened when Johnson caught a severe cold after sitting for hours each winter day with the chiefs in his courtyard. The cold aggravated all his chronic illnesses, especially his gout. He emerged from the council exhausted and in desperate need of relief. Nontheless, Johnson and the chiefs reached a preliminary understanding on the boundary and other issues.[126]

Johnson then disappeared for the next three months of crucial negotiations. Decades of stress and dissipation had ground down his health. In recent years ever worsening bouts of sickness forced him to bed for days and sometimes weeks. Yet his work never ceased. From bed he would not only coordinate policy by letter with Gage, the governors, his agents, and others, but he even presided over Indian councils. But the burdens of his duties and illnesses were becoming overwhelming. In late April 1768, he deemed it time for a long, much-needed vacation. After informing Gage of his intentions, he designated his son, Guy Johnson, his temporary replacement and then climbed painfully into his carriage for the long journey to take the sea waters at New London, Connecticut. There he would find little relief from his sufferings. In late May he sailed to Block Island for several weeks and then returned to the mainland where he traveled to Lebanon Springs, New York.[127]

Meanwhile, on April 26, 1768, Guy Johnson conducted his first Indian council. He met with a group of Mohican at Schenectady, New York to listen to their "tears" for "we have lost everything—the Patroon has got all our lands."[128] Guy Johnson could offer no more than a promise to look into the matter. He lacked his father's authority, expertise, and sympathy. In this and subsequent councils he glossed over specific issues while preparing the chiefs to attend the Grand Council later that year. But he offended the chiefs by skipping over protocol and conducting the proceedings far too rapidly. All that exacerbated rather than alleviated tensions. Whether the Grand Council would be convened was an open question. Chiefs at nearly every preliminary council brought rumors of warbelts and rising anger. Would the frontier explode again in war?[129]

While the Johnsons negotiated to close the link in the northern boundary, John Stuart and his agents worked just as feverishly to accomplish the same in the south. They had made enormous progress over the previous five years. From 1763 until 1768, Stuart sewed up a boundary between British and Indian lands across the southern frontier through a series of councils and subsequent treaties. The first stretch—Georgia's—was negotiated and signed into treaty on November 10, 1763 at the Augusta Congress. West Florida's frontier was delineated with the Choctaw and Chickasaw at Mobile on April 27, 1765, and with the Creek at Pensacola on May 28, 1765. Negotiations among North Carolina, South Carolina, Virginia, and the Cherokee dragged on intermittently from 1765 until 1768. The Cherokee signed preliminary agreements with South Carolina on October 19, 1765 and North Carolina on February 5, 1766. A final agreement was struck at the appropriately named Hard Labour, South Carolina council on October 14, 1768. A month later, on November 13, Virginia and the Cherokee agreed to a boundary west of the Kanawha River. In doing so the Cherokee surrendered their hunting grounds in Kentucky, the "dark and bloody ground" they squabbled over with the Ohio valley tribes. That boundary would be fleeting. The Fort Stanwix Treaty, signed nearly at the same time, would push that boundary as far west as the mouth of the Tennessee River.[130]

To the relief of all, William Johnson's three-month vacation ended on July 15 when he returned to his home and took back the Indian superintendency from his son. His desk was stacked with letters detailing various problems. He soon forged a key agreement. The Kayaderosseras proprietors finally agreed to make concessions to the Indians. On August 5, the patentees agreed to pay 5,000 pounds more to the Mohawk for a much more limited concession. The decades spent wrangling over that concession were as much the result of the scanty and often illegible records as the claimants' greed. But its resolution helped ease tensions on the Grand Council's eve.[131]

The Indian council at Fort Stanwix was one of the largest and longest ever held in American history. For over six weeks, from September 19 to November 6, 1768, 3,102 Indians from at least sixteen tribes gathered to negotiate and feast at Fort Stanwix, New York. For the British, in addition to Johnson and his staff, at various times Pennsylvania governor John Penn,

New Jersey governor William Franklin, commissioners from Virginia and Pennsylvania, and their entourages attended. Johnson performed a dual role as Indian Superintendent and New York commissioner.[132]

The logistics and expense of feeding so many people were immense. Far more Indians arrived than were expected. Food stocks rapidly diminished; their exhaustion would imperil the congress. Johnson ordered his supplier to "send a large quantity of provisions up here as soon as possible, otherwise it must overset the design of this congress, as it cannot be supposed that hungry Indians can be kept here, or in any temper without a bellyfull. I need not add further than to wish that the great work in hand may not be frustrated (after all the expense & trouble we have had) for the want of a timely supply of provisions."[133] Those vital provisions did arrive just in time to avert disaster.

The council cost a small fortune. When the accounts were tallied, the expenses came to 21,923 pounds, of which 17,932 pounds were paid to the Six Nations for land cessions, 978 pounds to various chiefs, 883 pounds for supplies from Gilbert Tice, 665 pounds for supplies from Duggart, 302 pounds for 54 fat cattle from John Wickwier, 271 pounds to Jeles Fundas for supplies, and 106 pounds in presents to Stockbridge and Abenaki Indians. Then there were 46 separate accounts worth less than 100 pounds, of which most were for less than 10 pounds, and a separate account marked 758 pounds worth of provisions delivered to the council.[134]

But it was worth it. After three weeks of negotiations, speeches, and feasts, the Treaty of Fort Stanwix was signed by British and Indian leaders on October 24, 1768. Johnson was elated: "The line is settled beyond my expectations & more favorably than was proposed by the Crown."[135] The line started at the Hudson, followed the southern Adirondack Mountains to west of the carrying place between the Mohawk and Onondaga watersheds. From there it extended due south until it reached the Mohack branch of the Delaware River, and followed that to the mouth of the Poackton branch, where it was drawn west to the Susquehanna River. It followed down that river to Awandoe Creek and then west up it and along Burnett's hills to Tiadagnton Creek, down it to West branch and then up it and over the divide. From there it was drawn west to Kittanang on the Allegheny River and then downstream until where the Cherokee (Tennessee) River flows into the Ohio River.

Johnson committed an extraordinary act in negotiating the boundary as far west as the Tennessee River, whose mouth on the Ohio was just 40 miles from the Mississippi. Since 1764 he had lobbied Whitehall to do so, despite the fact that it would be a gross violation of the 1763 proclamation. On December 23, 1767, the Board of Trade finally rejected the request and insisted that the Kanawha River be the westernmost boundary. Johnson violated the King's orders in drawing that line at the Tennessee. Cunningly he also briefly raised Iroquois prestige by granting them the power to dispose of lands that they did not own and whose loss they would not mourn. He paid them handsomely for that "concession," along with the Shawnee and Delaware, who did hunt in Kentucky, and agreed to give up their land only with extreme reluctance.

But the Cherokee also claimed that land and were willing to part with it only to the Kanawha River, as instructed by Whitehall and negotiated by Stuart. The southern superintendent and Cherokee protested the Fort Stanwix Treaty. The result was a compromise. Whitehall rejected the Tennesee River boundary but instructed Stuart to redraw his line westward. Under the Treaty of Lochaber on October 22, 1770, the Cherokee agreed to a line etched due south of the Kanawha River mouth and in 1770 from the Scioto River mouth. Thus did the Fort Stanwix Treaty knock open the gates to the "dark and bloody ground" that Daniel Boone, scores of other longhunters, and eventually hundreds and thousands of settlers would stride through, leading to a generation of warfare with the Indians there. But that is another story.

Despite that controversy, the Fort Stanwix treaty forged the final links in a series of boundaries previously negotiated. The line zigzagged back and forth across the Appalachian watershed which Whitehall's 1763 proclamation designated as the proper division between Americans and Indians. The frontier fell far east of that boundary along the western ends of Florida, Georgia, South Carolina, and North Carolina. It was at the boundary between North Carolina and Virginia where the line shot west over the Appalachian watershed and sliced across eastern Kentucky to the Ohio River, and then up it and beyond east of the watershed once again, where it would pass back and forth until the Hudson River. The boundary line combined with trade rules to satisfy the outstanding conflicts which had provoked the Indian uprising of 1763. "Amherst's War" symbolically ended with the Fort Stanwix Treaty.

NOTES

1. Pennsylvania Assembly to Benjamin Franklin and Richard Jackson, January 19, 1767, in James Sullivan and A. C. Flick, eds., *The Papers of William Johnson* (hereafter cited as *Johnson Papers*), 14 vols. (Albany: State University of New York, 1921–1965), 12:418, 417–19.

2. Journal of Indian Affairs, March 2, 1765, *Johnson Papers*, 4:530.

3. Proceedings of Johnson and Indians, April 29 to May 22, 1765, in E. B. O'Callaghan and Berthold Fernow, eds., *Documents Relative to the Colonial History of the State of New York* (hereafter cited as NYCD), 15 vols. (Albany, N.Y.: Weed, Parsons, and Co., 1856–1887), 7:726, 718–38.

4. Proceedings of William Johnson with Indians, April 29 to May 22, 1765, NYCD 7:718–41; William Johnson to Lords of Trade, July 1765, ibid., 7:746.

5. Cadwallader Colden to William Johnson, June 13, 1765, *Johnson Papers*, 11: 786–88.

6. Thomas Gage to William Johnson, February 25, 1765, *Johnson Papers*, 11: 640, 603–5.

7. William Johnson to Lords of Trade, July 1765, NYCD 7:747.

8. William Johnson to George Croghan, March 9, 1765, *Johnson Papers*, 11: 629, 627–30.

9. William Johnson to Thomas Gage, January 30, 1766, *Johnson Papers*, 5:17–20.

10. Illinois Historical Collections 10:456.

11. Council with Indians and d'Abbadie, March 1765, NYCD 10:1159–61.

12. William Johnson to Thomas Gage, July 6, 1765, *Johnson Papers*, 11:830, 830–32.

13. Thomas Gage to William Johnson, June 22, 1765, *Johnson Papers*, 11:802–4.

14. Francis Fauquier to William Johnson, July 22, 1765, *Johnson Papers*, 11:863; William Johnson to Francis Fauquier, September 17, 1765, ibid., 11:941–42.

15. Thomas Gage to Lord Halifax, June 8, 1765, in Clarence Edwin Carter, ed., *The Correspondance of General Thomas Gage with the Secretaries of State, 1763–1775* (hereafter cited as *Gage Correspondance*), 2 vols. (1931–1933) (reprint, Hamden, Conn.: Archon Books, 1969), 1:61.

16. Alexander McKee to William Johnson, June 18, 1765, *Johnson Papers*, 11: 796–97.

17. Thomas McKee to William Johnson, June 1, 1765, *Johnson Papers*, 11:759–61.

18. Thomas Gage to William Johnson, June 3, 1765, *Johnson Papers*, 11:763, 762–64; Thomas Gage to William Johnson, June 10, 1765, ibid., 11:784–85.

19. Thomas Gage to William Johnson, May 5, 1766, *Johnson Papers*, 5:201.

20. Orders for Regulation of Trade, January 16, 1765, *Johnson Papers*, 11:535–36.

21. Michilimackinac Traders to William Howard, July 5, 1765, *Johnson Papers*, 11:825–28; From Baby et al. to William Johnson, July 6, 1765, ibid., 11:828–29; Lawrence Ermatinger to William Johnson, September 17, 1765, ibid., 11:942–43.

22. William Johnson to the Traders of Michilimackinac, July 2,1765, *Johnson Papers*, 11:816–17; William Johnson to Thomas Gage, August 9, 28, 1765, ibid., 11:878–80, 914–17; Thomas Gage to William Johnson, August 18, September 8, 1765, ibid., 11:902–5, 927–28.

23. William Johnson to Thomas Gage, January 7, 1766, *Johnson Papers*, 5:4, 1–5.

24. Thomas Gage to William Johnson, February 3, 1766, *Johnson Papers*, 5:30–31; Thomas Gage to Barrington, December 18, 1765, Report of Forts in North America (2 enclosures), *Gage Correspondance*, 2:318–24; Thomas Gage to Barrington, May 7, 1766, ibid., 2:349–52.

25. William Johnson to George Croghan, March 9, 1765, *Johnson Papers*, 11: 627–30; Thomas Gage to Welbore Ellis, April 27, June 1, August 10, 1765, *Gage Correspondance*, 2:283–85, 293–94, 295–97, 301–2; Thomas Gage to Thomas Whately, April 27, 1765, ibid., 2:285–86.

26. Thomas Gage to Lord Halifax, February 23, 1765, *Gage Correspondance*, 1: 51.

27. Council Minutes, St. Ange to Thomas Gage, April 28, 1765, Gage papers, William L. Clements Library, Ann Arbor, Mich. (hereafter cited as CL).

28. Alexander Fraser to William Johnson, May 18, 1765, *Johnson Papers*, 11:743–44.

29. Alexander Fraser to Thomas Gage, May 26, Gage papers, CL.

30. John Stuart to William Johnson, March 30, 1766, *Johnson Papers*, 12:53–57.

31. George Croghan to William Johnson, February 18, 1765, *Johnson Papers*, 11:576–77.

32. Charles Grant to Henry Bouquet, March 9, 1765, in Sylvester K. Stevens, Donald H. Kent, Autumn L. Leonard, Louis M. Waddell, and John Totteham, eds., *The Papers of Henry Bouquet* (hereafter cited as *Bouquet Papers*), 6 vols. (Harrisburg: Pennsylvania Historical and Museum Commission, 1972–1994), 6:763; Robert Callender to Henry Bouquet, March 11, 1765, ibid., 6:764–66; Croghan Purchases Account, March 21, 1765, ibid., 6:774; Nathaniel McCulloch to George Croghan, March 12, 1765, *Johnson Papers*, 11:635–36; Lieutenant Colonel Reid to Thomas Gage, June 4, 1765, in *Minutes of the Provincial Council of Pennsylvania* (hereafter cited as MPCP) (1852) (reprint, New York: AMS Press, 1968), 9:269–70.

33. Thomas Gage to William Johnson, April 15, 1765, *Johnson Papers*, 4:717, 717–19; John Penn to William Johnson, March 21, 1765, ibid., 11:643–45; Thomas Gage to Henry Bouquet, March 21, 1765, *Bouquet Papers*, 6:772–73.

34. William Johnson to Thomas Gage, April 27, 1765, *Johnson Papers*, 11:704, 704–5.

35. William Johnson to Board of Trade, May 24, 1765, NYCD 7:716, 711–18.

36. For other estimates, see Thomas Gage to William Johnson, March 31, 1764, *Johnson Papers*, 4:702–4; William Johnson to John Penn, April 12, 1765, ibid., 4:710–11; Frances Wade to William Johnson, April 26, 1764, ibid., 4:729–30.

37. Henry Bouquet to Thomas Gage, April 10, 1765, *Bouquet Papers*, 6:781, 780–81.

38. William Johnson to George Croghan, April 17, 1766, *Johnson Papers*, 12:78–80; Instructions to George Croghan, April 20, 1766, ibid., 12:80–82.

39. William Johnson to Thomas Gage, April 3, 1765, *Johnson Papers*, 11:664–65; William Johnson to John Penn, April 3, 1765, ibid., 11:666–67; William Johnson to George Croghan, April 8, 1765, ibid., 11:680–82; William Johnson to John Penn, June 7, 1765, ibid., 11:776–79; Thomas Gage to Henry Bouquet, April 4, 1765, *Bouquet Papers*, 6:779–80; John Penn to William Johnson, May 23, 1765, *Johnson Papers*, 11:746–47; John Johnston to William Johnson, March 13, 1766, ibid., 12:42–43; John Penn to Thomas Gage, June 28, 1765, MPCP 9:275–77; Thomas Gage to John Penn, July 5, 1765, ibid., 9:281.

40. Indian congress, May 10, 1765, *Johnson Papers*, 11:728; Indian Congress, May 9–11, MPCP 9:256–64.

41. George Croghan to William Johnson, May 13, 1765, *Johnson Papers*, 11:738, 737–38; List of Prisoners, May 10, 1765, ibid., 11:720–21; Indian Congress at Fort Pitt, May 9–11, 1765, ibid., 11:723–34; George Croghan to William Johnson, May 12, 1765, ibid., 11:736–37; George Croghan to Henry Bouquet, May 12, 1765, *Bouquet Papers*, 6:789.

42. Proceedings of William Johnson with Indians, July 4, 1765, NYCD 7:750–58.

43. George Croghan to William Murray, July 12, 1765, *Johnson Papers*, 11:841; George Croghan to Alexander McKee, July 13, 1765, ibid., 11:845–47; Journal of Croghan Transactions with Western Indians, May 15 to September 25, 1765, NYCD 7:779–88.

44. George Croghan to William Johnson, July 12, 1765, *Johnson Papers*, 11: 838, 836–41.

45. Thomas Gage to William Johnson, August 12, 1765, *Johnson Papers*, 11: 882–83.

46. Indian Congress, Ouiatenon, July 13, 1765, *Johnson Papers*, 11:847–50.

47. George Croghan to William Johnson, July 12, 1765, *Johnson Papers*, 11: 839.

48. George Croghan to William Johnson, August 17, 1765, *Johnson Papers*, 11: 899–902.

49. John Campbell to William Johnson, September 16, 1765, *Johnson Papers*, 11:939, 938–39.

50. Surrender of Fort de Chartres, Sterling, October 10, 1765, NYCD 10:1161–65.

51. Thomas Gage to Henry Bouquet, May 15, 1765, *Bouquet Papers*, 6:789–93.

52. Henry Bouquet Last Will and Testament, June 25, 1765, *Bouquet Papers*, 6:795–97.

53. Henry Bouquet to Elizabeth Chew, July 2, 1765, *Bouquet Papers*, 6:798.

54. Henry Bouquet to Margaret Oswald, July 2, 1765, *Bouquet Papers*, 6:799–800.

55. Thomas Gage to William Johnson, August 15, 1765, *Johnson Papers*, 11: 890, 890–93.

56. Lord Halifax to Govenors in North America and West Indian Islands, August 11, 1765, NYCD 7:646.

57. Secretary Conway to Governors in America, March 31, 1766, NYCD 7:823–24.

58. William Johnson to Thomas Gage, October 12, 1765, *Johnson Papers*, 11: 930–32.

59. William Johnson to Thomas Gage, January 7, 1766, *Johnson Papers*, 5:4.

60. William Johnson to Lords of Trade, November 16, 1765, NYCD 7:777, 775–79.

61. George Croghan to William Johnson, November 1765, NYCD 7:787, 787–88.

62. Ibid., 7:787–88.

63. John Stuart to William Johnson, March 30, 1766, NYCD 10:56. See also John Preston Moore, *Revolt in Louisiana: The Spanish Occupation, 1766–1770* (Baton Rouge: Louisiana State University Press, 1976).

64. William Johnson to Thomas Gage, December 12, 1766, *Johnson Papers*, 12: 227–29; Edward Cole to George Croghan, October 25, 1767, ibid., 5:753–55.

65. Thomas Gage to William Johnson, March 17, 1766, *Johnson Papers*, 12:44.

66. William Johnson to Henry Seymour Conway, July 10, 1766, *Johnson Papers*, 5:319; Advantages of an Illinois Colony, July 10, 1766, ibid., 5:320–30.

67. For example, see Warrant and Instructions to Alexander McKee, March 24,

1766, *Johnson Papers*, 12:49–52; Lord Shelburne to William Johnson, September 13, December 11, 1766, ibid., 5:374–76, 447–49.

68. William Johnson to Lords of Trade, June 28, 1766, NYCD 7:835, 834–36.

69. Thomas Gage to William Johnson, May 19, 1766, *Johnson Papers*, 12:91–92; John Penn to William Johnson, March 11, 1766, ibid., 12:41–42.

70. William Johnson to William Franklin, June 20, 1766, *Johnson Papers*, 12:108.

71. Thomas Gage to Henry Conway, May 6, 1766, *Gage Correspondance*, 1:91.

72. Ibid.

73. Thomas Gage to William Johnson, June 22, 1766, *Johnson Papers*, 12:11–12; from Thomas Wharton et al., June 6, 1766, ibid., 12:101–2; John Penn to Francis Fauquier, November 15, 1766, MPCP 9:344–45; Francis Fauquier to John Penn, January 5, 1767, ibid., 9:349–50; Thomas Gage to John Penn, December 7, 1767, ibid., 9:403–4.

74. Indian Proceedings, August 13–30, 1766, *Johnson Papers*, 12:167–70.

75. Merchant Protest to William Johnson, January 22, 1766, *Johnson Papers*, 12:4–8; Memorial of Montreal Merchants, March 30, 1766, ibid., 12:57–61; Memorial of Montreal Merchants, April 15, 1766, ibid., 12:71–72; Memorial of Traders, September 20, 1766, ibid., 12:186–90; Thomas Gage to William Johnson, December 1, 1766, ibid., 12:225–26.

76. William Johnson to Thomas Gage, June 14, 1766, *Johnson Papers*, 12:105.

77. William Johnson to Montreal Merchants, May 15, 1766, *Johnson Papers*, 12:91, 90–91; William Johnson to Montreal Merchants, February 20, 1766, ibid., 12:19; William Johnson to Thomas Gage, March 22, 1766, ibid., 12:48–49.

78. Account of Losses, March 31, 1766, *Johnson Papers*, 12:63–64.

79. John Campbell to William Johnson, February 24, 1766, *Johnson Papers*, 12:29–31; Donald Campbell to Thomas Gage, April 10, 1766, ibid., 5:160.

80. Donald Campbell to Thomas Gage, May 10, 1766, *Johnson Papers*, 5:161, 159–61; William Johnson to Thomas Gage, May 27, 1766, ibid., 5:224.

81. Thomas Gage to William Johnson, June 16, 1766, *Johnson Papers*, 5:272, 271–72.

82. Normand MacLeod to William Johnson, August 4, 1766, *Johnson Papers*, 12:150.

83. Proceedings of William Johnson with Pondiac and Other Indians, July 23 to July 31, NYCD 7:858, 854–67; William Johnson to Lords of Trade, August 20, 1766, ibid., 7:851–53.

84. William Johnson to Baynton, Wharton, & Morgan, September 16, 1766, *Johnson Papers*, 12:182.

85. George Croghan to William Johnson, September 10, 1766, *Johnson Papers*, 12:99.

86. John Stuart to William Johnson, June 1, 1766, *Johnson Papers*, 12:99, 176–77.

87. William Johnson to Thomas Gage, February 20, 1766, *Johnson Papers*, 12:20–24; John Stuart to William Johnson, March 30, 1766, ibid., 12:56–57; John Stuart to William Johnson, June 1, 1766, ibid., 12:98–99; Thomas Gage to Lord Shelburne, December 23, 1766, *Gage Correspondance*, 1:115–18.

88. Personnel of Indian Department, December 9, 1766, *Johnson Papers*, 5:442–46.

89. Lord Shelburne to William Johnson, December 11, 1766, *Johnson Papers*, 5:447–49.

90. Account of George Croghan, February 22, 1767, *Johnson Papers*, 12:264–65; George Croghan to William Johnson, February 23, 1767, ibid., 12:265–66.

91. Thomas Gage to William Johnson, March 23, 1766, *Johnson Papers*, 5:94.

92. Thomas Gage to William Johnson, April 13, 1767, *Johnson Papers*, 5:536.

93. Thomas Gage to Robert Rogers, March 19, 1764, Gage papers, CL; Thomas Gage to Barrington, January 15, 1766, *Gage Correspondance*, 2:331–32.

94. Thomas Gage to Henry Gladwin, March 23, 1764, Gage papers, CL.

95. Thomas Gage to Robert Rogers, January 10, 1766, *Johnson Papers*, 12:1–2.

96. William Johnson to Thomas Gage, January 25, 1766, *Johnson Papers*, 12:9, 8–11; William Johnson to Thomas Moncrieffe, January 30, 1766, ibid., 12:11–13.

97. Thomas Gage to William Johnson, February 3, 1766, *Johnson Papers*, 5:30; Thomas Gage to William Johnson, June 2, 22, 1766, ibid., 12:100–101, 110–11.

98. William Johnson to Robert Rogers, June 3, 1766, *Johnson Papers*, 5:238–39.

99. Thomas Gage to Lord Shelburne, February 22, 1767, *Gage Correspondance*, 1:123.

100. Orders and Regulations, 1767, *Johnson Papers*, 12:246–48; Regulations for the Indian Trade, January 15, 1768, ibid., 12:409–13.

101. Lord Shelburne to William Johnson, June 20, 1767, *Johnson Papers*, 5:567; William Johnson to Guy Carleton, January 27, 1767, ibid., 5:479–83; Guy Carleton to William Johnson, March 27, 1766, ibid., 5:520–23; Guy Carleton to Lord Shelburne, March 28, 1766, ibid., 5:524; Thomas Gage to William Johnson, April 5, 1767, ibid., 12:295–96.

102. Thomas Gage to William Johnson, July 12, 1767, *Johnson Papers*, 12:335–36; Thomas Gage to William Johnson, June 28, 1767, ibid., 5:573–74.

103. George Croghan to William Johnson, June 3, 1766, *Johnson Papers*, 5:560.

104. William Johnson to Lord Shelburne, October 26, 1767, *Johnson Papers*, 5:762–64.

105. Jehu Hay to William Johnson, August 1767, *Johnson Papers*, 5:648.

106. Jehu Hay's journal of Indian transactions, August 29?–September 13, 1767, *Johnson Papers*, 5:669–76.

107. Howard H. Peckham, ed., *George Croghan's Journal of His Trip to Detroit in 1767* (Ann Arbor: University of Michigan Press, 1939).

108. Thomas Gage to William Johnson, October 4, 1767, *Johnson Papers*, 12:366–68.

109. Henry van Schaack and Other Traders to Jehu Hay, September 4, 1767, *Johnson Papers*, 5:653, 653–56; Jehu Hay to Henry van Schaack and Other Traders, September 4, November 26, 1767, ibid., 5:657–59, 826–30.

110. Report of Indian trade, Fort Pitt, Alexander McKee, 1767, *Johnson Papers*, 12:396–97; Report of Indian Trade, Fort Detroit, Jehu Hay, 1767, ibid., 12:398–400; Report of Indian Trade, May 14, 1767–November 24, 1768, ibid., 12:660–61.

111. George Croghan to William Johnson, October 18, 1767, *Johnson Papers*, 12:374, 372–75.

112. Thomas Gage to William Johnson, November 9, 1767, *Johnson Papers*, 12:376, 376–78.

113. Thomas Gage to William Johnson, November 9, 1767, *Johnson Papers*, 12: 380.

114. Robert Johnston to William Johnson, August 24, 1766, *Johnson Papers*, 12: 161–62; Robert Johnston to William Johnson, September 25, 1766, ibid., 12:198–99; Robert Johnston to William Johnson, August 20, 1767, ibid., 12:353–54; Jean Baptiste Cadot and Alexander Henry to William Johnson, August 21, 1767, ibid., 12:355–56; Memorial of Benjamin Roberts, August 21, 1767, ibid., 5:632–34; Benjamin Roberts to Guy Johnson, August 22, 1767, ibid., 12:356–57; John Christie to William Johnson, February 24, 1768, ibid., 12:438–42; Robert Johnston to William Johnson, February 24, 1768, ibid., 12:443–45; Frederick Spiesmacher to William Johnson, February 25, 1768, ibid., 12:449–51; Jehu Hay to William Johnson, April 25, 1768, ibid., 12:479–80; Frederick Spiesmacher to William Johnson, May 6, 1768, ibid., 12:491–92; Benjamin Roberts to William Johnson, October 29, 1768, ibid., 12:612–15; Deposition, October 29, 1768, ibid., 12:615–16; Robert Rogers to William Johnson, September 23, 1766, ibid., 12:193–94; Robert Rogers to William Johnson, August 14, 1767, ibid., 5:615–16; Robert Rogers to William Johnson, September 4, 1767, ibid., 12:357–58; William Johnson to Shelburne, October 28, 1767, NYCD 7:988–90; Nathaniel Potter Deposition, September 28, 1767, ibid., 7: 990–92; Colonel Hopkins to Robert Rogers, April 9, 1766, ibid., 7:993–94; Thomas Gage to Lord Shelburne, January 23, March 12, 1768, *Gage Correspondance*, 1:161, 164–65; Thomas Gage to Barrington, March 12, 1768, ibid., 2:454. For a good collection of the conflicting evidence, see David A. Armour, ed., *Treason? At Michilimackinac: The Proceedings of the Court Martial Trial Held at Montreal in October 1768 for the Trial of Major Robert Rogers* (Mackinac Island, Mich.: Mackinac State Historic Parks, 1972).

115. Norman Gelb, ed., *Jonathan Carver's Travels Through America, 1766–1768: An Explorer's Portrait of the American Wilderness* (New York: John Wiley and Sons, 1993); Armour, *Treason?*, 47–56.

116. William Blyth Testimony to Will Allen, January 17, 1768, MPCP 9:414–16; John Penn to Cumberland County Magistrates, January 19, 1768, ibid., 9:416–17; John Penn to Lancaster County Magistrates, January 19, 1768, ibid., 9:418–19; John Penn Proclamation, January 19, 1768, ibid., 9:420; John Penn to Thomas Gage, January 21, 1768, ibid., 9:422–23; John Penn to William Johnson, January 21, 1768, ibid., 9:424–25; John Penn to Newoleeka, January 23, 1768, ibid., 9:428–30; Governor's Council, January 25, February 3, 4, 1768, ibid., 9:430–31, 446, 450–51; John Penn to Wighaloosia, January 28, 1768, ibid., 9:436–37; Edward Shippen to John Penn, Janaury 29, 1768, ibid., 9:438; John Penn to Sheriff, January 24, February 2, 1768, ibid., 9:444–45, 441; Assembly to Governor, February 2, 5, 1768, ibid., 9:447, 554–58; John Armstrong to John Penn, January 24, 29, 1768, ibid., 9:444–45, 448–49; John Armstrong to John Penn, February 7, 1768, ibid., 9:462–63; Sheriff Holmes to John Penn, February 7, 1768, ibid., 9:463–65; Assembly to Governor, February 16, 1768, ibid., 9:465–66; Governor to Assembly, February 16, 1768, ibid., 9466; John Penn to William Johnson, February 18, 1768, ibid., 9:468–69.

117. James Cunningham Disposition, February 4, 1768, MPCP 9:450–51.

118. Thomas Gage to Lord Shelburne, April 24, 1768, *Gage Correspondance*, 1: 170.

119. Thomas Gage to Shelburne, October 10, 1767, *Gage Correspondance*, 1: 152–53.

120. Thomas Gage to Barrington, March 10, 1768, *Gage Correspondance*, 2:450, 449–50.

121. Lords of Trade to Lord Shelburne, December 23, 1767, NYCD 7:1004–5; Thomas Gage to William Johnson, April 18, May 3, 1765, *Johnson Papers*, 6:200–201, 211–13; Lord Shelburne to William Johnson, December 19, 1767, ibid., 6:22–23; Lord Shelburne to Thomas Gage, December 19, 1767, ibid., 6:23; John Blair to William Johnson, March 10, 1768, ibid., 6:143–44.

122. Thomas Gage to William Johnson, March 15, 1768, *Johnson Papers*, 12:466, 465–67; March 13, 1768, ibid., 6:146–48. For other letters concerning the fort debate, see William Johnson to John Penn, January 2, 1768, *Johnson Papers*, 12:401–2; Thomas Penn to William Johnson, January 7, 1768, ibid., 12:405–6; William Johnson to John Penn, February 18, 1768, ibid., 12:432–34; William Johnson to John Penn, February 29, 1768, ibid., 12:453–55; Thomas Gage to William Johnson, May 8, 1768, ibid., 12:493–94; Thomas Gage to William Johnson, August 7, 1768, ibid., 6:312–14.

123. Cadwallader Colden to Lords of Trade, June 8, 1765, NYCD 7:744–45; Memorial of William Johnson, July 8, 1766, ibid., 7:843–45; Committee of Council to Lords of Trade, July 8, 1766, *Johnson Papers*, 5:313; William Johnson to Daniel Burton, November 8, 1766, ibid., 5:413–15; Philip Sharpe to William Johnson, May 16, 1767, ibid., 5:551; Lords of Trade on William Johnson memorial, February 10, 1767, NYCD 7:896–99.

124. Thomas Gage to Lord Shelburne, August 17, 1768, *Gage Correspondance*, 1:189.

125. Northern Superintendency's Expenses, March 24 to September 25, 1768, *Johnson Papers*, 12:640–43; Dispersements to Indians, March 26 to November 14, 1768, ibid., 12:644–49.

126. Journal of Indian Affairs, March 1–3, 1768, *Johnson Papers*, 12:456–58; William Johnson to Thomas Gage, March 5, 1768, ibid., 12:459–60; William Johnson to George Croghan, March 5, 1768, ibid., 12:461–62; William Johnson to John Penn, March 16, 1768, ibid., 12:467–69; William Johnson to George Croghan, March 16, 1768, ibid., 12:472; William Johnson to Thomas Gage, April 8, 1768, ibid., 6:184–87.

127. William Johnson to Thomas Gage, April 23, May 24, 1768, *Johnson Papers*, 12:476–79, 513–51.

128. Indian Conference, April 26, 1768, *Johnson Papers*, 12:481, 480–82.

129. Guy Johnson to Thomas Gage, May 4, 20, 30, June 16, July 5, 1768, *Johnson Papers*, 12:488–90, 507–10, 519–21, 525–27, 543–45; Indian Conference, May 9, 19, 24–27, June 8–28, July 10–16, 1768, ibid., 12:497–500, 504–7, 515–16, 529–43, 548–50; Thomas Gage to Guy Johnson, May 16, 29, June 5, July 11, 1768, ibid., 12:500–502, 517–18, 522–23, 546; William Johnson to Henry Moore, September 20, 1768, ibid., 6:398–404.

130. For the best acount, see John Richard Alden, *John Stuart and the Southern Colonial Frontier: A Study of Indian Relations, War, Trade, and Land Problems in the Southern Wilderness, 1754–1775* (New York: Gordian Press, 1966).

131. Kayaderosseras Proprietors to William Johnson, 1767, *Johnson Papers*, 6:39–41; William Johnson to Henry Moore, August 5, 1768, ibid., 6:309–11.

132. Indian intelligence, September 30, 1768, *Johnson Papers*, 12:599–601; Agreement between Mohawks and Mohicans, September 30, 1768, ibid., 12:603–4; William Johnson to Thomas Gage, October 13, 1768, ibid., 12:605–7, Congress at Fort Stanwix, September 15 to October 30, 1768, ibid., 12:617–29.

133. William Johnson to John Glen, October 16, 1768, *Johnson Papers*, 12:607–8.

134. Account against the Crown, December 9, 1768, *Johnson Papers*, 12:665–68; Account for Provisions, December 17, 1768, ibid., 12:672.

135. William Johnson to Thomas Gage, November 13, 1768, *Johnson Papers*, 6: 454.

8

Consequences

"Whom See We Now, Their Haughty Conquerors"

They take us for a lump of earth which they break in their hands and give us to the winds to blow away.

—Pontiac

History is lived forward but written in retrospect. We know the end before we consider the beginning, and we can never wholly recapture what it was like to know the beginning only.

—C. V. Wedgewood

"Amherst's War" may have been the bloodiest and most destructive Indian war in American history. About 500 British troops died during the war and another 50 captives were tortured to death.[1] As for civilians, George Croghan believed that the Indians "killed and captivated not less than two thousand of his Majesty's subjects, and drove some thousands to beggary and the greatest distress . . . and . . . plundered of goods . . . to the amount of not less than one hundred thousand pounds."[2] That might have been an exaggeration. The best count found that Indians killed 31 around Fort Pitt, 88 between Lake Erie and Fort Pitt, 34 between Fort Pitt and Bedford, and 48 between Bedford and the Susquehanna, for 170 dead altogether. At least 88 traders in the Ohio valley were killed when the uprising broke out and their goods were stolen. Another 200 or so may have been slaughtered elsewhere along the frontier that year and the next.[3] The Indians suffered as well. Gladwin estimated that 80 or 90 warriors had been killed around Detroit. The Indians may have lost around 60 warriors at Bushy Run. But they got off fairly lightly elsewhere, except for the peaceful Conestoga Indians. Perhaps no more than 200 warriors died in battle. Hundreds more Indians, however, died from the smallpox unleashed by Captain Ecuyer.[4]

Were any lessons learned from that war, which was so costly in lives and money? If nothing else the war clearly revealed the truth of the saying "an ounce of prevention is worth more than a pound of cure." Bouquet, for one, harbored no doubt over who was responsible for sparking the conflagation: "We have evidently brought upon ourselves this Indian war by being too saving of a few presents to the savages which properly distributed would certainly have prevented it."[5]

All along Johnson had argued that the causes of and solutions to Indian problems rested on British attitudes and actions: "Our people in general are ill calculated to maintain friendship with the Indians. They despise those in peace whom they fear to meet in war. This with the little artifices used in trade, and the total want of that address and seeming kindness practiced with such success by the French, must always hurt the colonists. On the contrary, could they but assume a friendship and treat them with civility and candour, we should soon possess their hearts and much more of their country than we do now."[6]

Croghan offered the most in-depth analysis of why the war began and how it could be won. He rhetorically asked, "if we make a boundary with the Indians and pay them for the lands east of such a boundary, why should we indulge them with any favours annually? I answer, custom and good policy as amongst themselves a neglect of renewing their Treaties of Friendship is looked on as an open violation of the peace of Nations. The expense of giving favours to the many additional Tribes of Indians as are now in alliance with Britain since the reduction of Canada must be considerable, but I dare say it will be found the cheapest and best method in the end to cultivate a friendship with them in this manner." After all, war brought Britain "nothing but fatigue and the devastation of our frontiers, and load the nation with debt."[7]

As for winning the war, Croghan saw nothing but folly with the notion of "marching an army at an immense expense into their Country, and driving a parcel of wretches before us who we know won't give us a meeting, but where they have the advantage of either beating us or running away, and then content ourselves with burning their villages of bark huts, destroying their corn, and driving them into the woods—This cannot be called conquering Indian nations." The Indians simply flee to new villages where they live to avenge themselves on frontier settlements.

How then could peace and prosperity with the Indians be secured? Croghan argued that the Indians "are to be governed only by love and fear . . . know how to flatter their vanity so as to gain their confidence. . . . Justice, honor, and our own interests demand [this] from us." Fear could only be promoted in the Indians by the British fearlessly punishing any Indian transgressions.

Why were Johnson and Croghan, America's leading Indian experts, along with Gage, adamantly opposed to trying to settle the war with military means? Those men were hardened realists with a clear-eyed vision of how to promote a prosperous, secure, expanding British Empire. Quite simply, war did not pay. It cost far more to fight than feed Indians. Pacifying Indians through appeasement reaped enormous wealth for the empire through more trade and pared military budgets. Wars destroyed property and productive lives; diverted skilled hands from scythes, pens, or looms to muskets, reins, and oars; deepened the nation's debt; and, even after they sputtered out, left hatreds that provoked the next bloody round. Amherst's "get tough" policies backfired. Containment hurt and appeasement enhanced Britain's imperial interests.

Were these "lessons" translated into policy? "Amherst's War" can only be understood in the context of British policies toward its new empire from Canada's conquest on September 8, 1760 to the Fort Stanwix Treaty on October 24, 1768. During those eight years, British policy makers struggled to find a balance between Indian and colonial demands that could best advance the empire's peace and prosperity. The war was the catalyst in the transition from Amherst's tragically flawed policy of denying Indian needs to Gage's policy of trying to satisfy them.

Whitehall's October 7, 1763 Proclamation, calling for a strict boundary between colonial and Indian lands, served as the new policy's foundation. For five years, from the 1763 Uprising to the 1768 Fort Stanwix Treaty, a debate raged over just what policy could best safeguard Britain's conflicting interests in the new empire. Whitehall, Gage, and Johnson were the major participants, while Parliament and various Indian agents, governors, merchants, and moralizers also contributed.

The final treaty at Fort Stanwix capstoned the new policy and essentially ended "Amherst's War." It was preceded by scores of agreements and formal treaties by which the northern and southern Indian Superintendents tried to realize the spirit, if not the letter, of the Crown's 1763 Proclamation calling for a strict boundary between colonial and Indian lands. In addition, trade was strictly regulated and gifts, especially munitions, were generously bestowed. The Indians had won the war not just on the battlefields but, much more importantly, at the peace councils.

Nonetheless, no British official saw the Fort Stanwix Treaty as anything more than a fleeting expedient, a means to buy time before the pressures of American encroachment proved overwhelming to the tribes. Gage admitted that "it is not to be foreseen how this measure would tend to preserve tranquility for any length of time; for if means cannot now be fallen upon to restrain the people from passing the present boundaries, they will in a short time go beyond them again, wherever they shall be fixed, for the same reasons and under the same pretense, that they do it now."[8]

Was the new policy successful? For a while the appeasement policy kept a troubled peace. But treaties were only as good as the official efforts to live up to them. When the expeditions of Bouquet and Bradstreet returned from the wilderness in late 1764, the frontier would be peaceful (aside from the occasional murder or robbery) for another decade until Lord Dunmore's War of 1774, prompted by an influx of squatters on Indian lands. That war bled into the frontier war during the American Revolution. American Indian policies would fluctuate between repression and appeasement for the next 120 years, with results similar to the policies of Amherst and Gage.

That frontier wars would periodically erupt was to be expected. After all, when the 1763 Proclamation reached America, few colonists believed that the settlements would ever stop in their tracks just because of treaties signed with Indians. The promise of an Appalachian boundary was seen as a temporary expedient to help pacify the Indians amid a war. That view, of course, proved to be true. Within a few years of the 1768 Fort Stanwix Treaty, squatters had penetrated that boundary in several places and colonial governors demanded adjustments.

Finally, what fate met the war's best-known leaders?

From 1760 to 1763, Whitehall had received many reports critical of Jeffrey Amherst from Johnson, Croghan, and various governors. His policies had nearly lost Britain's newly won western empire and cost untold numbers of lives, property, and expenditures. So was Amherst cashiered or at least censured when he reached London?

As irony would have it, after a brief eclipse the man most responsible for that savage war rose ever higher on a heap of honors and sinecures. After Amherst's return to London, Whitehall merely ignored him, and only for a while. The general's political connections prevented anything harsher and eventually got Sir Jeffrey named honorary colonel of the 3rd Royal Regiment in 1768, governor of Guernsey in 1770, lieutenant general of ordnance in 1772, a life peer as Baron Amherst in 1776, general of the army on March 19, 1778, colonel of the 2nd troops of Horse Grenadiers in 1779, commander in chief of all British forces on March 20, 1782, and field marshall in 1796.

The Cabinet may have been corrupt but was not completely incompetent; Amherst was not sent to quell the American rebellion. The general's last military action was about as glorious as any in his career—he sent troops to suppress the Gordon Riots in 1780. In his eighty-first year he died peacefully on August 31, 1797 at his estate, "Montreal," in Kent, most likely to his last breath clinging to the belief that his harsh policy toward the Indians was correct while generous conciliatory policies were nothing but liberal soft-headedness.

The man most associated with the war met his demise much sooner. By 1766, Pontiac's status among his own people reached rock bottom. Rumors spread that his tribe had even beaten and driven him like a stray dog. When Jehu Hay sent him an invitation, in April 1768, to council at Detroit, Pontiac politely refused with a tacit admission of how far he had fallen: "I have no complaint whatever against the English. It is only my young men who have shamed me. This has obliged me to leave my village. It is solely against my own nation that I am offended, by several insults they have made me, saying that I was never chief."[9]

Pontiac's death was filled with tragic irony. The man who more than anyone else led the Indian uprising of 1763 would die not on the battlefield against the British invaders but in an Indian village by one of his own race. In March 1769, Pontiac and 30 warriors arrived at Cahokia. Trouble soon brewed between Pontiac and the local tribes, especially the Peoria, who decided to assassinate the fallen chief and drive off his followers. On April 20, the nephew of Peoria Chief Makatachinga, or Black Dog, slinked up behind Pontiac as he walked down the street and bashed in his skull with a war club. Pontiac probably died unaware of any danger and devoid of any pain. Adding to the irony, Pontiac was most likely buried not in wild nature but across the river in an unconsecrated grave in downtown St. Louis.[10]

Perhaps the most appropriate way to end this tale is to quote Pontiac's farewell address in the play "Ponteach," attributed to Robert Rogers:

> The torrent rises, and the tempest blows;
> Where will this rough rude storm of ruin end?
> What crimson floods are yet to drench the earth?
> What new formed mischiefs hover in the air?
> And point their stings at this devoted head?
> Has fate exhausted all her stores of wrath?
> Or has she other vengeance in reserve?
> What can she more? My sons, my name is gone;
> Nothing remains but an afflicted King,
> That might be pitied by Earth's greatest wretch . . .
> Was I not Ponteach, was I not a King,
> Such giant mischiefs would not gather round me.
> And since I'm Ponteach, since I am a King,
> I'll shew myself superior to them all;
> I'll rise above this hurricane of fate,
> And shew my courage to the Gods themselves.[11]

NOTES

1. Howard Peckham, *Pontiac and the Indian Uprising* (Princeton, N.J.: Princeton University Press, 1947), 239.

2. George Croghan to Lords of Trade [January 1764?], in E. B. O'Callaghan and Berthold Fernow, eds., *Documents Relative to the Colonial History of the State of New York* (hereafter cited as NYCD), 15 vols. (Albany, N.Y.: Weed, Parsons, and Co., 1856–1887), 7:603, 602–7.

3. Ourry return of killed or taken in Department of Fort Pitt, September 30, 1763, in Sylvester K. Stevens, Donald H. Kent, Autumn L. Leonard, Louis M. Wad-

dell, and John Totteham, eds., *The Papers of Henry Bouquet* (hereafter cited as *Bouquet Papers*), 6 vols. (Harrisburg: Pennsylvania Historical and Museum Commission, 1972–1994), 6:410–11; Trent List of Indian Traders Killed or Captured, September 30, 1763, ibid., 6:412–13.

4. Henry Gladwin to Jeffrey Amherst, November 1, 1763, in Charles Moore, ed., *Gladwin Manuscripts* (Lansing, Mich.: Robert Smith, 1897), 675–77.

5. Henry Bouquet to Thomas Gage, November 30, 1764, *Bouquet Papers*, 6: 713, 711–15.

6. William Johnson to Board of Trade, June 28, 1766, NYCD 7:836, 834–36.

7. George Croghan to Lords of Trade, [January 1764?], NYCD 7:604, 602–7.

8. Thomas Gage to Lord Shelburne, January 22, 1768, in Clarence Edwin Carter, ed., *The Correspondance of General Thomas Gage with the Secretaries of State, 1763–1775* (hereafter cited as *Gage Correspondance*) (New York: Archon Books, 1969), 1:157.

9. Pontiac to Jehu Hay, May 10, 1768, enclosed in George Turnbull to Thomas Gage, Gage collection, William L. Clements Library, Ann Arbor, Mich.

10. For a discussion of different accounts of Pontiac's death, see Peckham, *Pontiac and the Indian Uprising*, 309–18. For a stark announcement, see Thomas Gage to Lord Hillsborough, August 12, 1769, *Gage Correspondance*, 1:233.

11. Allan Nevins, ed., *Ponteach, or the Savages of America: A Tragedy by Robert Rogers* (1914) (reprint, New York: Lenox Hill, 1971), 256.

Index

About the Author

WILLIAM R. NESTER is Professor in the Department of Government and Politics at St. John's University in New York. He is the author of numerous books which explore various aspects of international relations and political economy, and two books on the American frontier. He is a lifelong student of the American wilderness and the frontier.

ISBN 0-275-96770-0

HARDCOVER BAR CODE